ON MY HONOR

ON MY

H ★ O ★ N ★ O ★ R

Boy Scouts and the Making of American Youth

★ JAY MECHLING ★

THE UNIVERSITY OF CHICAGO PRESS
CHICAGO AND LONDON

JAY MECHLING is professor of American studies at the University of
California, Davis.

The University of Chicago Press, Chicago 60637
The University of Chicago Press, Ltd., London
© 2001 by The University of Chicago
All rights reserved. Published 2001
Printed in the United States of America

10 09 08 07 06 05 04 03 02 01   1 2 3 4 5

ISBN: 0-226-51704-7 (cloth)

Library of Congress Cataloging-in-Publication Data

Mechling, Jay, 1945–
   On my honor : Boy Scouts and the making of American youth / Jay Mechling.
     p. cm.
   Includes bibliographical references and index.
   ISBN 0-226-51704-7 (cloth : alk. paper)
     1. Boy Scouts—United States. 2. Boys—United States.　I. Title.
HS3313 .M43 2001
369.43'0973—dc21

                          2001035165

For Devon Jay and Tyler Tristan

two men for the 21st century

CONTENTS

ACKNOWLEDGMENTS

Authors sometimes write pages of thanks for books they write over a period of a year or two. What am I to do with a book written over a period of twenty years? Give it a try, I suppose, and apologize in advance to any I have forgotten to mention.

My first thanks go, of course, to the men and boys of Troop 49. They have been generous, patient, and friendly. I have enjoyed many long hours of conversation with the Scoutmaster I've called "Pete" here. I am enormously indebted, too, to my former student, called "Tad" here, for introducing me to the troop and the troop to me. Tad and I have talked and corresponded a great deal about the troop over many years, and he remains the perceptive American studies culture critic to this day.

As I explain in my introduction, over the years I have presented portions of this research in papers at scholarly meetings and in the pages of academic journals and edited books. Many colleagues across the nation heard and read these attempts to make sense of my materials, and I am thankful to them all, from questioners in crowds to the referees of the articles, the book chapters, and the draft of this book. Dee Seton Barber and her family showed me generous hospitality when I visited them in Santa Fe and Dee opened her father's papers for me there. The staff at the Seton Museum at the Philmont Scout Ranch in Cimmaron, New Mexico, was very helpful during my research there, as was the staff in the national office of the Boy Scouts (when it was still in New Jersey). Tim Curran generously spent an afternoon talking with me in the early stages of his lawsuit against the Boy Scouts of America. Over the years, my students have heard this research and some have written research papers of their own, teaching me about their own Boy Scout and Girl Scout experiences. Michael Zuckerman, as always, was a remarkable reader and critic. Brian Sutton-Smith provided seminal

thoughts on the nature of play and provided continuing encouragement for this project; he has been a treasured intellectual playmate.
Other valued intellectual playmates include Gary Alan Fine and Simon
Bronner, who share my interest in and writing about the folk cultures
of children and who are sometimes my coauthors on other projects;
Michael Cowan, a fellow Eagle Scout whose Yale American studies
senior thesis on the Boy Scouts I read even before we met at the 1975–
76 Yale National Humanities Institute and began our quarter-century
friendship; Bruce Hackett, another Eagle Scout, sociologist, and colleague at the University of California–Davis; and Michael L. Smith and
Jon Wagner, my buddies in our writing group, who were among the
few people who read the entire manuscript and who offered detailed
advice, from argument to style. Their suggestions improved this book
immensely. Two anonymous readers for the University of Chicago
Press offered helpful suggestions. The thoughtful advice and enthusiastic support of my editor, Doug Mitchell, helped me revise the manuscript. Finally, David S. Wilson, my longtime colleague and friend,
who was himself a Scout holding "the gentlemen's rank," has shared
with me endless conversations about the Boy Scouts and American
culture.

Thanks are due to institutions, as well. The 1975–76 fellowship at
the Yale National Humanities Institute, a project of the National En-
dowment for the Humanities, provided the time and company of nineteen other fellows to read, talk, and write in the very first stages of this
work. I still draw upon the intellectual capital I accumulated that year.
Several grants from the Research Committee of the Davis Division of
the Academic Senate of the University of California supported research
travel to libraries and research collections connected with this project.

American studies staff members at UC Davis over the years have
assisted my research in many ways, from typing article and book chapter manuscripts (precomputing, of course) to managing my research
accounts. Gerry Baker, Judith Ryan, Carol Beck, Lesley Byrns, and
Kay Allen always provided cheerful, professional help, and I am grateful
to them all.

My parents, of course, supported the Cub Scout and then Boy Scout
experiences in which this book began, so once again I can thank my
father and my late mother. Thanks, too, to my Scoutmaster, Nate Wei-
ner, back in Miami Beach so long ago.

When I first began thinking of this research as a book-length project,
I intended to dedicate the book to Elizabeth Walker Mechling, my
spouse and frequent coauthor on other projects, and to Heather Shawn
Mechling, our daughter. They were the ones who put up with my

occasional absences to go into the mountains to "play in the woods" with the Boy Scouts. My daughter was only seven years old when I began the work, but the book has taken so long that my daughter is now married and the mother of two sons. So I beg forgiveness from my wife and daughter and ask their blessing as I dedicate this book, after all, to our grandsons, Devon Jay McGlone and Tyler Tristan McGlone, two boys who will be new men for the twenty-first century.

INTRODUCTION

Americans are worried about their boys. Large numbers of boys roam the streets without much adult supervision or even surveillance. They gather in peer groups and seem to flaunt adult values in their dress and speech. Large numbers of them are foreign-born.

These male peer groups—gangs, really—engage too often in aggressive and violent behavior. Sometimes they direct their violence against property, but at times the boys show disturbing cruelty toward animals. And then there is the violence they visit on one another. One sociologist's book, *The Boy Problem,* has labeled this the most challenging social problem for the generation.

Adults look everywhere for someone and something to blame for the disturbing behavior of boys. Some blame the advanced state of society and its creation of too much leisure time for children and adolescents. Some blame mothers and female teachers for "feminizing" boys. Most agree that boys' nature is driven considerably by their biology, that male children struggle with impulses created by eons of human evolution, impulses pushing them toward strong peer group loyalty, very physical play, hierarchical relationships, competitiveness, aggressiveness, and violence. Experts advise that, rather than trying to fight against this biological nature of boys, we should create youth programs that will accommodate boys' natural instincts and shape them in socially constructive directions. The experts also lobby for single-sex schools and recreational programs; only then, they say, can we attend to the special developmental needs of boys.

The America I have just described is the America of the year 1900.[1] Among the interesting ways that the 1890s and the 1990s resemble each other is the "crisis of masculinity" felt by the white middle class and discussed broadly in the media of the time. In both decades, the "boy" emerged as a symbol around which to have the public conversation about masculinity. A future historian or anthropologist looking back at the newspaper stories, magazine articles, and television stories from the 1990s will see plenty of signs of worry about boys, worry often bordering on fear. In some of these stories, boys are violent predators, gathering in "posses" bent on raping girls or in full-fledged gangs engaging in an assortment of crimes, ranging from petty theft to murder. In other stories, the boys are spree killers who, deranged by the violence displayed in the music and videos and computer games they consume, arrive at their middle school or high school armed with automatic rifles and bombs, reenacting in real life a fantasy scene from the film *Basketball Diaries,* starring teen idol Leonardo DiCaprio. In still other stories, the boys are more victims than perpetrators; they are more at risk than girls on most social indicators, from dropping out of school to committing suicide to being murdered.

The national media really began giving priority to this story in the late 1990s, when it was white, suburban, middle-class boys, rather than black and Latino kids in the inner city, who began displaying and falling victim to the violence, aggression, and risks. What could turn some of the smartest and most respected teenage boys in a suburban high school into serial rapists or killers? Some magazine articles offered up for parents an inventory of warning signals that your kid might be in danger or a danger to others. Middle-class parents thought that they knew how to read their sons, had confidence that they could tell the good boys from the bad boys; now they were not so sure. "He seemed like such a nice boy" was the testimony of neighbors about more than one teen killer.

In the search for someone or something to blame, violent media images seemed a likely target, as did drugs (especially marijuana). Parents, teachers, and public officials began trying to control children's access to violent video games, computer games, theatrical films, and music lyrics. Teenage boys constitute the major audience for action-based, violent video and computer games, so that genre of teen entertainment drew considerable attention.

Of special concern, largely due to what was learned about the boys responsible for the Columbine (Colorado) High School shooting, was the teenage "Goth" (from Gothic) cultural style, which features black clothing, black trenchcoats, and distinctive body ornamentation. Unconcerned with the teens' finely tuned understanding of distinctions in cultural styles—between, say, grunge and Goth—the adults went after anything that did not look like a clean-cut, wholesome adolescent. Of course, some of the teen killers and rapists had that clean-cut look, but it was easier for the adults to target "the freaks."

What emerged from all these media accounts was the parents' growing sense that their children—especially the boys—were leading private lives hidden from the adult gaze and supervision. Some social conservatives blamed the social movements of the 1960s for creating an ideology that legitimated parental freedom and self-fulfillment at the expense of parental responsibility. Leftist critics tended to blame a stage of late capitalism that elevated consumption goods over human relationships.

Also at stake was a debate over the nature of boys. Americans have tended to think of children as innocent unless corrupted by some force. In the nature versus nurture debate, Americans in the twentieth century landed most often on the nurture side, thanks to the rise of behaviorism in scientific psychology and to the pervasive American faith in self-improvement and societal progress. The rise of sociobiology, cognitive science, and the brain sciences in the last two decades of the twentieth century pushed thinking in the other direction, toward thinking about the existence of biological foundations for the creation of gender.

The problem with all this adult fretting about boys is that very few adults tend to look closely at the actual everyday lives of normal boys. The 1990s advice books on "the boy problem" were written mainly by practicing clinical psychologists, who (by the very nature of their professional roles) tend to see troubled boys or boys somehow at risk. Similarly, the boys in the media accounts tend to be boys in trouble, boys in gangs and other equally marginal, transgressive groups. Everywhere we look, it seems, we see a boy problem, and we seek ways to rescue boys from a society that views them as dangerous, as toxic.

The Boy Scouts of America (the BSA) was founded in 1910, largely in response to the 1890s crisis of masculinity, and ninety years later the Boy Scouts continues to be enmeshed in debates over the appropriate meanings for manhood. I recount some of this ninety-year history later in this book, but my point here is simply that the Boy Scouts in the first few years of the twenty-first century must be understood, at least in part, as a nineteenth-century solution to the cultural trauma experienced as a result of the twentieth century's assault on traditional understandings of what it means to be a boy and a man.

For some observers of the Boy Scouts, a return to some nineteenth-century values—such as duty, honor, and integrity—is just the thing this society needs in the twenty-first century. "Character Counts," proclaims the organization's latest advertising slogan, a slogan adopted even before the Clinton White House scandals made character the litmus test for candidates in the 2000 presidential election. Other observers of the Boy Scouts see its nineteenth-century values as peculiarly antiquated. These same observers would say that the socially conservative view of Scouting substitutes nostalgia for a clear view of history and, therefore, poorly prepares young men for the adult lives they will spend in a complexly multicultural United States. The most critical observers of the Boy Scouts often compare the organization to the Hitler Youth, seeing in this parallel not only the uniforms and militarism but also an intolerance and an inflexible commitment to "one truth." For one group, the Boy Scouts offers a corrective to many of America's problems; for the other group, the Boy Scouts is an example of the problem. Either way, the Boy Scouts of America touches the lives of millions of boys. The organization claimed to have nearly 3.5 million registered Scouts in 1999, and on April 4, 2000, the BSA announced that it had registered its 100 millionth member (Mario Castro, from Brooklyn, New York) since 1910.[2]

The correction to both of these skewed views of the nature of boys and the nature of the Boy Scout experience lies in the study of boys' lives in what social scientists call "natural settings," those places and occasions in the everyday lives of boys where we get some glimpse of who they are and how they fashion their lives. A Boy Scout troop is such a setting. This book aims to set aside everyone's preconceptions about the meaning of the Boy Scout experience and to look at how a living group of boys and men in California constructs that experience at the troop's annual summer encampment in the mountains.

We need this correction even more as recent events have put the Boy Scouts center stage in the public debates over what is becoming of our boys. The 1990s saw a series of lawsuits filed against the Boy Scouts of America around what came to be called "the three G's"—God, gays, and girls. As I shall examine at length later in this book, the national organization had to defend itself against suits by boys who were excluded from the organization because they were atheists, by gay men who were excluded from membership, and by girls who were rejected in their bid to join.

In these cases—certainly in the God and gay cases, but even in the gender cases—at stake was the model of boyhood, and presumably the model of adult masculinity the organization saw at the center of its mission. One need look no further than the Scout Oath and the Scout Law for the qualities of this masculinity. The Scout Oath, adopted at the creation of the BSA in 1910 and sworn by each boy with right hand raised and three middle fingers held upright to represent the three points of the oath, reads

On my honor I will do my best
To do my duty to God and my country
And to obey the Scout Law;
To help other people at all times;
To keep myself physically strong,
Mentally awake, and morally straight.

Honor, duty, God, country, strength, and morality establish the masculine ideal the Boy Scouts sees as being as relevant in the twenty-first century as the nineteenth. To leave no doubt what qualities are valued in the adolescent boy, the Scout Law to which the boy swears obedience has twelve points:

A Scout is Trustworthy, Loyal, Helpful, Friendly, Courteous, Kind, Obedient, Cheerful, Thrifty, Brave, Clean, and Reverent.

In defending itself against the lawsuits, the BSA insisted that its declared identity, mission, and message surrounding the creation of the ideal boy meant that it could not accept girls, atheists, or gay boys and men as members or as leaders.

In the 1990s, the California and New Jersey Supreme Courts came to different conclusions in two cases of Eagle Scouts expelled from the Boy Scouts when, as young adults, their homosexuality became public knowledge. The Supreme Court of the United States heard the New Jersey case and settled the matter on June 28, 2000, with a 5–4 decision in favor of the Boy Scouts of America. That highly publicized decision may have boosted the visibility of the Boy Scouts as a viable "answer" to "the boy problem" at the turn of the twenty-first century, but it also plunged the organization even deeper into what scholars and journalists have come to call the culture wars between those arguing for moral absolutes and traditional values, on one side, and those arguing for a more pluralistic approach to morality and understandings of truth, on the other.[3] While many applauded the Court's decision in favor of the Boy Scouts, others have condemned the organization's position.[4]

So, as I said, all this attention to "the boy problem" amid the larger culture wars in the United States makes this an especially compelling moment to inquire into the nature of the Boy Scout experience. This book is not a history of the Boy Scouts, though I'll tell a bit of history along the way. A basic premise of this book is that the national office of the Boy Scouts of America does not represent the experience of "being a Boy Scout." That office has the authority of the headquarters of a national corporation, but the twelve-year-old boy does not experience the Boy Scouts through the national office and its bureaucracy. The boy experiences Scouting through a living group of men and boys who make up his troop, and within the troop the boy is a member of a smaller group (usually no more than eight boys) that is his patrol, with its own name, badge, and other signs of identity.

If we are to understand what it means for the average boy to be a Boy Scout, then we must look closely at the everyday details of that experience. This book does not look at every boy or at every troop. But I do offer this intensive case study of a single troop and its annual summer encampment as a place to begin understanding that the boys themselves and their somewhat autonomous peer folk cultures have a great deal to do with creating the experience of being a Boy Scout. A Boy Scout camp experience follows neither the local adult male leaders' agenda (which might differ from the official organization's agenda, we'll see) nor the adolescent male peer group agenda; rather, what happens at camp (and in the troop while not in camp) is a third thing, a unique culture created by the interaction between all these forces— the official Boy Scout program, the program as put into practice by the adult leaders, and the sometimes resistant male adolescent peer culture.

The dynamic, interactive nature of the Boy Scout experience means that the organization does not create a single sort of boy or man. Despite the national organization's wishes (maybe fantasies), having a uniform program does not guarantee that the troops crank out a uniform product—the God-fearing, highly moral, heterosexual adult male of Boy Scout rhetoric. Culture is a great deal more messy than that. All sorts of boys and men belong to the Boy Scouts, and together they create multiple versions of the Boy Scout experience and multiple versions of adult men. My aim here is to show how this dynamic cultural process works in one troop. Troops and the experiences of boys within them will vary some across time and space, but if we focus on the dynamic process where adult intentions and adolescent male intentions negotiate the meanings of masculinity, then we will be in a better position to understand "the boy problem" and the wisdom of seeing the Boy Scouts as a potential solution. I want this book to bring to our public talk about boys, masculinity, and the Boy Scouts the perspective acquired through extensive fieldwork among the boys.

I am a Boy Scout. Actually, I am an Eagle Scout, the organization's highest earned rank. Note that I don't say that I "was" an Eagle Scout; as Pete, the Scoutmaster in this study, says, "Once an Eagle, always an Eagle."

This book was a long time in the making. It began in a real sense when I joined the Cub Scouts in 1953 at age eight in my hometown of

Miami Beach, Florida. As was common in the baby boom families created just after the war, my parents were determined that I would have all the luxuries of childhood their Depression-era teen years denied them. This included tap dance lessons and Scouting. My mother was not my first Cub Scout den mother, but eventually she volunteered to help and became a den mother herself. I worked my way through the Cub badges, including Webelos, which introduced me to the next step in my Scouting career, a Boy Scout troop. I was an eager and active Boy Scout, awarded my Eagle rank in December of my fourteenth year. I was a camper and then a camp counselor at the South Florida Council's camp in Sebring for a few years, and I was a member of the Order of the Arrow, the elite service fraternity within the Boy Scouts.

As is often the case for adolescent boys, other high school activities eventually dragged me away from the organization. Still, my Scouting experience and my proud identity as an Eagle Scout continue to define my understanding of myself, including my love of teaching, which began when I first taught another boy how to tie a knot. I come to the study of the Boy Scout experience with the mixed strengths and weaknesses of the insider. This is not a scientifically "objective" study, if ever such a thing is possible, especially outside the laboratory and in the natural settings of everyday life. My fieldwork with this troop always had as its comparative background my own experiences as a Scout, and it always had as its sense-making framework my ongoing interdisciplinary training and practices, as I drew upon history, folklore, anthropology, sociology, psychology, rhetorical criticism, and other scholarly fields to understand what I was seeing and hearing.

I first met this troop—I call them Troop 49, not their real number—in the mid-1970s, while I was still a young assistant professor of American studies at the University of California, Davis. I had begun writing about the numerous Boy Scout novels that began being published for boy readers as early as 1910, and I mentioned this in one of my classes. One of my students, an American studies major, came up to me after class and said, "You know, if you want to study a really interesting Boy Scout troop, you should come visit mine." And I did. That student is the "Tad" (a pseudonym, as I have given all members of the troop) in this book.

Tad and I first went up to the troop's encampment in the summer of 1974. I was fascinated enough with what I saw that I decided to begin writing about the troop and the ways these boys and men constructed the Boy Scout experience. Over the next several years, I joined the troop in camp a number of summers—1976, 1979, 1981, 1982, 1989, 1990, 1996, 1998, and 1999. In between, I sometimes visited the troop's other activities during the school year—other campouts, Eagle Courts of Honor, and so on. By the late 1970s, I had begun publishing academic journal articles and book chapters on the Boy Scouts, primarily about Troop 49, and for different scholarly audiences, including folklorists, anthropologists, sociologists, psychologists, and historians. Doing fieldwork with adolescent males in a natural setting like a Boy Scout summer encampment posed some interesting methodological problems, which I address in a methodological appendix to this book.

For a while, I had the notion that my "Boy Scout book" would be a compilation of the articles and book chapters I had published elsewhere, but the increasing visibility of the Boy Scouts in the so-called culture wars of the 1990s and the accelerating public alarm over the purported "crisis" in American boyhood convinced me that I needed to write this book for the general audience. The Boy Scouts is enmeshed in some very important public policy questions facing American society, and if we are to make wise public policy in these matters, then we need to see boys and the Boy Scout experience as they actually are, rather than as the abstract social types adults construct in these debates. I also want to speak to the audience of parents, volunteer Scout leaders, coaches, and teachers who work every day with male adolescents. As a folklorist of children's cultures, I want the adults who work with boys to develop a deep respect for the creativity and resilience of the boys' peer cultures and to take these boys' cultures into account as they shape organized institutional experiences for the boys.

Reconceiving the audience for this book meant adopting a writing style and narrative strategy different from the essays I had already published. Most of my fieldwork was at the troop's summer encampment, where one encounters what is probably the most distinctive and intense version of the troop's culture. As an all-male society secluded in the woods and cut off from outside influences and as an institution that structures the lives of the men and boys twenty-four hours a day, camp offers the clearest natural setting for studying how the participants struggle with constructing the meanings of masculinity, honor, friendship, and more. I decided, therefore, to write this book as a coherent narrative account of a two-week encampment by the troop.

This account, however, does not record an actual two-week encampment. I have constructed the two weeks from the events and conversations I witnessed and participated in over several different summers. The pieces all happened, just not necessarily in the order and combination I have recounted here. The boys and the men in this book are, in most cases, composites, with the important exception of Pete, who was the Scoutmaster through this quarter century of my fieldwork with them. Thus, Todd, the Senior Patrol Leader, is a composite of several Senior Patrol Leaders whom I've met over the years, though I have tried to give him (and every other character here) a real personality. The boys in this narrative represent both "types" and real boys. I hope my writing gives them life. Similarly, I have also sometimes presented as a single conversation what really took place in several conversations across a somewhat longer period of time. Taking the boys' (and sometimes the men's) point of view means capturing their natural language, including obscenities. These are real men and boys, not the ones imagined in the Boy Scout *Handbook*.

Also on the topic of narrative strategy, in writing this book I have used footnotes to explain some things that would interrupt the flow of the narrative. There are other important topics that I wanted to introduce but did not want to bury in the footnotes. Borrowing a narrative strategy used by sociologist Peter L. Berger, I have inserted these as various excurses or interludes between some chapters, and these asides could stand alone as interpretive essays. The book can be read without these excurses, but not as profitably, I think.

I was always straightforward with the troop about what I was doing. That I was Tad's university professor gave me access to the troop, and I explained to the Scoutmaster and the boys that I was doing research and writing about them because I was interested in their troop's culture. I guaranteed them anonymity, but that promise was as often met with disappointment as relief. What good was it, the boys wondered aloud, to write about their troop when nobody would know which troop it was? But I have honored that promise. My intent is not to embarrass the troop or its sponsor, a church, but to describe the Boy Scout experience as it is actually created and understood by a group of men and boys.

I also aim to say something important about American culture, and I think there is a warrant for my claims in my long-standing experience with the troop I studied. This is not to say I am unaware of the dangers of generalizing. My research and frequent conversations with people who have been Boy Scouts persuade me that both these things are true: there is a remarkable similarity in the Boy Scout experience across space and time, *and* the nature of the Boy Scout experience is considerably variable. The personality and leadership style of the Scoutmaster make a great deal of difference, for example. A Scoutmaster who is a police officer or military officer might be keen on proficient military drills, whereas some Scoutmasters consider the marching and drilling to be "Mickey Mouse." Some Scoutmasters are strong, charismatic leaders, so much so that the troop is a projection of their personalities.

Other Scoutmasters are low-key, even passive. Troops sponsored by religious organizations are likely to have a tone different from that of troops sponsored by men's fraternal and service clubs. Although the Boy Scouts is primarily a white, middle-class organization, there are important exceptions, such as troops organized specifically for poor kids, or for kids of a particular racial or ethnic group, or for kids with disabilities.

The boys and adult leaders in the troop I studied are white and middle-class, broadly defined. They live in a relatively large town in California's great Central Valley, and they experienced Scouting in the mid-1970s through the 1990s, which means they were born between 1965 (the eleven-year-olds I saw the summer of 1976) and 1988 (the eleven-year-olds I saw in 1999). I have observed generations of boys socialized into the troop's culture, so that I have been able to watch some of the eleven-year-olds mature into older Scouts and, finally, into troop alumni. The troop now contains as members the sons of some of the boys I met my first few years of working with the troop. I have been able to observe continuities and discontinuities in the troop's culture over time as some traditions disappeared and new ones were "invented."

Throughout my work on this book, I have struggled with the problem of finding the appropriate critical distance for writing about an institution that is so much a part of me. As I look back on my own Scouting experiences, for example, I see some events and elements that I now would criticize. There was too much militarism at the South Florida Council camp, but it seemed like fun at the time. There was a good portion of sexism and perhaps even some misogyny—a genuine and aggressive dislike for and disrespect toward women—in our adolescent folk culture at camp. Certainly, there was homophobia—"the irrational fear or intolerance of homosexuality"—in our jokes and verbal dueling.[5] And I am sorry to say that our use of Indian lore somehow mixed a genuine respect for the Native American with a verbal disrespect for real Indians; we worked hard at recreating the costumes and dances of the Great Plains tribes, while ignoring the Seminole people who lived not far from our camp. I can assuage my late 1990s progressive male guilt by reminding myself that the late 1950s were a different time, a Cold War culture with masculinity problems of its own (How many of the Scouts I knew at the Council camp went to Vietnam? How many came back?).[6] But the continuities between Scout camp in the late 1950s in Florida and in the late 1990s in California are too many to celebrate a victory of "progressive" masculinity over Cold War masculinity.

I invite the reader into the world of the men and boys of Troop 49 as they camp for two weeks high in California's beautiful Sierra Nevada. I imagine that people with very different backgrounds, with very different perceptions of the Boy Scouts, with very different views on masculinity, and with very different politics will be reading this book. I take seriously our public policy debates about the lives of children, and I am alarmed that so much of our adult talk about children—especially about boys, in this case—is so uninformed by fieldwork-based knowledge of the lives of real children in natural settings. I am alarmed, too, that we are having some very heated public policy debates about the Boy Scouts of America without examining closely the nature of the lived Boy Scout experience. This book does not offer a final answer to these public policy questions, but it does seek to add something the policy debates have not had so far—that is, a view of Boy Scouts' lives from their point of view. What I offer might provide evidence both for those who see the Boy Scouts as a problem and for those who see it as a solution. But at least we'll be arguing social philosophy with some knowledge of how things are.

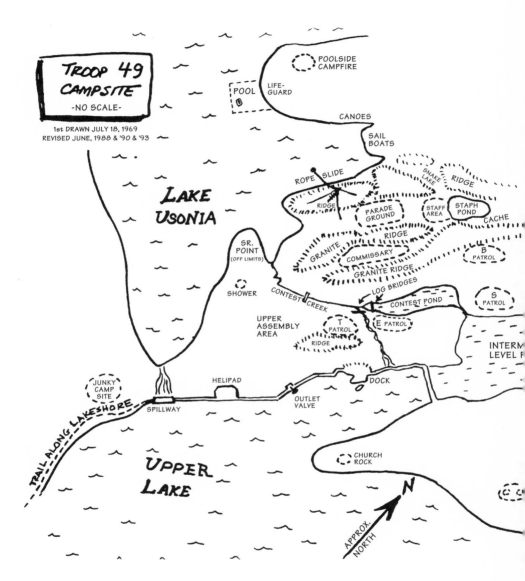

Map of Camp Usonia

DAY 1

Sunday

E-THE-FLAG AREA
ALL & ARCHERY

KYBO

★ ★

I have a rule that I turn off my car's music when I ease off the state highway onto the crushed rock and dirt road that carries me toward the high mountain lakes where Boy Scout Troop 49 has camped each July for the past thirty years or so. In fact, I usually pull over into the small paved area of a marked vista point a scant quarter mile before the turnoff, silence my engine, and get out to look at the view of the Sierra Nevada at that elevation, about seven thousand feet. The dark green of the tall pines against the grays and whites and mottled green of the granite has a stark beauty compared to what I've left behind, but it is the immense distances and scale of the mountain view from that vista that entice the motorist to stop, stretch, and move imaginatively into that landscape. My music comes on again when I restart the car, but already I have taken an important step in my transition from the everyday world to the world of Troop 49's encampment.

My journey that Sunday morning began in the broad, flat floodplain of California's great Central Valley. Backpack and assorted camping comforts in my car, I drove east across the valley during the coolest part of the day. Temperatures easily reach over one hundred degrees on summer days, and the hot air rising from the valley floor late in the morning can make the Sierra Nevada foothills seem even hotter, so I tried to leave my home early enough to get above the foothills by mid-morning. The drive takes three to four hours, depending on traffic, so I took along plenty of cassette tapes to entertain me. The valley and the foothills have their own beauty, even in the summer, but I was accustomed to them, and the yellow-brown of the hills reminded me of the heat I was trying to escape. The months between May and October are the dry season in California, and the valley rarely sees a cloud, much less rain. By July, the beauty and charm of the valley summer have grown old, and that morning my mind rested on the mountain forests and lakes that were my destination. For most of the drive, I kept the windows closed, the air conditioning working furiously against even the early morning heat, and the tape player wailing blues and jazz between the more numerous opera tapes.

The trip from the Pacific Coast east to the Nevada line carried me through a dizzying variety of ecological systems.[1] The flat valley's expanse of tomato fields, orchards, and rice fields slowly gave way to rolling foothills—yellow and brown in the summer, a lush green in the wet winter months. Native trees were few, and the sight of a few green oaks against a velvet yellow hill made the heat almost bearable. I was thankful when the foothills finally gave way to the mountain forests, officially the yellow pine belt and then the lodgepole pine belt, as I climbed higher and higher.

That particular Sunday I drove past the turnoff to the camp. Ten miles beyond the turnoff is a small village with a country store and cafe serving the locals and the recreational tourists. A national forest surrounds the highway for miles at this elevation, dotted by several campgrounds and lakes attracting summer campers and anglers.

My goal that morning was not to eat at the little cafe, as I sometimes do as my ritual farewell to normal food, but to check the large mailbox marked "Troop 49." Boys away at camp for three weeks like to get mail, even if they don't like to write letters and postcards in return, and it is customary in the troop for a visiting dad or other adult to check the mailbox before coming into camp. Occasionally, the box contains a note to see the store proprietor for a package too large for the mailbox. These parcels usually are the "care packages" parents send to their sons, and if there is one thing the boys welcome more than mail, it is a care package filled with cookies, candy, popcorn, and anything else requested in the last postcard home.[2] Tucked among the candy and cookies are toothpaste, books, comic books, extra socks, underwear, and likely a letter from Mom.

I gathered the mail and the two small packages and headed back down the highway toward the turnoff that would carry me toward the camp. My favorite B. B. King tape, *Live at the Regal,* was still playing when I turned off the highway onto a narrower blacktop road that sloped down toward the river. That's when I enforced my rule: when you turn off the highway, turn off the music. I rolled down the windows so I could smell the pine trees and other scents of the forest. The blacktop only runs for about three miles, to a point where a bridge crosses a small river. A campsite to the right, along the river, is the reason the Forest Service paved the road that far, and after I crossed the bridge, I braced myself for the bumpier ride on the unpaved, but graded, road of crushed rock. I glanced at my odometer and made a mental note of the mileage. I had about eight more miles to drive on this road, generally climbing higher into the mountains, but I knew that the mileage was my best guide to the location of a turnoff that most people miss.

Each time I do it, the drive from the valley floor to the lakeside camp feels like a ritual transition from the space and time of ordinary, everyday reality to the ritual space and time of the Boy Scout encampment. I move from the familiar and ordinary landscape of the Central Valley through the transition zone of the foothills and into the mountains themselves, first along a comfortable major highway, then along a simpler blacktop, then along a rustic crushed-rock road, and then along a truly primitive, bumpy logging road to the place where I park and load myself up for the last part of my journey—the walk to camp. Each stage in the journey leaves behind the more familiar and more civilized, easing me into the wilderness setting. Turning off my air conditioner and my tape player is part of the ritual process.

The world of our everyday lives, our ordinary and taken-for-granted reality, is only one of several realities we may experience. Realities are "framed" much like a picture frame encloses and defines the boundaries of a painting, telling us what counts as the painting and what does not.[3] For those who study culture, social scenes are framed, usually unconsciously, by the participants. In the give-and-take of their conversations and other interactions, the participants engage in the ongoing construction and maintenance of a frame that defines the social scene. The frame provides the terms and rules, so to speak, for interpreting the scene. People know both how to behave and how to interpret the behavior of others in a scene thanks to the tacit frame they create through their collaboration. In this sense, social reality is a conspiracy between the participants. To "conspire," as the Latin root has it, is to "breathe together," and I can think of no better metaphor for the conspiracy that is the social construction of everyday reality.[4]

The conspiracy has its rough spots. Frames can be fragile. For example, children understand and can participate in playfighting because they know the difference between the frame "This is a fight" and the frame "This is a playfight." We are most aware of frames, perhaps, when they are broken, as when we violate the norms of a scene and create discomfort all around. A too-hard poke, intentional or unintentional, can turn a playfight into a real fight.

So the culture critic in me experiences the drive from the valley to the mountains as a slow transition from one frame to another, from one social reality to another. The travel, the changing scenery, the changing temperature, the changing smells, the changing road surfaces, and other clues all help mark the changing frame. The men and boys of Troop 49 leave behind them the everyday reality of home, school, neighborhood, summer jobs, hanging out at the mall, and so on to enter a new frame, "This is Boy Scout camp." Or, better yet, "This is Usonia," for the members of the troop tend to refer to their camp experience by the name of one of the two reservoirs beside which they camp.[5]

I watched my odometer carefully when I thought I was near the turn and recognized it without doubt. I turned left and drove upslope along this spur, less maintained by the Forest Service than even the graded gravel road. Another mile or so along that bumpy road, little more than a logging road, brought me within view of Upper Lake, the reservoir just above Usonia. I found a slightly protected place to park my car and loaded up for my hike into camp. I slipped off the casual deck shoes I wore for the drive and put on the socks and hiking boots that would be my main footwear for the encampment. My backpack held the clothing and other items I would need. Once I had the pack frame on my back and adjusted properly for the weight to ride comfortably on my hips, I grabbed my aluminum chair in one hand and a grocery bag full of mail and goodies in the other. The boys like visitors to bring in mail, but the adult Staff likes visitors to bring in pretzels, potato chips, cheese, and even beer and wine for the Staff's campfire. Thus loaded down, I walked down through the pine trees the twenty yards to the lake.

I paused at the lakeshore to take in the view. Upper Lake is an artificial reservoir created by Pacific Gas and Electric Company (PG&E) for its hydroelectric plant downriver. To my right, I could see the lake and the high Sierra Nevada peaks that ring its view. The lake is at 7,000 feet, still in the yellow pine belt of the Sierra, but the visible peaks in the distance rise to over 9,500 feet and are bare granite. Off to my left I could see the dam that holds Upper Lake. Below that dam, I knew, was Usonia Lake, the second reservoir and the one after which the troop named its camp. Across that dam was the troop encampment, so I began walking along the shore of Upper Lake toward the dam.

It was late morning, a day both typical and beautiful. There were only a few tufts of cirrus clouds in the sky. Just beautiful blue sky, bright sunlight, tall stands of yellow pine and lodgepole pine contrasting with the granite landscape, a soft wind blowing across the dark blue lake. As I approached the dam, I could hear two familiar but conflicting sounds. One was the faint splashing of water pouring through a spillway near the bottom of the dam. PG&E releases varying amounts of water from Upper Lake into Usonia, and then from the Usonia dam into the river and on to the hydroelectric power plant downstream. Over the sound of the water, I could hear the voices of teenage boys at play. I was near camp at last.

The last part of my walk was the most treacherous. I had to walk across the dam balancing my backpack, chair, and bag of mail and goodies. The dam top is about two feet wide, but the spillway is a low hump of cement rather than a flat surface, so footing is not as secure as one might like. It always looks more treacherous than it really is—I think. Falling to my right would land me in the lake; falling to my left was a more terrifying possibility, as I could see myself tumbling down the rocky face of the dam. I survived the crossing, as I always did, but I felt that I had earned my entrance into camp. I had passed my last test in the journey begun four hours earlier in the suburban Central Valley.

The first person I encountered was a boy who looked about eleven, one of the first-year campers, I guessed, who was sitting on the dam, fishing. I smiled and said, "Hi"; he returned my greeting but seemed a bit cautious. I was a stranger, after all. I visit camp only every two or three years, which means that the first-year campers do not know me. The boys I knew three years ago were fourteen that year, members of the Senior Patrol. I needed to be introduced to the new campers, such as this young fisherman.

Stepping off the dam, I encountered a cluster of older and younger boys at an area designated as the Upper Lake Waterfront. Just beyond the swimming area was the boating area, where a few of the troop's canoes, rowboats, sailboats, and two powerboats were beached on the rocks. I could see I had arrived during the morning free swim period. About eight boys, teamed as "buddies" for safety, were swimming ten yards offshore, climbing all over an eight-by-four-foot floating rectangle (a war surplus balsa life raft, without the webbing) they called the donut. They were engaged in a customary game of King of the Donut, a game similar to King of the Mountain, in which a boy tries to maintain his domination of the donut by standing on it and pushing or wrestling challenging boys into the water. The boys standing around on shore were older, and I recognized them as Seniors, some of whom I knew when they were younger scouts. I was challenged, properly, by Todd, who did not recognize me even though I had met him a few months earlier at his Eagle award ceremony. He was Senior Patrol Leader, I knew, and I supposed from his whistle, bathing suit, and clipboard that he was also the Waterfront Director that year. He was on the high school swimming team and was also a Red Cross–certified lifeguard.

"Hi, Todd," I said, smiling and extending my right hand to shake his. "I'm Jay Mechling. We met at your Eagle Court of Honor." Todd smiled back, finally realizing why I looked vaguely familiar. He gave me a firm handshake.

"Oh, yeah," he said. I asked him where I could find Pete, the Scoutmaster. "He's back in the Staff Area, taking a nap. You know where that is?"

"Yeah," I replied. "Thanks, I'll see you guys later."

I walked down the slope from the dam into the cool shade of the tall pines that dominate the campsite. I had to take my bearings a bit. The troop was camped at a site they called G.O.N.U., which stands for "Good Old New Usonia." This was the Camp Usonia site the troop used when I first began visiting them in the 1970s. But the troop has used several different sites over the years. Troop 49's original Camp Usonia site, now known as "Old Usonia," was one they shared with a San Francisco Bay area troop, Troop 8.[6] Pete had been a member of Troop 8 and as an Assistant Scoutmaster helped establish the camp for Troop 8. When he moved to the valley and became Troop 49's Scoutmaster in 1957, he began the Troop 49 tradition of having its own summer encampment at Usonia. Old Usonia is near the Usonia Lake dam.

At some point, the troop moved to "New Usonia," the site near the Upper Lake dam. But in the early 1980s, the then district ranger—the head honcho of the Forest Service for that area—began hassling the other troops who were using various sites around the two lakes. The ranger seemed to harbor some basic antipathy toward the Boy Scouts, according to Pete, and he instituted a rule that campers must limit their camp to seven days. He no doubt thought that his arbitrary rule would force the troops to camp elsewhere. But the ranger did not seem to know about Troop 49's encampment, so he never gave them direct orders to limit their camp to seven days. The troop decided to "go underground," as Pete explained it, and moved its site to a spot across the creek from Old Usonia.[7] This spot, dubbed "Usonia III," is where Camp Usonia was held during most of the 1980s.

New Usonia and Usonia III are about twenty minutes apart by motorboat, much longer on foot or in a vehicle. Not many vehicles can get
that far on the Forest Service fire trail that goes around Usonia. Only
four-wheel-drive vehicles and Pete's 1952 Chevrolet pickup truck,
with its high-ratio "Granny gear," can make it into that camp. Eventually the troop was able to move back to New Usonia, hence the name
"Good Old New Usonia." So, while I had known this campsite from
my first visits, I had not been there for over ten years and needed to let
the terrain sink in for a few moments and stir some memories. Finally,
I headed off in the general direction of the Staff Area (see map facing
page 1). As I walked through one of the patrol sites (later I would learn
that it was the Tiger Patrol site), I could see some boys goofing off
during this free period. Some were talking; some were reading, re-
clined on their sleeping bags and foam pads. Others were swinging
lazily in their nylon hammocks. The boys in the patrols do not sleep in
tents, but they sometimes rig tarps for shade or, since most patrol sites
are wooded, for some protection from rain. I smiled, said, "Hi," without explaining my presence, and continued on my way.

The Camp Usonia site is very rocky, with large granite ridges probably ten or fifteen feet high in places and running in parallel lines
through the site. Between the ridges are relatively sandy areas where
most of the camp activities take place. The ridges provide some privacy
between activities and help mark areas set aside for those activities. To
get to the Staff Area, I walked across one granite ridge and through the
flat Commissary Area, and then across another ridge into the more
expansive Parade Ground.

The Commissary Area holds a large, walled tent with a covered
porch. Under the porch is the Commissary table, a white camp box
on legs, and some aluminum lawn chairs. The tent contains the food
disbursed meal by meal to the patrols, and in the shade beside the
Commissary tent are several coolers holding perishables. Wet burlap
bags cover the coolers, relying upon evaporation for much of their
effect.

The Parade Ground has three distinct areas. A tent by the ridge
holds camp equipment, such as Coleman gas lanterns, shovels, rakes,
and other tools. On the far side is an open-air "dining fly" that shades
a table; this is the Advancement Area, and the granite rock beside the
table is known as Advancement Rock. The third area in the Parade
Ground is the Assembly Area, with its twenty-foot flagpole. Logs and
stones mark a square around the flagpole, with four identifiable spots
along three sides, one spot for each patrol. The Senior Scouts and adult
Staff stand along the fourth side. Hanging from the rope and shower

curtain hooks at the top of the flagpole are the American flag and the troop flag.

Just past the Parade Ground is the Staff Area. The "front door" of the area is marked by a hotel bellman's bell sitting on a waist-high rock, and the Staff Area itself is another thirty feet or so into a stand of trees. Anyone but Staff must "knock" on the "door" by ringing this bell, wait for an acknowledgment, and declare his purposes or needs. In other words, the Staff Area is out of bounds for the boys unless they are invited in. I count as Staff and did not "knock" on that Sunday morning; besides, I knew Pete was trying to take a nap, and I did not want to disturb him. He was, just as I imagined, asleep on his camp cot and surrounded by an assortment of bags and boxes. The Staff Area is shaded by a clump of tall pines and has several lawn chairs, a few tables laden with books and clipboards, a large toolbox that is the Staff first aid kit, a few coolers, cots, and other amenities meant to make camp comfortable for the adult men. There are no tents; everyone at Usonia sleeps under the stars and canopy of tall trees.[8] The Staff Area is always messy and cluttered, subject to occasional frenzies of trying to clean up and bring order to things, but it feels comfortable. I found an unused cot under two pine trees near the granite wall that helps enclose the Staff Area and set down my things.

I had been resting only a few moments when Aaron came into the area. Aaron is in his mid-twenties, an alumnus of the troop, and was serving that summer as Camp Director. Aaron had graduated from college and moved to Los Angeles, but he had such loyalty to the troop and to Pete that he agreed to spend his two-week vacation as Camp Director. In that office, he is second in charge after Pete (see fig. 1). Other troop alumni (all bearing the official rank of Assistant Scoutmaster), dads, and other adult males visiting camp are subject to the Camp Director's authority. Aaron and I greeted each other softly so as not to disturb Pete's nap, and I inquired how camp was going.

Aaron replied that the four-and-a-half-day hike taken the week before had gone well and that camp seemed to be off to a good start. Camp Usonia really lasts three weeks, but the troop spends only two of those weeks at the campsite. Camp begins with a three- to five-day backpacking trip in the mountains, ending at the campsite. Troop alumni and dads have set up camp by the time the tired boys arrive on Friday. Setting up camp is an elaborate matter, for the troop has a large truckload of equipment for making the encampment as comfortable as possible. Basic to the setup is "ULMUD," the Usonia Lake Municipal Utilities District. ULMUD is a vast system of black and gray polyurethane tubing that provides running water for every patrol site and the

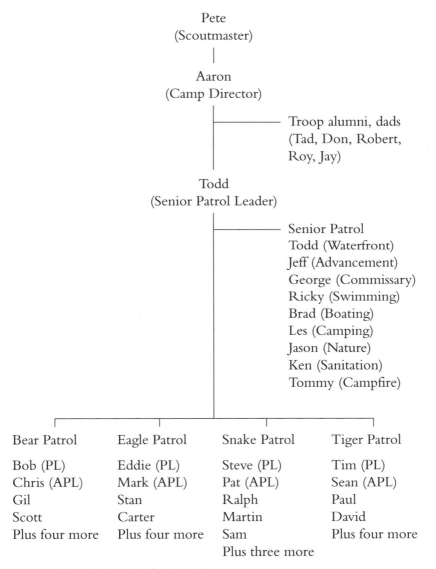

Figure 1. Organization chart for Camp Usonia

Staff Area. Since camp lies below the level of Upper Lake, ULMUD can siphon water from the lake, filter it, and store it in large barrels and tapped containers at the campsites. ULMUD even includes a camp shower, with hot water provided by coils of black tubing lying on the granite rocks in the sun, an efficient solar water heater.

Besides ULMUD, the alumni and dads assemble large wooden tables and benches for each patrol site, assemble the patrol boxes for each site, erect the few tents that store food and equipment, set up the water-front, bring in the boats, erect the flagpole, and set up the KYBO. The KYBO is the camp latrine. The alumni must dig a rather deep hole in the sand, cover it with the two-seat wooden construction made by Pete years ago, and shelter the KYBO with a tarpaulin that provides privacy from the back and overhead shelter from the sun and occasional rain. The KYBO is open-air on all other sides, and at both Old Usonia and G.O.N.U. the site for the KYBO has been chosen with an eye to providing campers a scenic view while they're taking care of business. "KYBO," as a traditional name for a camp latrine, goes far beyond Troop 49, though people seem not to agree on whether KYBO stands for "Keep Your Bowels Open" or "Keep Your Bowels Operating." In any case, the KYBO it is.

There were over forty boys in camp, Aaron explained to me, a healthy number and a sign that the troop was prospering. Todd, the Senior Patrol Leader, was the next in command beneath Aaron and was the person who bore the most responsibility for making sure the day-to-day activities of camp ran smoothly. Todd was sixteen, and his office, Senior Patrol Leader, really meant two things. First, he was Patrol Leader of the Senior Patrol, the patrol of boys aged fourteen through seventeen. The Seniors were the camp counselors, dividing among themselves various duties for camp management and various responsibilities for teaching Scout skills. Jeff was the Advancement Director, responsible for overseeing the Scouts' work on skills and their advancement through earning badges. George was Commissary Director (or "Commy Czar"), in charge of the food. Todd was, as I had supposed earlier, the Waterfront Director. As one of the two Seniors certified as instructors in lifesaving by the American Red Cross, Todd was the camp's official lifeguard and taught the swimming and lifesaving classes. Ricky (also certified) helped Todd teach swimming, Brad taught boating, Les taught camping skills, and Jason taught nature skills. In addition to some merit badge and skill award classes, Ken was in charge of camp sanitation. And Tommy was Campfire Director. One of Todd's duties as Senior Patrol Leader was to keep track of the performance of all these Seniors in their various roles and report to Aaron or to Pete any problems he detected in Senior performance.

The Seniors, though, are a fairly tight fraternity within the troop, so it is likely that the Senior Patrol Leader deals with a troublesome Senior himself without drawing Pete's or Aaron's attention to the problem. The Seniors have their own campsite, Senior Point, out on a thickly forested, rocky promontory that juts into Lake Usonia, well below the rest of camp. Senior Point is off-limits to the younger Scouts and, significantly, to the adult Staff as well. Pete will violate the sanctity of Senior Point only in order to fix a problem that would threaten the entire encampment itself, and even then he calls out, "Knock, knock," as a warning of his approach.

Pete and the other adult leaders of the troop expect the Seniors to perform their duties responsibly and to demonstrate leadership throughout camp. A boy advances in the troop by learning skills and passing tests of those skills in order to earn badges. The new boy earns Tenderfoot by mastering some basic knowledge of the Boy Scouts and some basic skills. He then earns individual skill awards (cooking, camping, swimming, etc.), working toward the ranks of Second Class and then First Class Scout. The next step is to earn merit badges toward Star, Life, and finally the pinnacle rank, Eagle Scout. But a boy cannot become an Eagle Scout just by earning the requisite number of badges. He must design and execute an approved community service project. And he must demonstrate leadership. Camp Usonia is where the Seniors best get to show Pete and others whether or not they possess this undefined quality of character. Some boys in the troop have earned enough badges for Eagle but have never received that rank because they have failed to show leadership. Some boys simply never muster the assertiveness and interpersonal skills necessary to lead. Others fail their leadership test by "fucking up," as Pete and the alumni put it. Every Senior knows that his performance at Camp Usonia is scrutinized twenty-four hours a day for evidence of leadership—and for evidence of "fucking up."

The second sense in which Todd is Senior Patrol Leader is that he is senior to the other four patrol leaders. The Scouts themselves, boys aged eleven through thirteen, are divided into four patrols—the Bears, the Eagles, the Snakes, the Tigers—and each patrol has a Patrol Leader (PL) and an Assistant Patrol Leader (APL) with authority over the four to six boys in the patrol. An old tradition in the troop is that the names of the four patrols must begin with the letters B–E–S–T, and the troop refers to itself as "Troop 49, the BEST Troop!" The patrols stand and report during assemblies in that order—BEST—and often do other things in that order. The names of the four patrols have remained fairly stable over the years. To become a member of the troop and to be assigned to a patrol, therefore, is to become a member of a relatively small group that has a character and a history.

From the folklorist's perspective, the patrol is the boy's most basic "folk group" in the troop.[9] When people have some ongoing experience with one another, they may come to establish group traditions, such as oral routines or customary rituals, that help individuals feel "at home" in the group. The folklore and folkways of the group may come to mark its identity, to provide ways of teaching new members what it means to belong to the group, and to provide ways of dealing with tensions within the group. The patrol is the group with which the boy spends most of his time. It is the group with which he eats and sleeps, works and plays.[10] A boy may have friends, even best friends, in other patrols, and these friendship dyads count as folk groups, too; but his own patrol is the one where he is expected to develop the most loyal friendships. Sometimes boys are very unhappy in a patrol and wish to be transferred to another patrol, but Pete will do that only if it serves the best interests of everyone concerned, not just the unhappy boy.

Troop 49 itself is small enough to count as a folk group, and there are a good many customs and traditions—"C&Ts," the troop calls them—that belong to the troop as a whole. Yet, if it is accurate to say that the boy "experiences" the Boy Scouts not through the national organization but through a concrete, embodied troop of particular men and boys, then it is also accurate to say that the boy experiences Troop 49 (at least at Camp Usonia) primarily through the particular small group of boys in his patrol. Being a Patrol Leader or Assistant Patrol Leader is the boy's first leadership role in the troop, and it is a difficult role for the average thirteen-year-old who fills it. He is responsible for the success or failure of the small-group folk culture that emerges slowly over the three weeks at camp. The Patrol Leader who shows leadership skills has a good chance of being chosen Senior Patrol Leader when he is older and a member of the Senior Patrol.

These, then, were the forty-odd boys in camp that summer, nine Seniors and over thirty Scouts. The third group at Camp Usonia was the adult Staff. To be "adult" in this context simply means to be over eighteen. Beyond Pete and the Camp Director, the adult Staff may vary from day to day. Troop alumni, from those in college to those in their thirties, tend to show up now and again, usually for weekends.[11] Most of these alumni are on the troop's records as Assistant Scoutmasters. Dads show up, but usually only for specific duties, such as helping out with an overnight patrol hike. The adult Staff usually forms its own folk culture, with traditions of its own, despite the transience of its population. The Staff, as we have seen, has its own campsite as secluded from the gaze of the Scouts as is Senior Point, and the Staff has its own small campfire site for the after-campfire campfire, that is, a Staff-only campfire after the troop's or patrols' campfires and after all the Scouts and Seniors are (supposedly) bedded down for the night.

The folk culture of Camp Usonia exists on several levels. There is the folk culture of the individual patrols, a folk culture determined to some extent by the dynamics of the folk culture of early-adolescent white, middle-class males. There is the folk culture of the Senior Patrol, the product of the dynamics of the folk culture of middle- to late-adolescent white, middle-class males. And there is the folk culture of the Staff, adult white, middle-class males. Each folk culture has its own character, and each interacts in complex ways with the other two cultures. The power and vitality of these cultures dominate the scene in relation to the "official" Boy Scout agenda of the camp. Neither the boys' agenda nor the adults' agenda for camp dominates; what emerges is a dynamic culture that results from the interaction of these three folk cultures. In a very real and important sense, the culture of Camp Usonia is a culture created at the borders where these three cultures meet.

Of course, Aaron and I were not talking of such things that Sunday morning. We were chatting generally about how camp was going. Pete stirred a bit and opened his eyes. Once they focused on me he flashed a smile. "Why, hello, Jay Mechling." "Hello, Pete," I replied. Pete sat up and swung his legs off the cot, and he sat there for a few seconds. "That nap did me some good," he said. Some may scoff at the amenities of Camp Usonia, holding that camping must entail roughing it in order to be an authentic camping experience, but there is much to be said for comfort in a long-term camp. Restful sleep keeps the men and boys healthier and happier. I noticed that Pete was sleeping on a four-inch-thick foam pad, covered with sheets and a sleeping bag opened like a quilt. Comfortable shoes, including some that looked like bedroom slippers, were lined up underneath the bed on a scrap of carpeting.

Pete was born in the San Francisco East Bay and had become a member of the famed Troop 8 when he was twelve. Troop 8 had a long history, dating back almost to the founding of the Boy Scouts of America in 1910, and Pete loved the troop's rich folk culture of customs and traditions. Pete attended the University of California, Berkeley, and became a teacher of high school mathematics. He and his wife moved to the Central Valley in the 1950s and raised their three children, two older sons two years apart and a daughter. The two sons had become Scouts, but their troop was poorly organized and Pete stepped in to help out. One thing led to another, and before long Pete was the Scoutmaster. Over the years, Pete has fashioned Troop 49 after his best experiences in Troop 8. Pete brought to Troop 49 several of the C&Ts of Troop 8, but the folk culture of Troop 49 has built upon that base to create a distinct culture of its own. Pete is still friends with leaders of Troop 8 and keeps in touch with some of the Troop 8 alumni. When Troop 8 camps at Old Usonia, Pete always manages to go over and visit with them.

Pete's two sons were among the troop's first Eagle Scouts, and they are among the alumni who make a special effort to visit Camp Usonia whenever possible. Pete himself never earned Eagle, though he was a Life Scout, the rank just below Eagle. Accordingly, the troop calls Life the "gentleman's rank," something like the "gentleman's C" grades that Harvard and Yale men of years ago took as evidence that they had old wealth and did not need to work hard to earn A grades, as did the new rich. Pete is very proud not only of his sons but also of every Scout who has earned Eagle in the troop. In fact, Todd's Eagle of a few months earlier was the fiftieth Eagle in the troop's history and the occasion for a gala celebration. This number is especially impressive among Boy Scout troops, but it is all the more impressive because it is well known that Troop 49 is no "Eagle mill"; it does not crank out Eagles. In fact, Pete has resisted over the years the gradual relaxing (in his view) of the official requirements for Eagle, so the troop has its own standards that are stricter than the official organization's. More than fifty Eagles over thirty years testifies to the strength of this troop's culture.

Pete's work and identity as a high school mathematics teacher affect his performance style as a Scoutmaster. Pete had originally intended to be an engineer, and he brings to everything he does the engineer's careful attention to order, sequence, and detail. But being a teacher also means that he is used to teaching lessons, both formal and informal, to adolescents. He knows how to break down a task into separate steps that boys can master, and he is accustomed to dealing with behavior problems.

Pete's individual personality, of course, also shapes his performance of the role of Scoutmaster. Pete is a tall man, probably six feet three inches, and though he is lean (not skinny), he is athletic enough to provide a strong presence. His beard is as curly and graying as his hair, and his voice is deep. All this amounts to an imposing presence that helps, no doubt, in keeping control over the four dozen boys and young men who are his moral and legal responsibility for the three-week encampment. He has an excellent sense of humor and jokes easily with everyone at camp. He is empathetic and has worked with adolescent boys long enough to read their nonverbal communication as accurately as their verbal. He can be soft and compassionate and confesses that he cries easily under the right circumstances. But he also can be firm, sometimes too firm for his liking. Pete has had a problem with his temper since he was a teenage Scout himself, and he works daily on strategies for keeping his temper under control. The fact that Pete *might* holler at a boy is usually enough to keep the boy in line, and some of the folk narratives told and retold in the troop are about occasions on which Pete lost his temper.

The fact is that a Scoutmaster's personality and communication style play a large part in the overall character of the experience of being a Boy Scout. As I have talked to men over the years about their own Boy Scout experiences, it has become clear to me that many of the experiences of the organization remain amazingly stable across time and place. But it is just as clear to me that the crucial variable in creating differences in the experience is the Scoutmaster. A Scoutmaster who loves military drilling will drive away some sorts of boys; a passive Scoutmaster who cannot control rowdy teenagers will drive away others. The personality of a troop in many ways reflects the personality of the Scoutmaster, and any generalizations about the Boy Scout experience must take this into account.

"What time is it?" Pete asked Aaron, suddenly realizing that it was Sunday and that Church Service was on the agenda for the late morning, just before lunch. Aaron replied that it was 10:45, only five minutes or so before the troop needed to be assembled for Church. Pete rose, walked the few steps to the water spigot lashed to a board that was, in turn, lashed to the trunk of a tree, and brushed his teeth. He reached for his Scout uniform shirt and neckerchief which were hanging on a wire hanger hooked on a low branch of the pine tree. Normally, uniform shirts and troop neckerchiefs are worn only for ceremonial occasions—the raising and lowering of the flags, Church Service, and the Investiture of new Scouts—occasions requiring the presence of the uniform to signal that these are serious, solemn events. The uniforms help frame such events as rituals distinct from everyday life at camp.

I heard a referee's whistle blowing and Todd bellowing out from a high spot on one of the granite ridges, "Five minutes to assembly. Five minutes to assembly." Where other troops may have a bugler to sound assemblies and other activities, Troop 49 uses the whistle and lung power.

I went into my pack for my own Scout shirt and neckerchief. On the Parade Ground, the Scouts and Seniors were beginning to assemble by patrol. Todd stood facing the flagpole, with the Bear Patrol to his left, the Eagle and Snake Patrols facing him across the square, the Tiger Patrol to his right, and the Seniors and Staff closing the square behind him. He called the troop to attention and asked the Patrol Leaders for their reports. As was custom, the Patrol Leaders saluted Todd and responded in their BEST order whether all boys were "present or accounted for." Todd then called the troop "at ease." These assemblies and the flag ceremonies are about as military as this troop gets.

Pete asked Todd for the floor and introduced me to the troop as a longtime friend of Tad and of Troop 49. Todd led the traditional Troop 49 welcome: "Hip-hip-hooray! Hip-hip-hooray! Hip-hip-hooray!" Pete had more news—namely, that I had brought in some mail. That pleased the boys and, I imagine, was more impressive than the fact that I knew a troop alumnus. Pete handed the mail to Todd, and the Seniors led the troop in singing the traditional mail call song:

Mail call, mail call, maaaiiiil call

(Tune: "The Farmer in the Dell")
What a terrible death to die,
What a terrible death to die,
What a terrible death to be mailed to death,
What a terrible death to die.
Mail call, mail call, maaaiiiil call.

Then, without pause:

(Tune: "Here We Sit Like Birds in the Wilderness")
Here we sit like birds in the wilderness,
Birds in the wilderness,
Birds in the wilderness,
Here we sit like birds in the wilderness
Waiting for the mail to come.[12]

Mail call is a very public event, sparing nobody. Todd calls out the name of each boy as he reads it off the postcard or envelope, but postcards are in danger of being read aloud to the group, and envelopes are in danger of being sniffed to see if they contain perfumed notes from girlfriends back home. There was considerable joking and teasing throughout mail call, but I could see that the boys most hurt were the ones who had received no mail.

After a few announcements, Todd asked the troop, when they were dismissed, to follow him in single file "and reverently" up to Church Rock for services. Todd called the troop back to attention, surveyed how well the boys were doing that, and then said, "Dismissed." He began walking toward Church Rock, and the patrols, again in their BEST order, followed him. The Seniors and Staff fell in behind.

We followed Todd through camp and up to the Waterfront, then along the lakeshore to a smaller dam. We crossed the dam and then veered off to the right and up the steep granite slope toward a rocky promontory that overlooks Upper Lake. When we reached the peak, two Seniors were standing there with stacks of yellow mimeographed booklets, "Worship Service at Usonia." These Seniors were the ushers, and they gave each boy and man a book as we filed by. All sat down and took in the magnificent view. From this promontory, the troop can see many of the major Sierra Nevada peaks that are part of the Usonia landscape.

This is what humanistic, cultural geographers would call an "affective landscape," or a "landscape of memory." [13] This place means more to the troop than the U.S. Geological Survey topographical quadrangle maps can render. These boys can draw the profile of that Sierra horizon from memory (they have done it in my presence). They know the names of the peaks. They have climbed some of those peaks, and oral tradition within the troop connects those peaks with particular backpacking trips—the Cinder Cone they climbed in 1987, for example—and memories of those trips. Some of the names of the features of the physical landscape are official; some are folk names given by someone in the troop, accepted by others, and passed on to subsequent generations of campers through oral tradition. Landscape, memories, and meaning are inextricably linked for the troop. From Church Rock, we can see their landscape of memory.

The grandeur and scale of the view from Church Rock helped frame the scene as a solemn ritual, so the boys sat quietly, refraining from their usual banter, poking, and other adolescent play. Todd asked the boys to turn to page 5 in the yellow booklet and led us in a responsive reading:

We Thank Thee

Leader: For the glory of the stars, the majesty of the mountains, and the beauty of the trees—
Response: We thank Thee, O Lord.
Leader: For the changing seasons, that bring the snow to the peaks and then water to the valleys—
Response: We are grateful, O Lord.
Leader: For the songs of birds and the laughter of little streams—
Response: We offer our thanks, O Lord.
Leader: For the friendship of our fellow scout, the affection of our parents, and the freedom of our nation—
Response: We lift up our voices in thanks.
Leader: As we remember Thy gifts, show us ways we can be of service to others.

On the trail that we walk, help us to enjoy the lights
and the shadows, taking joy from the light and strength
from the shadow.

Response: Lord, this is our prayer.

Then Pete rose to speak his "sermon." The theme was love. The best kind of love, he explained, was not physical or sexual love, but caring about each other. "I love you all," he said, "and I get signs that you feel the same way about me. I love this place. I feel close to God here. I often wonder, when I'm in church, whether God is there. Never mind why I wonder that. But I never doubt it when I'm at Church Rock." Pete continued with the observation that the Scout Law is just about perfect to live by and that two important points of the twelve points of the Scout Law are the first and last: "A Scout is Trustworthy" and "A Scout is Reverent." "They really go together well."

Pete alluded to an event during the backpacking trip the past week. Trustworthiness was key in that event, and related to Reverence. Pete returned to love. "God is love. That's a good definition. It all connects—God, love, Trustworthiness, Reverence." Pete sat down, and Todd rose again to lead the troop in singing "America, The Beautiful" from the book. Todd then closed the service with a benediction read from the book: "May the grandeur of the lakes, and the mountains, and the beauty of all that grows, enter our souls, bringing us strength and joy and peace. Amen."

Church over, we all rose and filed back down the slope, past the two Seniors who collected the service booklets. When we got back to the Staff Area, I barely had time to change from my uniform shirt to a T-shirt before I heard George blow his whistle and call out "Commissary Emissary! Commissary Emissary!" This is a folk term within the troop for the boy designated for that day by each patrol to fetch the patrol's cardboard box of provisions for each meal. I searched out George to ask him which patrol was to have me as their "guest" that day for meals. The Eagles were the lucky patrol, so I walked to their patrol site, the farthest from the Staff Area.

As I strolled up, I could see a few of the boys setting the camp table with paper towels as placemats; the rest of the patrol was standing around, waiting for the cooks to finish getting ready for lunch. Each day two boys were designated the cooks, one boy as KP (borrowed from military jargon for "Kitchen Police," naturally), one or two boys to collect firewood for the patrol campfire, and so on. The Patrol Leader was responsible for creating and posting on the side of the patrol box a duty roster showing the rotation of all the boys through the various roles that had to be performed. Every boy performed every role in turn, but being the cook is an especially sensitive role, and older campers show little enthusiasm for sitting down to a meal prepared by a first-year camper. Anything can happen, and adolescent appetites are at stake.

I greeted everyone, including Eddie, the Patrol Leader. I chose the place with the plastic Solo cup holder marked "G1" in black marker ink. G1, I knew, stood for "Guest #1," and adult Staff was always G1 at a patrol meal, while Senior guests were G2 and G3. The lunch was simple. On the table were two loaves of soft "marshmallow" bread, one white and the other whole wheat. For the sandwiches there was a pile of yellow American cheese, sliced and bearing the telltale black fingerprints of a cook who did not wash his hands before handling the cheese. "Oh, gross," groaned one of the older Scouts. "Butt head," said Eddie to the young Scout who set out the meal, "didn't you wash your hands? Go wash them now!" The hungry Scouts made do with the cheese, applying mustard, mayonnaise, and even peanut butter to the bread. The boys passed around large plastic pitchers of Kool-Aid.[14]

There was enough cheese for two sandwiches each, but some of the boys were still hungry and made themselves peanut butter and jelly sandwiches. Patrol boxes are always stocked with bread, peanut butter, and jelly, because of Pete's philosophy that food ought to be available at all times to help the boys stay healthy and energetic. One of the older Scouts in the patrol laid out two pieces of bread and said, "Have you guys seen this?" He spread peanut butter on one slice of bread and mayonnaise on the other. When he closed the sandwich, the boys around him said something like "Gross." "P, B and P," he said, confusing the boys who knew that "P, B and J" stood for "peanut butter and jelly" but were unfamiliar with the variant. "Peanut butter and pus" he grinned, taking a bite from the sandwich. "It's delicious." Boys groaned again and turned away from him, unable to watch.

One of the cooks brought the patrol's cardboard Commissary box to the table and distributed the candy bars and gum that were the dessert for lunch. I took some gum (the least favorite dessert) and then followed the troop custom that guests thank the cook and ask permission to leave. I walked back to the Staff Area, taking the long way around so I could stroll through the other patrol sites. Lunch is followed by a brief "siesta" period so the cooks can clean up and the rest of the boys can relax a bit before the rest of the day's activities. Most of the boys do rest during siesta; some actually nap, but most lie reading or talking softly in their "bunks." Their reading may consist of comic books or novels (Stephen King novels were popular one summer) or, most likely, Boy Scout *Handbooks* and merit badge pamphlets. Advancement classes require reading done as "homework," and the siesta is about the only quiet time boys have for this reading.

Patrol sites are pretty much alike in their elements. The patrols camp in traditional sites; the Eagle site at G.O.N.U., for example, was selected years ago by the Eagle Patrol. At the site dining areas are the large, wooden picnic tables and the patrol boxes. The patrol boxes are $2 \times 3 \times 2$ feet, made of ⅝-inch plywood, and hinged on one of the long sides. Chains keep the hinged side hanging parallel to the ground as a working surface for the cook. In the box are basic supplies—salt and pepper, sugar in a recycled peanut butter jar, jelly, peanut butter, bread, dry cereal, dishwashing detergent, scouring pads, matches, paper towels, and assorted other items. Sometimes the patrols paint their boxes to individualize them, and the Tiger Patrol box has the best paint job I've seen—the black and orange stripes of a tiger. Each patrol also has a Coleman gas camp stove for cooking, a considerable advance from earlier days when patrols had to cook on large and inefficient wood-burning stoves.

The routines around preparing food and cleaning up after meals are among the most elaborate of the troop's camp routines, and the subject of some humor and campfire skits. Sanitation is a subject that Pete takes very seriously. In part, he worries about the impact of the troop's camp on the environment and wants to minimize that effect. There are separate containers for different sorts of garbage. Burnable trash, such as paper plates and towels, goes into a large garbage bag tied to a tree. Tin cans must be washed out and have both ends and the label removed; the can is then squashed flat and put into the patrol's "can can." Foil and nonburnable plastic also go into the "can can" to be separated out later. "Clean garbage" goes into a large white bucket labeled as such with a marker. Clean garbage—the leftover food and drink that has not been consumed—will go through elaborate treatment before being buried. Each patrol site had a small pit for disposing of used dish-water and a small pit criss-crossed with twigs and pine needles for disposing of the cooking grease left over from bacon or hamburger. The cool grease flows through the needles, while bits of food are captured and burned later with the needles.

Pete also worries about sanitation because of the effect on health, morale, and the camp program of boys coming down with stomach and intestinal ailments because soap was not rinsed off a cooking pot or grease off a griddle. Because the boys eat with disposable plastic utensils off paper plates and bowls and drink from disposable Solo cups in reusable plastic holders, the only washing involved with KP is of the pots, pans, and utensils used in cooking the meal. Those on KP duty have plastic tubs for washing and rinsing the cooking implements, which are hung out to dry. Todd makes an official inspection of each patrol site every morning after breakfast and morning assembly. Todd awards points to patrols based on the cleanliness and neatness of their sites, and he attends carefully to the patrol kitchen. Pete occasionally will make his own surprise inspections, and certainly he inspects a patrol's sanitation when he is a guest at a meal. Pete has been known to become very angry over unsanitary conditions and practices.

Aside from the outdoor kitchen and dining room, each patrol site has its bedroom, the area where the boys have spread out their camp mattresses (foam or inflatable) and their sleeping bags, duffel bags, backpacks, and assorted belongings. Each patrol has a small campfire site for patrol campfires, and each site has a handmade patrol flag.

As I walked by them, I noted how each patrol site seemed like the others, but how each also had its own character. The program of the Boy Scouts of America and of Troop 49 aims at making the patrol the Scout's primary folk group, hoping that out of their close association these boys will build a rich folk culture reflected in patrol flags, patrol yells, patrol hats, and patrol spirit. Sometimes the strategy works. With the right combination of boys and a skilled Patrol Leader, a patrol can become a tightly bonded "gang." [15] But just because a group meets the logistical conditions for a folk group does not mean it will develop a folk culture. Some small groups never succeed in creating a satisfying small group culture, and that's as true at Camp Usonia as elsewhere.

Finally, I was back at the Staff Area and stretched out on my cot for a brief nap myself. I wanted to avoid the "mountain sickness" that sometimes comes to valley people during their first day or two in the mountains. It takes a while for the body to adjust to the lower oxygen supply at the high altitude, and I have suffered through the headaches and slight nausea that come with this adjustment. I had dozed a while when I heard Todd's whistle and his yell, "Second period! Second period!" I rose and decided to find and sit in on one of the advancement classes.

"Advancement" is the word used to refer to the part of the camp program devoted to learning Scout skills and earning the awards and badges that mark proficiency in those skills. Advancement is the most official part of the agenda at camp, and most of the boys count on earning a number of badges (perhaps even a new rank) at camp. Some of the boys were down at the Waterfront working on swimming, lifesaving, rowing, canoeing, and sailing skills. Some were at a nature class, working on skills awards and merit badges having to do with nature study, ecology, and the like. The boys working on campcraft skills were learning how to build an emergency shelter. Most advancement classes involve the boys in doing something physical, but the classes also involve some "book learning," reading from the *Handbook* or from merit badge pamphlets, and even some tests of this book knowledge. The boys' outlook on this bookish aspect of advancement pretty much follows their attitudes toward school. The good students don't mind it; the poor students hate it. I chose to join Pete at the Snake Patrol site, where he was working with the first-year campers who had not yet earned their first rank, Tenderfoot.

When an eleven-year-old boy joins the troop, he must learn the basic information and philosophy that earn him the rank of Tenderfoot. These boys resemble pledges in a fraternity, in that they are not yet full members of the troop. The most significant mark of this in-between status, apart from the lack of any rank badge on their left breast uniform pocket, is the absence of a neckerchief around their necks. Their status also excludes them from the circle of Scouts that closes the troop campfires. The new boys must stand in the center of the circle, not yet included in the fraternity.

The troop neckerchief is one of the most important markers of identity for this troop, for it is one of those areas where the troop departs from the official BSA procedures and creates its own C&T. Official BSA neckerchiefs are large right triangles of cloth of a single color. The neckerchief was an element of the original Scout uniform at the organization's founding in 1910, and though there has always been some opposition to the military style of the Boy Scout uniform, the justification for the neckerchief included its usefulness as a bandage in administering first aid.[16] At the time of its founding, each troop selects a color for its neckerchief.

Pete brought with him from his boyhood troop the tradition of creating a distinctive two-color neckerchief. Troop 49 takes two neckerchiefs, one gold and the other maroon, and sews the two together along the long side of each triangle. Troop tradition holds that the gold represents "sunshine and happiness, especially at Usonia," while the maroon represents "the two stars on the Scout badge, truth and knowledge." The neckerchief is then folded and worn so that the gold half comes over the right shoulder and the maroon over the left. This is the "correct" way to wear the troop neckerchief, and the folk group enforces this rule by taunting and teasing the boy who gets it wrong. The standard reminder to a Scout who has it on backward is to ask, "What color is blood?"

The six new boys around the dining table at Snake site had not yet earned their troop neckerchiefs. As I quietly approached the group, I could see that each boy had in front of him a copy of the most recent *Handbook*.[17] Pete was asking one boy, "What's the Scout motto?" The boy smiled; this was an easy question. "Be Prepared." Pete smiled. "Yes. And do you know the Scout slogan?" At this question, the boy's smile of triumph turned to a frown of puzzlement, helped not in the least by the eagerness of a few boys around the table to give the right answer. After a few seconds, when it became clear that the first boy was not going to come up with the answer, Pete allowed another to provide it: "Do a good turn daily."

In order to earn their Tenderfoot badges and be invested in the troop, these first-time campers would have to master the basics of the Boy Scout values, learning the Scout Oath and the twelve points of the Scout Law "by heart," as they say—an interesting way to say "memorized" in this context. Pete held up his right hand in the "Scout sign," with the palm forward, the middle three fingers straight, and the thumb folded across the pinkie.

"These three fingers stand for the three points of the Scout Oath or Promise." Pete showed them how the three-fingered Scout sign is turned into a military-style salute and then showed them the left-handed Scout handshake; "With the left hand because it's nearest the heart," said Pete.

Pete then asked the boys to open their *Handbooks* to the page listing the twelve points of the Scout Law. He asked the boys to read the brief descriptions accompanying each law, but he then began to talk at length about the seventh and tenth laws, "obedient" and "brave."

"Let's look at what it says 'obedient' means. 'A Scout follows the rules of his family, school, and troop. He obeys the laws of his community and country. If he thinks these rules and laws are unfair, he tries to have them changed in an orderly manner rather than disobey them.' Notice that 'orderly manner' part about changing unfair rules. What if your Patrol Leader makes you do KP and it's not your turn? What should you do?" Pete paused and looked around the table.

"Do it, then talk to the Patrol Leader," said one boy.

"And what if the Patrol Leader still says 'too bad'?"

"Go to a higher authority," said the same boy, confidently.

"Right. If you think something's unfair, then check with the Senior Patrol Leader or one of the adult leaders." Pete then turned their attention to the *Handbook*'s explanation of "brave."

"It says here, 'A Scout can face danger even if he is afraid. He has the courage to stand for what he thinks is right even if others laugh at or threaten him.' What that means is that there are two sorts of brav-

ery—physical and moral. There are lots of ways to show you are physically brave, but there's a big difference between being brave and being
stupid, isn't there?" The boys nod agreement. "I don't want you to be
doing anything dangerous just for the thrill. Moral bravery is harder,
lots harder." Pete spent the next few minutes spinning out some examples of moral bravery, of the ability to resist friends' temptation to
do something wrong. The whistle sounded, announcing the end of this
advancement period, so Pete gave them a reading assignment out of the
Handbook and dismissed them.

With the second advancement period over, boys from all over camp
wandered back to their patrol sites and listened for Todd to whistle and
announce free swim. Most boys had changed into their swimsuits and
headed for the Waterfront, while a few preferred to remain in camp,
goofing off. The cooks for the evening had a rather shortened free
activity time, as George soon called, "Commissary Emissary" and the
cooks trudged to the Commissary tent to pick up the boxes of food for
dinner.

I walked back to the Staff Area with Pete.

"A few years ago I would have talked about civil disobedience, the
Civil Rights movement, the antiwar movement, and a whole bunch
of other things in that lesson about obedience, but now these kids
wouldn't understand a thing I've said. They've had no experience with
civil disobedience." We walked a few more paces, and Pete continued.
"Camp started real well this year," he told me with great satisfaction;
sometimes the troop has had a rocky start. "The backpacking trip went
well and the kids are really up for camp." Pete was pleased that Aaron
had agreed to come up and be Camp Director. As Pete and I caught up
on a few things, we heard cooks shouting, "Dinner is served," from
their patrol sites, so we headed off to different patrols.

I arrived at the Eagle site to find the table set as before and the Scouts
waiting for me. I recognized the dinner that was being served. USDA
surplus canned beef and gravy had been heated in one large, No. 10 tin
can, with its bail (handle) made from a coat hanger—the traditional
Boy Scout substitute for a cooking pot—while instant mashed potatoes
had been prepared in another. Canned peas completed the meal. The
twelve-year-old cook, who was working on a cooking skills award, and
his younger assistant moved slowly around the table, serving generous
dollops of mashed potatoes and asking each diner if he wanted his meat
on the potatoes or on the side.

Les, the Senior who was G2 for the evening, groaned at the menu.
"I see we're having S.O.S. tonight," he said cryptically, looking around
the table for a reaction. A young Scout took the bait. "What's that

mean?" "Shit on Snow," answered Les, smiling. "I kind of like it," said one boy down at the end, but his patrol buddies looked at him like he was from another planet. Complaining about the food and making gross comments about it were an important tradition at camp; there's no place for actually liking the food.

Like it or not, the hungry boys devoured all the food there was. Once everyone was finished, the cook brought over a can containing the evening's dessert, instant butterscotch pudding, which he dished into the Solo cups in front of each boy. Instant pudding made with too much liquid is a fairly runny substance, so he could have poured the pudding into our cups. "Oh, good, scours," said Les, noisily slurping his pudding. "What's that mean?" "Oh, you know, scours . . . what farmers call the diarrhea calves get. Scours." Les got the reaction he wanted, as the boys made faces and shouted, "Gross!" But they ate the pudding. The boy who finished first jumped up and grabbed the can, which still held a few spoonsful of pudding, and quickly poured what was left into his cup. "You homo," shouted the boy sitting next to him, and they started to scuffle over the remaining pudding, but it was too late. Eddie, the Patrol Leader, shouted, "Cut that out!" He was refer-ring to the physical scuffling and the greedy behavior, not to the epi-thet, because he, like the others, took for granted that "homo," "fag," and "queer" are acceptable taunts at camp, at least out of earshot of certain adults.[18]

Homophobia, the fear of and hatred toward homosexuals, is a cen-tral theme at camp.[19] The social construction of masculinity is high on the agenda of a Boy Scout camp. When most boys arrive at camp, they are still children physically and emotionally. At age eleven, these boys come from a folk culture (in the schoolyard and the neighborhood) that marks the differences between boys and girls with jokes, games, taunts, teases, and stories.[20] During the years they come to camp as Scouts, these children become adolescents, experiencing hormonal and other changes in their bodies.

The problem for boys at this age is that they have no clear signal that they have become physically mature. The girls they know back home have such a marker—menstruation—and girls' periods are a subject of the sex talk of these boys. Without such a marker (nocturnal emission, "wet dreams," are a poor substitute and certainly not the occasion for talk), boys are left with sex talk as their primary mechanism for estab-lishing that they are leaving childhood behind and are becoming men. Sex becomes a major topic of their conversations, and the talk makes it clear that having heterosexual relations is the desired outcome of their maturation and socialization.

Homophobic taunts play a crucial role in this social construction of masculinity. Part of the performance of a heterosexual male identity is the put-down of the feminine—the feminine in women and the feminine in men. In fact, as one folklorist notes, to put down the opponent in a male contest of ritual insults metaphorically puts the other male down in the female (i.e., passive and submissive) position in sexual intercourse.[21] The insults feminize the "downed" male, even when their content is not homosexuality. Misogyny—the expression of dislike for and disrespect toward women—and homophobia work together in this economy of the social construction of male heterosexuality.

The ritual male insults so pervasive in camp really serve a double purpose. The content of the insults—calling someone a "homo" or "fag" or making a joking comment like "Is that pubic hair in your teeth?"—affirms for both participants that homosexuality is to be despised, that to be a man is to be other than a homosexual. But the ritual insults also accomplish another important piece of business in the social construction of masculinity, namely, the social construction of heterosexual male friendship.

Ritual male insult contests require the collaborative construction of a play frame. The participants somehow signal to one another a play frame in which the insults (normally fighting words) are taken to be playful, in the "what if?" mode. The participants usually establish the play frame through facial expressions and tone of voice, the initiator inviting the other to respond in kind.[22] The great paradox of ritual insulting is that it takes a great deal of trust to engage in this play frame. Play frames are somewhat fragile in any case, but the ritual aggression of the playfight really tests the ability of the players to sustain the frame and to repair it in case of damage. Ritual insulting can get out of hand and turn into a real fight if a participant taps an off-limits topic. The ritual formulas of male insult contests, most elaborate in the African-American genres of sounding and playing the dozens but found just as commonly in white male folk groups, serve to maintain the play frame and to keep the stylized male aggression from turning into actual male violence.[23] Fierce insulting, then, requires great trust. The very fact that these boys can trade insults in the play frame speaks to the strength of their relationship.[24]

Male friendship becomes problematic at Boy Scout camp. Back in the home world, especially before the onset of puberty, male friendship is a relatively simple matter. But sexual maturity complicates male friendship. Adolescent males come to see each other as sexual competitors for the attention of young women, but just as important is what the males are going to do about the possibility of sexual behavior with other males. The social construction of heterosexual male identity requires some definition of the close feelings—some might say affection—male friends feel toward one another. These young men must define their feelings as normally heterosexual, as different from homosexual affection. Homophobic insults between close friends help accomplish this categorization of feelings. "We can call each other 'queer,'" says the play frame, "because we aren't queer. Our closeness as friends is not sexual."

Boy Scout camp intensifies the problem of heterosexual male friendship. Unlike the home world, the camp puts males together in a "total institution," in which all the participants eat, sleep, and live to-gether twenty-four hours a day.[25] Male friendships arise naturally in this setting, and boys may become very close. For the adolescent boys, the intensity of this experience and the intensity of the friendships arising from it may be confusing. The adolescent male folk culture seeks to settle this confusion by providing the play frames that assure the boys their affections for one another are not sexual. The ritual insults accomplish this, but so do other play frames. Play in the nude, for example, can achieve the same goal. Years earlier, before the national office for-bade such play, the troop had a tradition of nude swimming during free swim, and I observed more than one game of King of the Donut played at Usonia III without swimsuits.[26] The playfight frame permitted nude wrestling on the donut and, paradoxically, helped confirm the heterosexual orientation of the players. "We can play in the nude," says the frame, "because we do not see each other as sexual objects."[27]

So this is why Eddie and the others at dinner treated so matter-of-factly the "homo" taunt over the last of the pudding. Dinner finished, we asked permission of the cook to leave, and I wandered back to the Staff Area. Pete, Aaron, and I chatted while we gave ourselves quick sponge baths at the spigot. The daytime climate in the Sierra is hot and dry in the summer, and even walking stirs up dust that leaves a thin layer on the skin. We all felt the need to clean up a bit before donning our Scout uniform shirts and neckerchiefs for evening flag assembly. Before long Todd blew his whistle, announcing "Five minutes to as-sembly," and by the time we walked out to the Parade Ground, the boys and Seniors were pretty much assembled in their large rectangle around the flagpole. Patrol Leaders reported who was absent and for what reason, and three boys from the Bear Patrol took their position in a corner of the rectangle. On Todd's command, they presented them-selves to him with Scout salutes, did a clumsy about-face, and went to the flagpole. Once they had untied the ropes, Todd called out, "Scouts, salute," and all present saluted as the color guard lowered the two flags.

Todd called, "At ease," once the flags were lowered, but it took a while for the boys to fold the flags correctly (a skill they learn for Tenderfoot). Lining up again in their color guard formation, the three Scouts marched off to put the flags into the footlocker until the next morning, when another color guard would raise the colors in assembly after breakfast.

The flag ceremony over, Todd announced that there would be a Whiffleball game that evening before patrol campfires. There were no other announcements, so Todd called the troop to attention, looked around to see that everyone had complied, and then said, "Dismissed." One of the Seniors, Les, grabbed the Whiffleball equipment (a hollow, slotted, plastic baseball and lightweight, hollow, plastic bat) and led the troop up to the Games Area. Like the sacred spaces—Church Rock and the Investiture site—the play spaces are set aside from ordinary space at camp. The spaces are not far from camp, but their separateness helps frame the activities as different from everyday, taken-for-granted reality. The short walk to the Games Area constitutes the same sort of transitional journey the boys experienced earlier in the day as they walked up to Church Rock.

Once everyone had gathered in the Games Area, Les chose two boys to be team captains and had them choose sides, as boys would for sandlot baseball. Whiffleball is a version of baseball, but the ball does not travel far. Ordinary softball or baseball would be impossible in the rocky and partly forested terrain; the ball would be lost the first time anyone got a decent hit. Whiffleball solves that problem. Les showed the two teams where each base was and pointed to trees that marked the foul lines. The boys began to play. I watched for about half an hour, then went back to the Staff Area to rest and write some notes in my journal. It was getting darker, and soon the boys returned from the game and dispersed to their patrol sites for the evening's patrol campfires. The patrols are supposed to have genuine campfire programs, miniature versions of the troop campfires, but as I strolled through the camp, I noted that the patrols were sitting quietly around their campfires, talking about the day and telling stories about school and the home world. Throughout these conversations, the boys stared at the campfires, fascinated as we moderns all are with the fires that have become largely ornamental.

The Seniors were gathered at the advancement table. It was dark, and they had all changed into the down parkas and other clothing that would insulate them against the cold Sierra night. Two Coleman gas lanterns sat on the table, hissing and glowing brightly. Pete was not there yet. The Seniors were engaged in their usual banter when Les made a face and said, "Whew. Who cut the cheese?"

"Why," asked Brad, the presumed offender, "do you want to lick the knife?" Some other Seniors observed that the canned beef dinner was coming back to haunt them.

The purpose of the meeting was to finalize plans for Insane Day, scheduled for Tuesday afternoon. Insane Day is a troop tradition, a sort of Scout Olympics pitting patrol against patrol in contests for points. It is the responsibility of the Seniors to plan the day's events. Pete came up to the table, flashed his smile at everyone, and sat down. "Now, tell me, what have you got planned for Insane Day?" Todd consulted his notes and began to describe the events and which Senior was responsible for organizing each. Pete would interrupt him occasionally to ask a question or make a point. About halfway through Todd's presentation, I heard a soft fart and looked over in Brad's direction. He was looking at Ricky, smirking, and I saw Ricky shift his weight and fart. Suddenly I realized that there was a farting contest going on in the midst of the dialogue Todd and Pete were having about Insane Day. Soon Jeff joined in, and none of the Seniors was paying any attention to Todd and Pete. The farting contest—a folk event, I suppose—had completely undermined the meeting.

But things had gone too far, and Pete stopped midsentence to look around the table. His eyes squinted in anger. "Are you all listening to this? Because you'd better. Insane Day is an important tradition in the troop. Other Seniors worked hard to make Insane Day fun for you when you were campers, and you owe it to these campers to do the same for them. So listen up." Sheepish looks around the table; the meeting resumed.

Pete was especially interested in the new plans for a theme for the day. One of the troop's C&Ts is "always to have new C&Ts," a lovely paradox that describes well the dynamic tension between creativity and tradition, between invention and convention, in folklore. This year the Seniors decided to invent a new tradition. The Insane Day theme would be "The Return to Gilligan's Island," a reference to the television series perennially in reruns. The "Gilligan's Island" theme would provide the frame for all the day's events. Seniors would dress up as different characters from the series, and each contest would refer somehow to the circumstances of the series—namely, a group of people stranded on an island. The troop goes out to an island in Lake Usonia for Insane Day, so the idea had lots of promise. The Seniors were building props, costumes, and so on. They were very excited about putting this new face on an old tradition, and I could see Pete was very pleased with their ideas and enthusiasm. "That's great," he said as they described each idea. The meeting was drawing to a close. "We'll meet again tomorrow night, just to be sure everything is in place for the next day. Now let's have some 'wins.'"

"Wins" is a tradition borrowed from organizational studies, a strategy in which members of a group are asked to describe their wins for the day—that is, events or things they are happy about. "My win," began Todd, "is that we had a really great hike this year and we are having a really great start of camp." Everyone in the circle applauded Todd's win. "My win," said Jason, "is that we're back in camp and eating real food." That got especially hearty applause. "My win," said Ricky, "is that I didn't get the shits on this hike." All laughed and applauded, remembering a past hike in which Ricky came down with diarrhea. And so it went around the circle. "My win," said Pete, "is that we have a really great group of Seniors this year and that they have a great plan for Insane Day." Hearty applause. That seemed the end of the wins. Just then, Todd asked me, "Hey, Jay, what did you do last night?" This question startled me, and I must have looked puzzled, but before I could say anything, the Seniors began to sing to me with great gusto a song that (I learned later from Tad) had become a new C&T for ending Senior meetings:

(Tune: "Funiculi, Funicula"—traditional Italian song)
Last night I stayed at home
And masturbated,
It felt so good, I knew it would.
Last night, I stayed at home
And masturbated,
It felt so nice, I did it twice.

Chorus
Womp it, stomp it, beat it on the floor,
Wrap it around the bedpost, make it cum some more
Some more, some more, some more, some more,
Some people go for intercourse
But me, I beat my meat! Hey![28]

We all laughed and the meeting broke up.

By now, most of the boys were in their sleeping bags, talking softly about girls, sex, and other bedtime topics before going to sleep. Back in the Staff Area, though, we had one more ritual to observe—the Staff campfire. Aaron was lighting the fire in "the den," the small Staff campfire site fifteen feet or so from the area in which we slept. I brought up three aluminum camp chairs and set them in a semicircle around the fire, while Pete carried over a small cooler, which we used as a side table between the chairs. The mountain night was getting even colder, and we all welcomed the fire's warmth. Pete opened the cooler, removing a jug of white wine, three glasses, and a hunk of white cheese. I opened the bag of pretzels I had brought while Pete poured us each a bit of wine and cut several slices of cheese, which he passed around on a paper plate. We sat quietly for a while, enjoying the snacks and watching the fire.

Staff campfires of this sort are a tradition of the troop. Relaxation before going to bed is part of what happens, and a glass of wine or a beer helps the men, including visiting fathers and alumni, unwind. But the more important function of the Staff campfire is to discuss the existing and brewing problems at camp. This is the sort of meeting a hospital staff might have at the end of the day. Sometimes the talk is trivial and playful. Sometimes the talk is serious, contemplative, philosophical. Crises in camp, problems with homesick campers, interpersonal problems between campers, problems with Seniors who are fucking up, and other sorts of problems that arise daily are the proper subject for talk at Staff campfire. We were only a day or two into camp, and no serious problems had arisen yet, so Pete was pretty mellow and said again how pleased he was that camp was off to a good start. "I really like the Seniors' plans for Insane Day. That should be neat."

I shared with the group Les's wordplay with food at lunch, and Pete look displeased. "He was testing you, Jay. I would never allow that sort of talk at the table, and he knows it. He was trying to see what you would do. I just know I'm going to have trouble with him at camp."

As we sipped our wine, the talk turned to alcohol, probably for my edification. Pete is aware of the contradiction, a dilemma as he sees it, of our drinking. The Boy Scouts of America has a strict policy of "no alcohol at official events," and the troop is sponsored by a Protestant church that frowns on alcohol consumption in any case. But adolescent boys drink, and that poses a potential problem. Moreover, the adult drinking at camp could be seen by some as hypocritical. Pete is torn on the matter because he thinks the small amounts of wine and beer consumed at the Staff campfires are important for "getting loose" and having productive talk about problems in camp. The consumption is so small that there is no danger of an adult's becoming drunk and incapable of responding to a sudden emergency, but the BSA identity and the church sponsorship pose problems in justifying this adult drinking.

The troop has had problems with alcohol. Years ago the policy was one of toleration. Senior Point normally is off-limits to everyone, so if the Seniors in those early years smuggled in alcohol and drank it quietly and invisibly, the adults would not have known it. What Pete called a "discretionary policy" was in force. If the Seniors were discreet and their drinking was undetectable and did not affect the performance of their duties, then the adult Staff would not raid Senior Point and confiscate the alcohol. But in the mid-1970s, the Seniors began abusing the policy, and word got back to parents and the church sponsor. So now the "discretionary policy" has been replaced by the "taboo policy." Alcohol and drugs are strictly forbidden. At the Senior Retreat before camp, Pete made every Senior promise that he would not bring alcohol or drugs to or use them in camp.

To complicate matters, the boys' parents vary considerably in their toleration of their sons' drinking. One father told me, "I know that my son is going to experiment with drinking, and the way I figure it, I would rather he learn how to drink with Boy Scouts than with some guys on a canal bank." What this father and other fathers recognize is the role of drinking in the adolescent's social construction of masculinity. The question for these fathers is not whether their sons will drink; personal experience and national statistics on teenage drinking answer that question. The question is whether their sons will drink as responsibly and as safely as possible. So Troop 49 bears this added responsibility. The new, strict policy about alcohol makes the drinking at Staff campfire that much more problematic, and Pete worries what to do.

As we talked about these matters and I volunteered the comment I heard from one of the fathers, I tried out one of my scholarly observations on the Staff. I explained that anthropologists, beginning with Radcliffe-Brown, have noted that in some societies the mother's brother is the adult male who takes responsibility for training his nephew in the skills, rights, and obligations of the men in the society.[29] That arrangement frees the father to be the friend of his son, because he has no real responsibility for the son's socialization. It seemed to me, I said tentatively, that middle-class American culture is settling into a similar pattern. Psychology and other sources of advice in child rearing want American middle-class fathers to become the chums of their sons, to spend "quality time" with them. To do this, the fathers feel they must surrender their normal socialization duties to some other adult males in the society, and it is the athletic coaches and the Scoutmasters who most often take on the role of teaching the boys discipline, skills, morals, and a general philosophy of life. That might include advice about drinking, sex, and a number of things the boys will not discuss with their fathers. In effect, then, the fathers are turning over to other adult males the "superego" training of their sons.

Pete was very interested in this line of reasoning, and he agreed that's what was happening in a great many cases. We talked about this a bit more, settling nothing and certainly not deciding to forgo alcohol at future Staff campfires. But the fire was burning down and we were getting sleepy, so we packed up our things and brought them back to the Staff "bedroom." We lined up along the edge of the Staff Pond to urinate (in the folk lingo, "piss") before climbing into our sleeping bags, and it struck me how comical, almost, was this taken-for-granted male bonding ritual of pissing together. I lay awake a brief while, looking at the stars. At seven thousand feet, away from any lights and during the new moon, the starry night was spectacular. I slipped into a deep sleep, warm in my down bag as the clear night got colder still.

The "Problem" of God
in the Boy Scouts

The Sunday service at Church Rock raises questions relevant to the first
"G" of the three legal challenges to the Boy Scouts begun in the
1980s and punctuated by the U.S. Supreme Court decision of June 28,
2000 — God, gays, and girls. Lawsuits are nothing new to the Boy
Scouts, but these lawsuits began during a period of heightened culture
wars in American society, and each of the three topics of these suits
pokes at the sensitivities, worries, and anger one sees elsewhere in the
culture wars. My account of Troop 49's Sunday religious service provides the occasion for an extended comment on the first "G," the matter of religion in the organization.

In April of 1985, the National Council of the Boy Scouts of America ruled that a fifteen-year-old Scout, Paul Trout of Charlottesville,
Virginia, "should be expelled from the Scouts because he doesn't believe in God."[1] Apparently, Trout mentioned in his interview with the
advancement committee for his promotion to Life that he does not
believe in God (or maybe that he does not believe in God as a Supreme
Being, a distinction that makes a difference). Carl Hunter, director of
the Stonewall Jackson Area Council, was quoted in the press as saying, "The Scout Law requires a young man to be absolutely loyal to

God and country and to be reverent toward God. You can't do that if you don't believe in a Supreme Being."[2] The American Civil Liberties Union (ACLU) took up Trout's case, but by October the national organization reversed itself and readmitted Trout. The organization's explanation was that Trout had said merely that he "did not believe in God as a supreme being," and they chose to interpret his views as a disagreement over the definition of God. "So the organization's national executive board decided to delete from its literature any definition of God . . . while reaffirming the Scout Oath's declaration of duty to God."[3] I shall return to this issue of defining God, but let me move ahead to 1991.

By the summer of 1991, the BSA had two more lawsuits on its hands. The families of eight-year-old Mark Walsh of Chicago and of nine-year-old twins Michael and William Randall of Anaheim, California, had launched separate suits after their sons had been expelled from Cub Scout troops for saying they did not believe in God. The Cub Scouts is the organization created in 1930 by the BSA for younger boys, aged eight to eleven, with the young boys organized into "dens" supervised by a "den mother" and a larger unit, the "Cub Pack," usually led by a male pack leader.

The BSA had finessed the Trout case by framing it as a mere dispute over the meaning of the word "God," but these suits pitted avowed atheists against the BSA requirement that members believe in God. The National Council's stance was that the BSA is a private group that can admit and exclude members by criteria particular to the organization. "Also supporting the status quo," explained a *New York Times* story, "are the Church of Latter-Day Saints, or Mormons, which formed the first Scouting council in America in 1913 and which remains the largest single Scout sponsor, and the Roman Catholic Church, the fourth-largest Scout sponsor. The two churches, which together support more than a quarter of all Scout troops, contend that the Boy Scouts has every right to keep certain people out, whether as Scouts, volunteers, or staff members."[4]

Public schools, it seems, sponsor the largest number of Scouts, which provided fuel for the plaintiffs' view that the BSA is a public organization. But the public schools "do not speak with the unified voice of the Mormon or Catholic churches," notes the *New York Times* reporter, who also points to a basic contradiction in the BSA practices regarding religious belief. "Officials say the organization was founded for boys who believe in God and should remain true to those principles," he writes. "But while the organization accepts Buddhists, who do not believe in a Supreme Being, and Unitarians, who seek insight from many traditions but pointedly avoid setting a creed, it does not tolerate people who are openly atheist, agnostic, or unwilling to say in that Scout oath they will serve God." [5]

In fact, it was precisely this contradiction that the twins' father, James Grafton Randall, acting as their attorney in the case, hammered as he cross-examined witnesses for the organization.[6] In a decision with significant implications, Orange County Superior Court Judge Richard O. Frazee Sr. ruled in June of 1992 that the Boy Scouts could not exclude the twins "because of their beliefs, or lack of them." [7] More shocking still, the state supreme court refused to hear a petition from the Orange County Council of the Boy Scouts of America.

Meanwhile, the Girl Scouts of America faced a similar challenge. In November of 1992, James Randall filed a suit against the Girl Scouts on behalf of a six-year-old San Diego area girl and her father, challenging the Girl Scouts' pledge to "serve God" as a "religious test oath" that violates the Constitution.[8] Within a year, the Girl Scouts had changed their pledge, permitting girls to replace "God" with "words they deem more appropriate" while reciting the Girl Scout Promise. "The group's leaders said the measure . . . acknowledges growing religious and ethnic diversity among the nation's 2.6 million Girl Scouts," explained a newspaper account of the national convention that voted overwhelmingly for the new policy. "In regions with large Asian and American Indian populations, the group has had trouble recruiting girls whose religious tradition does not include a Judeo-Christian concept of God. . . ." [9]

The Girl Scouts found a comfortable solution to the dilemmas of religious diversity, choosing a route that would make the organization open to every girl.[10] What kept the Boy Scouts from doing the same thing? When reporters bothered asking boys themselves what they thought about excluding boys from the organization because they didn't believe in God, the reporters found "mild to strong support for changes." [11] And this is what I would expect from my long association with the Scouts, both as a Scout and as a researcher observing a troop for over twenty years. The "professional Scouters," the bureaucrats who work for the national office of the Boy Scouts of America, feel compelled to speak authoritatively about what is good or bad for children and adolescents without actually asking any young people what they think about it.

So why did the National Council dig in its heels on this issue? What was so much at stake that the Boy Scouts could not follow the example of the Girl Scouts and move to accommodate religious diversity?

Part of the answer lies in the historical connection between Christianity and an aggressive version of masculinity. It is useful to examine a bit of history on this connection. And perhaps the best way to get at this history is to look briefly at the five main figures who came together to create the Boy Scouts of America—Ernest Thompson Seton, Daniel Carter Beard, Edgar M. Robinson, John L. Alexander, and James E. West—for these men embodied much of the ambivalence and tension that connected Christianity with masculinity at the turn of the twentieth century.

Born in Victorian England (1860) and raised in Canada, Seton established himself as an artist, naturalist, and author of animal stories before he embarked on his boys' work near the end of the century.[12] In the 1890s, Seton began to formulate his "Woodcraft Idea," a theory for youth work based on the Darwinian instinct psychology of G. Stanley Hall. The model woodcrafter, thought Seton, was the American Indian, and in 1898 Seton (at the urging of Rudyard Kipling) began casting his Woodcraft Idea into the form of a novel. Over the next few years, Seton worked simultaneously on the novel, *Two Little Savages: Being the Adventures of Two Boys Who Lived as Indians and What They Learned* (1903), and on a handbook for the organization he envisioned. In 1902, *Ladies Home Journal* agreed to establish a new Department of American Woodcraft for Boys, helping Seton launch his organization by publishing a Seton article each month. The appearance of *Two Little Savages* in 1903 and *The Red Book, or How to Play Indian* in 1904 cemented Seton's national reputation as a leader in youth work, and he was asked to chair the committee that met in 1910 to found the Boy Scouts of America.[13] Seton was made the first Chief Scout of the organization, and he wrote large portions of the first *Handbook for Boys* (1911), a manual that resembles the *Birch Bark Roll* as much as or more than it does the first British handbook written by Lord Robert Baden-Powell. Seton increasingly felt alienated from the Boy Scout leadership, accusing the New York businessmen and bankers in their numbers of abandoning the Woodcraft Idea he had in mind as the ideological foundation for the movement and as the feature that distinguished it so well from Baden-Powell's militaristic model. In 1915, the conflict came to a head over the fact that Seton had never become an American citizen. The position of Chief Scout was abolished, and amid very bitter public exchanges Seton left the Boy Scouts to redevote himself to his Woodcraft Indians.

Two aspects of Seton's thought in this period are relevant to our understanding of his conception of God. First, Seton looked primarily to American Indian religions as the model for spirituality and ethics. Seton consulted written documents and live informants to distill "The Indian's Creed." Whereas "the redman" believed in many gods, he accepted "one Supreme Spirit." To prove his thesis that the "redman's religion" could revitalize twentieth-century white society, Seton described in detail the "redman's" traits: he was reverent, clean, chaste, brave, thrifty, cheerful, obedient, kind, hospitable, truthful, honorable, and temperate, the model of physical excellence.[14] In short, Seton embraced American Indian religions more than traditional European faiths, and he was as likely to hold up the famed Shawnee chief Tecumseh as a model of spiritual manhood as he was Christ. So, while it is accurate to say that Seton believed in God, he believed in a Supreme Being far from the one portrayed by most Western religions, and I think it is unlikely that he would have wanted to exclude from the Boy Scouts any boy or man who expressed doubts about the traditional understanding of God required by the present organization.

But Seton left the organization. What of Beard and the other founders? Daniel Carter Beard was no more conventional in his religious views than was Seton. Beard's childhood in Cincinnati prepared him for the same wedding of art and nature we see in Seton's thought.[15] His father, James N. Beard, was a prominent artist, and his mother's family (the Carters) enjoyed great entrepreneurial success in the Ohio Valley. The Swedenborgian theology of John Chapman, better known as Johnny Appleseed, provided the moral canopy over the artistic and entrepreneurial values that Beard learned in his childhood home, as both the Beards and the Carters had converted to this faith early in the nineteenth century. After formal training in both engineering and art, Beard gained his fame in New York as an illustrator for *St. Nicholas,* a magazine for children, and compiled a series of articles he wrote and illustrated into his first book, the classic *American Boys' Handy Book: What to Do and How to Do It.*[16]

In 1886, Beard joined Henry George's single-tax movement and wrote his own single-tax novel, *Moonblight.*[17] By 1889, Beard's fame led Samuel Clemens, writing as Mark Twain, to seek him out to illustrate *A Connecticut Yankee in King Arthur's Court,* an assignment Beard relished. The politics and morality of the novel appealed to Beard, and he was especially attracted to Twain's theme of sham and the relationship between appearance and character. Beard's illustrations for the novel became controversial because of his use of contemporary public figures (such as Jay Gould) as models for his characters as well as his explicit attacks on the church and the capitalists. Twain was pleased with Beard's *Connecticut Yankee* illustrations, but many critics saw the illustrations as propaganda, and Beard was blacklisted as an illustrator.

Frustrated with the political and economic arenas of reform, Beard returned to boys' work in 1905. William E. Annis, the new owner and publisher of *Recreation,* hired Beard as the magazine's editor. In addition to the conservationist agenda they shared, including the conservation of American Indian cultures, Beard and Annis wanted to use the monthly magazine to launch a youth movement. The July 1905 issue introduced The Sons of Daniel Boone, a new department of the magazine. One purpose of the new organization was to enlist young people in the magazine's conservation work. But equally important to Beard was the movement's promise to promote "manliness" through democratic organization (boys would create local chapters called "forts"), outdoor fun, woodcraft (the study of nature), and handicraft (the making of things as first illustrated in his *Handy Book*). There was no central bureaucracy for the movement, and Beard's monthly articles and the other material he wrote were all that linked the local chapters. By 1908, however, twenty thousand boys were members of the Sons of Daniel Boone.

Conflicts within the organization led Beard to sever his ties with *Recreation* in 1906 and join *Woman's Home Companion,* where he continued writing for The Sons of Daniel Boone. Beard's clashes with the women editors of the magazine led him to resign in 1909 and use *Pictorial Review* as the new magazine for promotion of his youth-movement ideas. A legal battle ensued with *Woman's Home Companion* over the rights to the name "The Sons of Daniel Boone," and when the parties finally settled, the magazine kept the name and Beard kept the rights to his articles. Beard chose Young Pioneers as the name for his new movement and filled the movement's handbook with stories of pioneer heroes like Davy Crockett and Johnny Appleseed.[18] These movements were in place in 1910 when Beard joined Seton and others to establish the Boy Scouts of America.

If neither Seton nor Beard was religious by the usual, mainstream standards in 1910, certainly we can say that Edgar M. Robinson, John L. Alexander, and James E. West embraced the Protestant "muscular Christianity" that linked physical fitness and moral rectitude at the end of the nineteenth century. Robinson and Alexander came from successful careers organizing youth work for the Young Men's Christian Association (YMCA), and West, the first chief executive of the BSA, also had YMCA experience as well as a law degree.[19] But even in their most religious moments, Robinson and Alexander and West resembled Seton and Beard in their greater concern that boys acquire the virtues of manhood. Alexander wrote the "Chivalry" chapter for the first *Handbook,* and a long paragraph on "A Boy Scout's Religion" is the only mention of religion in the entire *Handbook.* "The Boy Scouts of America maintain that no boy can grow into the best kind of citizenship," explains Alexander, without recognizing his obligation to God. . . . The recognition of God as the ruling and leading power in the universe, and the grateful acknowledgment of His favors and blessings is necessary to the best type of citizenship and is a wholesome thing in the education of the growing boy. . . . The Boy Scouts of America therefore recognize the religious element in the training of a boy, but it is absolutely non-sectarian in its attitude toward that religious training.[20]

Alexander goes on to explain that the Boy Scouts leaves religious train-ing to the boy's own religious organizations; that is not the work of the Boy Scouts.

A careful reader of Boy Scout *Handbooks*, Scoutmaster *Handbooks*, and other Scout literature from the founding through the 1940s would have to conclude, I think, that insisting upon an aggressive religious stance was not high on the BSA's agenda. Of course, it was true that the Boy Scout Oath created by the 1910 committee to "Americanize" elements borrowed from Baden-Powell's movement had boys promise to do their best to do their duty to God, but the first *Handbook*'s rheto-ric around religion is remarkably subdued. The explanation of the twelfth point of the Scout Law, "A Scout is Reverent," emphasizes both duty and tolerance: "He is reverent toward God. He is faithful in his religious duties and respects the convictions of others in matters of cus-tom and religion."[21] Nor does this rather relaxed approach change in the second (1911), third (1915), or fourth ("revised," 1927) editions.

It is only in the fifth edition (1948) that the authors of the *Handbook* began to expand their explanation of "duty to God" and "A Scout is Reverent." For example, "Your Duty to God":

You worship God regularly with your family in your church or synagogue. You try to follow the religious teachings that you have been taught, and you are faithful in your church school duties, and help in church activities. Above all you are faithful to Almighty God's Commandments.

Most great men in history have been men of deep religious faith. Washington knelt in the snow to pray at Valley Forge. Lincoln always sought Divine guidance before each important decision. Be proud of your religious faith.

Remember in doing your duty to God, to be grateful to Him. Whenever you succeed in doing something well, thank Him for it. Sometimes when you look up into the starlit sky on a quiet night, and feel close to Him—thank Him as the Giver of all good things.

One way to express your duty and your thankfulness to God is to help others, and this too, is a part of your Scout promise.[22]

The expanded discussion of the twelfth point of the Scout Law also lays down much more explicit instructions on what it takes for a Scout to be "reverent":

> Reverence is that respect, regard, consideration, courtesy, devotion, and affection you have for some person, place or thing because it is holy. The Scout shows true reverence in two principal ways. First, you pray to God, you love God and you serve Him. Secondly, in your everyday actions you help other people, because they are made by God to God's own likeness. You and all men are made by God to God's own likeness. You and all men are important in the sight of God because God made you. The "unalienable rights" in our historic Declaration of Independence, come from God.
>
> That is why you respect others whose religion and customs may differ from yours. Some fellows think they are smart by telling stories or making fun of people of other religions or races. All your life you will be associating with people of other beliefs and customs. It is your duty to respect these people for their beliefs and customs, and to live your own.[23]

We can see in this passage an elaboration of what was introduced first in Alexander's 1911 linking of belief in God with "the best type of citizenship." We see the wedding of religion and democratic ideology, of religion and patriotism. And we also see a continuation of tolerance and of what earlier *Handbooks* called "practical religion"—that is, the demonstration of duty and reverence to God by helping others.

It was also in this 1948 edition of the *Handbook,* used throughout the 1950s, that the Religious Awards Program appeared. The program required cooperation between the BSA and certain religious denominations, as it was the minister, priest, or rabbi who certified that the boy had performed the duties and service worthy of the award. The 1948 *Handbook* described religious medals for Roman Catholic, Jewish, Mormon, Lutheran, and Buddhist boys and a general Protestant medal called the God and Country Award.[24]

The Boy Scouts of America hit its golden age, both literally and figuratively, in the late 1950s; 1960 marked the golden anniversary of the organization. The demographics of the 1950s still have a lot to do with how the Boy Scouts thinks about itself. The baby boom was one feature of the 1950s, as the first wave of children born in that cohort (1946–62) pressed hard on the 1950s institutions aimed at serving children. I know because I am a member of that cohort. Born in July of 1945, I was eight years old when I joined the Cub Scouts in 1953. My third grade class had to meet in a one-room "portable" classroom because the South Florida school districts could not build new elementary schools fast enough to handle the suburban baby boomers. White, suburban, middle-class—these were the demographic features of the baby boom kids who flocked to Scouting in the 1950s. Being a good mother in the 1950s meant that you stayed home to raise the children, which included carting the kids to Scouts, dance lessons, Little League practice, and more. An organization that originally aspired to reach urban, working-class, and immigrant kids had become by 1960 predominantly white and middle-class.

The impact of the "symbolic demography" of the 1950s was just as significant. By symbolic demography, I mean the web of symbols and meanings that characterized the mainly mass-mediated narratives of American public culture.[25] The rise of television in the 1950s had a profound effect on the symbolic demography of the period, as television generated for the middle-class audience a great number of narratives about "American life" and "the American way," from the family sitcoms like *Father Knows Best, Ozzie and Harriet,* and *Leave It to Beaver* to Cold War narratives as obvious as *I Led Three Lives* and as subtly coded as *Gunsmoke.*

In many ways, the 1950s version of America and the 1950s version of the Boy Scouts of America are fixed in the minds of the white middle class, regardless of the realities of differences in the ways Americans experienced American life from 1945 to 1960. The mass media invented an American middle-class way of life, a way "we never were," as one historian puts it.[26] But it is this fiction, the 1950s version of middle-class family life, that has become "normative," that has become the "traditional" way of life to which all subsequent experiences have been compared.

Now consider the role of religion in this public culture of the United States in the 1950s. By any measure, Americans in the 1950s were a "religious" people. Membership in organized churches and other sects grew from 64.5 million in 1940 to 114.6 million in 1960.[27] Public opinion polls consistently showed that the vast majority of Americans believed in God and prayed to him daily. Religious leaders like Reinhold Niebuhr, Bishop Fulton J. Sheen, and Billy Graham became well-known figures in the public culture, and Protestant minister Norman Vincent Peale's 1952 best-seller, *The Power of Positive Thinking,* captured the optimistic tone and style of much of the public religion.[28]

Religion in the 1950s was tangled with national and international politics. Religion had become an important marker distinguishing between the Communists and the Western democracies. "They" were "godless communists," while we were religious. The World Council of Churches was founded in 1948, but Cold War politics soon disrupted that ecumenical move.[29] The National Council of Churches was founded in the United States in 1950, and that coalition of mainly Protestant, mainline, and liberal denominations represented about thirty million church members.[30] It is no accident that sociologist Robert Bellah published his first writings on "the American Civil Religion" in 1967.[31] Although Bellah sees evidence of this particular blend of Protestant Christianity and Enlightenment political theory in earlier public narratives, such as Lincoln's second inaugural address, it was living in Eisenhower's America of the 1950s that made so clear to everyone the ways Protestant Christianity and Cold War ideology became tangled in the definitions of America. Even writers on Jews and Catholics, for example, noted how acculturation to the United States "protestantized" other religions.[32] And this was the period when "under God" was added to the Pledge of Allegiance and "In God We Trust" was added to our money. The American flag, the civil religion, and patriotism entwined in the 1950s. The American Civil Religion enjoyed a powerful consensus in the public culture, even if people could not agree wholly on the political practices implied by that religion. Martin Luther King Jr. could invoke the Civil Religion as well as anyone, and the Civil Rights movement (which, in many ways, began with the Montgomery bus boycott late in 1955) drew upon religious energy from the start.

The Boy Scouts of America, that quintessential organization of 1950s America, proudly embraced this civil religion. The Boy Scouts was "nondenominational," to be sure, and there were religious badges representing each major religious group. But "nondenominational" could not include agnosticism or atheism in 1950s America, for "nondenominational" meant only that no one religious denomination could impose its theology and practices upon the organization. Boys from all faiths were free to join the organization, but "faith" was the key. A boy had to have a faith, for atheism—and probably agnosticism—was the characteristic of Communists, our sworn enemies.

The sixth edition of the *Boy Scout Handbook,* published in 1959, reflects the public religion of the 1950s in its revisions of the passages explaining "duty to God" and "reverent." "Your parents and religious leaders teach you to know and love God, and the ways in which you can serve him," explains the text about the Oath. "By following these teachings in your daily life you are doing your duty to God as a Scout."[33] The passage on "A Scout is Reverent" states the Civil Religion perfectly and is worth quoting in full:

Take a Lincoln penny out of your pocket and look at it. What do you see on it? Just above Lincoln's head are the words "In God We

Trust." Twelve little letters on our humblest coin. Not only as individuals, but as a nation, too, we are committed to live and work in harmony with God and His plan.

Most great men in history have been men of deep religious faith who have shown their convictions in deed. Washington knelt in the snow to pray at Valley Forge. Lincoln always sought divine guidance before making an important decision. Eisenhower prayed to God before taking his oath of office as President of the United States. These men had many things in common: love of the out-of-doors, human kindness, and an earnest vigor in working with God in helping make a better world.

You are reverent as you serve God in your everyday actions and are faithful in your religious obligations as taught you by your parents and spiritual leaders.

All your life you will be associated with people of different faiths. In America we believe in religious freedom. That is why we respect others whose religion may differ from ours, although for reason of conscience we do not agree with them.[34]

This passage effectively conflates duty to God and country as a single duty, the individual's duty to both but also the nation's duty to God's plan. The authors of the *Handbook* link Washington, Lincoln, and Eisenhower as practitioners of the nation's public religion, while still urging tolerance for sectarian differences under the larger umbrella of a public religion. Tellingly, this passage also revives a 1950s version of "muscular Christianity." The talk about "love of the out-of-doors" and about "an earnest vigor in working with God" echoes the nineteenth-century belief that a physically vigorous, aggressive masculinity would nourish and strengthen the spiritual and moral dimension of the boy's character.

By 1960 the Boy Scouts had two powerful visual icons at work reinforcing the role of religious faith and reverence in the socialization of American boys. First was the artwork of Norman Rockwell. Rockwell began his association with the Boy Scouts very early. In 1912, the national office had acquired *Boys' Life,* a magazine that had been created by an eighteen-year-old in Providence, Rhode Island.[35] Shortly thereafter, another eighteen-year-old, Norman Rockwell, began working for *Boys' Life* editor Edward Cave as illustrator for the magazine, for books, for Boy Scout calendars from 1925 into the 1970s, and for the covers of the 1927, 1959, and 1979 editions of the *Handbook* and the 1959 edition of the *Handbook for Scoutmasters.* William Hillcourt's generously illustrated book on Norman Rockwell's work on behalf of the

Boy Scouts tells the details of this association, details I shall not recount here. My point is that through *Saturday Evening Post* covers, his numerous illustrations of the Boy Scouts, and especially his "Four Freedoms" paintings used to sell war bonds during World War II, Norman Rockwell had become by 1960 the definitive illustrator of the American Civil Religion. In his caption for Rockwell's 1950 painting "Our Heritage," Hillcourt writes that in this calendar painting "Norman combined 'duty to God' and 'duty to country' in a single picture. There was an extra significance to this painting: that year more than fifty thousand Scouts took part in the Second National Boy Scout Jamboree at Valley Forge, Pennsylvania, where Washington has prayed during the dark days of the winter of 1777–78." [36]

Indeed, Valley Forge was the site for both the 1950 and the 1957 National Jamborees, only the second and fourth giant gatherings of Boy Scouts from all over the United States. [37] The national office chose as the visual image for these jamborees a profile of George Washington, kneeling in prayer and asking God's help for the soldiers huddled in the cold at Valley Forge. Of course, Washington was also praying for God's blessing on the whole enterprise of the American Revolution. [38] The image brilliantly condensed both the religious and the political elements of the American Civil Religion in the 1950s and even contained what I imagine was an unintended pun on Cold War. This official logo of the jamboree appeared on patches, jackets, coffee mugs, and any number of other memorabilia available to Scouts.

The national office of the Boy Scouts of America has never shaken off the symbolic demography of the 1950s. In 1992, the Anaheim twins' agnostic lawyer father, James Randall, told a *Los Angeles Times* reporter: "It's like dealing with the 1950s all over again—or at least all the bad parts of the 1950s," and the same reporter found that many "Scout elders say their adolescent experiences with compasses, intricate knots and Scouting comrades left deep impressions on them. 'It was one of the most meaningful times of my life,' said Edward C. Jacobs, once a teen-age Scout in Missouri, now Scout executive in Los Angeles, the country's second-largest council." [39] Here lies the significance of the actual and symbolic demographics of the 1950s—that so many adults running the organization were Scouts or young Scout leaders in the 1950s.

Repeated attempts to move the organization beyond the white middle class, many of them good-faith attempts, have met with little success and occasional scandal. [40] The 1970s move of the national headquarters from New Brunswick, New Jersey, to Irving, Texas, a suburb lying between Dallas and Fort Worth, symbolizes the symbolic demography of the movement. The national organization has chosen sides in the culture wars.

Talk of the culture wars has entered public discourse and everyday conversations to such an extent that most Americans have a pretty good sense of what this phrase means. This is a war over values and moral authority. As James Davison Hunter, one of the best writers on the wars, puts it, we are witnessing "polarizing impulses" from two camps.[41] For one group of Americans, the "orthodox," moral authority rests on "an external, definable, and transcendent authority," and this camp holds the cultural conservatives and moral traditionalists. For the other group, the "progressives," moral authority is not so fixed, as this camp tends "to re-symbolize historic faiths according to the prevailing assumptions of contemporary life." These are the "liberals" and "cultural progressives."[42] These categories cross and confound faith traditions, including secularists, who can be found in both camps. For Hunter and a number of other commentators on the culture wars, it is this new element of identity— not gender, not race, not social class, not religious tradition—that becomes the best predictor of a person's politics.

So for all these reasons the Boy Scouts of America could not compromise on the atheists' challenge at the end of the twentieth century. It does not matter that the founders of the movement, including Baden-Powell himself, had little interest in promoting religion beyond a very generalized belief in a Supreme Being, a fact that should make it as easy for the Boy Scouts as the Girl Scouts to change the oath (in practice, if not in wording) from a belief in God to a belief in a Supreme Being.[43] The religious conservatives who control the national office of the Boy Scouts see themselves as important troops in the culture wars. If religion, masculinity, and citizenship are as tangled as the rhetoric of the Boy Scouts and others seems to make them and if, as so many historians and social critics have suggested, there is evidence everywhere of a "crisis in white masculinity," a status revolution in which white males feel like the beleaguered class, then it makes sense that the men running the Boy Scouts see the atheists and their ACLU lawyers as agents of an assault upon masculinity and whiteness (symbolized by certain European religions and the very American religion of Mormonism).[44] The link between white masculinity and religion at century's end explained why the Boy Scouts would not make this compromise, while the Girl Scouts would; the Girl Scouts, quite simply, have no stake in the masculinity part of the tangle. There is more to be said on this religion-morality-masculinity complex, but I shall save that discussion for a later excursus on the other two "G's"—gays and girls.

Flag Ceremony—Piedmont Boy Scout Camp, Lake Lanier, Tryon, N.C.
(Asheville Post Card Co., North Carolina; postcard from author's collection)

Monday

★ ★ ★ ★ ★ ★ ★ ★ ★ ★ ★ ★ ★ ★ ★ ★ ★ ★ ★ ★

The sound of the whistle slowly entered my consciousness and I was fully awake when Todd shouted, "Reveille, reveille. Five minutes to Commissary Emissary." I sat up in my sleeping bag and gazed around the Staff Area. Aaron and Pete were awake but still lying down, gathering their energies for the day. We rose almost in unison, dressed, and wandered over to the spigot to brush our teeth and wipe the sleep from our eyes. Pete already has a beard, and I could see that Aaron was letting his beard grow for camp. Most of the older boys do this. Facial hair is a visible sign of manhood for the adolescent boy, and letting a beard grow during the three weeks of camp helps cement the male identity.

Soon another whistle and call from Todd announced morning color assembly. We were all wearing T-shirts in anticipation of the warm day, but we all wore troop neckerchiefs for the assembly. A morning person myself, I looked around the assembly and noticed the differences between the morning people and the night people. The Seniors seemed especially sluggish and tired, and I guessed they had stayed up late into the night, having their own campfire and talking about who knows what. After taking the patrol reports, Todd called us to attention for the raising of the colors. Once we were all "at ease," George, the Commissary Czar, read off his list of which Seniors and Staff would be dining guests at which patrols for the day. Some Seniors made announcements about their advancement classes, and finally we stood at attention again and were dismissed.

At the Snake Patrol site, where I was to have breakfast, Steve, the Patrol Leader, greeted me with a smile. I could see the cook was still working on breakfast, French toast. "Sorry we're a bit slow," apologized Steve. "Our cook hasn't done this before." Impatient, some of the boys raided the patrol box for the dry cereal that is always there and began eating. "Uh oh," said Steve, ominously, and I turned to see what had alarmed him. Pete was striding toward the patrol site. "What's holding you up? How come you aren't finished with breakfast yet?" Steve started explaining what the problem was, but Pete stepped in to show the cook what he was doing wrong.

"You need a hotter griddle," said Pete, kneeling to look at the weak flames coming from the Coleman stove. Pete pumped the fuel tank a few times and turned up the flames. "And you've made the toast too soggy. Look." Pete started a new batch of French toast, showing the cook how to do it. Pete turned to Steve, saying, "You'd better eat in a hurry or you'll all be late for the first advancement period." Then he shot off in the direction of the next patrol.

The boys, especially Steve, had been tense the whole time Pete was there. "He always thinks he knows everything," said one boy, known for having an attitude. "Shut up," said Steve, torn between sharing the view and knowing that as Patrol Leader he should have shown better leadership in keeping the meal on time. A thirteen-year-old Patrol Leader has to manage six to eight boys who range from the easygoing to the surly, from the very responsible to the very irresponsible. Patrol Leaders learn leadership skills under fire, more often from mistakes than from clear successes. Motivating tired teens is difficult for anyone, but most of all for another tired teen.

We all ate quickly and those on KP duty cleaned up the site as the others scurried for their first advancement period. Cleaning up after breakfast is especially important, because Todd inspects each patrol site during the first advancement period, checking for cleanliness, neatness, the status of safety equipment, and so on. Patrols earn points during these inspections and can use the points later in the week at a Nugget Auction at the troop campfire.

I decided to sit in on Les's class on orienteering, that is, using a compass and map to find one's way. The boys had had some exposure to these skills on the hike into camp, but Les wanted to go over these skills because the Scouts would need to be able to do a compass-and-pacing course as part of the Treasure Hunt coming up later in camp. Les patiently showed the boys how to "orient" a compass to a map, and then he let each boy have a turn. Each boy also needed to measure his own "pace"—a practiced step that has a uniform length—so that he could pace off distances and have a rough approximation of how far he had gone. These and other campcraft skills were meant to help provide the boys with some wilderness survival skills, in case they should ever need them. I left the class as the boys were still finding their compass readings and pacing off the triangular courses Les had given them.

A whistle announced the end of the morning advancement period and the beginning of free swim. I returned to the Staff Area to sit on my cot for a while and write in my journal. Soon Pete turned up, having just come from the KYBO.

"I forgot to tell you something, Jay. There are new rules this year for the KYBO. Last year there was a Scoutmaster in the Bay area accused of sexually molesting boys in his troop. It was a real shock to everyone; I know him and he was very well respected. The national office and the local Council have reacted by making a new rule, the 'rule of three.' There always have to be at least three people present when Scouts and adults are together. It can be two Scouts and one adult or two adults and one Scout, but it can never be one Scout and one adult. This means that there cannot be an adult and a Scout alone up at the KYBO. So you'll have to call out to see if anybody is there when you go to the KYBO, and if a Scout comes up while you're there, you'll have to ask him to wait until you're finished. I'm sorry, but that's the world we live in now."

I could see the sadness on Pete's face—not anger that there was another set of rules from the Council, but sadness that a Scoutmaster would break a trust and cast a pall over every adult leader, changing forever how adult men could relate to boys at camp. I thought of the reactions of many men working in children's day-care centers in the wake of some highly publicized child molestation cases. Male caretakers and elementary school teachers were afraid to touch, hug, and otherwise comfort children for fear of how the touching would be interpreted. Many experts worried publicly about the fact that men who should be hugging children in need of hugging could no longer do so. I guessed some of this was on Pete's mind as he told me the story.

"You know," he continued, getting more visibly angry, "what really bugs me is that the Council's first reaction was 'How can we keep from being sued?' I saw the video they created, supposedly to help train Scout leaders how to recognize signs of molestation and how to guard against it, but the whole tone of the video was toward covering the organization's ass. There was nothing about concern for the victims of molestation, nothing about counseling, nothing about how to talk with kids about sexual abuse. The whole thing was aimed at protecting the Boy Scouts against lawsuits." Pete's sadness had turned to disgust. The bureaucrats who ran the national and council offices of the Boy Scouts of America had proven once again to him how out of touch they are with the real experiences of boys and men in Scouting.

I spoke some words of understanding and sympathy, agreeing that it was too bad things had come to this. I thanked Pete for the warning and headed up toward the KYBO myself. The KYBO was set a hundred yards or so from camp. I found the toilet seats covered with a large piece of cardboard, on which Seniors had written in black marker: "Usonia Food Fund—Please Donate Generously." An inverted tin can covered a roll of toilet paper, and a large can of fire pit ashes and sand sat next to the seats. An improvised scoop invited the KYBO user to sprinkle the ashes and sand into the pit after each use, and a sign reminded the user to cover the seats after use. The flies find the KYBO every summer, and a generous use of ashes (like lime in the old-time outhouses) helps reduce that population. A broken canoe paddle sat against the rock beside the KYBO, and some Senior had drawn a face with an enormous tongue on the paddle blade. The paddle, called the "manure spreader," is for leveling off the contents of the pit as the piles get higher, a process which I preferred not to think about. After finishing my business, I walked back to the Staff Area to wash my hands and write a few pages in my journal about the theories I was formulating around the wordplay at camp. Lunch was announced, and I put away my things to join the Snake Patrol in a lunch of tuna fish sandwiches, Kool-Aid, and candy bars. I actually took a nap during siesta.

For second advancement period, I decided to go with Pete, who was going to teach the Scouts working on their Cooking Skill Award (required for the First Class rank) how to make "twist on a stick." Between the cooking of dehydrated food on the initial overnight hike and the regular rotation of cooking duties in a patrol, the boys get lots of opportunities to prove their abilities for the skill award. But the troop tradition is that every boy has to make twist or, alternatively, gingerbread, the old-fashioned way.[1] The boys had been instructed earlier in the day to dig small fire pits and gather some firewood, and by the time we arrived the boys had their fires burning. Pete laid out the ingredients and showed the boys how to combine the biscuit mix and water, roll out the dough into a long snake about an inch thick, and twist it around a stick. The stick was then suspended over the fire.

"Watch it closely," warned Pete, "and turn it every so often. You don't want it to burn on the outside and be uncooked on the inside. This should be edible, you know."

We watched as each of the boys created his twist on a stick and positioned it over the hot coals. Some boys were making every mistake possible, of course, but eventually each brought his product to Pete for the taste test. Some turned out fine, some were not done enough in the middle, but all told Pete was pretty happy with the outcome. The boys were devouring the twist as if it were a gourmet meal. "Good work," he said. "You all pass. Now put out the fires and go back to work on your menu plans." Pete gathered the materials he had brought, and we went back to the Commissary to put things away. On the way, we talked about how proud the kids were of their twist.

"The result of all that work really isn't worth it," chuckled Pete, "but it teaches the kids a *process* of fire building and cooking. It gives the kid a real sense of accomplishment because the twist comes out so well and tastes good."

"You know," I said, "I do all the cooking in our family. I really enjoy cooking. My mother didn't teach me how to cook. I learned all that in the Boy Scouts. While other kids were heating a can of beans to eat on a campout, I loved making an elaborate dish of some sort. Then, when my mother worked and couldn't be home to cook, I was able to cook for myself and sometimes for my parents."

Pete smiled. "I really want these kids to be self-sufficient like that. They are so used to having their mothers do everything for them. It's important that they learn how to take care of themselves; so they don't starve to death, for one thing."

Later I thought about what difference learning to cook might make in the gender socialization of these boys. In the home world, most of these boys probably thought of cooking and cleaning up after people as a mother's work, as women's work. But in an all-male society like the Boy Scout camp, there are no women to do this work. So boys and men fill all the roles, including the nurturant roles, such as feeding others.

I could imagine two possible outcomes to this experimentation with roles. On the one hand, a boy could come home from Scout camp with a new respect for nurturant roles and the realization that men and women can play all roles in a way more fluid than our present gender-based division of labor endorses. Perhaps all-male societies like the Scout camp help produce more androgynous men, men who value in themselves a broader repertoire of behavior and values, including those the society regularly ascribes to women.

On the other hand, I could just as easily imagine a boy getting home, handing his mother his bag of filthy clothing, and saying, "Here, these need to be washed. When's dinner?" His experiment with playing roles normally performed by women might just as easily lead him to think that these are really unpleasant roles (i.e., "Thank God we have mothers and other women to do these things!"). I wondered which outcome was more likely, and what conditions might push the boy toward the more androgynous one.

At the color assembly, Pete reminded everyone that there would be a troop campfire that evening. Todd dismissed the troop for a brief period of individual sports, during which the boys could play horseshoes or a number of other games in small groups. The mountain evening was turning cool, so I returned to the Staff Area to change into warmer clothes for the campfire.

The troop reassembled for the first troop campfire of the season. Todd led the boys single-file through camp and up toward the troop campfire site. At both Usonia III and Good Old New Usonia, the campfire site lies uphill and a few hundred yards away from the camp itself. As we snaked slowly across the granite incline, I considered how well early troop leaders had chosen the site. Each campfire site provides an exquisite view of one of the lakes and the Sierra Nevada peaks. Like Church Rock, each of these sites is special in the topography of the troop.

But if Church Rock is the site for sacred ritual in the troop, the campfire site provides a stage for a "social drama" that is part ritual and part play. A typical troop campfire includes moments that are among the troop's most sacred and serious and moments that are among its most profane and silly. Symbolic anthropologist Victor Turner was interested in the "social dramas" that groups create to enact the shared meanings of the group.[2] The drama metaphor permits folklorists, anthropologists, and sociologists to speak of front stage areas and back stage areas; of roles, costumes, and scripts; of conventional plots and formulaic narratives. Some social dramas are sacred and serious. Those ritual dramas affirm the accepted values of the group, announcing that things are as they should be. "Here is who we are, what we believe, and it is good."

Some social dramas are playful. Play resembles ritual in many respects.[3] Each is a carefully, purposefully constructed frame for stylized activities. But while the ritual frame affirms the group's realities, play assumes doubt. The play frame assumes the "what if?" mode, acting as if reality were different. In the play frame, people can play roles not usually open to them, invert usual categories and usual power relations, and generally experiment with other worlds as they could be.[4]

It is possible for a group to play because the participants know that they must return to the normal, normative order sometime soon. Play can be an escape valve, paradoxically strengthening the social order it mocks because it draws off doubt and discontent into the manageable play frame. But play can also be genuinely subversive, especially in the hands of the less powerful members of society. And adolescent males at Boy Scout camp are the less powerful in that scene.

The everyday campfire, then, is a rather complex folk event involving constantly shifting lines between performer and audience, between collective and individual performance, between genuine spontaneity and carefully rehearsed drama.[5]

As we approached the campfire site, we could see the fire already burning vigorously. Some of the Seniors had supervised a few Scouts earlier in the day in gathering wood for the campfire, and after dinner the Seniors had built the fire. The troop's custom is to have the fire burning as the boys approach; they dismiss as "hokey" the more elaborate procedure of ceremonial campfire lighting practiced by some troops and council camps.[6]

The campfire circle is a square, really, with logs and low rocks serving as informal benches for the boys to sit on, arranged by patrol. Older Staff members brought along aluminum lawn chairs for better comfort, and Pete brought his ukulele. Usually his ukulele is the only instrumental accompaniment at the campfire, though occasionally a Staff member brings a guitar.

Everyone was seated, finally, some boys chatting among themselves and some staring at the campfire, which was several times larger than the small fires they have at their patrol sites. The Seniors were milling around a bit, and I expected Tommy, the Campfire Director, to take charge and get the campfire going. But he seemed as casual as the others. Suddenly, Pete strummed an aggressive, extended chord on his uke and sang a deep, throaty "Oh . . . ," and the campfire began.[7]

The boys knew to come in on the next word after Pete's extended "Oh . . ." because the troop always begins its campfires with the same lively song:

Fireman Bill

My brother Bill is a fireman bold, 'cause he puts out fires.
He went to a fire last night I'm told, 'cause he puts out fires.
The fire it lit some dynamite,
Which blew poor Bill clear out of sight,
But where he's going he'll be all right,
'Cause he puts out fires!

This opening song not only sets a brisk pace for the campfire, but also is an inside joke, of sorts, at which all veteran troop members laugh uproariously after the last line. Guests and newcomers to the campfire rarely see the joke quickly enough to join the laughter, so everyone points at the puzzled outsider. Beginning with this traditional song reminds the troop that they have been here before, that they have a collective history and identity.

Tommy had worked earlier in the day on the design of the campfire program and at dinner had shown the tentative plans to Pete for his approval. Tommy had then written the list of campfire events in order on a paper plate that he referred to throughout the evening. Putting together a campfire program takes some skill, and not every Campfire Director is successful. The troop has a total repertoire of over one hundred songs, but probably only fifty or so come readily to mind as candidates for inclusion in a program.[8] The Campfire Director must pay attention to pace, alternating peppy songs with slow songs, depending partly on his own mood but more importantly on the day's activities and the probable mood of the troop. Amid the songs, the Campfire Director must intersperse troop yells and, under some circumstances, patrol skits and a story told or read by Pete. What's more, the Campfire Director must be sensitive to the "feel" of the unfolding program and must be able to make impromptu changes in the campfire program if, say, he needs an action song to pick up a sagging crowd or a slow spiritual to get control of accelerating rowdiness. This a lot to ask of a fifteen-year-old boy, but most learn how to be a successful Campfire Director.

"Okay," said Tommy, after referring to his paper plate, "the next song is 'There Was a Little Ford.'" Pete strummed a bit searching for the key, then began the song:

There Was a Little Ford
Oh, there was a little Ford, the cutest little Ford,
The sweetest little Ford that you ever did see.
The Ford was on the wheels, the wheels were on the ground,
The engine in the Ford made the wheels go 'round.
Match in a gas tank. Boom! Boom!

Oh, there was a little seat, the cutest little seat,
The sweetest little seat that you ever did see. (*faster*)
The seat was in the Ford,
The Ford was on the wheels, the wheels were on the ground,
The engine in the Ford made the wheels go 'round.
Match in a gas tank. Boom! Boom!

The song built increasingly longer verses in this same manner, adding a little girl on the seat, a little hat on the girl, a little flower on the hat, a little petal on the flower, a little bee on the petal, a little wing on the bee, and a little flea on the wing. The boys sang loudly and with great enthusiasm, taking obvious pleasure in the tongue-twisting, memory-testing string of lines in the long verses.

"Little Ford" ended with some chaos of laughter and talking, so Tommy moved swiftly to regain control and take advantage of the energy the song had created. "Let's do a yell now," he urged the group. "Everybody stand up. We'll do 'Go Back.'" On Tommy's hand gesture, the group began its yell:

Go Back
Go back, go back,
Go back to the woods.
You ain't, you ain't,
You ain't no good.
You ain't got the spirit
And you ain't got the class.
You ain't got the spirit
Troop 49 has.
Hip-hip-hooray!

The group cut off the last word sharply and listened for an echo, which came back crisply a second later. The boys all smiled and sat down again.

"Now we need a skit from the Bear Patrol," announced Tommy. Tommy stepped aside as the Bear Patrol rose and gathered for their skit in the smooth area deemed the stage for campfire programs. Although all the boys in a patrol are supposed to participate in a skit, only Bob, the Patrol Leader, and Chris, his Assistant Patrol Leader, were in this one, while the rest of the patrol merely stood around as "extras," observing the action. "Mine's bigger than yours," shouted Bob at Chris. "No way," Chris shouted back, "Mine's a lot longer than yours." Bob again: "Naw, mine's longer!" And Chris again: "Mine's longer!" "Okay," said Bob, "let's measure them." At this point, both boys pulled off their belts and hung them side by side to compare lengths.

A few laughs from the audience were accompanied by many groans of disapproval, as this skit was based on an old joke well known in the troop. Tommy asked three Seniors, whom he had chosen as judges for the patrol skits, to announce the points, up to five, they were awarding the skit. One Senior judged humor, another originality, and the third execution.[9] These points matter to the boys because they are added to the patrol's point totals for the Nugget Auction later in the week.

Tommy announced that the next song would be "My Bonnie," which is sung to the tune of the traditional song and even begins with the traditional verse. But by the second verse, it was clear that the troop was singing a parody version of the familiar song.

My Bonnie

My bonnie lies over the ocean, my bonnie lies over the sea,
My bonnie lies over the ocean, oh bring back my bonnie to me.

Chorus

Oh, bring back, bring back, oh bring back my bonnie to me, to me,
Bring back, bring back, oh bring back my bonnie to me.

Last night as I lay on my pillow, last night as I lay on my bed,
I stuck my feet out of the window, next morning my neighbors
    were dead.

Chorus

Oh, bring back, bring back, oh bring back my neighbors to me, to
    me, *(etc.)*

My bonnie has tuberculosis, my bonnie has one rotten lung,
My bonnie can cough up raw oysters,[10] and roll them around on
    her tongue.

Chorus

Oh, cough up, cough up, oh cough up raw oysters, cough up,
    cough up, *(etc.)*

My bonnie has tuberculosis, my bonnie has only one lung,
My bonnie spits blood by the bucket, and dries it and chews it for
    gum, by gum.

Chorus

Oh, dries it, dries it, oh dries it and chews it for gum, by gum, *(etc.)*

My bonnie leaned over the gas tank, the contents of there which to
    see,
I lighted a match to assist her, oh bring back my bonnie to me.

Chorus

Oh, bring back, bring back, oh bring back my bonnie to me, to
    me, *(etc.)*

The boys enjoyed singing this song, smiling all through it and putting emphasis on the most disgusting imagery. Parody and "grossing

out" are among the most powerful weapons in the child's folklore repertoire.[11] Both assault adult sensibilities, but the particular form of assault in this song is very telling. "My Bonnie" is about the human body, a subject that fascinates adolescents at a time in their life cycle when they are acutely aware of and sometimes embarrassed by their bodies. Their bodies are changing on them even as they sing the song; their voices are changing, they are growing hair in new places on their bodies, and their sweat has lost the sweet smell of childhood and reeks of the hormones surging through their systems. So their fascination focuses not only upon bodies, but also upon the grotesqueries, pathologies, disfigurements, and other abnormalities or unpleasant aspects of the body.

The gross-out song "My Bonnie" suggests that we might profitably think about the boy's body as a symbolic territory, a map of sorts, to which the boys return repeatedly for symbolic comment upon their social system. Their bodies and their group culture are equally problematic to adolescent males, so the humor in these gross-out parodies masks genuine confusion and anxiety. It is as if the boys can learn something about the normality of bodily and social systems by examining their abnormalities. All of these mental processes are condensed in the "gross" lore of these boys.[12]

With the fun of "My Bonnie" still in the air, Tommy announced that it was time for the Eagle Patrol to offer its skit. Eddie served as narrator and introduced the five characters played by the other members of the patrol: Artie, the bum; Mr. Smith; Mrs. Smith; the maid; and the butler. The players had used their Scout neckerchiefs in various ways to suggest the characters, but otherwise there were no costumes. "The scene opens," Eddie explained, "on a street corner."

Mr. Smith:	I want you to kill my wife for a dollar, okay?
Artie:	Okay, okay.
Mr. Smith:	Thanks.
	[The scene changes.]
Artie:	Knock, knock, knock.
Mrs. Smith:	Yes?
Artie:	Are you Mrs. Smith?
Mrs. Smith:	Yes.
	[Artie strangles Mrs. Smith, then strangles the maid and the butler; they all fall dead and Artie runs away.]
Narrator:	Okay, so Artie got arrested, and this is the next day on the corner at the newsstand. And I'm the newsman.

This [gesturing to another Scout] is just a man that's
walking by.

Man: I want to buy one of those papers. [He pretends to pay
for and receive paper, then reads.] "Artichokes three
for a dollar."

The audience let out a loud groan over the punch line, and Tommy
asked each of the three Senior judges for the points he was awarding
the skit. "Let's give that skit a watermelon cheer," said Tommy, as he
raised his hands in the mock gesture he wanted everyone to imitate.
"Ready? Slurrrrrp! Pttttttttttttttttttt!" (The audience does a very liquid
"raspberry.") Everyone but the Eagle Patrol participated, but even they
had a laugh at the watermelon cheer they received.

Tommy held his paper plate program near the light of the fire to see
what came next. "Ah, the next song is 'Gopher Guts.'"

Gopher Guts

(Tune: "The Old Gray Mare")
Great green gobs of greasy, grimy gopher guts,
Itty bitty birdy feet, mutilated monkey meat.
One pint portion of all-purpose porpoise pus,
And me without a spoon.

Immediately after this traditional verse,[13] the boys sing with gusto a
chain of lines that have been invented and added over the years.

But here's a straw!
Watch out, McDonald's!
Have it your way, have it your way! [to the
tune of a Burger King commercial jingle]

Like "My Bonnie," this song falls in the gross-out category, playing on
the same powerful symbolism of bodily excretions. But the song accomplishes two more things. First, it links the excretions, the material
passing out across the borders of the body, with food, the material passing into the body. "My Bonnie" actually did this with its conversion of
phlegm into raw oysters and coughed-up blood into chewing gum. But
things remain in the mouth in "My Bonnie," whereas "Gopher Guts"
completes the transformation of disgusting things into food. Second,
the song's alliteration and tongue-twisting juxtapositions are a form of
wordplay that the boys enjoy.

"The next song," Tommy told us, "is 'You Can't Get to Heaven.'"
I knew this song from my own Scout camp days and was eager to hear
what the troop did with it. The song establishes a formula into which

the boys insert their own content.[14] Once the boy learns the formula, he can become the center of attention briefly by creating a new verse for the group to sing. The troop has a small number of these songs and would never sing more than one of them at a campfire. If the traditional folk song, such as "Swing Low, Sweet Chariot," represents the most inflexible genre for the boys' meaning-making at a campfire, these chainlike songs are the most malleable, and hence potentially the most valuable outlet for the boys to express the urges and anxieties they are feeling.

The nature of the song precludes a printed version (it is listed in the troop songbook by title only), but the following is a typical verse:

You Can't Get to Heaven

Scout: Oh, you can't get to heaven . . .
All: Oh, you can't get to heaven . . .
Scout: . . . in Pete's old car . . .
All: . . . in Pete's old car . . .
Scout: 'Cause Pete's old car . . .
All: 'Cause Pete's old car . . .
Scout: . . . stops at every bar!
All: . . . stops at every bar!

Chorus

Oh, you can't get to heaven in Pete's old car,
'Cause Pete's old car stops at every bar!
Ain't gonna grieve my Lord no more!

While a single Scout is in charge of the verse he is inventing, the entire group participates in each verse in a call-and-response pattern and chorus reminiscent of gospel music. The formula is simple enough for the teenage boy; he must build a verse around a single couplet (e.g., car/bar). An important rule of the song is that everyone gets a chance to invent a verse, though nobody is forced to do so. The song has no fixed length and must be ended by some arbitrary factor (time, say, or the fact that everyone has had a turn). The Campfire Director must know when to end the song, and he signals this by initiating the traditional last verse:

> Oh, the Devil came out *(repeat response)*
> And shut the door *(repeat response)*
> That's all there is *(repeat response)*
> There ain't no more *(repeat response and chorus)*

Repeated singing of a chainlike song at campfires over the years establishes a number of "traditional" verses, that is, verses that are so clever and appreciated that the boys remember and repeat them from one year to the next. Any single performance of the song combines "traditional" verses with the totally new, the latter being candidates for new traditional verses. The song is an interesting showcase of sorts for the boys' display of verbal cleverness.

The most important feature of "You Can't Get to Heaven" is the part of the formula that permits the boy to insert the name of a member of the group. The combination of a person's name and the couplet makes a verse an opportunity for either an insult or some neutral statement (rarely a compliment). The insults are good-natured and in fun, but they are "cuts" nonetheless, and a common pattern is for the target of one verse to come back a verse or two later with a verse aimed at the original perpetrator. As in other forms of ritual verbal insult, the quicker and more clever the retort, the better.[15] In the example I have quoted, the verse deals with alcohol, a subject of great interest to these boys.

It was getting late, and I could see that Tommy was editing his program as he saw that time was running out. He called for the Snake Patrol's skit, but only Steve, the Patrol Leader, and Pat, his Assistant Patrol Leader, rose to take the stage. Steve began pantomiming in a way that made it clear he was a bartender.

Steve: Hiya, Fred. Where ya been?
Pat: I had to serve ten in the pen.
Steve: Was it long?
Pat: Well, it was at first, until I found a pet ant.
Steve: A what?
Pat: A pet ant. I trained it to play the piano and tap dance. [pause] Oh, wow, bartender. Look at this ant!
Steve: Oh, sorry. [He smashes the ant on the bar.]

The skit actually got some applause, and the Senior judges seemed to like it. Tommy then quickly called for the skit from Tiger Patrol. Again, only Tim, the Patrol Leader, and Sean, his Assistant Patrol Leader, came forward to do the skit. Tim stood while Sean crawled on his belly up to Tim and pretended to knock on the door.

Tim: Yes? Who is it?
Sean: I ran out of gas and crawled here for two days. I'm a traveling salesman. Can I please spend the night here?
Tim: Okay, but there's just me here. I don't have a daughter.
Sean: Can you tell me how far it is to the next farmhouse?

Everybody laughed at this enactment of an old joke, and the Seniors awarded a generous number of points to the Tiger Patrol.

"We don't have time to sing 'Mountain Dew,'" Tommy apologized, and there was some disappointment. But the boys were getting tired, too, and seemed not to mind too much that the campfire was nearing its close. "We'll sing 'Swing Low, Sweet Chariot.'" That slow, soft song set the contemplative tone for the rest of the campfire. Tommy asked, "Who's got a win?" Hands went up, and Tommy called on a series of boys to say their win; a few named the troop campfire their win for the day. The group applauded after each boy's win, and sometimes a boy raised his hand again later to give a second win. Finally, there were no more hands, and Tommy concluded with his own win and then led the troop in a recitation of the Outdoor Code, from the *Handbook:* "I will be careful with fire. I will be clean in the outdoors. I will be considerate in my outdoor manners. I will be conservation minded."

"Everybody up for the 'Vesper Song,'" said Tommy, and we all stood.

Vesper Song

(Tune: "O, Tannenbaum")
Softly falls the light of day,
As our campfire fades away.
Silently each Scout should ask,
"Have I done my daily task?
Have I kept my honor bright?
Can I guiltless sleep tonight?
Have I done
And have I dared
Everything to be prepared?"

Then each boy and man placed his left hand on the right shoulder of the person to his left, leaving his right hand free for the gestures that came with the rest of the ritual closing. The group recited in unison the Scoutmaster's Benediction, while making the Scout sign with the right hand:

> The twelfth point of the Scout Law:
> A Scout is Reverent.
> May the Great Scoutmaster of all Scouts
> Be with us until we meet again.

Finally, the group softly sang "Taps," gesturing with the outstretched hand still in the Scout sign:

Taps

Day is done, gone the sun,
From the lakes, *(hand pointed toward ground)*
From the hills, *(hand lifted to shoulder level)*
From the sky. *(hand lifted toward sky)*
All is well, safely rest. *(arm lowered slowly)*
God is nigh. *(hand brought across heart)*

"This was a good campfire," said Pete. "It had lots of spirit. Tomorrow's Insane Day, so I want you to get a good night's sleep. Are there any announcements?" A few Seniors made announcements about logistical details for the next day. Business done, everyone gathered their things while two Seniors began dousing the fire and others lit the camp lanterns that would provide some light for walking back down the rocky slope, across a short stretch of dam, and back into camp. The boys headed for their patrol sites and sleeping bags, the Seniors for one last meeting with Pete over Insane Day. Everyone was cold and tired, but Pete insisted on talking through the day, step by step. Pete knows that something as elaborate as Insane Day takes very careful planning, and he doesn't want to overlook any potential problems.[16] Finally satisfied with the plans, Pete asked Todd to lead the group in Senior wins. Although many of the Seniors had offered a win at the troop campfire, the Senior meeting is the place for the boys to offer wins associated with their teaching or other leadership roles. After Todd offered the last win, Pete bid the Seniors good night, and we returned to the Staff Area for our campfire.

Back in the Staff Area, we found that Tad (troop alumnus, Eagle Scout, and my former student from the university) had arrived with all his gear. Tad is roughly Aaron's age and is an attorney. Like Aaron, Tad had decided to spend his vacation with Troop 49. Tad and I embraced, and we each grabbed a lawn chair for the Staff campfire.

As we began, I reflected a bit on the spiritual warmth of the troop campfire's closing. Everything at the close of the campfire conspires to create a frame of sacred ritual and bonding, from the beauty of the site itself to the awesome display of stars overhead to the unbroken circle of touching at the end. I could see that the boys, too, were touched by the power of the closing sequence, for they exhibited none of the usual disorderly sabotage of the sacred frame that one sees, for example, during the flag ceremony. The ritual frame worked for this group.

This troop of Boy Scouts faces every day a series of major and minor threats to its collective unity and identity. The division of the troop into four smaller patrols dominates most of the everyday activities of camp life. Patrol members sleep, play, and eat together. They stand together at assemblies and compete together against other patrols for inspection points, in games, and in contests for the best campfire skit. At times, this competition is intense, yet the group must also maintain its identity as a troop. The boys need a ceremonial occasion to remind them of their collective identity as members of Troop 49 and to temper the competitive, divisive feelings that are encouraged throughout the day. The troop campfire, especially its ritual closing, accomplishes such bonding.[17]

The circle itself certainly symbolizes what the ceremony is accomplishing, but it is important, I think, that the circle is around a campfire. The fire itself may be the most potent symbol in the ritual.[18] Ernest Thompson Seton recognized the symbolic power of the campfire, based (he thought) on a human instinct he called "reverence for fire," and like psychologist G. Stanley Hall, Seton believed that the adolescent was an especially spiritual person.[19] One of the nine principles of Seton's earlier movement, the Woodcraft Indians, was "The Magic of the Campfire."[20]

Pete, Aaron, and Tad agreed that the campfire has a mystical power that fascinates the boys. Indeed, we Staff were all staring at our fire as we talked. We also talked briefly about how the day had gone, and Pete worried a bit about Tommy. Tommy seemed very tentative in directing the campfire, and Pete wondered if he'd made a mistake appointing him to that position. "We'll see how the next campfire goes," said Pete. We ended the Staff campfire early. We were all tired, and the next day would be full.

Camp Read, Mahopac, N.Y.
(photographer and publisher unknown; postcard from author's collection)

Tuesday

★ ★

Somehow I slept through the reveille whistle and came to consciousness only in time to hear the call for morning flag assembly. I arose quickly, threw on some clothes, and hustled to the assembly. During the announcements, Pete outlined the day for the boys. The morning would follow the regular schedule, but after lunch everyone would assemble for the beginning of Insane Day. After getting a few more items of business out of the way, Todd dismissed us, and we began our routine morning.

I went down to the Waterfront to watch the lifesaving merit badge class being taught by Todd. A Scout must earn the swimming merit badge before working on lifesaving, so the class was small. Todd was showing the boys a standard lifesaving grasp, from behind with the lifesaver's arm slung over the victim's left shoulder, across the chest, and under the right armpit. This position permits the lifesaver to kick and stroke with one hand while supporting the victim on his hip to help keep his mouth above the water. The boys were attentive, and Todd let each practice the hold on him.

This class reminded me that one of Pete's main worries is drowning. He is responsible for the lives of all these boys, and there are many ways a boy can get hurt in the mountains. But drowning is a constant threat around so much water. In fact, one of the stories at camp that year was of a boy—a teenager in a family of non-Scout campers on another part of the lake—who had drowned earlier that summer. The story goes that he wanted to take a shortcut across the lake, so (without disrobing at all) he put his wallet in his mouth to keep it dry and began swimming. Something went wrong, and he drowned. This sort of story bothers Pete, naturally, adding renewed emphasis to his constant vigilance regarding the rules around the water. Even strong swimmers drown, especially when swimming alone. Another reason for the buddy system practiced by the Boy Scouts during free swim.

On the other hand, the Scout program empowers boys by teaching them skills, including lifesaving and first aid skills. There is even a medal for "saving life," and for years every monthly issue of the organization's magazine, *Boys' Life,* carried a graphic story of "Scouts in Action," telling the story of some Scout who saved a human life, sometimes at risk to his own. The origins of this medal for heroism date back to the founding of the Boy Scouts in 1910 and are rooted in the larger historical and cultural context of that period.[1] The medal represents the organization's ongoing message that selfless service to others is a highly prized value in the organization. Giving the boy the lifesaving skills he might use some day to save a life fulfills one important element of the motto, "Be prepared!"

A whistle announced that the advancement period was over, and the boys got out of the water, toweled off, and ambled back toward their patrol sites for lunch. Talk at lunch focused on the Insane Day activities coming up. The older boys assured the first-year campers that the day would be fun, but I could see that the new campers were suffering some anxiety in anticipation of this unknown event that had been built up so much. Bob, the Bear Patrol Leader, emphasized that it was important for the patrol to win points during the day's contests, and he reminded the boys that they needed all the points they could get for the Nugget Auction.

Not long after lunch, Todd assembled the troop. The Scouts were dressed in bathing suits, T-shirts, canvas shoes of one sort or another, and patrol hats. Most of the Seniors had already left for "T.I.," the island in Lake Usonia where we would spend the rest of the day. My assignment was to take one of the small outboard motorboats over to the island with a load of supplies for the picnic dinner, but I wanted to see the beginning of the events in camp. The boys would depart from the Usonia Waterfront, taking about a half hour to canoe the distance to T.I. I could observe the activities here and still beat the troop to the island in my motorboat. What I wanted to watch was the unique way the Seniors had devised to get the boys down to the canoes.

Todd led us all over to the Rope Slide, which consists of a ¾-inch polyvinyl rope slung through a fifteen-foot pole jammed into a natural "socket" in the rocks at the edge of a cliff about twenty-five feet above the water. One end of the rope is anchored to a submerged stump about thirty feet out from the base of the cliff. The rope goes through a hole bored in the top of the pole, and the other end is connected by means of a block and tackle to a tree about sixty feet from the pole. Hanging from the rope is a large pulley with another rope attached to it for retrieving the pulley from the water end of the slide. A boy climbs the ladder attached to the pole, reaches overhead to where the rope goes through the pole, weaves his hand (for safety) through a loop in the wide webbing attached to the pulley, and firmly grips the knot above the loop. The boy then turns away from the pole to face the water and, pausing to gather his courage, launches himself down the rope slide to the water. The whine of the pulley on the rope, the boy's adrenaline-pumped scream, and the splash in the waist-deep water makes for loud and exciting fun. The troop had been building rope slides each year for several years, but this site was the most dramatic.

Todd explained that the Rope Slide was the first contest of Insane Day and that he would award points to the patrols based on the "fancy rides" of their members. Once everyone in a patrol was down the slide, they were to go to their assigned canoes, put on their life vests, and await further instructions. The patrols went in their BEST order.

Things went smoothly for a while. Some of the boys elected to take a rather normal ride down the slide, but the more daring tried tricks such as pulling their feet into a ball or spinning. The very last boy to ride the slide was Paul, a first-year camper and member of the Tiger Patrol. Paul climbed the pole to the rope, but once he had grasped the pulley, he froze, unwilling to push himself out for the ride down the slide. Pete stood below Paul, gently encouraging him and reassuring him that he could do this. Paul began crying, insisting that he couldn't do it. When, after more soft encouragement, Paul still would not push off, Pete sternly bellowed, "You *can* do it." Paul finally took the plunge, as his Patrol Leader, Tim, and the rest of the patrol cheered him on. Once in the water, Paul smiled and admitted, "That was fun." After splashing in the water with his patrol, Paul and the others waded over to their canoes. Pete pulled Tim aside as the others put on their life vests. "Paul almost chickened out up there. Help him. Don't embarrass him by drawing attention to it." Tim nodded in agreement and joined the others.

I pushed my aluminum boat out from the shore and started the small outboard engine. The boat was loaded heavily with boxes of food and supplies for supper, but I knew that even at my slow rate of progress I would beat the boys to the island, for after canoeing through a narrow strait connecting a smaller part of Usonia with the larger part, they would face a wide expanse of water between them and T.I.

As I motored through the strait and spied T.I. in the distance, I reflected a bit on the little drama back at the rope slide. The tenth point of the Scout Law is "A Scout is Brave." The *Handbook* talks about two sorts of bravery. One is the sort that sends a person into a dangerous situation to rescue someone. But the *Handbook* talks mainly about another sort of bravery, the courage to "do what is right when others call you a coward or chicken for doing it."[2] The BSA endorses an old-fashioned individualism, what David Riesman called "inner-direction," a nineteenth-century individualism in which the person relied upon an inner "moral gyroscope" in order to do what is right in a situation.[3] This nineteenth-century bravery helps the boy resist peer pressure to do something he would rather not do, and for the BSA of the late twentieth century this has primarily meant peer pressure to take illicit drugs.

But the first sort of bravery certainly is an issue for these boys as they work at the social construction of masculinity. The aggressive, competitive individualism favored in American males implies risk-taking. The rope slide was a test of manhood, in this sense, and Paul almost flunked the test. If he had chickened out, then I imagine his life at camp would have been miserable, and he probably would have gone home early. Pete's abrupt change to authoritative command and his later comment to Tim were an attempt to head off any teasing and taunting Paul might have received for his momentary display of cowardice.

About halfway across the lake, I could make out the topographical details of T.I. and the human figures on its shore. The name "T.I." has an important history, according to Pete. Pete's old Berkeley troop first named it "Tit Island" when they began camping at Old Usonia in the early 1950s. The island is fairly small, mainly a mound of sparsely forested sand rising from the lake, but two large granite boulders sit side by side in plain view from Old Usonia—hence the folk name. Later the Berkeley troop shortened the named to "T.I.," a common nickname used in the San Francisco Bay area for Treasure Island, the landfill island created for the 1939 World's Fair. "T.I. is also sometimes referred to as 'Chest Island,'" Pete once told me, with a smile, "but neither name refers to treasure."

When I got closer to shore I could see the Seniors lined up as a water brigade passing five-gallon buckets of water from the lake up the sandy rise to where they had dug the Poison Pit. This pit, about five feet deep and six feet across, was lined with tarpaulins to help hold the water they were pouring into it. The pit would become central to the games later in the day.

Once Jeff was satisfied that the pit had enough water in it, the Seniors began preparing for the arrival of the Scouts, whom we could see on the far horizon. The Seniors had created elaborate props and costumes for the day's theme, "Gilligan's Island: The Final (We Hope) Episode."[4] The set consisted of a cardboard replica of the wrecked *Minnow,* a footlocker doubling as a treasure chest, a cardboard grass hut, and other assorted props. George carried a cardboard "movie camera" for shooting the episode. Things were ready none too soon, as the canoes were approaching the island. The Seniors hid in a clump of small trees so they could not be seen from the beach. Pete held all the boys in the canoes a few feet from shore until all had arrived. Then Tommy, costumed perfectly as Gilligan, came running down the sandy beach, shouting, "Skipper, Skipper, we're saved, we're saved! The Scouts are here!" He tripped and fell, in character, and on that signal the other Seniors appeared to sing the *Gilligan's Island* theme song. Jeff then took over and with his cardboard director's bullhorn explained that the troop had come upon a set where a movie, *Gilligan's Island: The Final (We Hope) Episode,* was being shot. Jeff introduced George, his cameraman, and the Seniors, dressed as characters from the television series. Sometimes only a hat or other prop suggested the character, but Jason and Ricky, the two Seniors playing Ginger, the movie star, and Mary Ann, the assistant to the Professor, tied their hair back and gave their shirts a Calypso tuck to resemble girls' halter tops. They even stuffed their shirts with paper towels to enhance the illusion (or, more truthfully, to parody the illusion). Les was dressed as the Skipper, captain of the *Minnow.* Brad was the Professor, and Ken was dressed as Mr. Howell. Mrs. Howell was mysteriously absent, and a running joke throughout the day was for a Senior to ask, "Where is Mrs. Howell?" Jeff explained to the Scouts that their arrival had "saved the day," as the hired extras had failed to show and the Scouts could now take their place in the filming of the episode.

Jeff then announced the first event, the Hat Contest. Each boy was to wear a special hat that he'd prepared in advance, and two of the Seniors went down the line of boys, inspecting each hat. Finally, they announced the winner in each category: original, organic, storebought, troop spirit, and best all around. Next Jeff led the boys up the beach toward the Poison Pit. Mary Ann ran up to the Professor, holding two watermelons up to "her" breasts. Mary Ann explained that she had found something to eat, and the Watermelon Eating Contest began. This contest is a traditional one for Insane Day. The Seniors turned over an aluminum rowboat, stern end at the edge of the Poison Pit, and Mary Ann placed one of the watermelons on this makeshift table. The patrols took turns in their BEST order. Kneeling on both long sides of the table, the boys were to eat the watermelon as fast as they could, at first without using their hands. After thirty seconds, they could use their elbows and after sixty seconds their hands. They were not finished until all the red melon flesh was gone. A Senior kept time with a stopwatch, and the winning patrol would earn points. Mary Ann took a canoe paddle and with one sharp blow sliced the watermelon in half, signaling the beginning of the contest.

I had watched this contest several times over the years, and I noticed a small change in the behavior of the patrols not participating. Traditionally, the spectators tried to disgust the patrol eating the watermelon, attempting to slow them down by suggesting that they were eating something revolting. In years past, several of these comments had had to do with menstruation, something like "You're eating your girlfriend's period!" Even then, the adults present would discourage those comments, asking the boys to "keep it clean." The tradition endured a while, but by this summer apparently an explicit rule had been imposed against making such comments. Instead, the boys sang "Gopher Guts" and made other, nonsexual comments about what the boys were eating. Once an older boy made a comment about "your girlfriend," but a sharp glance from Jeff ended that.[5]

When the Bear Patrol had finished and its time was recorded, the Seniors tipped the boat up and washed all the debris (rinds, seeds, leftover red flesh, and juice) into the Poison Pit. Each patrol took its turn devouring a watermelon. By the time the Tiger Patrol had finished, the Poison Pit was full of watermelon debris, but the water level was down a bit from seepage through the not-quite-watertight lining of tarps, so Jeff announced that the next event would be a Water Brigade to refill the pit. The job was framed within the *Gilligan* story as the lagoon's going dry and needing to be refilled.

The next event for points was the Solo Cup Race, a traditional relay race. "Solo" is a brand of plastic and paper goods used in camp. "The Skipper needs a clean shirt," Jeff told the boys, so each patrol had to fill a washtub with water. Racing against each other, the patrol members in turn were to carry a Solo cup full of water with their teeth a distance of thirty or forty feet to a washtub and run back to give the cup to the next boy. Once everyone had had a turn, patrols earned points based on how much water was in their washtub. During the race, the Seniors playing Mary Ann and Ginger stood by the washtubs, taunting the boys with sexual postures and come-ons. Mary Ann (Ricky) would turn "her" backside to the boys and wiggle it provocatively in their faces, while Ginger (Jason) mainly pretended to show "her" breasts. The younger boys were trying to concentrate on the task of the relay, but some clearly were amused that these two Seniors were dressed as girls and adopting stylized, sexualized performances of femininity. The other Seniors thought it was hilarious.

With that event finished and the winning points determined, Jeff led the troop back down to the shore for the traditional Relay Race around the island. The runners had to stay in the water, and around the "Titties" it was necessary to swim briefly, so orange life vests took the place of batons in the race. Jeff stressed that runners would not be allowed to proceed until the vests were on properly. Jason (as Ginger) climbed up to sit on one of the "Titties." He was posted there as a safety measure and held the long aluminum shepherd's crook used by lifeguards to fish people out of the water; but all the while he stayed in character and shouted flirty things at the boys as they swam by.

The next event was one invented by Pete. The Steamroller required the boys to lie on the ground side by side. The line of boys moved like a tractor's caterpillar tread, as the boy at the far end rolled himself across the other boys and into the position at the front of the line, in the direction they were moving. The lines of boys quickly turned into tangles, and there was plenty of playfighting to add to the confusion. The first patrol to cross the finish line collected the most points, with other patrols collecting points based on the order in which they finished. The boys were laughing as they got to their feet and dusted themselves off—apparently this contest was a hit.

The next event was designed to wash off the sand and dirt the boys had accumulated during the Steamroller. Jeff took the boys down to the waterline and explained that Mr. Howell had hidden his money in the watermelon and he needed someone to bring it back to shore. Jeff heaved the Greased Watermelon (a melon slathered with margarine) into the water and said, "Go get it." The crowd rushed into the water, with shouts of "Smear the queer" when one particularly athletic boy got the watermelon first. Progress was slow, for it is very difficult to hold the greased watermelon, especially when other boys are grabbing for it. From shore, the contest looked like a slow motion rugby match, and just as violent.

At one point, one boy shouted at another, "Stop fucking choking me!" They exchanged shoves briefly, and Pete called them both out of the water. "First," he began, "you know the troop rule about swearing. Ralph, you should say to Martin, 'Stop hecking choking me,' right?" Ralph smiled and nodded. "You know," Pete continued, "you two are friends, and this sometimes happens to friends. Why don't you shake hands, make up, and get back into the game?" They did so tentatively.

Pete came back over to me and explained that he had discovered during the last year that he had to make a new rule about swearing. It seems that there was an incident in which one of the Scouts said "fuck" in front of outsiders. So Pete has asked the boys to clean up their language so that they will not bring embarrassment or disgrace to the troop. Everyone is to say "hecking" now instead of "fucking," and "heck" in the place of "shit," "damn," or "hell."[6] Pete is still working on this himself. "You know," Pete said to me softly, "Ralph there literally did one of those slips, like the classic joke. The kids at camp say 'fucking' so much that they forget themselves when they get back home. Ralph asked his sister to 'pass the fucking butter' one evening at dinner. His father was amused, but his mother just about fell out of her chair. So I have realized that we'd better cool it with swearing in camp." We looked back to the boys to see that the game had ended with a broken watermelon, so no patrol won the points.

We were nearing the end of the contests, with the two most important to come. The traditional penultimate contest is the Tug-of-War. Jeff explained that the Scouts would have to pull the *Minnow* off the rocks. A long, heavy rope lay beside the Poison Pit. A rag tied to the middle of the rope marked the center line, and the Bear and Eagle Patrols took up their positions at each end of the rope. Jeff held the center of the rope over the Poison Pit and then signaled for the boys to begin. A boy is "out" when he touches the water in the Poison Pit, and each team is trying to drag its opponents into the pit. The pit had become pretty disgusting by that time. Besides the water, dirt, and watermelon debris, Brad and Ricky had urinated into the pit when Pete wasn't looking. This was the revolting soup into which the boys were trying to drag each other.

The patrol that won the first contest tugged against the Snake Patrol, and the winner of that round tugged against the Tiger Patrol. The winner of that contest tugged against the Seniors, who won, as expected. In the final tug between the Seniors and the Staff, the Seniors won, but the adults let go of the rope, knowing better than to touch the poison. After each round, both teams would pose for the traditional victory picture, all of the losers in the pit wearing their watermelon rind "hats," with the winning team standing behind them, gloating.

Finally, the troop was ready for the last contest of the day, Poison Pit. Everyone present grasped the wrists of his neighbors to make a huge circle with the Poison Pit the center. I noticed that Ralph and Martin were joining hands in the circle; they had made up and were cementing their friendship through that grip. At Jeff's signal, everyone began trying to pull some other part of the circle into the pit. A person is out if he touches the water, and if two people break their grip, they are out as well. The game was very physical, with portions of the circle cooperating to pull other portions into the pit. But as the circle got smaller, the cooperation ended, and it was "every man for himself." Finally, the circle was too small to encircle the pit, so the ring of boys began beside the pit. Eventually, two people were left to push and pull each other until one threw the other into the pit. By that time, almost everyone but the victor had been in the pit and had been down to the lake to wash off the poison.

Poison Pit ended the contests, as it always has, and the patrols teamed up to build two cooking fires and began preparing the dinner of hot dogs, soup, and potato chips. As the fires burned down, the boys toasted marshmallows to make S'mores, the traditional sandwiches of toasted marshmallow and chocolate bar squished between two graham crackers. At meal's end, the troop thoroughly cleaned the island, packed all the supplies and debris into the boats, and made the trip back across the lake.[7]

Everyone changed clothes for the brief color assembly and then everyone was dismissed for patrol campfires. There was a brief meeting with the Seniors on advancement. Pete was concerned that every boy should be working on four badges or requirements, and once that was worked out, the meeting ended. Pete congratulated the Seniors on a "great Insane Day" and then bid them good night. Everyone was tired from the physically grueling day, but Insane Day is a favorite among the boys and Seniors, and everyone felt the hard work had been worth it.

We gathered as usual for our Staff campfire, and I steered our conversation toward the issue of swearing, which had come up earlier in the day. Pete felt really ambivalent about having to make an explicit rule about swearing. He saw that it was necessary in order to protect the troop, especially because a church was their sponsoring organization. But Pete also knew that one of the unofficial things boys learned at camp was "how to swear." Camp was a safe environment for learning that masculine skill.

Pete poured us all another glass of wine and turned more philosophical. "I believe that boys are born with naturally good or bad dispositions. I'll admit that there are a few boys I don't like, usually because they have lied to me. I can't stand liars. And I'll admit I have my favorites. One of them is Todd. I see myself in him, at his age. He's a lot like me. And he's going through a tough time now. He's getting very interested in sports and girls in high school, and he has less and less time for the troop. He loves the troop, but he's drawn to this other life and he knows that's the direction he'll go. He and I had a talk about this, and he started crying when he admitted to himself and to me that he would be drawing away from the troop. I started crying, too. I cry pretty easily, and, as I said, he's a lot like me." We all sat thinking for a while, staring at the fire.

This is a problem the Boy Scouts have had for decades—how to keep the interests of the boy once he reaches middle adolescence and gets interested in school sports, girls, and all the other activities high school has to lure away the teenager. The organization turned the Explorer movement (for boys aged fourteen and older) into a coeducational movement in 1969, but this strategy only partly succeeded in holding the boys.[8] Troop 49 has done better than most troops, but clearly Pete and Todd were grieving the impending separation.

Pete resumed talking. "We have a problem with David, the kid in Tiger Patrol. He's homesick. He's moping around, missing assemblies, and generally messing up morale in that patrol. I had a talk with him and decided to arrange for his mother to pick him up Thursday. I don't want a kid in camp who ruins it for the others. Maybe he'll snap out of it by tomorrow, but if not, he'll have to go." We launched into a brief discussion of homesickness in general and how boys usually get over it before long.

I thought to myself that the need to comfort a homesick boy created another example of the ways an all-male social group had the potential for inviting more nurturant behavior in the boys. One way to deal with the homesick boy is to ridicule him, in essence to infantilize and feminize him (somewhat equivalent moves in male friendship groups), and that happens sometimes. But in Troop 49, an older boy, especially the Patrol Leader, is often encouraged by Pete to take responsibility for talking with the homesick kid in a compassionate and nurturing way. Showing leadership in this troop means showing some nontraditional, more androgynous masculinity. I wondered to myself whether this lesson carried back to the home world of the boys or whether the troop and camp setting provided a safe frame for behavior otherwise too risky in the traditional adolescent friendship group.

Almost as if he had heard my thoughts, Pete spoke to my question. "I owe Scouting a lot in my own adolescent development," reflected Pete. "That's why I continued in Scouting, to contribute to these boys' development. I was a real wimp in ninth grade, not very strong, at the bottom of the hierarchy at my school. I wanted to be 'cool,' but I didn't know how. When I joined the Boy Scout troop in my hometown, I gradually developed lots of self-confidence as I moved up in seniority and leadership posts. But I sensed a real split in my personality. I had become this cool, confident, competent kid in the Scout troop and a different sort of kid at school. When I was fifteen, I contracted polio at the end of Scout camp, where I was looked up to by my peers as the camp's assistant hike master, a real macho job. I was confined to bed for nine months, so I had a home teacher for all of eleventh grade. This gave me a lot of time to think about the two personas I had and to figure out how to be more like the one I liked and was proud of. So when I returned to school for the twelfth grade, I was able to leave any traces of wimpdom far behind me. Naturally, I remained active in Troop 8, not just because I enjoyed it but because it was the 'touch-stone' of my new beingness.

"When I graduated from the university, got married, and moved to the valley to teach high school, I still camped with Troop 8 in the summer, but I lost contact with Scouting in my new town. When my oldest son turned eleven, I got involved in the local troop he wanted to join. In a year, I became Scoutmaster, and everyone welcomed the fact that I brought into the troop all of the C&Ts I had learned as a Scout in my home troop. So I like that continuity between the two troops. But we have our own identity, too."

We were all quiet for a minute or two, staring at the fire as it burned lower.

"Kids this age," continued Pete, "want to be cool. But being cool is a problem at camp. Being cool means being detached, being aloof, you know? None of this is a good quality for camp. I'm really getting pissed at Ricky's being cool about things, especially when he calls for a buddy check during free swim."

Aaron agreed. "Yeah, so many of the Seniors try to be cool, so they don't do their jobs."

"A few years ago, Jay," Pete said, turning to me, "I began trying to substitute 'class' for 'cool.' I want the kids to acquire class, so we always talk about how classy we do things in Troop 49, the BEST troop!" Pete beamed. "We're much classier than other troops in the area Council. Kids can be proud of being members of a classy troop. And what I like about classy is that it connects the kid to the troop, gives him some obligation to act in a classy way. Not like being cool. That's very alienating."

Pete had hit on a very interesting tension being negotiated by these kids. He wanted them to substitute being "classy" for being "cool," but in Pete's comments I saw that he realized he was expecting the kids to be very aware of the contexts of these two behaviors. He wanted them to behave classy all the time, to bring only positive impressions about the troop to everyone. But Pete was realistic enough to know that, once back in their junior high schools and high schools, these boys would revert to the cool pose so common in performances of masculinity. He just wanted them to leave the cool pose at home when they came to camp.

What we were talking about, really, was the adolescent male's stylized performance of masculinity. The cool pose feels empowering to the boy; it becomes part of his performance of masculinity, and at the same time it can be used by the boy as a form of resistance against adult power in institutions, usually against the power of the parent and the power of the teacher. The power of the cool pose may be illusory, though. Pete called it "alienating," and that it is. It may be psychologically alienating, but it also runs the risk of condemning the kid to a limited future. The self-confidence of the cool pose and the self-confidence of the classy performance of masculinity empower the boy in different ways, and the classy performance is more likely to help him acquire the "cultural capital"—the linguistic competence, the cultural knowledge, the practice at interpersonal relations—he will need to improve his social standing. The pleasures of the cool pose, the pleasures of mere resistance, are fleeting compared with the real power one might acquire by acting classy.[9]

Besides, the concept of acting classy grounds the kid's identity and performance of masculinity in the group rather than in the individual's personality. Even a group of boys performing the cool pose is little more than a gathering of individuals performing for one another. Performing classiness requires a collective effort, a group performance of an identity. These are two very different sorts of performances, and Pete has complicated the lives of these boys by asking them to balance somehow these two styles of performing adolescent masculinity.

The campfire had burned down to faintly orange embers, and it was getting very cold. We were all tired, so we put away the bags of pretzels we had been passing around, put away the wine bottle and cooler, and crushed the empty aluminum beer cans to tuck them away in garbage bags, well out of the sight of any Scouts or Seniors who might have the need to come into the Staff Area the next day. We assume that the Seniors, at least, know what goes on at our campfires, just as we can guess what goes on at their campfires out at the Point. But the delicately constructed contract holds that nobody is to acknowledge these things. That's being "classy."

I stripped to my underwear and climbed quickly into my down sleeping bag. Tired as I was, I lay awake for a time looking at the stars and thinking about the day's doings. I had observed three or four Insane Days over the past several years, and after the second I had begun formulating some ideas about the meaning and importance of the day. Each subsequent Insane Day refined my understanding, especially in reminding me how dynamic and changeable a "traditional" activity can be.

That Insane Day is an important social drama is clear enough to me. It requires its own space and time, carefully set apart from the everyday place and time of camp. T.I. is an almost mystical place, a place where the play frame is elaborate and sturdy. The Scouts and the Seniors love the day, considering it one of the three most important special traditions they have at camp (the campfires, especially the Nugget Auction, and the Treasure Hunt are the other two). Certainly on the level of the official agenda of the Boy Scouts and the troop, the boys get to practice skills they learn at camp, from canoeing to how to put on a life vest. And since physical fitness is an explicit goal of the organization, the athletic events help develop the boys' strength and coordination.

But by far the more important agenda served by Insane Day is the symbolic agenda. Beginning with the challenge of the Rope Slide, the day provided one opportunity after another for each boy to display to himself and to the others that he is a man. And each event seemed to carve out for special attention a different piece of the social construction of masculinity. The Rope Slide required a display of courage. The relay races required each boy to think of himself as a member of the team and to give his best effort for the team. This might not seem peculiarly male, but that is because it is only since Title IX of the Education Amendments of 1972 was passed that young women have had access to the same sort of experiences with competitive team sports that men have enjoyed. Learning teamwork through sports has been an important element in the social construction of American masculinity since the nineteenth century, and some feminist scholars have argued that women have been disadvantaged in the modern corporation to the extent that the corporation is a male world modeled on the competitive sports experience.[10] Through competitive team sports, for example, men learn that you don't have to like someone to play cooperatively with him, that you are expected to push the boundaries of the rules and cheat until caught, that cheating is part of the game, that there are rules governing cheating, and that anger is not an appropriate response to the aggression that goes on in an athletic contest.[11] The rules of male contest are meant to ensure that competitive aggression does not slip into violence, and boys' commitment to procedural justice (in contrast with girls' commitment to a more negotiated notion of justice) probably stems from the importance of rules in preventing interpersonal violence.[12] Male friendships tend to be forged in groups larger than female friendship groups, so the sports team becomes for men a model of the friendship group. These are the things the boys are learning as they participate in the relay races of Insane Day.

I find very interesting the pairing of the Steamroller and the Greased Watermelon Contest. Both of these are team events involving body contact between the boys, which leads me to think a bit about what sorts of body contact these boys have in the normal course of the day. These boys are enduring the bodily changes of puberty. They have a heightened awareness of their bodies. Suddenly, they can no longer take their bodies for granted as fixed and dependable entities. Camp further intensifies this body awareness. Gone, for example, is the bathroom technology of toilets, bathtubs, sinks, and showers. Bodily excretion now becomes a visible process, and human feces and urine become objects that must be dealt with somehow. Personal cleanliness becomes problematic, as some boys will accumulate layers of dust and dirt until forced to bathe. Privacy takes on new meanings in its loss, as boys urinate and defecate in each other's presence.

Getting dressed and undressed takes on new meanings. The boys' first experience with this public nudity probably is in the locker room in middle school or junior high school, and camp recreates this drama. The cool boy is supposed to be casual about dressing and undressing in front of the other boys; indeed, a boy who attempts to hide himself modestly from others will be derided. At the same time, these boys who are dressing and undressing in front of each other have bodies at different stages of maturity. Some are still boys, others have the bodies of men. Some are short, waiting for their growth spurt; others have had the spurt and are lanky and somewhat uncoordinated in handling their new bodies. Some have pubic hair, while others still wait for that sign that they are becoming men.

What all this adds up to is that the boys' bodies at camp have entered their consciousness in new and surprising ways. Now add to this development the more general problem of men touching men in American culture. By the time the boys reach age eleven and join the troop, they are well socialized in American norms of male body contact. Their peer culture makes it clear that males are to touch each other only in aggressive and, more commonly, in stylized, mock aggressive ways. Boys are not to hug and touch each other affectionately. Playfighting becomes the acceptable, stylized way for boys to touch each other, so in early adolescence these boys exchange friendly punches to the upper arm and sometimes engage in full-fledged playfighting.

As in the case of the boys' verbal dueling, the exchange of ritual insults, the playfight provides the classic example for framed play. The participants communicate to each other the message: "This is play. This is not a real fight. The actions we'll engage in now will look like a fight (e.g., snarling, baring teeth, wrestling), but they will not mean what they would mean if we were having a real fight." Central to the playfight is the paradoxical nature of play, that is, the fact that things do not mean what they seem to mean or what they would mean in a different frame.

For these reasons, playfighting provides an acceptable frame for American males to touch each other, even intimately. There is plenty of horsing around in the course of everyday life at camp, as teasing or ritualized verbal insult may slip into a physical playfight. Leaders sometimes discourage the physical playfight, fearful that the frame can too easily break and the playfight become a real fight, resulting in injury. Most times, however, playfighting runs its course and provides a "safe" frame for two things to happen. First, the playfight features stylized aggression. The symbolism of the fight is more important than its reality, so the playfight permits aggression without the danger of real violence and real harm. Second, the playfight provides something missing in the boys' lives—body contact. At home, their mothers may still hug them, but in the all-male setting of camp these boys are without any nurturing body contact. The boys won't hug and touch each other affectionately, as that raises the confusion about homosexual feelings. And adult leaders are far less likely to hug and otherwise touch the boys now that the fear of sexual molestation is so explicit in the organization. Research with animals shows the severe psychological damage that results when researchers deprive primates and other higher mammals of touching by others. Even in stressful situations (or perhaps especially in stressful situations), humans will find ways to touch. Robert Horan has written about the importance of playfighting for a community of boys in a group home. Those boys had their own horrible personal histories of touching. They were deprived of affectionate touching as they grew up, and their experience with touching from adults came in the form of sexual molestation or physical beatings. These boys hungered for human touch, but playfighting was the only acceptable way they could get that touching in the peer group.[13]

The boys at camp are not the deprived and abused population Horan studied in the group home, but they have the same need as those boys, the need for touching. Informal playfighting provides some of that touching, but so do more formal frames of games and sports—which brings me back to the Steamroller and the Greased Watermelon Contest of Insane Day. These games provide play frames in which it is "safe" for the boys to touch one another. In the Steamroller, they literally roll across each other, becoming a tangle of bodies and experiencing close to full body contact. This induces giggling and laughter in the boys, who clearly enjoy the sensation.

The Greased Watermelon Contest most resembles organized sports, especially rugby and football. Like those sports, the Greased Watermelon Contest provides a ritualized playfight frame that requires boys to grab each other rather aggressively. This is rough-and-tumble play usually associated with males. But what are we to make of the cries of "Smear the queer" as boys try to grab and pile onto the boy with the watermelon? Several years ago folklorist Alan Dundes offered a rather controversial interpretation of the folk speech surrounding American football, arguing that the folk speech reveals the latent homosexual content of the game. Football provides ritualized homosexual combat in which the victors feminize the losers.[14] Later Dundes put that interpretation into a larger context of competitive male sports and warfare. The informal game of Smear the Queer is the paradigmatic case. In all these frames, says Dundes, the folk speech and metaphors support the notion that they are forms of ritualized male homosexual combat.[15]

The way Dundes phrases his argument invites strong denial, and I think he would have been better off not calling the games "male homosexual combat." That phrase makes it seem as though Dundes is arguing that males who play these games are latent homosexuals, and that is not the point. True, Dundes's psychoanalytic approach relies upon Freud's view that all humans are bisexual in their potential sexuality, but the homosexuality in the folk speech of these boys at play is in the service of the social construction of male heterosexual orientation. The aggressive male heterosexual identity in this ritualized combat relies upon assaulting the masculinity of the opponent, and the most effective way to assault the other's masculinity is to feminize him, to make him play the feminine, passive, receiving role in sexual intercourse, the role of the penetrated rather than that of the penetrator. As Dundes notes in his essay on verbal dueling, to put down an opponent refers to putting the opponent in the "down," female position for intercourse.[16] Power, not sex, is the subject of the ritualized male combat. The game of Smear the Queer is not primarily about latent homosexuality, though if Freud is right, there may be an element of that in the game. More important, the game is about sustaining the boys' ongoing social construction of their heterosexual male identity.

Recall the frame break that happened during the Greased Water-melon Contest. Two boys, normally the best of friends, somehow lost control of the playfighting frame and began to have a real fight. Pete had to pull them out of the game and have a talk with them. There is always danger lying just beneath the surface of these playfights. The frames are easily broken, and lying on the other side of the fragile frame is the threat of real male anger and violence. The boys protect them-selves from this violence through the rules of the game and through the stylized nature of the aggression.

These thoughts about the meanings of the Steamroller and the Greased Watermelon Contest help solve another puzzle of Insane Day. The final game, Poison Pit, seems anomalous in the context of the other Insane Day games. Every other contest pits patrol against patrol, but in Poison Pit the men and boys participate as individuals. The Poison Pit itself demands attention both as a literal and as a symbolic center of the day's doings. The day begins with digging the pit, and the Watermelon Eating Contest and Tug-of-War focus attention on the pit. The pit acquires more importance as it accumulates watermelon debris and urine. The game always comes at the end of the day's con-tests; no matter what other contests come and go in Insane Day over the years, the day always ends with the Tug-of-War and the game of Poison Pit.[17]

The boys of Troop 49 play the game because it is "traditional," but they have changed other traditions on Insane Day. Why is this game so compelling to them? What I have just said about other male contests during the day helps make sense of Poison Pit. The game features touching and body contact of the sort we see in the Steamroller and the Greased Watermelon Contest. The game is an elaborated version of King of the Donut. Boys in that game enter into a playfight in which one male (the king) defends his territory (the donut) against assaults from other males. So Poison Pit resembles other male contests in which one male exerts his superiority by defending his territory and physi-cally overpowering the opponents. The winner of Poison Pit does just that. It is he alone who does not come in contact with the poison. It is he who puts his opponents down into the pit, feminizing them.

But are these features of the game sufficient to explain its centrality in the Insane Day events? No, not in themselves. I believe the details of the game tap some unconscious levels of meaning that help account for the game's power. Appeal to unconscious meanings necessarily introduces a theory of the unconscious, and in what follows I shall suggest a psychoanalytic understanding of the game. Only after I had seen Poison Pit played a few times and puzzled over its meanings was I persuaded that the psychoanalytic approach to this particular game helped explain a number of details that otherwise made no sense.[18]

Key to this interpretation is the willingness to see the island as a metaphorical woman. The folk speech supports this view. Recall that the island is dubbed T.I., Tit Island, and that when approached from the water it resembles a supine woman. The boys dig into this woman's belly a pit, a "hole," a metaphorical vagina, which they fill with water. The misogyny we found earlier as part of the folklore constructing a male identity explains why poison might be associated with a woman's genitalia. For these boys, young women's genitals and menstruation are mysterious, perhaps dangerous, matters. We do not have to go far in the folklore and anthropological literature to find male beliefs that women's vaginas are dangerous (also dirty and smelly) and that menstrual blood pollutes. But we have more symbolic details, for recall that the watermelon rinds, flesh, and seeds are swept into the pit and that the folk speech of these boys makes explicit the metaphoric connection between the red melon flesh and menstrual blood. The seeds can only add to this metaphor. Moreover, the boys often urinate into the pit, a rather aggressively male act that suggests urinating into a vagina. At the very least, the urine contributes to the sense that the poison pollutes. The male contest is to see who can put the other boy down into the metaphorical vagina. So the symbolic power of the pit is twofold: it literalizes the put-down of the other male into the passive, inferior, female position, and it punishes the other male by bathing him in symbolic dirt—menstrual blood and urine—which he must wash off in the lake.

If I am right, playing this game helps the boys express and tame the ambivalent feelings they have about female sexuality. There are signs here of fear, disgust, and contempt, but these are matched by evidence of envy and mystery. The game provides a safe way to explore these themes indirectly, through symbols standing for the real matters troubling them. The boys would not use this language to understand the game. Indeed, if I could persuade the boys that these unconscious meanings are encoded in the game (and it seems unlikely I could), they would probably stop playing the game. It would no longer seem a satisfying, fun game. Its psychological value to them lies precisely in the fact that it conceals its meanings.[19]

Finally, I need to account somehow for the transvestitism I saw in some of the Insane Day performances. The "Return to Gilligan's Island" frame for the day involved having two of the boys dress as women. This was the first time I had seen a sustained performance of cross-dressing at the camp. Earlier episodes were brief performances of female roles in patrol skits at campfires. Here at Insane Day the boys saw a sustained performance of two Seniors they knew well dressing as females and mimicking the speech and body language of females.

There is a long tradition of this sort of role playing and cross-dressing in all-male organizations. Dramatic productions at boys' prep schools and at men's colleges long have required men to play the parts of women, and the recent public debates about permitting openly homosexual men to serve in the military has led to a public discussion of the folk traditions of men dressing as women in the military, especially the Navy, for such occasions as theatrical performances and traditional hazings. Despite their conflation in public talk, cross-dressing and role playing should not be confused with homosexuality, but men's briefly playing the roles of women in all-male groups does make problematic in that framed space and time what it means to "act male" and "act female."

Like many other public performances of male cross-dressing, Jason's and Ricky's performances exaggerated femininity. They tried to walk like girls, they teased the boys with their fake cleavage, and they waved their behinds in the faces of campers trying to concentrate on a contest. I won't say their performances were "campy," in the sense Susan Sontag and others mean when talking about stylized performances in the gay community, but they came close.[20]

When a folk group like this troop has to deal with a collective anxiety or tension, such as those surrounding the troublesome project of creating heterosexual male adolescents out of male children, it may turn to a number of ways to address this anxiety. As Barbara Babcock-Abrahams explains, drawing on the work of Mary Douglas, there are several different approaches to dealing with a cultural anomaly or ambiguity, but the most interesting to anthropologists and other culture critics is the strategy whereby a group takes an ambiguity and makes it the center of elaborate ritual[21] or of elaborate play—and that is the case here. The cross-dressing at Scout camp draws upon the power of inversion.[22] The playful inversion of gender and the extreme, stylized version of "female" performed during Insane Day, combined with the participants' knowledge that this a framed event apart from everyday life, actually serve to reinforce the male heterosexual norms at camp. The process resembles the high school male football players' dressing in cheerleader costumes and performing exaggerated versions of femininity at "powder puff" football games, where the cheerleaders and other women play roles not usually open to them; they get to play football for an audience. In both cases, heterosexual male norms and the distinction between male and female are reaffirmed.[23]

Finally, the folklorist in me notices the role of mass-mediated, popular culture in the Seniors' "invention of tradition" in these Insane Day doings. Recently, scholars have been very interested in the invention of tradition, in the ways communities create new things or events and label them "traditional" as an ideological move in the public struggles over the power to name and define people and their places.[24] But the "folk" usually understand this process full well and employ the strategy when it serves their implicit and explicit goals. One day Tad, my former student, and I were doing some executive task at camp, and Tad turned to me with a mischievous smile and said, "You know, Jay, of all our C&Ts at camp, our most important C&T is always to invent new C&Ts." He smiled broadly at that, and we both knew it was true.

On this particular Insane Day, the Seniors had taken a rather old troop tradition and had elaborated it with a new frame appropriated from popular culture. The Seniors are old enough to have a double consciousness about *Gilligan's Island;* that is, as younger kids they probably took it on its own level as silly, fantasy fun, and now as high school teens they are able to see the campy cult possibilities in the show.[25] This appropriation of popular culture by an adolescent folk group makes a good case, I think, for the resilience of children's folk cultures in the age of television.

Just about every adult in the United States is familiar with the public debate over the effects of mass-mediated, popular culture on the lives of children. Much of the debate centers on images of violence and sex, but a slightly different concern—one shared by some scholars and parents alike—focuses on the ways television comes to replace the imaginative, creative aspects of children's folk cultures. Neil Postman expressed this view most clearly in his 1982 book, *The Disappearance of Childhood,* which argues, among other things, that television "disappears" childhood by making every adult "secret" accessible to children.[26] Postman and others also fear other aspects of the effects of television. Children now seem glued to the television some four or five hours a day, often as solitary viewers, instead of engaging in imaginative play alone or in groups. Critics worry that children are losing their ability to imagine things, to be creative, to learn sociability in groups, and so on. Now video games have joined television as the villains in this debate.[27]

The folklorist who studies children's lives necessarily takes a different view. The close study of children's folklore and folk cultures finds that

these are not such fragile constructions that the mass media will eradi-
cate them. Rather, we find a dynamic relationship between children's
folklore and the popular culture created for and marketed to kids.[28]
Sometimes the popular culture appropriates children's folklore, in effect
selling back to the kids the thing the kids themselves created. Sometimes it is the kids who do the appropriating, taking materials from
popular culture and converting those materials in service of their own
folk cultures. Often the children take control by creating parodies of
the popular culture, and that's what the Seniors did by creating a comical narrative frame, "Gilligan's Island," for the traditional Insane Day
games. The Seniors exercised the power of the television audience by
putting the media narratives to their own social and psychological uses.

Eventually the day's events took their toll, and, finally warm inside
my sleeping bag, I dropped off to sleep.

Nature Staff, Camp Sebring, South Florida Council, 1961
(author on far right; photo from author's collection)

Wednesday

★ ★

At the sound of the Commy Czar's whistle and his bellowed "Reveille, reveille," we all shuffled slowly over to the wash area at the back of the Staff sleep area on the edge of the Staff Pond. The late night Staff campfires were beginning to take their toll on us. We seemed to be moving more slowly that morning. Some of us urinated into the mucky edge of the pond, while others took their turns at the cold water spigot for brushing our teeth and washing our faces. Having performed our morning toilet, we walked the brief distance to the morning color assembly. The Seniors also seemed more tired than usual, probably as a result of the hard work and play of Insane Day. After colors and a few announcements about the day (this was to be a regular day of advancement classes), we were dismissed for breakfast.

As I approached the Tiger Patrol site, I could see Tim standing over the shoulder of one of the cooks, a small, first-year camper who was stirring the milk for the morning's cold breakfast of cereal, fruit, and bread. The troop uses dry milk, which is distributed to the patrols in quart packets. It's a trick to get the dry milk to dissolve in the cold, hard lake water. The cook had filled a plastic quart container with water and was stirring the milk frantically, aware that Tim was watching over his shoulder.

"You've got to get rid of those 'flavor nuggets,'" advised Tim, referring to the lumps floating at the top in spite of all efforts to get them to dissolve.[1]

"Yeah," added Sean, the Assistant Patrol Leader. "It's gross to put that on the cereal unless you get rid of the 'flavor nuggets.'" The poor cook had a look of combined frustration and panic. Finally, all seemed satisfied with the consistency of the milk, and we sat down for breakfast. Most of the talk replayed funny moments from Insane Day. I noticed that David, the first-year camper we had talked about at Staff campfire, was being very quiet, sullen really. I could see why Pete was worried about the effect David's attitude might have on the other kids.

After breakfast, the Scouts scattered for advancement classes, and I decided to sit in on Jason's nature class. I had been a nature counselor at my own Boy Scout camp at age sixteen, and I was interested to see what Jason would do in this very different environment. Nature classes are of two sorts. First, boys must meet nature skill requirements to earn each of the early ranks. To earn the rank of Tenderfoot, for example, the boy is required to identify local poisonous plants and show he knows first aid for treating exposure to those plants.[2] To earn Second Class rank, the boy must "identify or show evidence of at least 10 kinds of animals (birds, mammals, reptiles, fish, mollusks) found in your community," and to earn the First Class rank the boy has to "identify or show evidence of at least 10 kinds of native plants found in your community." Second, there are merit badges in the area of nature study. For the more advanced ranks—Star Scout, Life Scout, and Eagle Scout—the boys must earn merit badges, each of which has its own set of requirements as laid out in a merit badge pamphlet. The pamphlet also gives the boy information about the subject of the merit badge and provides a bibliography for further reading on the subject. The Star rank requires six merit badges, the Life rank five more, and the Eagle rank ten more (for a total of twenty-one). The twelve badges (or categories) required for Eagle are the merit badges in First Aid, Citizenship in the Community, Citizenship in the Nation, Citizenship in the World, Communications, Personal Fitness, Emergency Preparedness or Lifesaving, Environmental Science, Personal Management, Swimming or Hiking or Cycling, Camping, and Family Life. The other nine badges for Eagle are electives that the boy can choose from a large number of badges, ranging from Agribusiness to Woodwork.

The presence of nature requirements in the Boy Scouts is a legacy of the turn-of-the-century, Progressive Era origins of the movement.

Ernest Thompson Seton had credentials as a naturalist.[3] The growing nature conservation movement influenced the Boy Scout requirements during those early years, as Progressive Era figures like Theodore
Roosevelt and Gifford Pinchot made great efforts to support the Boy
Scouts' teaching conservation to young men. Among the merit badges
appearing in that first Boy Scout *Handbook* were badges for Conservation and Forestry. So by 1920 the advancement program of the Boy
Scouts directed the boys' attention to nature through at least three
routes—through the pervasive sense of the recreational value of going
out into the wilderness, through direct instruction in natural history,
and through an ethos of protecting and conserving nature.

Jason was standing at the end of the table at the Bear Patrol site,
talking about one of the requirements: "Make a 3-hour exploration of
a forest, field, park, wetland, lake shore, ocean shore, or desert. Make
a list of plants and animal life you recognize."[4] Jason explained that the
overnight hike could count as their observation, and he started naming
some of the plants and animals at that elevation. He had brought along
a few of the nature identification guides from the troop's library, and
he pointed to the trees and a few of the flowers we could all see from
where we were sitting. "This should be easy for you," said Jason. He
then went on to read another requirement: "Study a plot of ground
1m-sq. (10 sq. ft.). Report on the plants and animals you find." Again,
Jason gestured toward the nature guides and told the Scouts that there
would be plenty of insects and plants in any square meter at the edge
of camp.

The boys seemed listless, tired already from their experiments at
staying up as late as they could, and Jason's monotone didn't do much
to enliven the class. This class involved a lot of reading and probably
seemed too much like school to some of the boys; many boys prefer
the badges where they actually get to do something, like cook a meal
or learn how to upright an overturned canoe. Most of the half-dozen
boys in the class were taking notes, but others seemed bored. A poisonous snake or two, I thought, would liven up this class. No poisonous
snake appeared, so the class ended, and the boys moved on to their
second class and eventually to a free period before lunch.

After lunch, Pete had a long Scoutmaster's conference in the Staff
Area with David, the homesick boy from Tiger Patrol. Pete regularly
has these sorts of conferences with boys having or causing problems,
and the troop alumni jokingly refer to these as "Pete's 'being wonderful' sessions." Pete himself will say something like "I was 'being wonderful' with [so-and-so] this afternoon." In this case, Pete was hoping
to give David one last chance to change his attitude before being sent

home. Pete listened thoughtfully as David complained that the boys in the patrol were making fun of his last name, turning it into a slang word for penis. Pete told a story about a high school friend of his son's named Michael Hawk. His friends would call him "Mike Hawk" ("my cock"), and he learned to go along with the joke. "In fact," continued Pete, "I was sometimes called 'Big Peter' by my friends, and I learned to take that in good fun and tease them back somehow. You're going to have to show them that you can take some ribbing," said Pete, defusing the power of the name ridicule. Pete then raised the matter of David's moping around.

"Do you want to stay in camp?"

"I guess," murmured David, but it was not an answer Pete was prepared to accept.

"Your 'I guess' sounds like a question. I want a firm yes or no." It took a while, but Pete got the firm "yes" from David; he would stay. Pete would call his mother and tell her not to come up. David left the Staff Area with a bounce in his step. He had committed himself to a change in attitude.

Pete asked me to sit up at the Waterfront to provide adult supervision for the swimming and boating classes and for the free swim and free boating period following the afternoon classes. When free swim began, a few boys came up to the dam to swim and play in the water. Ricky made sure the boys were with buddies and would blow his whistle every once in a while and shout, "Buddy call . . . 1, 2, 3, 4, 5, 6, 7, 8, 9, 10," giving buddies that much time to find each other and hold their clasped hands above their heads. Once all the buddies were accounted for, Ricky called, "Clear," and the water play resumed.

I was reminded of Pete's complaint at last night's Staff campfire about Ricky's lackadaisical tone of voice while giving orders. "He gives orders like he's asking a question," Pete had said. Pete had mentioned this to Ricky a few times, but Ricky's newfound assertiveness was always short-lived, and he would lapse quickly into his casual way of asserting his authority.

That afternoon Pete was walking up the short rise to the dam when he heard Ricky's lazy buddy call. Pete also noticed that Brad did not have his bullhorn nearby to hail the sailboats and rowboats in case of an emergency. Clearly angry, Pete told all the swimmers to get out of the water immediately, and he called out to the boats to come in to the beach. The swimmers looked puzzled, unsure why they must get out, so they hesitated to obey. This made Pete even angrier. "Get out now," he roared, and they did. Finally, all the boats and swimmers were on shore, and Pete sent them away.

Pete then commenced to lecture Ricky and Brad on the need to have Scouts obey orders immediately. "You act like 'Joe Cool' up there. You call 'Buddies' like you're bored. Do you understand what I mean?"

Nothing in Ricky's face hinted that he understood Pete's point.

"Look, teenagers believe in the 'three I's,'" continued Pete, enumerating them on his fingers. "They think that they're immortal, that they're immune, and that they're infertile." The boys laughed. "They don't fear getting disease, and they don't fear knocking up a girlfriend, and they don't fear the water. So they *must* be made to fear the Seniors so that they'll obey them. Understand? You've got to be harsh at first and then ease off if you need to."

The boys nodded in agreement.

Pete instructed Ricky to draw up a new, more comprehensive set of Waterfront rules, have Pete approve them, and post them. Pete was in the middle of his suggestions about the rules that needed to be listed on the sign when one of the older Scouts ran up, obviously excited about some news.

"Pete," he began, "there are some Girl Scout leaders up near the dam and they want to know if we want to have a campfire together tonight. They're camping on the other side of the Intermediate Level Pond. Can we?"

Pete had a pained look on his face. He looked at Aaron, who had joined us on the trail back from the Waterfront. "What do you think?"

"Well, you know how the boys act around girls. They show off, get silly, get really out of control. I don't think it's a good idea."

"Me neither," agreed Pete. He turned back to the obviously disappointed Scout. "Tell them . . . no, wait. You'd better go up there, Aaron. Tell them 'Thanks, anyway,' but we have a set program and joint campfires don't fit in very well. Make it a gentle and polite brush-off." Pete then finished his suggestions to Ricky and Brad about the explicit rules for the Waterfront.

It was almost time for dinner, so we returned to the Staff Area to clean up. Dinner was one the boys actually enjoy, though outsiders fail to see the attraction. As I came into the patrol area, I could see the cooks grilling slices of Spam. Once the Spam was browned, the cook poured a large can of fruit cocktail over the meat and sprinkled the concoction with brown sugar. They served the Spam and fruit over rice. Everyone enjoyed the sweet, greasy meal. After dessert, I asked to be excused and returned to the Staff Area to dress for color assembly.

In the middle of the folding of the flags, Ralph, who was a member of the evening's color guard, turned away suddenly and vomited. He ran off into the bushes, and Pete warned the others to "ignore it. He'll be okay." Once the colors were put away and everyone was "at ease," Pete offered (as he often does) a detailed critique of how that color guard had performed its duties. At the end of some serious criticisms about how to do things better, Pete said, "And then, to make things worse, one of the color guards barfed." Everyone laughed, including Ralph, who had rejoined his patrol. "There have been others feeling sick over the past few days. There's a 'one-barf flu' going around, so don't worry about it." Thus, Pete smoothly defused the embarrassment Ralph was probably feeling by publicly making fun of the fact that people barf and by pointing out that it's no big deal. Pete knows that Ralph works hard at being classy, and he helped him out.

After a brief period of individual sports, Todd assembled the troop again for the walk up to the campfire site for the evening's troop campfire. On the way up to the site, I could see two campfires. One, ours, was the closer, but a few hundred yards away, across the marshy area called the Intermediate Level Pond, was the Girl Scout troop's campfire. While most of the girls were standing around the campfire, singing, a few were off to the side, gazing at our campfire site through a pair of binoculars that the girls were passing around. The boys returned the attention; a few at the near edge of our campfire area were blinking their flashlights in the direction of the girls, though none of the boys knew Morse code, I was certain. I suppose teenage hormones have their own way of communicating across vast expanses. This carrying on confirmed for Pete and the Staff that the decision to have separate campfires had been a wise one.

The campfire began traditionally, with "Fireman Bill." Again Tommy was directing the campfire from his trusty list written on a paper plate. "The next song," announced Tommy, "is 'Salvation Army.'" I expected to hear a traditional Salvation Army song, but instead the troop sang a chainlike song that alternated a sung chorus with spoken verses of the "Yay! Boo!" type:

Salvation Army

Chorus
Salvation Army, Salvation Army, throw a nickel on the drum, just
    to save a dirty bum,
Salvation Army, Salvation Army, throw a nickel on the drum and
    be saved.
Testimony time! *(spoken)*

> *Verses*
> Scout: In our town, all the girls wear grass skirts.
> All: Boo!

Scout: The boys all have lawn mowers!
All: Yay!
Scout: In our town, the girls wear wooden dresses.
All: Boo!
Scout: The boys all have wood peckers!
All: Yay!
Scout: In our town, the bar is two feet wide.
All: Boo!
Scout: And a mile long!
All: Yay!
Scout: In our town, there's a cop on every corner.
All: Boo!
Scout: Hanging from the lamppost!
All: Yay!

Just these few verses from among the dozens I heard that night exemplify the themes the boys introduce into their chainlike songs if given the chance—sexuality, alcohol, and resistance to authority. The song establishes and celebrates a collective fantasy about sex with girls, about endless drinking, and about the elimination of official power figures. These topics are highly charged for adolescents, and in these respects the "Yay! Boo!" cycle resembles other male adolescent lore.

Pete spoke up, addressing Tommy. "Let's have a yell, now." The troop stood and faced a distant mountain ridge, aiming to get maximum effect of an echo. "Cut off the end really sharp," instructed the Campfire Director, "so we'll get a good echo."

TR
T–R, T–R, T–R–O–O,
P–For, P–For, P–Forty–Nine
T–R–O–O–P–Forty–Nine,
T–R–O–O–P–Forty–Nine
Hip-hip-hooray! Hip-hip-hooray! Hip-hip-hooray!

The boys had, indeed, crisply cut off the last syllable, and after a second's silent pause we heard the "RAY" bouncing from peak to peak. "Awwright!" the boys murmured in agreement as they sat down again.

Tommy announced that the next song would be "I Don't Want No More of This Old Life," including new verses that the patrols had invented the previous evening at their patrol campfires. The song begins with the chorus; then there is a pause, during which any boy may sing a verse. The boys began with the five verses traditional in the troop.

I Don't Want No More of This Old Life [5]

Chorus

Oh I don't want no more of this old life,
Gee, Mom, I wanna go,
Oh, how I wanna go,
Gee, Mom, I wanna go home.

Traditional verses

1. The chicken in the BEST Troop, they say is mighty fine,
    One jumped off the table and started marking time.
2. The Kool-Aid in the BEST Troop, they say is mighty fine,
    They put it on cuts and scratches instead of iodine.
3. The biscuits in the BEST Troop, they say are mighty fine,
    One rolled off the table and killed a friend of mine.
4. The water in Lake Usonia, they say is mighty nice,
    But if you were to ask me, I'd say it's just like ice.
5. The hiking in the BEST Troop, they say is really neat,
    But they forgot to tell me about my blistered feet.

There was a brief calm; then the Campfire Director asked someone to offer a verse newly invented for this campfire.

6. The hiking in the BEST Troop, they say is really neat,
    But they forgot to tell me about the blistering heat.
7. The KYBO in the BEST Troop, they say is really clean,
    But if you were to ask me, it smells like Listerine.
8. The chicken à la king, they say is really hot,
    But if you were to ask me, it tastes a lot like snot.
9. The campfires in the BEST Troop, they say are a drag,
    But if you were to ask me, I'd say they're really rad.[6]
10. The KYBO in the BEST Troop, they say is mighty fine,
    But every time I get up, my butt's covered in grime.[7]

To this point, the boys had observed the relatively new rule against personal slams, that is, verses commenting on individual boys. But patrol slams were still permitted, governed only by the rule that you could not sing anything you would not sing in front of your mother (the famous "mother test"). So the slams began.

11. The Eagle Patrol in the BEST Troop, they say is really cool,
    But if you believe what Eddie says, you're just a fool.
12. The Eagle Patrol in the BEST troop, they say is really hot,
    But if you were to ask me, I'd say they have the trots.[8]

13. The Eagle Patrol in the BEST troop, they say is mighty hot,
But if you were to ask me, I'd say they eat my snot.

This last verse was getting more insulting and dangerously near the edge of the "mother-approved" zone, so the next boy returned to safer territory—food.

14. The chicken à la king in the BEST Troop, they say is mighty hot,
But if you were to ask me, I'd say it gives the trots.

A longer pause hinted that the boys had run out of their new verses, so Aaron offered an impromptu commentary on what was on everybody's mind:

15. The Girl Scouts are so close, I can almost smell their hair,
But everybody knows I cannot go over there.

The laughs acknowledged the truth that the nearness of the girls had been a distraction, and Aaron's verse cleverly reminded the boys that the Girl Scout campsite was off-limits. The song closed with a rousing chorus.

Picking up on the high energy left from singing the song, Tommy asked everyone to stand again for another yell. "This time, let's do 'Matadora,' and let me hear that echo. Let those Girl Scouts know who we are. Ready?"

Matadora

Matadora, troubadora, cuspidora, boys!
Listen while the BEST troop makes with the noise!
Rack 'em up, stack 'em up, siss boom bay!
Troop 49, hip-hip-hooray!

Again the echo bounced back clearly, and the boys were pleased. With a quick check of the song list penciled on his paper plate, Tommy announced that the next song would be "Hasenpfeffer," a troop favorite.

Hasenpfeffer

(also known as "Days of the Week")
Today is Monday, today is Monday. *(slowly)*
Monday—hasenpfeffer. *(faster)*
Is everybody happy? Well I should say!

The song continues, adding Tuesday—string beans, Wednesday—soup, Thursday—roast beef, Friday—fish, Saturday—cold cuts, and Sunday—church. The boys like the song for its challenge to the memory and oral dexterity, and the subject, food, is dear to them.

"Now," said Tommy, "I want to call up Aaron to lead us in 'Saints.'" Aaron put down his guitar, rose, and took a place by the fire.

"This is a song we've sung over many years in the troop," explained Aaron, "and I want to hear some enthusiasm. We used to sing this back in the seventies, so when we get to the verse 'When the revelation comes,' you can sing it the way I learned it—'When the revolution comes.' So, let's go."

Saints

Oh when the Saints go marching in,
Oh when the Saints go marching in,
Oh, Lord, I want to be in that number,
When the Saints go marching in.

Oh when the moon has turned to blood, *(etc.)*
Oh when the sun refuses to shine, *(etc.)*
Oh when the revolution [revelation] comes, *(etc.)*[9]
Oh when they gather 'round His throne, *(etc.)*
Oh when they crown him King of Kings, *(etc.)*
Oh when the Saints go marching in, *(etc.)*

As is troop tradition, the boys screamed each word of the last verse, so by the time the song was finished, the boys had worked themselves into a highly agitated state. Aaron praised their performance and returned to his seat.

Tommy wanted to slow things down a bit and change the mood to get the boys ready for Pete's story, so he announced that the next song would be "Usonia," a song written by a member of the troop in the late 1970s and now a traditional song at campfires.

Usonia

Chorus
Usonia, what a wonderful place to be.
Oh, the magic of the mountains and the scenery.
We've got two whole lakes,
Got half a dozen peaks,
Clean air to fill our lungs.
What a wonderful place to spend three weeks,
What a wonderful way to have fun.

Verses
So I joined up with Troop 49 'cause I heard that they were great.
They spend three weeks at summer camp

At a place called Usonia Lake.
They camp at *(chorus)*

We hike out 'most every year, upon the dusty trail.
Sometimes we hike in the sun and wind,
And sometimes in the hail.
All hail to *(chorus)*

I remember '74, yes a time I do recall,
When we climbed to the top of Dardanelles Cone
And we had fun one and all.
Had fun at *(chorus)*

We came up a week ago, our future so unclear.
But we took the chance and we're glad we did,
And we're coming back next year.
Back up to *(chorus)*

Whereas the boys personalize their chainlike songs with references to individuals and to well-known things around camp, "Usonia" invokes something more like a collective memory of experiences. While none of the boys singing in the 1990s remembers the 1974 climb of a prominent volcanic peak in the area, the peak is visible from the campfire site, and the verse stands for the hike and experiences the boys shared the previous week. The song helps make the troop a "community of memory."[10]

The song had quieted down the group, as Tommy expected, so they were ready for Pete's "scary" story. Sometimes Pete reads a published short story from one of the numerous paperbacks he collects for such occasions. But on this night he was going to tell a "true" story, the "Story of Sapp's Cabin," which turned out to be a traditional contemporary legend, the sort of scary story kids at camp are used to hearing and telling one another.[11]

The campfire ended as usual, with everyone standing to sing the "Vesper Song" and then, linked by left hands resting on right shoulders, reciting the Scoutmaster's Benediction and singing "Taps." Pete thanked the boys for a great campfire, "lots of great spirit!" He reminded them that the hike to LBAS (Little Bare Ass Slide) was the next day. He asked if there were any announcements. None were offered, so he said, "Good night, Scouts." Tommy and Jason began putting out the fire with the buckets of water and shovels they had brought. As we walked slowly down the hill toward camp, we could see that the Girl Scouts had ended their campfire. Later Pete and Aaron again agreed that they had made a wise decision not to have a campfire program with the Girl Scouts.

The Senior meeting had a troubled start. This was to be a faculty meeting for the Seniors to plan the next day's morning advancement periods. Jeff, the Advancement Director, did not have his binder with him, and even after he fetched it from Senior Point, he did not have the information he needed to give Pete about each boy's progress so far.

Pete stared silently at Jeff and the others. "Do you know what 'backing up to the pay table' means? Any of you?"

Nobody seemed to know.

"It's a metaphor from the military," continued Pete. "'Backing up to the pay table' refers to getting something you supposedly earned—like your pay or a merit badge—knowing all the while that you did not earn it. A kid is cheated if a Senior allows him to get a badge without feeling like he really earned it." Pete paused to let this sink in. "Like Todd, for example," said Pete, turning to Todd with a smile meant to convey that this lesson would include some friendly ribbing. "Todd admits that he didn't really earn the Reptile Study merit badge he used toward Eagle."

"Well, yeah, but I had extra badges," explained Todd, a bit nervous that he was being used as the example here.

"Yeah, that's true," admitted Pete, still smiling, "but you didn't feel too good about that badge, did you?"

"No," admitted Todd.

"So it's very important that you do these advancement classes right. This is very important service you do for the Scouts, and I won't tolerate your fucking up another kid's advancement. One year I kept two Seniors from getting Eagle that fall because they messed up some kids' advancement. They eventually got their Eagles, but I wanted them to learn that lesson. Duty to others. These classes are your duty."

After offering a bit of advice about some of the classes, Pete left for the KYBO, and the Seniors continued their meeting briefly, preparing for the day hike.

"Whoa, did you fart?" said Ricky to Tommy, turning and making a face. Innocently, Tommy asked: "Why? Was I supposed to?"

The Seniors finally sang the masturbation song and broke up the meeting to return to the Point.

Once we had the Staff campfire going and had gathered our chairs and snacks, Pete continued talking about the importance of advancement. "You know, Jay, we have had some families leave the troop because of our high standards. We're not an 'Eagle mill,' cranking them out. It's harder to earn Eagle in Troop 49 than in any other troop in the Council, and when you get Eagle in the troop, you can be very proud of what you've accomplished. Some kids and their families want the fast track to Eagle, so we tell them to move on. That's not the Troop 49 way."

I commented that I had read in the *Handbook* the latest list of merit badges required for Eagle and was surprised to see the new (to me) Family Life badge there.

"That's the work of the conservative 'traditional religious values' people who have taken over the national office. They're trying to make sure parents do their duty and are as involved as possible in the boy's life, but this is a potentially traumatic badge for a boy. So many boys now don't come from an intact, 'traditional' family. That badge just dredges up lots of unhappy stuff for some kids and causes nothing but hurt. I wish they wouldn't require it for Eagle, but there's no chance of that."

"Hey, Woody," said Aaron to me, using the nickname for whoever is sitting nearest the wood pile for feeding the fire. I got the message, reached over, and picked up two larger pieces of wood for the fire. Pete continued.

"I hate it when a Senior fucks up a kid's advancement. Advancement is the most important thing we do at camp. Wait, that's wrong, having fun is the most important thing we do at camp. But advancement is important, and it can be fun, too. It adds a sense of accomplishment to reinforce and validate the fun times.

"Actually, Jay, I expect the kids, including the Seniors, to fuck up. It's natural. I think the troop offers a 'safe' environment for fucking up, at least for the minor fuck-ups that don't endanger lives. In school or in sports, a kid can fuck up and never get out from under it. But in the troop a kid can fuck up, even be sent home from camp, and still turn out to prove himself competent and trustworthy.

"Sometimes there are kids that mean well and just plain fuck up for no visible reason. It has taken me a while, but I finally have come to the realization that I can still love a kid who fucks up." I was intrigued by Pete's notion that the troop provided a safe space for kids to fuck up and still redeem themselves.

Changing the subject after a long silence, I asked Pete and Aaron about a campfire song I had remembered from the last time I was at camp. The song was entitled "Dead Puppies," and Aaron had just brought the song to the troop from his few years of living and working in Los Angeles. Dr. Demento was a famous disc jockey in L.A. who often played what are called novelty songs, and Aaron had heard the song several times on the radio.[12] The song bore the mark of the sick humor that the boys would love:

Dead Puppies [13]

Chorus
Dead puppies, dead puppies,
Dead puppies aren't much fun.

Verses
Puppy died late last fall,
That's him rotting in the hall.
Dead puppies aren't much fun.

They don't come when you call,
They don't do much at all.
Dead puppies aren't much fun.

Mom says puppy's days are through,
She will throw him in the stew.
Dead puppies aren't much fun.

"We don't sing that song anymore at the troop campfires," said Pete, looking at Aaron with a smile. "See, there was this kid last year, a first-year camper, who was very upset when we sang the song. Later I asked him what the matter was, and he told me the story. He had pleaded with his parents to let him get a puppy the previous summer, and they finally relented. But his father told him he was responsible for taking care of the dog—feeding it, walking it, and so on. Well, one day the dog got out through a hole in the fence—a hole the kid's father had asked him to fix—and the dog was hit by a car and killed. The kid was devastated, but the father blamed the kid and was really nasty and mean about it. Our song touched off that very sore point. The poor kid was in tears. So I promised him we wouldn't sing the song anymore. But, you know, I kind of liked that song. I miss it."

"We could sing it now," offered Aaron, who had brought his guitar to the Staff campfire. So we sang the song, slowly, softly, and with dramatic sadness, after Pete's story, loving every bit of its irony.

Talk turned to the Girl Scouts nearby. "You saw how the boys acted tonight. It would never work to have a campfire with the girls. Once, when we had a bicycle camp at a county campground in Marin, there were girls all around, and we couldn't get anything out of the boys. They were too busy showing off for the girls."

"Yeah," agreed Aaron, remembering that campout. "They really act differently around girls. Their hormones won't let them think of anything else."

I changed the subject again, returning to the notion that a kid could redeem his fucking up. I asked Pete what kid now in the troop had improved the most.

"Well, Jay, that's a good question." He paused a few seconds. "I think it's Jeff. He came into the troop as a 'wimp.' Not a 'sissy.' A sissy doesn't want to change. He's always looking for sympathy and wants to be babied. I have no use for sissies. A wimp, on the other hand, knows he's a wimp and wants to change, but he doesn't know how. That's pretty much what I was as a kid when I joined the Scouts, so I know the type well. Jeff has really blossomed. I take some credit for that, for creating the sort of troop that makes it possible for a kid like Jeff to change so much and for spending many hours of 'being wonderful' with him about strategies for not being a wimp."

Pete paused briefly in thought and then continued.

"I think that for me and for Jeff, the key is that a troop like ours lets you change, lets you move up in status, ability, and confidence. Teen culture pretty much labels you, and you're stuck with that status all through junior high and high school. But not Troop 49. A kid can really change."

After a few more observations on the disrupting influence of girls, we put out the fire and retired for the night.

Hidden Valley Scout Camp, Loysville, Pa.
(photographer and publisher unknown; postcard from author's collection)

Thursday

★ ★

We arose as usual and had a regular morning of advancement classes. Late in the morning, the troop assembled and Todd went over the plan for the day hike. The Staff and Seniors would take the troop across the lake to the Old Usonia campsite, where we would pick up the jeep trail that would lead us to LBAS. Pete would drive the truck around the lake and meet us at LBAS with the supplies for lunch.

LBAS and BBAS (Big Bare Ass Slide, what else?) are two sites along one of the forks of a river that feeds the lakes. They are traditional swimming holes where the troop will usually break a hot and dusty hike with a cool and relieving dip in what is pretty cold water, even in July. In some years, this water is coming from still-melting snow. LBAS and BBAS are part of the symbolic geography of the troop, like T.I. and Church Rock. The troop is surrounded by a landscape named sometimes by others but most often by them. Naming the landscape makes it theirs, and giving the landscape obscure, coded names (like the initials LBAS) helps make sure that the meaning of the names stays within the troop. The names are what a folklorist would call "esoteric lore," meaning that the names are part of the folklore known only to the troop and are invoked as part of the performance of the unique identity of the troop. Part of being socialized into the troop as a first-year camper is learning this esoteric lore, including the names of the special features of the landscape.

We crossed the lake in boats and canoes, arriving at Old Usonia by around 11:00. We formed a single line and began the hike. The boys were carrying only water bottles, as they needed no other equipment. Aaron led the way and asked me to take the end of the line, to deal with the stragglers. Part of my job was to keep the slowest walkers up to pace, but the most important thing was to make sure we didn't lose any boys. The first part of the hike took us across what the troop calls Devil's Slide, a large expanse of sloping rock that rises behind Old Usonia. As we walked diagonally across the face of this slope, we got an increasingly grand view of the two lakes. After reaching the top, we descended again into a wooded area with a stream running through it, and we stopped to appreciate the cool shade. A little further up this same stream was the place where we would be swimming later. Aaron drew everyone's attention to a grove of quaking aspen trees, their leaves fluttering in the breeze, showing, alternately, their green topsides and silvery undersides. In the fall, these same aspen leaves turn yellow, just about the only color in the Sierra (there are some reds; almost everything else is evergreen).

Refreshed, we resumed the hike, and before too long we came in sight of LBAS. It's a beautiful spot where the stream tumbles down the rocks in a long, gentle series of falls. The name comes from a large rock with a sheet of water flowing over it, creating a gentle slide about thirty or forty feet long. Slick green algae on the rock's surface makes it a true slide, and there are other, smaller slides in the same area. Erosion has created shoulder-deep and shallower pools. The variety of water action, in places crashing over the rocks, in other places still as a bathtub, is what makes it so much fun to play here. The boys gathered into their patrols and stripped off their clothes. Most had bathing suits on under their shorts; some wore just jockey shorts in lieu of a bathing suit. Before the National Council handed down the "rule of three," there would always be some Seniors skinny-dipping on this traditional trip, in the true spirit of Little Bare Ass Slide. The older boys seem to feel much more comfortable with the nude play than do the younger boys, who show modesty about their still-developing bodies. Even under the "rule of three," some Seniors still pull their shorts down a bit to slide bare-assed down the slick rock, but they no longer show their genitals.

Aaron and I stretched out in the shade of a large pine tree, keeping an eye on the troop but also simply enjoying the beauty of the mountains.

Although visiting LBAS is about having fun, the experience also offered those tests of manhood I see so often in the male group. One test, of course, was the hike itself, showing who had the physical stamina to keep up with the pace Todd set. The hike exposed the "weak sisters," as one folk phrase of this male group has it, the boys who struggled to keep up and occasionally lapsed into whining about being hot and tired and about hurting from blisters on their feet. The next test, now lost, was the opportunity for nudity. The older, physically mature Seniors were the ones most likely to strip naked and frolic in the water. But most boys, including some of the younger and physically slighter Seniors, wore something, even if it was just their underwear. Some who wore jockey shorts in those years had left their swimsuits at camp because at the outset of the hike they had intended to swim bare-assed but at the last minute chickened out. It seemed to me that the transition from clothed to unclothed was still a powerful marker of mature masculinity for the boys in this troop. The third test was going down the slide. Many boys tried it; some worked hard at playing elsewhere in the stream.

After about half an hour, Pete arrived in the truck. Todd called all the boys in for lunch as the cooks retrieved the patrol boxes from the back of the truck and made Kool-Aid to wash down the sandwiches and fruit. The boys were hungry, but they jabbered excitedly to each other as they ate. Playing in the very cold water had stimulated them. As the boys were finishing their lunch, Pete stood up and called their attention to a nearby clump of trees. He was giving them a quick lesson in tree identification, showing them in that small area the three different conifers common at that altitude.

While we were relaxing after lunch, and Pete was some distance away, napping in the shade of a tree, some of the boys played a prank called Atomic Sit-Ups. Knowing Pete's firm rule against any sort of hazing or other form of humiliation, the boys never would have tried this within his view or earshot. Gil asked Mark, a boy from another patrol, if he had ever heard about Atomic Sit-Ups. Mark said he had not, so the boys explained to him that if you hold a person and touch him in a certain way, then he cannot do sit-ups. Mark agreed to try to do a sit-up under these circumstances. The boys used a T-shirt to blindfold Mark and had him lie down carefully on a level area of rock. They had him clasp his hands behind his head, and they placed their fingers on his stomach. Meanwhile, Gil, whose bathing suit had ripped in back while he was sliding down the rocks, straddled Mark with his buttocks toward Mark's face. "Now try to sit up," the boys told Mark. He was able to sit up, of course, but his face came up square in Gil's ass.

The pranksters all laughed uproariously, while Mark wiped his face with the T-shirt blindfold he had torn off once he had realized what had happened. "Gil, you queer," shouted Mark, obviously embarrassed.

Everyone was laughing, so it became clear to Mark that he had better not take this prank too seriously. He protested a bit more, warning Gil that he would get even, but even Mark smiled in recognition that this was a pretty good joke. What Mark had realized, probably without being able to say it, was that he had been tested in the ways males test one another in friendship groups. As part of the initiation into a group, a male may be subjected to pranks and practical jokes. There is mild aggression in these pranks, just as there is mild, stylized aggression in male ritual insults, but the proper response is to take the joke well. "Taking the joke" shows deference to the group and bonds the victim to the group. The prank amounts to a ritual of victimization and submission, which, paradoxically, helps make the victim an equal of sorts. But the male friendship group also has its understood hierarchy, and pranks help maintain that hierarchy.[1]

It is quite a different matter for a boy to be the constant target of jokes, and the danger of that practice emerging is why Pete feels so strongly about any pranks that humiliate a boy. "I can barely tolerate hazing among true peers," Pete later told me, "and I certainly cannot abide it when there is any power relationship involved." In that case, the group is not initiating the boy with ritual humiliation but engaging in aggressive, mean-spirited humiliation meant to send the boy away from the group. Sometimes boys do fall into this role, but they don't stay in the troop long. One way to make himself a candidate for such a role is to take a prank too seriously, to overreact to the prank, to refuse to accept the construction of the play frame. Mark was smart enough to laugh at himself and to accept the play frame. His reaction maintained his membership and status in the group, and his promise to get even was a signal that he accepted the reciprocal relationship initiated by the prank. The play frame itself, quite apart from its content at any moment, communicates relationship, and in the case of pranks the play frame ensures that the participants understand that pranks are possible only between boys who trust one another deeply.

The content of the prank was not unimportant, either. That Mark retaliated immediately with "Gil, you queer" acknowledged that Gil had put him into a submissive position, almost literally "kissing Gil's ass."[2] The prank also metaphorically enacted a sexual practice, but I doubt these boys understood that. Mark's throwing an antigay epithet at Gil, however, was his way of countering all these layers of meaning that had made him the submissive male—that is, the feminized male—in the prank.

The boys cleaned up their areas after lunch and put the boxes and trash back into the truck. Aaron was going to drive the truck back to camp while Pete took over the hike. We hiked about another hour and swung back toward camp. Along the way, Pete stopped and showed the boys another traditional swimming site, the Jacuzzi, a swimming hole with a waterfall the boys can sit under. About half the boys stripped again to their bathing suits, and we spent about a half hour there, while some played in the water and others explored the sides of the stream. Finally, we were on our way again, hiking back to Old Usonia, where we climbed into the boats and canoes for the trip back across the lake to G.O.N.U. It was late afternoon by the time we secured the boats and canoes and climbed up the rocks to camp.

Back in the Staff Area, we found Robert, a troop alumnus about twenty years old. Robert was taking a long weekend off from work to visit the troop. We exchanged greetings, and Aaron gave Robert a brief report on how camp was going. We were washing up for dinner when George, the Commy Czar, came to the "door" of the Staff Area.

"Knock, knock," he said, and we turned to look at him. He was holding a dead mouse by the tail. Pete asked him to come in.

"We caught this mouse in one of the traps we had set in the Commissary tent. I wanted to show it to you. What should I do with it?"

"Well, I don't want it. Throw it out into the bushes," said Pete, and he headed off to the KYBO.

"Leave it there on the rock," said Robert, which George did. George left and Robert picked up the mouse and brought it over to where he had been sitting. "Fresh, not stiff yet," he said mischievously. He sat down and began working on making a hangman's noose with a short length of binder twine. He put the noose around the mouse's neck and hung the mouse from a branch. "This will warn other mice to stay away from our food," he said with a smile.

Pete returned from the KYBO and didn't see the mouse at first. When he did see it, he didn't show too much surprise and Robert explained his purpose. "Only until it starts to smell," warned Pete.

Patrol campfires followed dinner and individual sports. After such a tiring day, the boys needed something more quiet and restful than a troop campfire. I walked from one patrol site to another, but there seemed not to be much in the way of campfires at any site. In the main, boys were milling about in small groups or lounging in their sleeping bags. So I worked my way back to the Staff Area and began talking with Aaron and Robert.

"Knock, knock," came the call from the dark edge of the Staff Area. It was Todd, with three Scouts in tow. "Is Pete here?" asked Todd. "No," replied Aaron, explaining that Pete was off taking a shower.

Todd then began telling the story of these three boys, who, I could see, were wet to their waists. Todd had been making his rounds of the patrol sites. At the Snake Patrol's site, he had heard sounds in the Contest Pond (another marshy area). He had been suspicious of this patrol, because on an earlier visit just after dinner he had heard Scouts shouting across the pond to some of the girls camping with the Girl Scout troop. He had warned them then to stop. On his return visit, Todd had climbed a low rock separating the patrol site from the pond, held out his lantern, and discovered these three Scouts huddled in the water, trying not to be seen. They were attempting to wade across the pond to speak with a thirteen-year-old Girl Scout on the other side. Todd called them out of the water and, saying nothing else, led them immediately to the Staff Area.

I could see that Aaron was unsure how to handle this. He and Robert gave the boys a brief lecture about violating the rules and how serious an infraction this was. But they were reluctant to say more, not wanting to diminish in any way the impact of Pete's certain lecture and decree of punishment. During this brief lecture, the Scouts offered no defense and said very little, mainly gazing at the ground in some combination of shame and fear. We sat there for a while in silence, awaiting Pete's return. As it was getting cold, I suggested that Todd take the boys back to their campsite to change into dry, warm clothes and bring them back promptly to wait for Pete. He did so, and about ten minutes later they all returned, properly dressed for the rapidly falling temperatures.

When Pete returned from the shower, Aaron quickly summarized the events, and Pete asked us if he could be alone with the three Scouts. We Staff members moved fifty yards or so over to the table where the Seniors were holding a planning meeting for the Nugget Auction to be held at campfire the next evening. Throughout the meeting, I kept glancing over at the Staff Area where I could see Pete talking calmly, but quite seriously, with the three Scouts. His talk with the Scouts lasted nearly an hour. As the three boys headed back to their patrol site, Pete ambled up to us.

"I'll get caught up on your Nugget Auction plans later," began Pete. "For now, I want to talk with you about something else." He opened the aluminum lawn chair he had brought with him from the Staff Area and sat at the head of the table.

"The Staff 'night out' is coming this weekend, and I want to remind you all that the troop has a 'taboo policy' regarding alcohol. There are two important ingredients in the taboo policy. First, you should never, never ever do anything that will jeopardize the existence of the troop. Second, you should never do anything that will make a fellow Senior uncomfortable, like pressuring him to drink or smoking dope in his presence. I've sent Seniors home before for violating the taboo policy, and I'll do it again if I have to. You all promised me at the Senior Retreat before camp that you would abide by the taboo policy. I want to remind you of that promise."

He looked around the table. "Can you all agree to the taboo policy?" They all nodded their heads in agreement.

"The taboo policy represents putting 'duty before self.' That's what Scouting is about. That's what being a Senior is about. Duty before self. Now good night and get a good night's sleep."

The meeting broke up, the Seniors returned to the Point, and we four Staff members huddled around the Staff campfire for the usual day's debriefing.

Pete told us that he was not sending home the boys from Snake Patrol. They were "beached"—that is, excluded from water activities other than advancement classes—for violating the camp rule about going into the water without a lifeguard present. But Pete made it clear that he considered the presence of the thirteen-year-old girl to be a mitigating circumstance. She was a temptress, he said in something close to these words, who got the boys into trouble for doing what came naturally to them. Aaron and Robert agreed with Pete's assessment that thirteen-year-old boys simply cannot help themselves in the presence of thirteen-year-old girls. "You can keep them apart," said Aaron, "but you can't keep them from yelling back and forth." Aaron smiled, as if to agree that hormones overcome male judgment every time.

"I have a theory," said Pete, still thinking about the approach-avoidance experiences boys have with girls in these years, "that boys learn pretty early—maybe by kindergarten—that girls are very judgmental toward them, that girls try to make the boys behave according to the expectations applied to boys. This has got to rankle boys, unconsciously. Maybe this even teaches boys some misogyny, a word you like, Jay." Pete smiled at me with this dig. "Boys and girls seem to me to be genetically incompatible in their early years in terms of their personal goals. All boys want to do is play and maybe occasionally learn something that interests them. They certainly have no interest in conforming to some imposed regimen. Girls, on the other hand, seem to take naturally to conforming, or at least in having others, especially boys, conform to whatever it is the girls think it is important to conform to.

Girls can be quite righteous about it and see no fault in being so. Boys don't see that at all. I think they simply don't care to see it. So, at a very early and formative age girls learn to be very disapproving of boys, and boys learn to view girls as ridiculous creatures without minds of their own. Then, not too much later than all this, sexual nuances enter the scene. But I don't think the boys ever get over that strong sense that the girls disapprove of them."

Pete changed the subject and asked Aaron how the Senior meeting had gone. The Nugget Auction is one of the three "most fun" special activities at camp, along with Insane Day and the Treasure Hunt, and Pete wanted to be sure that the Seniors were prepared for the next night's campfire auction.

"They seem prepared," began Aaron, "but they seem pretty listless, tired. More tired than they ought to be. In fact, I've noticed that all week."

"Yeah, so have I," agreed Pete. "Something's up."

"Well," chimed in Robert, "I think I know what it is. I ate dinner with the Tiger Patrol and some of the Scouts were talking about the fact that the Seniors have a box full of *Playboy, Penthouse, Hustler,* and other porn magazines out on the Point. They're probably staying up late at night looking at those magazines."

"Yeah, I'll bet that's it." Pete arose from his chair, walked out onto a rock, and faced toward Senior Point. Cupping his hands into a megaphone, Pete called out, "Todd, I want to see you! Now!"

Pete returned, smiling. "He'll shit in his pants wondering what trouble he's in now."

Within about five minutes, Todd arrived at the Staff Area, and called out, "Knock, knock." We had moved back down from the Staff campfire site, and Pete asked Todd to come in. Todd looked uncertain, no doubt wondering what he had or hadn't done.

"It has come to my attention," began Pete, "that there is a box of smut on the Point. Is that right?"

"Yes," gulped Todd, almost as a question.

"We've noticed that the Seniors seem more tired than usual. I suspect that they're staying up late, reading those magazines. Is that right?"

"Yes." Todd's eyes were getting bigger, as he tried to guess what was coming next.

"Well, I'm not going to do anything about this now. You can keep the smut, but I want the Seniors to be getting enough sleep to run the camp programs. The minute I think the camp program is suffering because the Seniors aren't getting enough sleep, I'm going to confiscate the smut. How do you feel about that?"

"That's fair," Todd agreed, clearly relieved. "I'll take care of it."

"Now go back to the Point, deliver this ultimatum, and get some sleep!"

Todd left a lot less nervous than he arrived. We walked back up to the Staff campfire. After putting some more wood on the fire and passing out some of the beers Robert had brought, we continued talking about the Senior smut problem.

Pete sighed. "I know that part of growing up is figuring out sex, and I don't begrudge them those magazines, though *Hustler* is really gross. I'm willing to respect troop tradition and not snoop on what happens on the Point, but when what happens there interferes with the camp program, I get really angry. I won't tolerate that." Aaron and Robert agreed. They also agreed that, while *Playboy* and *Penthouse* seemed harmless enough, *Hustler* was pretty obscene.

Aaron had brought out his guitar, and he strummed it lightly as a sort of invitation for us to stop talking and sing a bit. He began "Dead Puppies," and Pete explained to Robert why the troop didn't sing that song at campfire anymore. "But *we* do," said Aaron, and we all sang the song, softly but with feeling.

"How about 'Dead Mousies'?" asked Robert, inspired by the nearby grossness of the expired rodent, and we all understood immediately what he had in mind. He had issued an invitation to "invent" a new tradition, to create a parody campfire song about the dead mouse hanging in the Staff Area. So after Robert suggested a chorus to Aaron's soft strumming, we took turns inventing verses for our song.

Dead Mousies

(Tune: "Dead Puppies")

Chorus
Dead mousies, dead mousies,
Dead mousies are well hung.

Verses
Dead mousies drip a lot.
Can't help but make a spot.
Dead mousies aren't much fun.

Dead mousy ran around,
Now his tail's pointing to the ground,
Dead mousies aren't much fun.

Poor Pete, too much booze,
Tried to suck the mousy's ooze,
Dead mousies aren't much fun.

Tired, we ran out of inspiration and ended the song. It was unlikely that this parody song would become a Staff C&T; it probably would last no longer than this one camp season. But the process of creating the song was what was important. We had created a sick parody of a song that, itself, was a sick song. Like the chain songs sung by the boys at campfires, our parody song provided a formula for inventing verses that permitted us to engage in playful insults. Here, in a microcosm, was a perfect example of the dynamic process of innovation and tradition, of invention and convention, that marks folklore.

The fire was low and we decided to go to bed. We gathered the debris of our snacks, spread the embers of the fire, and retreated to our warm sleeping bags. The night was especially cold.

Salute to Old Glory—Camp Lenape, B.S.A., Medford, N.J.
(Artvue Post Card Co., New York City; postcard from author's collection)

DAY 6

Friday

★　★　★　★　★　★　★　★　★　★　★　★　★　★　★　★　★　★　★

At the color assembly the next morning, Pete asked Todd for the floor and began talking seriously.

"You all know that there have been two incidents lately that touch on my greatest worry. You know what my greatest worry is? Drowning. I worry about a Scout's drowning. Drowning is permanent. Death is permanent. This probably comes from my boyhood fear of the water. Anyway, it's what I worry about most, and the way some of you have behaved in the last few days does not reassure me much. At your age, you believe in the three false I's—and they are false. You falsely believe that you're immortal. You falsely believe that you're immune. And you falsely believe that you're infertile. You think you won't die. So we must substitute your fear of the Seniors for your fear of the water.

"The other day, up at the Waterfront, I discovered that some Scouts were violating the rules and that some Seniors were not enforcing the rules. I think we've solved that problem." Pete turned to survey the Seniors. "Right?"

"Right," murmured the Seniors involved.

"The Seniors have posted a new, more explicit set of Waterfront rules, and I expect you to read and follow those rules. The Seniors are under strict orders to enforce those rules. Now, last night, under the influence of a hormone attack caused by the Girl Scouts, we had another violation of the water safety rules." A wave of giggles and knowing looks swept through the crowd.

"IT'S NOT FUNNY!" bellowed Pete. "Drowning is permanent! That's what I am talking about. You are not taking the water safety rules seriously, and if you don't, I'm going to beach everyone. Understand?" The boys all nodded assent. Pete glared at the boys for a few moments and then changed the subject.

"Another thing. We're going to have a Staph Bath inspection this afternoon before free swim. When you hear Todd blow the whistle and call for the Staph Bath inspection, assemble in the Snake Patrol area. We're going to inspect you for signs of chapped skin. The air is very dry here, and the natural oils in your skin evaporate. That, with the heat and dust, can cause chap, a redness to your skin, especially on the arms and legs and ankles and around your mouths. Some of you have that already. I can see it from here. If you don't do anything about that, the chap starts to ooze and crust over. It actually becomes a scab."

"Yeah, Usonia Scum," chimed in Jeff. Pete smiled.

"Yeah, Usonia Scum. That can lead to cracking and bleeding and infection. That's bad. So you need to correct it before it gets that far. You know that there's a pump bottle of skin lotion at every washstand. Use the lotion on your skin after you wash up. If you have the crusting, then you need to rub off the crusting with a nylon scrubby you use to wash pots. It'll hurt a bit, but you have to get that crust off and apply lotion. If it's too bad, we have first-aid cream in the Staff Area. Come to the inspection clean, okay?" Everyone nodded. Pete turned the assembly over to Todd, who called everyone to attention and then dismissed the troop.

At breakfast with the Eagle Patrol, the talk was all about the previous night's doings. Everyone in camp had heard about the Scouts caught trying to wade over to the Girl Scout encampment, and there was general surprise that the Scouts had not been sent home. The boys also knew, somehow, that the girls were leaving that day, so this female disruption of their program and attention was about to end.

After breakfast and the early morning routine, I decided to sit in on Jeff's first aid class. "First Aid and Life Saving" was a chapter in the first *Handbook* (1911), and these skills have always been a big part of what is meant by the Boy Scout motto: "Be prepared!" The early ranks require basic knowledge of first aid for everything from scrapes to fractures and poisonous snake bites, and the First Aid and Lifesaving merit badges have been required for Eagle since the organization's beginning.[1] Watching Jeff teach his class of boys how to use their Scout neckerchiefs as bandages and as slings for a sprained or broken arm made me think about this casual empowering of these boys to help themselves and others. The movement's emphasis on "duty" and "preparedness" was creating in these boys at least the expectation that they could help others. They really could save a life some day.

Pete called for a brief Senior meeting during siesta. Because he had been busy dealing with the three Romeos the previous night while the Seniors had been meeting, Pete wanted to go over plans for the evening's Nugget Auction. The Nugget Auction takes place at a troop campfire and is the occasion for the patrols to spend the points they have earned throughout the week, through daily inspections, contests, and so on. The patrols bid their points in the auction for cookies, candy, soft drinks, popcorn, and other assorted treats. The Nugget Auction is one reason why the Staff keeps tight control of the care packages the boys get from home. If the flow of extra goodies from home becomes too great, the value of the goods at the Nugget Auction goes down and robs the auction of its fun.

"You all remember how much fun the Nugget Auction was for you as a camper," began Pete, "and I want tonight's auction to be as much fun for these campers. I am sorry I had to miss the meeting last night, but you know what I was dealing with. You also know by now, I hope, the conversation I had with Todd about Senior smut."

The Seniors exchanged sheepish looks.

"Yeah, exactly. I don't care what you do on the Point so long as . . . so long as," with the repeated phrase Pete's volume increased, "what you do doesn't threaten the program. If you're too tired or show up to assemblies chronically late, then that affects the program, and that affects the quality of the camp experience the Scouts are having, and that concerns me. I expect you to put duty before self."

The Seniors nodded general agreement.

"Fine. I don't want to have to say anything more about this. Now, let me hear the plans for the Nugget Auction."

Todd outlined the plans they had come up with the night before. The Seniors wanted to maintain two variations that had been growing into traditions over the past few years. First, they wanted to create a much more explicit television game show frame for the auction. "It'll be *Let's Make a Deal,*" explained Todd, "with Tommy as 'Studly Balls' [instead of Monty Hall] and Jeff as 'Don Hard-on' [instead of Don Pardo], the announcer."

Pete smiled. "Okay, let me hear more." Encouraged, Todd continued.

"Second, we want to make more of the handmade zonks for the patrols to keep, sort of make them valuable trophies." Long ago the Seniors adopted the term "zonks" from *Let's Make a Deal* for the worthless prizes the patrols were tricked into bidding for. In earlier years, the zonks had been things like boxes of "Senior Trash," but increasingly the Seniors were putting effort into making nonfood prizes (like a cardboard "skateboard") that were not treats, but that weren't exactly zonks either. So the Seniors had created a new category of creative prize that they took some pride in, and they wanted to elaborate that tradition.

"Fine," said Pete. "I like that. Is everything plotted out?"

"Yeah," replied Tommy. "We'll have nine prizes and four zonks, with songs in between."

"Okay, if that's all, then go on to your first afternoon advancement period." Most of the boys dispersed, but Todd and Jeff hung back to talk with Pete about something.

I headed for the Waterfront to watch the advancement classes there and to snoop a bit for Pete, who had asked me to check on whether the Seniors seemed to be enforcing the new rules. I perched on a comfortable rock and gazed out over the Waterfront and lake. The day was clear and sunny, as always, with just a few puffs of cumulous clouds forming over the mountains far beyond the lake. The Sierra creates its own microclimates throughout the year, and the usual pattern is for the days to begin absolutely clear and for a few clouds to appear in the afternoon, as water from lakes and streams evaporates in the fierce sun. Usually, a breeze comes up in the afternoon, sweeping across the lake and giving the campers some relief. The breeze had come up a bit early that day, so I was quite comfortable sitting on that sunny rock and watching the swimming and canoeing classes.

Pete came strolling up about forty-five minutes later and called for Brad, who was helping the Scouts lift one of the canoes out of the water and turn it over on top of two sawhorses so that the water would drain out.

"Brad, I want you to double-check that the Scouts put on their life vests properly. Look at that Scout." Pete pointed to one of boys, who obviously had secured his vest incorrectly. "Make them do it over and over again until they get it right."

"I'll take care of it."

As Pete and I walked back to the Staff Area, Pete told me his theory of what he calls the "Four Decodable Coverts."

"These are the things a teenage boy will say to you in order to be evasive, and I never let them get away with using them with me. First, there's 'Sir.' This means 'Fuck you.' Then there's 'I guess.' This means 'Yes, but I don't want to think about it.' There's a variant of this one called 'maybe' or 'probably.'"

I asked Pete if "I suppose so" is a variant of number two.

"No, it's more likely to be number three, which is 'If you say so.' That means an emphatic 'no' along with a 'fuck you.' Number four is 'Whatever.' This is a nonanswer and can mean number two or number three. In either case, it must be pursued. You can't let them get by with it. Actually, all four are evasions and must be pursued for the real answer. For example, if I ask a kid if his 'I guess' really means 'Yes, but I'd rather not think about it,' and the kid smiles at that, then I know that he realizes he can't get away with leaving his answer as that. Sometimes they say 'I guess' in response to my suggested interpretation, and then they realize they just trapped themselves into the truthful answer, see the humor, and give up on ever using that evasion again.

"Actually, I've recently discovered a fifth decodable: 'Not really.' This definitely requires further pursuit. It could mean 'No, but I don't want to think about it.' Or a definite 'no' (without the 'fuck you'), but softened so that it won't be hurtful. The first case is an evasion and cannot be allowed. The second may or may not call for further discussion.

"The age of all these kids, eleven to seventeen, is an age of denial. The kids will deny that something's happening when they basically know it's not OK. I can usually pursue the 'decodable coverts.' It's deceit that angers me more than anything. I really hate it when a kid lies to me, but that's different from denial."

Pete's five decodable coverts and his subsequent comments made me wonder about the relationships between the folk psychologies of people like Scoutmasters and athletic coaches and the more academic adolescent psychologies of professors and therapists. So much theory of the psychology of the adolescent arises from clinical settings that I wondered what different pictures we might have if we generated the theories more inductively from adolescents in natural settings, like Scout camps and softball teams and gatherings at the mall. Pete seemed to me to have a very firm grasp of male adolescent psychology, mostly gained inductively, as far as I could tell.

As Pete had promised, Todd blew the whistle just before the sched-uled free swim and shouted, "Staph Bath inspection in five minutes in the Snake Patrol area." As I walked in that direction, I smiled at the pun. This was a "Staph Bath" in its search for chap and bacterial infec-tions on the boys, but it could become a "Staff Bath" if the Staff had to clean a boy who was not doing a good enough job on himself. Once the troop had gathered in the Snake Patrol campsite and Todd had asked the Patrol Leaders for roll call, Todd turned the assembly over to Pete. Pete was sitting at the Snake table with an array of items spread out in front of him: a washcloth, a nylon scrubby, a large fiber brush used to clean tents and such, and a very large metal brush used for scraping grills.

"We're going to have an inspection. I'm going to look at your skin to see if you are doing a good enough job keeping yourself clean and healthy. If you are not bathing yourself well enough with a wash-cloth," he continued, pointing to the washcloth, "then we'll make you use this," pointing to the scrubby. "If you still don't clean yourself well enough, then the Staff will bathe you using this," he said, point-ing to the stiff fiber brush, "and if you still don't keep yourself clean, then we'll use this," pointing finally to the steel brush. The boys' eyes widened at the thought, not knowing how much truth was in what Pete said.

Most of the boys wore only their bathing suits for the inspection, and others took off their shirts and shorts, stripping to their underwear. Pete and Aaron moved around the large circle, from patrol to patrol, looking at each boy's exposed skin, examining the ankles especially carefully. Every so often Pete would show a boy where he would have to use a scrubby to get rid of a crusty patch. This was a boring process for the boys, and they were anxious to get on with their free swim, but Pete would not be hurried. He knew that it was important to keep these boys healthy, that an infection can send a boy home, and he was not going to let potential infections go untreated. Once Pete and Aaron had made the rounds, threatening a few of the Scouts with the fiber brush if they didn't do a better job of keeping themselves clean, Pete let Todd dismiss the troop, and they scattered for free swim and other unstructured fun.

Dinner with the Eagle Patrol turned out to feature the infamous chicken à la king, a mixture of canned chicken and mushroom soup served over instant mashed potatoes. Despite the meal's reputation in campfire songs, the boys devoured the meal and were disappointed when the food ran out. Those still hungry enough raided the patrol box to make peanut butter and jelly sandwiches.

After color assembly and individual sports, the troop assembled again to go up to the site for the evening's troop campfire and Nugget Auction. The boys had been looking forward to the Nugget Auction all day. The Nugget Auction occurs twice during the summer encampment, once after the first full week in camp and the second at the end of the last week, just before breaking camp. The Nugget Auction takes place at a troop campfire, but the boys' attention is on the auction itself and little else. The songs are mere fillers between the auctioning of items by the Seniors. Each patrol had over four hundred points to spend, and they were eager to spend them. The Seniors had been looking forward to the auction just as eagerly.

The Seniors had begun preparing for the Nugget Auction at least two days earlier. The true prizes in the auction are food prizes, such as six-packs of Coke, watermelons, potato chips, Oreo cookies, or cocoa. Some of the auction items are "open," that is, undisguised and in plain view. Most items, however, are hidden within cardboard boxes, so the patrols bid on the item blindly, gambling that the item inside is a real food prize and not a zonk. The Seniors relish thinking up creative zonks and constructing them for the auction. The Seniors love to burn the Scouts by making them bid precious points for zonks.

The campfire began in its usual way, with the singing of "Fireman Bill." Tommy then led a spirited rendition of "Chewing Gum." He introduced Les to auction the first item. Les came out from behind the boulder that hid the auction items, carrying a medium-sized cardboard box. "What am I bid for this item?" he began, and the Patrol Leaders started shouting out bids, raising their offers by only a few points each time. The patrols tend to bid their points sparingly early in the Nugget Auction, especially on "blind" items. The Bear Patrol succeeded in buying that first item for relatively few points (the average bid for a winning item is 80 points or so). The other patrols watched as Bob opened the box for his patrol. The other patrols naturally hoped that the Bears had spent 60 points on a zonk, but the box contained a slip of paper reading "Double Bid Points," which meant that the prize was worth 120 points added to their account for the auction. The Bears beamed broadly, taunting the other patrols for their foolishness in not buying the item.

Tommy retook center stage immediately and led the troop in singing "My Bonnie." Then he asked Ken to come forward with the next item to be auctioned. Ken held up for all to see a large package of Oreo cookies, an open prize that was probably what it appeared to be. The bidding was furious, and the Snakes finally won at a cost of 106 points. Tommy led two more songs and then introduced Jason with the next item, a closed cardboard box. The patrols were getting cautious; it seemed to be time for a zonk, so they bid slowly and reluctantly. The Bears took the box with a bid of only 50 points and were relieved to discover that it contained a bag of marshmallows that they could toast later at the patrol site. Again the Bear Patrol taunted the others, who were visibly disappointed that the Bears had not been zonked.

Brad stepped forward immediately with the next auction item, another cardboard box. This threw the patrols into a real quandary. A zonk was way overdue, yet the boys knew that the Seniors knew they would think this was a zonk and would trick the boys by making this another real prize. Things were getting very complicated. "Shake it, shake it!" the boys screamed at Brad, so he wiggled his hips while holding the box still. Those who got the joke laughed. But most had their attention on the box. The Patrol Leaders bid cautiously again, and the Eagles were able to buy the box for 49 points. Everyone watched as Eddie tore open the box; his face fell as it became clear to him that they had bought a zonk. He withdrew from the box a "Senior Communications Device," that is, a pair of tin cans connected by a string. The Seniors and others roared with laughter at the zonk, and Eddie and most of the other Eagles tried to show good humor despite their disappointment.

Tommy led another song and then asked George to bring out the next item, another cardboard box. A zonk out of the way, the patrols bid actively for the box George was hawking, and hawking well. The Tigers got the box with a bid of 75 points, and Tim greedily tore it open. Another zonk; this time it was "Senior Trash," assorted papers and other trash from Senior Point. Everyone had a laugh at the Tigers' expense, while the Tigers themselves began arguing about who had wanted the bidding to continue and who had said not to buy the box. Tommy led the troop in "Cigarettes, Whiskey, and Wild, Wild Women" before Jeff stepped forward with a six-pack of Coke. The Seniors had put duct tape across the tops and sides of the six-pack, an ambiguous clue the patrols had to reckon with. Experienced Scouts knew that the Seniors were capable of drinking the Cokes themselves, filling the empty cans with water, taping over the tops, and auctioning the six-pack as if it were "the Real Thing." But the Seniors were equally capable, the Scouts realized, of taping real Cokes to make the patrols suspicious. The patrols apparently were willing to take the risk, however, as the bidding was furious and ended with the Eagle Patrol's buying the Cokes for 138 points. Ripping off the tape, Eddie was much relieved to discover that the Cokes were real, and it was their turn to taunt the other patrols for losing out on a coveted treat.

The pace of the auction was accelerating now as Tommy asked Ricky to come forward with the next item, another cardboard box. With two zonks out of the way, the patrols felt confident in bidding for the box, and the Bear Patrol bought for 95 points what turned out to be a genuine treat—a large package of Twinkies, a popular snack cake. After singing "Clementine," standing to shout their "TR" cheer, and singing "PB & Jelly," the troop was ready for the next item, auctioned by Tommy himself. It was a cardboard box again, and the bidding was a bit lower as the patrols began to worry about another zonk. The Snakes bought the box for 62 points and were happy to find fruit rolls instead of some gag in the box (but fruit rolls are not considered a very desirable item, so the others hooted at them for buying a "semi-zonk" at a steep price). Les came forward again with his second auction item of the evening, a cardboard box. "Shake it, shake it!" the boys yelled, in what apparently had become a traditional routine between Scouts and Seniors because Les also wiggled his hips without moving the box. Buoyed by their recent success, I suppose, the Snakes ended up spending 77 points on this box, but their elation deflated quickly as they discovered the box was full of pine needles and twigs—"Senior Duff," a piece of paper explained.

After singing "Gopher Guts," which always puts everyone in a good mood, Tommy asked Ken to bring out his second item of the evening. The cardboard box raised little worry; the Snakes had just been zonked, and the Scouts knew that there were several traditional food treats that had not yet appeared as prizes. The Bears ended up buying the box for a mere 57 points and were pleased with the Jiffy-Pop popcorn they could make later back at the patrol site.

The campfire was running long, and Pete urged Tommy to hurry things up. Jason auctioned an "open" bag of potato chips, which the Bears bought for only 50 points. Other patrols were saving their points for the watermelon they supposed would be coming. With points to spare, the Bears were getting cocky and spent 50 points on the next item, a box with only other boxes nested in it.

Tommy began slowing things down, knowing that the mood would have to be less exuberant for the closing songs and recitations. After leading "Usonia," he brought Brad to center stage. Brad's box contained a six-pack of 7-Up, which pleased the Tigers. Tommy then brought out the long-awaited watermelon, but the duct tape on the watermelon served as a warning that it might be other than what it appeared to be. In the past, seniors have cut open a watermelon, eaten its insides, filled it with sand, and then taped it back together again for the auction. This time, though, the watermelon, which the Eagles bought for 100 points, turned out to be unadulterated. That was the last item, to the boys' disappointment, and the Seniors huddled briefly to determine which patrol had been least successful in the auction. The matter decided, Tommy stepped from the huddle to award the Snakes a long string of lollipops, "suckers" that stood for the patrol that bought the most or worst zonks.

After singing the traditional folk song "Sloop John B," the troop stood and went through the traditional closing sequence of the "Vesper Song," the Scoutmaster's Benediction, and "Taps." Pete congratulated the Seniors on a really good Nugget Auction and thanked the boys for their troop spirit. He reminded them that the patrol overnight was to begin the next day and said he hoped they would continue to make this a great camp. "Good night, Scouts," said Pete, and everyone wished him a good night in return.

Back at the Staff Area, we put together the usual ingredients for our Staff campfire. As we settled down, Pete asked me: "Jay, do you know the difference between the army and the Boy Scouts?" I smelled a riddle.

"No, Pete, what's the difference between the army and the Boy Scouts?"

"The Boy Scouts have adult leaders." We all laughed. The joke is funny in any case, but it is all the more funny and meaningful in the context of Troop 49 and Pete's attitude toward the military aspects of Scouting. The resemblance to the military has plagued Scouting since its inception. The Boy Scouts was founded in England by Lord Robert Baden-Powell, the military hero of Mafeking, a famous battle in the Boer War in South Africa near the end of the nineteenth century.[2] Troubled by what he saw as the slack physical and mental powers of the average British soldier, Baden-Powell decided to form a youth movement for British boys that would give them the sort of physical and mental disciplines and skills he would want to see in military scouts. The British Boy Scout uniform, accordingly, was very military in its appearance.

The military model was much more problematic for the founders of the Boy Scouts in the United States. In Seton's Woodcraft Indians, which he began in 1902, boys and girls were expected to make their own American Indian costumes, and Daniel Carter Beard's Sons of Daniel Boone wore homemade costumes modeled on pioneer dress. When these two men came together with YMCA workers and others in 1910 to plan the establishment of a Boy Scouts of America based on the British movement, the matter of the Americanization of the British movement took center stage, and a piece of that deliberation concerned the proper dress for the American Scouts. Seton and Beard reluctantly conceded to the pressures to create a uniform resembling the British uniform, with a few modifications. The uniform was military in look, nonetheless, and that caused some controversy.

The committee that founded the Boy Scouts of America in 1910 had some competition. Newspaper publisher William Randolph Hearst was sponsoring a group called the American Boy Scouts, and that movement had appropriated a very military uniform. Worse, the American Boy Scouts engaged in military drills with guns, and that alarmed people who did not like the idea of a paramilitary organization putting guns in the hands of adolescent boys. On this and other matters, the Boy Scouts of America had to work against the tendency for the public to lump together the two youth movements. Between 1910 and 1915, the national organization made several moves to consolidate its preeminence on the American scene. In 1916, the Boy Scouts of America received a charter from Congress, which sealed the fate of its competitors. Congress recognized the BSA as the rightful owner of the name "Boy Scouts," and the BSA used this new power to enforce its copyright. Even before receiving the charter, the national office had made several moves to assert its ownership of things officially Boy Scout. The office arranged for franchising the official BSA seal on manufactured items, from the uniform to camping equipment and personal jewelry. The national office created a chief librarian and committee to oversee the publication of "official" Boy Scout literature, including the popular novels being churned out by publishing houses. Grosset and Dunlap arranged with the national office to publish an official series, "Every Boy's Library—Boy Scout Edition," featuring some original fiction titles, some classic "boys' fiction," and nonfiction titles like Beard's *Handicraft for Outdoor Boys.*

So by 1916 the Boy Scouts had an official uniform protected by copyright. But that did not make the military association any less controversial, as by 1915 the country was having to contemplate the increasing militarization and belligerency in Europe. Beard and Seton, two men with mighty egos, clashed increasingly over this and other matters, a state of affairs that culminated in Seton's resignation as Chief Scout in 1915. After that, Seton turned his energies to revitalizing the Woodcraft Indians.

During World War I, the Boy Scouts of America participated in campaigns meant to emphasize the wartime homefront service of the young boys. Scouts participated in campaigns to collect needed scrap paper, iron, and other wartime resources. The Boy Scouts helped promote the sale of Liberty Bonds, and much of the patriotic iconography on posters and in magazines and newspapers during this period featured Scouts in uniform doing their part in support of the homefront war effort. The fictional boys in Boy Scout novels even went to war, most notably in Percy Keese Fitzhugh's Tom Slade series of seventeen novels, which began with *Tom Slade of the Moving Pictures* in 1915 and ended with *Tom Slade in the Haunted Cavern* in 1929.[3] The early novels establish Tom Slade as a tall, handsome, quiet sort of boy who goes from being a juvenile delinquent to being the most heroic and admirable member of his fictional Scout troop. Beginning with 1918's *Tom Slade with the Colors,* Fitzhugh took his character into the army and sent him overseas to fight in the war. Tom shows himself to be an all-American hero through a series of novels set in Europe—*Tom Slade on a Transport* (1918), *Tom Slade with the Boys over There* (1918), *Tom Slade, Motorcycle Dispatcher* (1918), and *Tom Slade with the Flying Corps* (1919).

The period between the wars did not raise many questions about the connection between the military and the Boy Scouts of America, though the visibility of uniformed youth organizations in the Soviet Union, Nazi Germany, and other totalitarian states doubtless caused some Americans to worry about the Boy Scouts. The Boy Scouts helped on the homefront of World War II much as they had during World War I. The creation of the United Nations and a broad public discourse endorsing the export of the "liberal democratic internationalism" originally conceived by Woodrow Wilson sparked the rapid postwar internationalization of the Boy Scout movement.[4]

The Boy Scouts of America maintained its military-style uniform over these years, through cycles of American attitudes toward the military. In the 1950s, the association seemed positive in middle-class eyes, and a great many troops emphasized a certain level of military drill in marching and other activities. At my own Scout camp at the end of the 1950s, I recall that a few of the older Staff leaders were students at the Virginia Military Institute (VMI), and they helped bring a military style and discipline to the camp.[5] Some teens in the 1950s and early 1960s were drawn to the structure of troops that emphasized the militaristic aspects of Scouting. Other teens hated that aspect of Scouting and left the organization if their parents would permit it. Troops varied in their adherence to military style, of course, but it was not until the mid-1960s or so that an increasing number of troops began cultivating a troop ideology rejecting militarism. The 1960s social movements and the antimilitarism of the counterculture had a great deal to do with this shift. In any event, Pete's home troop in Berkeley was never much into the military drill, and Pete became a Scoutmaster in the middle of an antimilitary period in American history.

By the mid-1970s, Troop 49 had come to take a certain pride in rejecting military drill. The troop wears the official uniform and has a proper color assembly to show respect for the flag and the country, but Pete never worries much about correct about-faces and the like. The troop has actually developed C&Ts meant to undermine the implied authority of the uniform.[6] During the Insane Day games, the troop rejects official hats and opts for specialized patrol hats, which are more personalized markers of troop identity. In fact, the Scout "uniform" in Troop 49 is anything but "uniform," and this troop is only one among many that treat the uniform in ways that break all the official Scout rules ("Wear your complete uniform proudly and correctly at all Scouting events," urges the 1990 *Handbook*).[7] Each *Handbook* since 1911 has been very clear that boys should wear only official Scout badges on their uniform shirts. Usually, the boy wears his earned badge of rank over his left breast pocket (over his heart) and "temporary patches"—that is, patches that commemorate an event (a hike, a camporee, a leadership conference, etc.)—over his right breast pocket. The left upper sleeve bears the Council patch, a large, colorful patch identifying the large geographical area in which the troop is located, plus the troop number and the badge of office (Patrol Leader, Troop Quartermaster, etc.), if any. On the right upper sleeve, the boy wears a patch of the U.S. flag and a patrol patch. The *Handbook* even provides templates for the proper placement and spacing of the badges.

But, as I said, Troop 49 adds to these official patches a number of patches unique to the troop. Sometimes these are even homemade patches (a very valued one made from moleskin with a Sharpie-drawn design recalls a fifty-mile hike). The troop never liked the move from red "community strips," which actually named the hometown of the troop, to the more general Council patches, which name large geographical areas and don't convey the local identity. So troop members are always on the lookout at garage and yard sales for old uniforms that bear the town's old community strip. These are highly valued in the troop and are worn in places that violate "correct usage"—but that's the point. This troop draws its identity precisely from breaking the rules.

It was common in the 1960s and 1970s to talk about some troops that were "Mickey Mouse," meaning they followed the rules unquestioningly and aped the military. Unquestioning obedience to authority had become problematic for Americans resisting or at least raising questions about the war in Vietnam, and since the seventh point of the Scout Law is "A Scout is Obedient," the organization had to address the complexities of what sorts of obedience Americans owed to authority. These were the issues Pete had been trying to get at with the investiture class of first-year campers he had taught earlier in the week, and he has a distaste for the uniforms, the drills, and the unquestioning obedience preferred in some troops.

All of this was the context for the riddle Pete told me at the Staff campfire. The joke reflected Pete's and the troop's rejection of the military and the military mind-set, all the while recognizing that in the public mind Troop 49 is a Boy Scout troop, with all of the meanings that entails. Troop 49 is nothing like what the defenders of the national movement imagine a Scout troop to be, but it also isn't anything like what the detractors of the movement think a troop might be. Carving out that unique space and identity feels good to the members of Troop 49, but they are always aware of the contradictions inherent in not being what they seem to be.

After telling his joke, Pete poked the fire a bit with a stick, added it to the blaze, and turned to more serious matters.

"You're probably wondering why Todd and Jeff hung back to talk with me at the end of this morning's Senior meeting. They wanted to talk about Ken."

Ken is the Senior who stands most at the periphery of the Senior Patrol. It is clear to anyone who spends any time around him that Ken is a slow learner. He is quiet, very shy really, with none of the language skills that would help him keep up with the other Seniors. Pete made sure that Ken's official role was "KYBO King," "Chief of Sanitation," not to punish him but, on the contrary, to give him a very structured job with straightforward rules and instructions. Ken does some advancement classes, but these are awkward because most of the younger kids are brighter and more physically adept than he is.

"I feel a special obligation to make sure Ken succeeds at camp," explained Pete, telling me the story that Aaron and Robert already knew. "Ken's father is very helpful with the troop, and we owe him for that. He sees the troop as a safe, important place for Ken. Ken is the product of a late-life pregnancy, so his parents are a good deal older than most kids' parents. They are very concerned that Ken learns how to be self-sufficient because they know that they won't be around for him forever.

"When Ken first joined the troop, he couldn't even tie his own shoelaces. True. My goal has been to make him as independent from his parents as I can. I've made sure that Ken is given responsibilities at camp, but I've also made sure that the other Seniors monitor him carefully. The trouble is that Ken isn't handling his advancement duties, so yesterday Jeff had to relieve him of one or two of those duties. I had a 'being wonderful' session with Ken just before that because I wanted to make sure he understood that he has to take responsibility for himself. I made it as clear as I could that I would not let him jeopardize other kids' advancement.

"Now it's Ken's own advancement that has people bugged. That's what Todd and Jeff hung around to talk about. Ken is a Life Scout, only a few badges from Eagle, and that's beginning to bother the other Seniors. We've had a covert policy of letting Ken earn badges with a performance below what we expected from others, but now that comes back to haunt us because Ken realizes he is just a few badges short of Eagle and has been talking in front of the Seniors and Scouts about 'when he gets Eagle.' Jeff was very candid in our conversation, saying he resented Ken's 'earning' badges he really didn't deserve. Todd wasn't as adamant about the badges, but he did say that since the troop requires evidence of leadership in addition to the badges for Eagle, and since Ken isn't capable of showing leadership, then did this mean that Ken wouldn't get Eagle, even if he had the badges? Or would that requirement be waived for Ken, too? Todd wasn't in my face about this, but he did see the upcoming dilemma. Do we let Ken earn all the badges for Eagle and then deny him Eagle?"

We all sat silently for a moment, thinking about the problem.

"You know," said Aaron, "this is like some other cases involving handicapped Scouts. It's a legal question—can they be excluded from earning ranks and badges?"[8]

"Yeah," replied Pete. "Somebody had to sue the national office to get them to change the requirements for Eagle so that boys in wheelchairs could still earn the badges for the rank."

"So what are you going to do?" asked Robert, turning to Pete.

"Well, I've decided to seek the advice of the Eagle alumni about what we should do in Ken's case, whether he should be allowed to get Eagle."

We pondered this solution as we watched the fire collapse into embers. Aaron reached over to add one more log.

Todd had put his finger on a persistent dilemma for the Boy Scouts, one with roots deep in a basic contradiction in American culture. The organization built its program according to the principle of status by *achievement*. If, as many critics think, the United States is an achievement-oriented society, compared with others that are more oriented toward ascribed status (by gender, race, social class, and so on), then the Boy Scout advancement program of badges and ranks reflects perfectly that ideology.[9] In theory, every boy can earn Eagle. The national criteria are clear. But in reality, as often happens, things are not so simple. Boys sometimes cheat or cut corners in the earning of badges, and not every troop enforces the same standards of performance for a given badge. And Troop 49 is not the only troop to grasp for criteria to ensure that only boys with the right sort of character achieve Eagle. Here, again, is that nineteenth-century concept—character—being invoked in the late twentieth century. At stake, too, is that not-quite-defined quality called leadership. How does a Scoutmaster know if and when a boy demonstrates leadership? These were vexing questions condensed in one crisis point for the troop—should Ken be permitted to earn the Eagle rank?

Pete had something else on his mind. "You know, I was watching Bill Moyers on television this past spring, and he used the word 'anomie' to describe the sense of meaninglessness many kids have today. And when I heard that word, it helped me think more clearly about what's wrong with kids today. Kids no longer have knowledge of values. I blame their parents, their grandparents really, the generation that came home after World War II. They created these lives filled with things, but kids now seem to have lost a clear sense of what is right and what is wrong. I find that I have to be so much more explicit with these kids than I had to ten years ago. I have to be so explicit with what is expected of them. And that bothers me."

"Yeah, I see it," said Aaron.

"Yet Todd and Jeff are really holding my feet to the fire on this one," Pete continued. "They want to uphold standards, and they have a strong sense of what's fair. Maybe I'm exaggerating this anomie idea, but it really made me think about the larger society and why I'm noticing these changes in kids."

We talked for about a half hour more, but fatigue and the beers were dragging our conversation to a slow halt. It was time to go to bed.

SCOUT BAY AT BOY SCOUT CAMP WAPELLO, DRAKESVILLE, IOWA

Camp Wapello, Drakesville, Iowa
(Artvue Post Card Co., New York City; postcard from author's collection)

Saturday & Sunday

★ ★

We had stayed up late at Staff campfire the previous night, so I slept
through the first reveille whistle and came to only when Todd was
calling out, "Five minutes to assembly." I rose and dressed quickly. After colors, Pete called on each of the Patrol Leaders in turn to see where
they were in preparations for the patrol overnight. They all felt pretty
confident that they would be ready to move out on time.

The weekend of the patrol overnight is an important tradition for
the troop, and it serves several purposes. First, it breaks the routine of
camp, sending each patrol off (not too far) to camp out by itself, under
the supervision of one or more dads. The overnight gives some of the
Scouts a chance to prepare meals for badges, the hiking itself may count
toward some badges, and the patrol gets a chance to develop some
closeness away from the other patrols. At the same time, the overnight
serves the important function of being the Senior and Staff "night off."
Pete permits the Seniors to hike out to a nearby resort town for a restaurant meal and some playtime, so long as they tell him where they
are going. Meanwhile, troop alumni and dads often come up on this
weekend for some playtime. The camp is empty, and the Staff and

other adults sail boats, go swimming, and otherwise "kick back" and relax.

Of course, the Senior night off has not always gone so smoothly. Some years ago a handful of Seniors got into trouble in the village for underage drinking, and that episode remains in memory a deep humiliation for Pete and the troop. That "indiscretion," as it is known in the troop, led to the taboo policy regarding alcohol. Too much is at stake for the boys and the troop to return to the discretionary policy of yore.

The dilemma Pete and other adult leaders face arises from the complex and contradictory attitudes Americans have about alcohol. Some researchers see a strong evolutionary, sociobiological basis for the human taste for intoxication.[1] I am not making a brief here for condoning teen drinking, which has real consequences in the world for the teens and for others. These consequences range from accidents caused by drunk driving to the results of having unprotected sex, including pregnancy and sexually transmitted diseases (though the same consequences result from adults' drinking). I am trying to step back from this highly charged topic in order to see it as a problem induced by the collision between human nature and culture, a collision we tend to organize and control by defining the teens as "incomplete" adults.

There is plenty of evidence that human beings seek intoxication. It gives them pleasure. Roger Caillois, who has written one of the most important books on the play instinct, includes "vertigo" as one of his four basic categories of play, and certainly intoxication should count as a sort of play.[2] There is plenty of evidence, too, that prohibition and "zero tolerance" by an "open" society like the United States do not work. So nature meets culture in the specific customs and formal rules a society may have regarding the use of alcohol. Alcohol has had an important place in the history of this society.[3] The United States has been a drinking nation from its beginning. Temperance and prohibition movements have come and gone, and Americans still drink. Recognizing the potential "disorderliness" of the "voluptuous panic" induced by alcohol, we do have laws governing drinking. For example, establishments selling alcohol must be licensed, and we have laws against drinking in certain public places, against drunk driving, and against underage drinking. There is nothing medical or biological, however, about this society's decision about what constitutes the legal drinking age. Indeed, what are we to make of the fact that eighteen-year-olds are considered legal adults for everything except drinking alcohol, other than the fact that eighteen- to twenty-one-year-olds do not vote in large enough numbers to change the drinking laws?

Not that the laws keep children from drinking. Children drink and adolescents drink plenty. While most adults still firmly believe that children shouldn't drink, attitudes toward teen drinking are more ambivalent. We do have biological definitions of sexual maturity, but what is the difference between "children" and "adolescents" when it comes to the matter of drinking? Some families actually permit or even condone underage drinking in the privacy of the home. Many adults believe that prohibition will not work with alcohol, so they stress responsible drinking. Many college and university student life staffs take this approach, rather than zero tolerance, as a way to cope with their untenable legal position—namely, that their students are legal adults for everything but drinking. Teachers and administrators at high schools and junior high schools cannot take this position, as their charges are legal minors altogether. But public advertising campaigns urge teens to "drink responsibly" if they are going to drink.

In this regard, the public battles over teen drinking resemble the arguments over teen sex. On one side are those who want the teens to "just say no" to sex and drugs, including alcohol. For these adults, part of being a moral, civilized human means controlling one's urges for pleasure. "True love waits," observes one sexual abstinence campaign aimed at teens, and the message is similar for alcohol—wait until you're twenty-one. On the other side are those adults who believe that the drives for sexual pleasure and the pleasure of intoxication are so great in teens that prohibition will not work. Their message is "If you must have sex, do it responsibly" and "If you must drink, do it responsibly."

It should surprise nobody that the official position of the Boy Scouts for ninety years has been against the boys' use of alcohol. The founding of the Boy Scouts coincided with a period of aggressive temperance movements, and the first *Handbook* (1911) had this to say on the subject of alcohol and tobacco: "Alcohol is not a stimulant, but is really a narcotic that is very depressing. It dulls rather than stimulates. The same is true of nicotine in tobacco. No growing boy should use either. The first athletes to drop out of a race are usually the drinkers and all trainers know that smoking is bad for the wind." [4] The "no growing boy" phrase leaves room for adult usage, and the author (George Fisher, M.D.) makes no moral judgment about alcohol and tobacco in general. The passage reads like a low-key warning or caution, emphasizing the effects of these substances on athletic performance. [5]

This 1911 passage remained unchanged in the 1915, 1927, and 1943 editions of the *Handbook*. Then, in the 1948 edition, the discussion of alcohol and tobacco disappeared altogether, to return in the 1959 edition with another rather low-key discussion of "Stimulants and Narcotics." The author (William "Green Bar Bill" Hillcourt) does not preach against alcohol but stresses its effects on physical and mental performance.[6] That section written by Hillcourt in 1959 also contained a brief mention of marijuana; but by 1972, the eighth edition, written by Frederick L. Hines, expanded its discussion of drugs to include marijuana, hallucinogens, stimulants, sedatives, tranquilizers, narcotics, and even glue (sniffed for the high).[7] Hines's separate section on alcohol took a stronger tone against the substance.[8] Now the talk is not of poor athletic performance but of accidents and emergencies. Bill Hillcourt's 1979 (ninth) edition tries still another strategy. "One look at a drunk staggering down the street," writes Hillcourt, "is enough to tell you that alcohol slows down the body and the brain. Alcohol can turn a strong man into a weeping child. It can change a person into a raving maniac. It destroys families. It kills people outright and by drunken drivers."[9] The tenth edition (1990) softens this tone and warns the boy reader that alcohol "will cloud your mind and affect your good judgment." The author notes that alcohol harms the liver and the brain, that alcoholism ruins families, and that drunken driving often ends in tragedy. "Thousands of teenagers die every year in crashes involving drivers who have been drinking."[10] Across the years, then, the Boy Scout *Handbook* generally has taken a rather understated stance toward alcohol use, mainly warning the boy against the effects of drink upon his physical performance, mental alertness, and good judgment.

Although these warnings seem sensible to the adult reader, I wonder what the boys think of them. It is easy enough to mouth these views for the small requirement buried in a long list of requirements—the boy probably handles it in less than a minute of interrogation by his merit badge counselor. Once again, the official stance of the organization may have little to do with the actual socialization of boys in the organization.

Troop 49's taboo policy is a test of the trust between Pete and each boy separately, and between Pete and the Seniors as a group. Pete trusted the Seniors of earlier times and, as a sign of that trust, maintained a discretionary policy; but they blew it. Now the Seniors live with a taboo policy. This year's Seniors know this history, and they were about to enter Senior night off with this policy in mind. Earning and keeping Pete's trust is very important to most of these Seniors, but it is still a test of leadership for Todd and the other leaders to keep this peer group trustworthy.

By midmorning, alumni and dads had begun arriving in camp, in anticipation of the overnight. Some dads would accompany the patrols out on their hiking and camping adventure, which is always at a site chosen by the boys but known to Pete. The weekend is a troop reunion of sorts, as alumni otherwise out of touch with the troop and each other take this weekend away from work and family to have some male fun in the woods. Pete loves seeing these alumni, people he has seen grow from insecure kids to mature, competent men.

As the morning wore on, large thunderclouds began covering the sun, and those with more experience in the mountains recognized that this was not the usual pattern of clouds. Large thunderheads often form in the late afternoons in the Sierra Nevada, but usually those thunderheads dissipate by sunset and pose no real threat of rain. But occasionally a mass of moist air swings out of Baja California and up into the Sierra, providing more significant moisture to clash with the heat rising from the valley. These unusual conditions create not just an isolated thunderstorm that comes and goes quickly, but more serious thunderstorms and rain. Those were the conditions that seemed to be coming upon us. Very dark, ominous clouds were building everywhere, and we could see lightning and hear thunder as the storm got closer.

Californians don't get to experience many thunderstorms, but Sierra thunderstorms make up in drama and ferocity for their infrequent appearances. And this storm seemed to be ready to live up to that reputation. The cool, crisp air being pushed in front of the storm had that smell and feeling familiar to those who grow up around thunderstorms, which created a mixture of excited anticipation and fear—fear because at seven thousand feet and in the wilderness, there are not a lot of safe places to ride out a thunderstorm. Tall trees, open rock, and a few canvas dining flies with metal-tipped poles did not offer many good options for cover in a violent storm.

Most of the Seniors and Scouts knew what had to be done, and those who didn't learned quickly from the others. Everyone had brought large plastic garbage bags for protecting their sleeping bags, clothes, and other personal gear, and some of the camp equipment had to be secured. The food would stay dry in the Commissary tent so long as the boxes were up off the floor. Sudden rainstorms bring too much water for the soil to soak up, so the storms usually create torrents of runoff water that can flow through campsites.

Pete found Aaron and asked him to spread the word to kids to put on their wool clothes and rain gear. Wet wool can still hold warmth, whereas wet cotton will conduct warmth away from the body. The main danger in these cool storms is that a boy will get very wet and cold, making him susceptible to hypothermia. Hypothermia is among the greatest dangers to hikers and campers in the Sierra Nevada in the summer, and there are needless deaths when a warm, sunny day turns cold and wet and the unprepared hiker slips into hypothermia. Most people in the Sierra know the symptoms of hypothermia—slurred speech, confusion, extreme sleepiness—and can help protect each other, but Pete would far rather prevent hypothermia than have to treat it. Besides, these boys think they are immortal. And, sure enough, I could see that some of the boys were not heeding the advice to get on wool clothes. Some continued to get ready for the storm wearing swimsuits, T-shirts, and sneakers.

I didn't need to be told twice. I went back to the Staff Area; got out my wool socks, wool Pendleton shirt, and Gore-Tex rain parka; changed my clothes; and then put my backpack and assorted belongings in a large plastic bag. We covered Pete's table and other things in the Staff Area with more plastic bags weighted down with substantial rocks, and I went back up to the Commissary Area, dressed for the storm.

From the vantage of a rock, I could see the sheet of rain moving across Upper Lake toward us. Aaron, a few alumni, and I took shelter under the dining fly at the Commissary tent, but we knew this was poor shelter for what was to come. The hail came first, and suddenly. Hailstones about the size of a thumbnail were pouring from the sky, and loud thunder claps accompanied the lightning that struck nearby trees. The pleasing aroma of burnt pine belied the danger we were all sensing, the terror we were all sharing, as we listened to the thunder and joked nervously about how close it sounded. The temporary security of our shelter was not to stay with us long, as the canvas fly began filling with hail and rain. The fly was not strong enough to hold up all that weight, so we pushed up on the fly at regular intervals to dump the hail and water, but even as we were doing this, I wondered if it was so smart to touch the wet canvas during a thunderstorm. My mind wandered unexpectedly to John Muir's story about lashing himself to a tree so he could experience a wild Sierra Nevada thunderstorm, and I could not imagine being out in the melee of such a storm.

Soon the hail gave way to mere rain, and then even that began to lighten a little. The wave of lightning strikes seemed to have passed with the front of the storm, so we relaxed a bit under our fly—wet, but safe. Pete came toward the fly with the patrols, dressed head to toe in the best rain gear. Following close behind him was Todd.

"Listen up," said Pete as we gathered around under the meager shelter. A few Seniors who had taken shelter under the advancement fly came over to join us.

"Lots of kids are soaked, so we've got to get them out of their wet clothes and into dry ones, preferably wool. If they don't have dry clothes, then we'll have to find them some. But it is very important to get them dry and warm. Part of getting them warm is giving them fuel, so we've got to feed them. George, forget whatever you planned for lunch. Give each patrol instant hot chocolate, candy bars, cheese, and bread. They can make cheese and peanut butter sandwiches, even in the rain. That'll give them energy." George nodded assent. Pete continued. "This is exactly the sort of situation that calls for leadership. It's easy to lead when things are going along great. But in a crisis, you have to draw on the real quality of leadership. So let me see you all out there, pitching in with whatever needs to be done to keep these Scouts healthy and to try to salvage some fun out of this. A thunderstorm is pretty exciting, isn't it?" Pete grinned, and we grinned back, but I thought that I would prefer to take this sort of excitement in small quantities.

Pete outlined a few more things he wanted the Seniors to do, and everyone scattered. The rain was letting up even more, and it seemed like the immediate crisis was over. I wandered over to the Snake Patrol to have lunch with them. They looked less unhappy than I thought I would find them. Most had on their rain gear, though one or two were still in their wet cotton shirts and shorts. I urged them to change, which they did. Everyone was hungry and enjoyed the warmth of the hot chocolate.

Pete called an emergency "Green Bar" meeting, that is, a meeting of the Patrol Leaders and Assistant Patrol Leaders, who wear (respectively) two and one green bars on their left uniform sleeves to designate their troop offices. Pete explained that the patrols could still have the overnight, but he wanted them to abbreviate their hikes and camp closer to camp than they had originally planned. After checking with each Patrol Leader about the status of their kids' clothing and gear and where they planned to camp, Pete dismissed them to get their patrols ready. Finally, Todd called an assembly, Pete gave the Scouts and dads a few last instructions, and then Todd dismissed them all to begin their hikes. Within a half hour, the camp was empty except for the Staff, a few alumni, and some extra dads, mostly the fathers of

Seniors. The Seniors had begun their night off and were nowhere to be seen.

The adults began to play. The rain had stopped, though the sky was still overcast, so some took out sailboats, while others just sat around and talked. I took the quiet time to write in my field journal, thinking about Pete's brief pep talk about leadership. "Leadership" is word often used in camp but never really defined, except by example. It is clear that a boy working toward Eagle Scout in the troop needs to demonstrate leadership. He does that in part by holding an office in the troop and by performing his duties responsibly. But leadership does not come with an office; one demonstrates leadership in an office. What is this thing called leadership?[11]

Sitting on my rock that day, I could not think of any occasions on which the term "leadership" had been defined for the boys. Days later, back with my books, I approached the question by looking at the successive editions of the *Handbook for Boys,* the *Handbook for Patrol Leaders,* and the *Handbook for Scoutmasters* to see what they had to say on the matter. Oddly, the *Handbook for Boys* has little to say on the subject. The first *Handbook*'s chapter on "Campcraft" by YMCA worker H. W. Gibson has only a brief paragraph on the topic, noting simply that a camping party needs "the best of leadership."[12] The only reference to the term in the revised fourth (1927) *Handbook* comes under the heading of becoming a Scoutmaster. "To give leadership, companionship, example, FRIENDSHIP and QUALITY to a group of earnest youth is a real privilege and an equal responsibility," explains that *Handbook.*[13] Finally, the 1943 revised edition makes explicit the leadership element to be required by Committees on Advancement before awarding Star, Life, and Eagle ranks. The Scout must prove through the testimony of others that he is "living up to his Oath and Law and Motto and Good Turn," and he must continue active membership in the troop. The third requirement speaks to leadership:

> 3) The challenging need of America is leadership—people who have ability and reliability enough to carry responsibility in business, in government, in church, everywhere. Leadership can only be learned by leading. Scout [*sic*] offers the opportunity to get this experience. Each Scout should use it by making an earnest, though modest, effort to serve through giving leadership to such activities and work and Good Turns as his own leaders deem wise. To help rather than merely to lead, is the ideal.[14]

Not much to help the boy reader here; a leader is one who leads.

The *Handbook* I had as a Scout in the late 1950s explains that leadership ability "counts largely towards your advancement" and that it "is not easy to be a good leader, but you can try to learn. If you are modest, keep your sense of humor, and remember some of your own troubles when you were new in the Troop, it will help you." [15] A good leader, it seemed from this passage, led by modest example. The sixth (1959) and seventh (1965) editions stress "taking initiative" as a sign of a leader, and the eighth (1972) edition really has nothing to say about leadership beyond recommending that a troop create a "leadership corps." [16] The ninth (1979) and the tenth (1990) editions talk about leadership in the context of the service project required for Eagle. "There is a major difference between the service projects for Star and Life, and the one you will complete for Eagle," explains the 1990 *Handbook*. "In the first two, you can be a follower. For Eagle, you must be a leader. You must plan, develop, and give leadership to others in a project of help to any religious group, school, or community. When finished, your project must be of real value." [17]

The various *Handbooks* for Patrol Leaders are richer resources for concrete advice about leadership. William Hillcourt's first *Handbook,* published in 1929, defines the "good patrol leader" in these terms:

A good patrol leader is enthusiastic, has unlimited faith in his boys and in the patrol.

He keeps moving, himself, along the Scout Trail of advancement and inspires the rest of the patrol to come along with him, as fast and as far as they can go.

He leads in Scout Spirit as well as in Scoutcraft; sincerely tries to set a good example for the rest to follow.

He does his best to understand his boys, to give them all the help and sympathy he can because he really cares for each and all of them from the depths of his heart. [18]

Hillcourt recommends against trying to be the "big boss" of the patrol; share your leadership, he advises, reminding the Patrol Leader that one of his responsibilities is to teach the other boys how to become leaders. "It is the 'Come on' attitude, not the 'Go on' attitude that makes for successful Patrol organization and real Patrol spirit." [19] Hillcourt's 1950 *Handbook for Patrol Leaders,* the one I used as a Patrol Leader in 1957, expands the description of the "good" Patrol Leader, but in the same terms and spirit as the earlier *Handbook.* [20]

Over the years, the *Handbook for Scoutmasters* has had lots of advice for Scoutmasters about the nuts and bolts of leading a troop, but in some ways those *Handbooks* are as lacking in concrete definitions of "leadership" as are the *Boy Scout Handbooks*. The fact that it is the Patrol Leaders' *Handbooks* that are most explicit about the practice of good leadership makes sense, given the fundamental reliance of the Boy Scouts on the patrol system. The patrol is the boy's gang, the small, face-to-face folk group where he most directly experiences "being a Scout" and where he learns to be a leader by observing a Patrol Leader.

Putting all these *Handbooks* back on the shelf, I realized what should have been plain to me when I was sitting on that rock enjoying the sunshine and fresh smells that followed the Sierra thunderstorm. I realized that none of these books helps at all to give boys an understanding what the troop means by "leadership." The meanings lie embedded in the practices. If I were to draw upon my ethnographic observations and list the practices of a "good leader" in the troop, the list would probably begin like this:

1. A good leader models the behavior he expects from others; he might not always live up to the ideal he sets, but he plainly tries.
2. A good leader puts the needs of others above his own; he is selfless rather than selfish.
3. A good leader has great empathy for others; he is sensitive to moods in others and tries to maximize the happiness of the group.
4. A good leader would not ask anyone to perform a task he would be unwilling to do himself.
5. A good leader persuades through language and the moral force of his ethos, not through physical strength or aggression.
6. A good leader has a good sense of humor, not least of all about himself; he can laugh at himself and can use humor to put others at ease and to manage some situations that can get out of control.

I began this list as a sort of thought experiment, and I suppose I could have generated more principles, but I wanted to see how this list compared with the qualities listed by Hillcourt, for example, and they're pretty close. They get taught and learned in the troop through dozens of everyday events, more often through the folklore of everyday life (jokes, pranks, stories, proverbs, etc.) than through direct instruction. So the troop needs no definitions; by the time he is a Senior, the boy in Troop 49 has a deep tacit knowledge of what is expected of him in the area of leadership.

At the Staff campfire later that evening, I got Pete to talking again about his "fuck-up" principle, which I knew was connected to his understanding of leadership.

"I'm totally serious about this," began Pete. "This is a serious philosophy that keeps me going in Scouts more than anything else. The fuck-up philosophy doesn't fit into the YMCA or the FFA [Future Farmers of America]. The Boy Scouts is the only organization I know—and what I'm about to say applies to fewer and fewer troops, unfortunately—where a boy is allowed to be a member and fuck up, and continue to be a member and continue to fuck up, and be given even more responsibility and continue to fuck up. There is an enormous toleration for fucking up. What other organization would let a kid fuck up more than twice, much less continue fucking up at higher and higher levels? Certainly not sports teams or clubs."

"Well, Pete," I said, assuming my anthropological voice, "what are the different types of fucking up? Can you draw me a typology of fuck-ups?"

Pete thought about this for a moment.

"Well, there's the first-year camper, Tenderfoot level of fucking up. You know, throwing rocks, going barefoot, that kind of thing. That's the level that the Patrol Leader has to deal with."

"Do the Patrol Leaders understand the fuck-up principle?" I asked Pete.

"Implicitly, yes, I think they do. For one thing, the Patrol Leader can't get rid of a kid the way the Staff can. The Patrol Leader is pretty much stuck with a kid in his patrol and has to deal with that kid's fuck-ups."

"Remember when Mitch was sent home two years ago?" interjected Aaron. "That kid exceeded the level of toleration for fucking up."

"Yeah, he did," agreed Pete. "He ran away from camp for two hours. That's not tolerable. I sent him home, and I had to ask him to leave the troop altogether. He was pretty demoralized by that, but I don't think I could forgive that level of fuck-up. To lose a kid up here is unthinkable."

"Back to your typology of fuck-ups," I prompted.

"Right. Another sort of fuck-up that any kid can do in his patrol is fail to do his KP duty after dinner. He promises he'll do it after campfire, and he still doesn't do it. The next morning, breakfast gets delayed because the stuff still needs to be cleaned, and everybody in the patrol is angry with him. Patrol Leaders have to keep on top of that one. And, of course, Patrol Leaders can fuck up, too. At YMCA camp, the leader of a cabin group is at least eighteen years old, but here the Patrol Leader is probably thirteen, maybe fourteen. And every kid, at some point, thinks about being a Patrol Leader."

"So how do you handle fuck-ups?" I asked, innocently.

There was nervous laughter around the campfire, at Pete's expense, I guessed.

"Well," said Roy, "sometimes he just blows up. Pete's temper—or fear of his temper, really—is highly motivating."

"Then there's the ass-chew," said Pete, once again taking control of the topic and trying to deflect the conversation away from his temper, which he tries hard to control. But at the phrase "ass-chew," everyone around the campfire responded with the traditional reply, "Gesundheit."

"As I was saying," continued Pete, smiling at the pun he had inspired, "sometimes there's the . . . lecture. And sometimes, of course, I'll take a boy off for a private conference of 'being wonderful' with him, of talking through his problem and getting him to see his options."

"And don't forget the 'I trusted you' lecture," suggested troop alum Don, who had been pretty quiet up until then.

Pete smiled. "Oh, yeah, I like that one. I have noticed that the Staff has learned to use that one. You have to be careful though. The 'I trusted you' lecture can't go on too long, or it loses its impact."

"Tell Jay what happened the other day with Ricky," said Aaron.

"Ah, yes. Recall that I was giving Ricky an ass-chew ["Gesundheits" all around] about stuff going on at the Waterfront—really more about his attitude than any single thing he was doing. And I asked him why some kid had done something under his charge, and he had the gall to say to me, 'Well, Pete, I trusted him not to do that, and a Scout is Trustworthy.' That really pissed me off. So here's a corollary to the 'I trusted you' lecture—it can't be used as a defense." We all laughed.

What this long, somewhat rambling and funny conversation told me was that over many years of working with adolescent boys Pete had developed a "folk theory" of sorts about this work. His folk theory, I felt sure, contained principles about adolescent male psychology (like the "three I's") and a repertoire of ways of getting boys to become the best men they could be. I resolved then to keep prompting Pete about these principles and to try to articulate them as a coherent theory based on experience.

Sunday morning dawned bright and cloudless, and we all slept in after the late night of talking. Breakfast was informal, and people spent the morning back in the sailboats or relaxing in some other manner. The patrols began straggling back into camp as the morning wore on, and by lunchtime everyone (including the Seniors) was back in camp to continue a regular day. Evening Vespers replaced the morning Church Service, so after evening colors we all walked up to Church Rock for a brief service of quiet songs and contemplation. The patrols had their campfires, and our own Staff campfire was low key. We were ready for week two of camp.

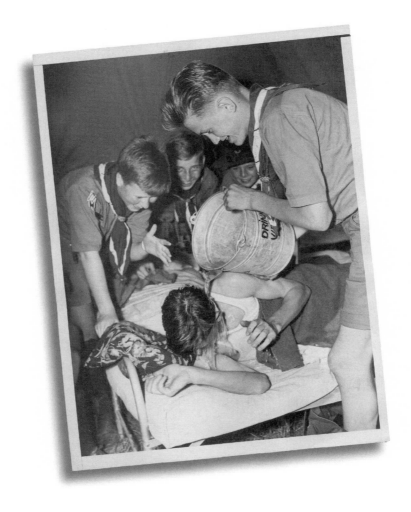

"Rise and Shine," 1927 Boy Scout Jamboree, Washington, D.C.
(photographer unknown; photo from author's collection)

Monday

★ ★ ★ ★ ★ ★ ★ ★ ★ ★ ★ ★ ★ ★ ★ ★ ★ ★ ★

I was in that twilight zone between sleep and consciousness when I heard Aaron's voice coming from his sleeping bag. "Where the hell is Todd? He's already ten minutes late with the reveille whistle."

I wiped the sleep from my eyes, rolled on my side, and reached down to where I had placed my watch on my shoes. Right; more like fifteen minutes late. Aaron was already out of his sleeping bag, pulling on his shorts and slipping into his sneakers. Aaron crossed the Parade Ground and clambered up the large rock ridge looking out over Usonia. He cupped his hands and shouted in the direction of Senior Point. "TODD! WHERE'S REVEILLE?"

"I knew this was going to happen," muttered Pete from his cot. "They're just too tired. Between the late nights with the smut and the Staff night out, they're too tired. I guess I'll have to 'be wonderful' with Todd a little more forcefully."

The truth is that we were all a bit tired. As we were getting ourselves out of our sleeping bags and dressed, Todd came hustling up.

"I'm sorry, Pete," he offered in a preemptive move. "My alarm didn't go off." Without waiting to hear from Pete, Todd turned and scrambled up the tall boulder beside the Staff Area, blew his whistle, and shouted three times: "Reveille. Commissary Emissary." He came back down the rock and stood at the edge of the Staff Area, knowing that he had a chewing-out coming.

"I'm really sorry, Pete." Todd was looking as contrite as he could manage through the fear.

Pete didn't look happy. "You're all just too tired, aren't you?"

"I guess." Whoops. One of the decodables. I tried to remember what this one meant in Pete's typology. Ah, yes. It means "Yes, but I don't want to think about it."

"What's that?" Pete asked, pretending he hadn't heard. Todd got it.

"Yeah. We're pretty tired."

"Right. So here's what we're going to do. I want you to collect all the Senior smut, put it in an empty cardboard box from the Commy tent, and put it . . ." Pete paused as he looked around. "Put it over there," he said, pointing to a place out of the way of foot traffic.

"We'll really be okay, and I won't let this happen again. I'll have Jeff set his alarm clock, too."

"Okay. Just let the Seniors know that I will not accept their shirking their duty just because they're tired. Let them go to bed earlier. Cut out the late night Senior campfires. They need to think of the Scouts and not themselves."

"I'll take care of it. Can I go now?"

"So long as you've got it." Todd nodded that he had and hurried away, back to the Point to deliver the unwelcome news that he was confiscating the Senior smut.

"So," said Don, "we're going to have a box of Senior smut in the Staff Area." He smiled. "We'll call it 'the library.'"

Pete smiled back. "Just don't let any Scout or Senior see you checking it out. Some of that stuff really is raunchy."

After the color assembly and the assignment of Seniors and Staff to patrols for the day's meals, Pete gave a little speech.

"I know from talking with some of you that you had a good overnight in spite of the storm we had. And that's great. I'm proud of your spirit. But you're probably tired, too." Pete paused and turned to look at the Seniors lined up on Advancement Rock, behind him. "I know the Seniors are." He smiled his broad Cheshire Cat smile, a controlled smile that indicated displeasure; the Seniors fidgeted. Pete turned back to the Scouts. "And I'll tell you what I told them. We have to keep our energy up for the program. You have patrol campfires tonight, but make them short if you need to. Tomorrow is the Treasure Hunt, and you'll need to be rested for that. This morning, after breakfast and patrol duties, I'm going to take the Green Bars on a tour of the area covered by the Treasure Hunt, so they'll know the traditional troop names for places. That'll be important for understanding the clues. You experienced campers will have to explain the Treasure Hunt to the new campers. The Treasure Hunt is a real old C&T in the troop, and it's lots of fun. So, remember, get some rest."

Pete turned the assembly back over to Todd, who called everyone to attention, paused, and then dismissed them.

After breakfast, the Green Bars assembled just outside the Staff Area, where Pete had said he would meet them. Pete returned (from the KYBO, I supposed), and he and I walked over to the boys. Pete made sure they were all there, and then we walked through camp toward Upper Lake and the dam. We crossed the dam single file and soon reached Pete's classic Chevy pickup. The boys piled into the back, and Pete and I sat in the cab.

The day smelled fresh, as if the thunderstorm had washed away the stale dustiness of the summer. The sky was cloudless again, and the light had a special clarity. A beautiful day in the Sierra. Pete's plan was to take the boys on a tour of the Treasure Hunt boundaries and traditional sites. This tour serves the important purpose of socializing the Green Bar leaders, introducing them to the traditional names the troop has for sites in the general area. Some of these names will turn up in the clues for the hunt, and Pete advised the leaders to take notes on the tour. We had to take the tour by truck because the boundaries are quite large—a few miles by a few miles.

Pete first took us in the direction we had gone on the day hike, stopping at each important site and indicating LBAS, Devil's Slide, and Silver Creek. Then we drove by LLBAS (Lower Little Bare Ass Slide) and the Rope Swing (a place on the creek where the troop once constructed a device for swinging out over the water and dropping in from a height of ten or fifteen feet). Then we drove past Bridge Camp, the bridge over Silver Creek, the King's Highway portion of the jeep trail, the Bleachers (a steep, very rocky portion of the jeep trail, so named because Pete and others strengthen their leg muscles for backpacking by running up this trail, just as they practice during the school year by running up the bleachers at the high school football stadium), the Lily Pond, and the Sandy Pits. Pete noted casually that those were the troop's canoe trailers we could see chained to trees near the Sandy Pits.

Pete stopped the truck at the Lagoon, a marshy area that was part of Usonia, and noted sadly that this was the spot where the boy from their own hometown, but not a Scout, had drowned a week before camp began. He reminded them that the boy had foolishly tried to swim across the lagoon in his clothes and with his wallet in his teeth and he had sucked water and drowned.

After letting that lesson sink in, Pete proceeded past the lakeshore and indicated the Cross up on the heights. We passed Chicken Creek, so named because it crosses the trail and, when the water runs a bit high, it looks impassable and the less adventurous adults park above the creek and walk into Old Usonia. (I learned the name one summer when I chickened out and parked my old VW bus without crossing the creek, thus giving myself a much longer hike into Old Usonia than was necessary.) Pete pointed out old license plates nailed high on tree trunks, marking an old ski trail. Eventually, we passed Sapp's cabin, now a charred ruin. Sapp's cabin is on an 1896 map of the area, explained Pete, and Sapp used to run cattle in that meadow. We swung back toward camp.

On the way back, Pete began telling me stories about his own days as a Scout camping in the area. He talked about the logging camp that was at Spicer's Meadow, about the railroad trestle he walked, about sleeping on an innerspring at the abandoned logging camp. Pete loved and missed the romance of those adventures.

The tour took about an hour, and when we arrived back in camp, the boys scattered to their assorted classes and duties. I was a guest of the Tiger Patrol that day, and as I came up to the table, all the others were already seated and passing the tuna salad for their sandwiches. The boys were in the middle of a discussion about the Treasure Hunt. Despite Pete's pep talk about the hunt being one of the troop's oldest traditions, the boys seemed to me to lack any enthusiasm for the game. Tim and Sean were doing their best to pump up the kids, but the experienced members of the patrol complained that the Treasure Hunt was a long day of walking, and the new campers sat silently, wondering whether they should worry about this Treasure Hunt thing.

"It'll be fun," Tim told the doubters. "And, besides, we need the points for the Nugget Auction." That argument seemed to carry some weight with the boys, but I had the feeling Tim was going to have to continue showing "leadership" in order to get these kids anywhere near high energy for the contest.

The afternoon followed the regular routine of siesta, advancement classes, and free swim. After evening colors, the troop broke briefly for patrol duties and then reassembled for the twilight evening recreation, a game of Capture the Flag. As we walked single file toward the Playing Field, I recalled the fun I had had in my own Scout camp days playing Capture the Flag and its variants, Capture the Staff and Color Wars. These are extremely popular games at Scout camps, other camps, and even in playgrounds and neighborhoods.

The roots of the modern game of Capture the Flag lie in eighteenth-century England, where it was first known as French and English or as Scots and English, the latter referring to border warfare. The formal structure of this game has remained remarkably stable over two hundred years.[1] It is a game of chase and capture, in which the goal is to penetrate the "enemy's" territory, seize the enemy's property, and return to safe territory without being captured and taken prisoner. Prisoners must remain in "jail" until freed by a teammate, and in some versions, a prisoner must be rescued before any more booty may be taken.[2] The booty varies from clothing to handkerchiefs (as in Gomme's description of French and English) to sticks.[3] The historians of this game see as part of its attraction the romantic model of "marauding raids of the Borders," and the English versions feature traditional taunts at the crucial border between friendly and enemy territory.[4]

The name "Capture the Flag" apparently appeared only when the game passed from being a spontaneous folk game to being a game "organized" by adults for children to play with some adult end in mind. The organized version appeared almost simultaneously in the British and American Boy Scout handbooks. There was considerable acrimony between Lord Baden-Powell and Ernest Thompson Seton over who brought into the movement a number of games, including Flag Raiding, the Scouting precursor to Capture the Flag. Seton's chapter on "Games and Athletic Standards" for the first *Handbook for Boys* (1911) and editions of Baden-Powell's *Scouting for Boys* from the same period have nearly identical descriptions of Flag Raiding. But in both cases, the authors had transformed the traditional folk game of French and English into a game that better suits the goal of training young men in the skills of scouting, stalking, and observing.

In Flag Raiding, there are two or more patrols of boys to a side, protecting in their own territory three flags (or, at night, three lanterns). An "outpost" protects the flags while each side "sends out scouts to discover the enemy's position."[5] As in war games, a scout seen by a stronger party is "out of action." At the end of play, sides tally points for flags captured, for sketches of enemy outposts, and for reports of movement of enemy scouts. With the stalking skill at its core, the game described in the early *Handbooks* is much more a game of strategy than of seizing property.

By 1915, the *Handbook for Boys* described the modern game of Capture the Flag. Play is between two troops or two teams chosen in a troop; members of one team tie handkerchiefs or neckerchiefs around their arms to distinguish themselves from the other team. Each team has a single flag mounted on a staff, which is placed within one hundred paces of the center boundary. Boys guarding the flag may stand no closer than fifty feet from the flag unless an enemy enters that circle. Scouts caught in enemy territory are captured if the captor can grasp and hold the intruder while shouting, "Caught, caught, caught." The captor accompanies the prisoner to the guardhouse, where he must keep a foot or hand on the prison base. A "friend" can free a prisoner by touching him, whereupon the two hold hands and have a "safe" return to their home territory. If an enemy seizes the flag but is caught before crossing into safe territory, the flag remains where the enemy is captured. A team wins by seizing the enemy flag and carrying it safely back to home territory or, if the flag is never captured, by having more prisoners than the other side at the end of the time limit.[6]

Successive editions of the *Handbook for Boys* and the *Handbook for Scoutmasters* from 1915 well into the 1930s clearly describe a game meant to reinforce Scouting skills and cooperation, while providing healthy, strenuous physical activity. But I was on my way that evening to watch a troop of Boy Scouts actually play the game, and I was curious to see how they would adapt this very old, very traditional, now very official game to their own folk culture.

Play resembles ritual in several ways, and this game of Capture the Flag was no exception.[7] The game is set aside in its own ritual time and place, removed from everyday life at camp. Insane Day on T.I., Capture the Flag on the Playing Field, Sunday morning service at Church Rock, the investiture ceremony in its secret spot, and troop campfires held at especially picturesque sites constitute the set of play and ritual occasions and sites for this troop. Capture the Flag differs from the others, however, in a few important details, one of which is the normal absence of adult Staff at the game. It was exceptional that I was tagging along as an observer. Usually, the boys play the game away from adult scrutiny, supervised by one of the Seniors.

The play space, I could see, was rather rugged, liberally sprinkled with trees, fallen logs, and granite boulders. It was a dangerous place to be running in under any circumstances, and the danger would increase as the mountain light faded. But the boys considered this an ideal playing field for the game, providing sufficient cover to make slow stalking as important a strategy as outright running. In fact, this feature of the play space was an equalizer of sorts. Whereas in a flat, open field the fastest runner has a decided advantage, in this terrain the slower runner can rely upon stalking, camouflage, and strategy to compensate for speed.

Jason, the Senior in charge, officially announced the game boundaries. The center line divided the play space into two roughly equal territories; the total space seemed to be a rectangle at least one hundred yards wide and two hundred yards long. Jason selected two younger

Scouts as team captains who alternately selected players until everyone was chosen. To distinguish themselves from the other team, one side took off their neckerchiefs. Each team had a few minutes to huddle, assigning positions and discussing strategy. The "flags" were Frisbees, and each team had to place its Frisbee where it was both visible and within the reach of the smallest Scout. Each team selected a spot for its jail, and the boys took their positions for the game to begin.

The "forwards" are the players who cross into enemy territory, usually for one or more of the following purposes: to capture the flag of the enemy and carry it back or throw it across the center line into safe territory without being caught, to divert the enemy defenders in such a way that another forward has a better chance of capturing the flag, or to free the prisoners held in the enemy jail. The "guards" are the players who stay within their own territory in order to defend the flag. They are permitted to cross the center line (as are all players), but their role in the game is to chase and capture enemy forwards who encroach upon their territory. Some guards may be assigned specifically to guard the flag. The troop rule is that these guards must stand "at least a Cadillac's length" away from the flag unless they are chasing an enemy forward. This rule, among others, turned out to be the subject of many disputes in the games I watched.

The third player position is that of "jailer," a position sometimes occupied by a Scout with a temporary physical impairment that keeps him from running. The jailer stands by the team's jail and watches over the captured enemy. The prisoners may not escape unless they are freed by a free forward, who must reach the jail, tag a prisoner (saying aloud "Free!"), and walk him hand in hand safely back across the center line.

Capturing is an important activity within this game. The capture of the enemy's flag is, of course, the goal of the game, the act that determines the winning side. Far more frequent is the capture of other players in enemy territory. The defender must chase, grab, and hold the enemy forward long enough to say aloud "Troop Forty-Nine!" The captured player must then cease resisting and go peacefully to jail, where he must wait until he is freed or the game ends.

This description of how the game is supposed to be played glosses too quickly over the features of the game as it was actually performed by the troop. The space over which the game was played was so large that it really was very difficult for the Senior in charge to supervise the game. Away from the watchful eyes of the Senior referee, the capture could become an invitation to violence. An explicit rule, "no fighting," confirmed the likelihood of conflict. At the very least, a capture was an event ripe for dispute, the word of one boy against another whether or not the forward was held for the required amount of time. The act of freeing prisoners created similar disputes, as did the capture of the flag. Scouts disputed over whether or not a defender was at least a Cadillac's length away from the flag. Since forwards capturing the flag were allowed to pass the flag-Frisbee while attempting to get it back into safe territory, there were disputes about whether a boy in possession of the flag was caught before he passed it. And so it went. The Senior referee sometimes stepped in to resolve a dispute, especially if it appeared that the parties involved were really angry about the infraction, but the usual course was to view the disputes as unimportant and sometimes even enjoyable events in the game. I saw several boys throw considerable energy into arguing each capture and freeing, just to see how far they could push the rules.

The style the boys brought to their play was as interesting to me as were the roles, rules, and disputes. The game was surprisingly verbal. Forwards would taunt each other across the center line and would shout changes of strategy to one another, and guards would shout warnings or call for help when an enemy forward crossed the line. Prisoners shouted to their own forwards to free them and would taunt the jailer with the epithet "base sticker," an insult that, for boys at least, carried some sense of a cowardly boy afraid to stray far from home. A feminized "momma's boy," in short, was most likely to be a base sticker. And, of course, the endless disputes were also highly verbal.

Each boy seeks out a role that suits his talents and personality. Forwards take joy in fast, elusive running or in slow, sneaky stalking. Both strategies entail a high risk of capture, and therein lies the excitement of the forward's role. Strategy in Capture the Flag also sometimes provides a boy the opportunity to sacrifice himself as a diversion so that others may have a better chance at capturing the flag. Guards tend to be no less athletic than forwards, but being a guard entails no direct risk of being captured and, consequently, of being out of action for some time. The guard is always "in play," so to speak; his pleasure comes not from risk or from sacrifice but from defense and from the act of capturing another. The jailer is, as I have said, the most passive player in the game and is almost always an injured or minimally capable player. Yet the job is an important one and provides the player with some sense of identity in the game.

The game ends either when one team captures the other's flag and returns it safely to home territory or when the set time limit is reached, in which case the winning team is the one holding the most prisoners. The time limits were short enough, usually ten minutes, that the troop could play three or more games before it got too dark. After each game, the sides would switch territories in order to balance out differences in terrain, and in some instances I saw teams trade players when it was clear that the "choosing sides" process had yielded an imbalance of talent.

I could not be everywhere during any one game, of course, but during some games I would sit on a high rock at the center line and have a full view of the action there and at the two jails. At other times, I would stroll back toward one flag or another to watch the play deep in one team's territory. I even played a few games, at the urging of the boys.

Unlike team games that focus players' attention on a ball or puck, Capture the Flag seemed chaotic. Small game events involving two or more boys were happening everywhere. At the center line, boys were taunting each other and making brief, teasing incursions a few steps across the line. Sometimes a group of boys would gather and make a sudden, massive "assault" across the line, sending the overwhelmed guards into a shouting panic. From my rock, I could see some boys sneaking across the center line near the edge of the playing field. And I saw, too, that "strategy" in this game included cheating, as I saw some boys moving around to the rear of the enemy's territory through terrain clearly out of bounds.

Running at the high altitude took its toll on the boys; bursts of running had to be followed by rest to catch their breath. And as the light faded, negotiating the rocks and tree stumps became increasingly tricky. A few times boys took nasty falls, and players in that area would take a "time out" to minister to the injured boy. Usually, the boy was not hurt badly—at most, rock "burns" or cuts on legs and hands; occasionally, a turned ankle put the boy on the sidelines for the remainder of the game. Play resumed as soon as the injury was assessed and resolved.

The game finished, the Senior in charge assembled the boys by patrol, determined that all were present or accounted for, and led the troop back to camp in the near dark. The boys were tired from the game, and the evening's program was to be patrol campfires, a relatively quiet affair. Most boys went to bed early that night.

Capture the Flag was familiar to me, and I recognized the boys' delight in the game. Only later did I come to realize how meaningful this game was in the overall tapestry of camp life. As I observed earlier about the first Sunday's church service and Tuesday's Insane Day on T.I., play and ritual are framed social scenes set aside from everyday life, and to understand Troop 49's summer encampment requires that we understand each framed world in relation to the others.

Play's power lies in its ability to produce paradoxical statements about itself, about ritual, and about the taken-for-granted reality of the everyday world. If the highly structured everyday world of camp is communicated in the simple declarative mood of "this is" or in the imperative mood of "you will," then we might say that the games of these boys are in the subjunctive, "as if" mood. The "as if" mood of play gives it the power to comment upon everyday life in ways that would be too frightening or too disruptive if done "for real." Both ritual and play help the participants reflect upon themselves and upon the social order. But whereas ritual affirms, play doubts.[8]

Like jokes, play doesn't select just any aspect of routine existence for its self-reflexive comment, but chooses especially conditions of contradiction or conflict.[9] Play dramatizes the problem in the social order, much as our jokes and our dreams dramatize our interpersonal problems.[10] Games and other expressive folk genres, folklorist Roger Abrahams tells us, give "a 'name' to the threatening forces both within and without the group," presenting "these names in a contrived, artificial form and context, giving the impression that the forces are being controlled."[11]

The characteristic of games that makes them good models of conflict would seem to be as threatening as the everyday world they were meant to dramatize if it were not that games often use disorder to affirm order of a different kind.[12] Games remind the player of the most amazing paradox of culture, namely, "that social cohesion is most fully sensed in terms of the antagonisms felt within the group."[13] This cohesion is doubtless the sort Victor Turner called "communitas."[14] How a game, one of the most structured forms of play, can lead the players through the conflict of competition, through disorder and doubt, to a new integration of communitas is surely among the most miraculous transformations of play.

Play works this transformation, in part, because the dramatized conflict is stylized, which is to say that the communication within the play frame takes full advantage of the expressiveness of metaphors and other cultural tropes.[15] We might say that a game has a "stylized presence" that does something more than just stand for the reality it is mirroring. The game experience itself might be one of those peak moments that define the meanings of human existence. The symbolism of a game encodes something not only about the structures and relationships of other realities but, just as important, about moods.[16] The taunts across the center line in Capture the Flag, for example, communicate a mood, but it is a mood stylized. The stylized communication of mood in a game contributes to the players' perception that conflict and chaos are under control, creating "an atmosphere in which pleasure may occur because the feeling of control is transferred magically from the formal expression to the situation itself."[17]

In this game, this stylized performance, the boys name the contradictory and threatening aspects of the social order of the troop and camp, transform those aspects through the structures and moods of the game, and finally confirm amid all the conflict of the contest a fundamental communitas that binds them. This much said, what might be the contradictions and conflicts this particular group of boys works out through the medium of Capture the Flag?

The conflicts turn out to cluster around authority and fraternity.[18] It should surprise nobody that a good deal of what goes on at a Boy Scout camp has to do with male power and authority. Among other things, games are dramatic models of power, so let us look at what the game of Capture the Flag does to and for the ordinary patterns of authority and power at camp.[19] At its outset, the game suspends the normal identities and rules of the camp. Normal identity in the troop is ascribed through the patrol. Capture the Flag is one of the very few games in camp (Poison Pit is another) where the contest is not between patrols. The game could be played with two patrols to a side, but it is not. Instead, choosing sides destroys the normal lines of affiliation and loyalty within the troop and creates new, temporary loyalties. The game also plays with identity in another sense, to the degree that the game provides three sorts of roles—forward, guard, jailer—to which the boys may gravitate. Each game role requires a different sort of skill level and temperament, and it is likely that these game roles (active chaser, active chasee, passive jailer) allow each boy to experiment with relative proportions of aggression and passivity in his personality.

Similarly, the game casts doubt upon the normal rules of camp. The certain, inflexible rules of camp life are set against the dispute-ridden rules-in-use of the game. The pervasive testing of rules and outright cheating in the game amount to a disorderly comment upon the rigid rules of camp. Moreover, the game challenges specific camp rules. Most obvious are the camp rules against running and fighting. The nature of the game space and its central element of physical capture make the game an easy outlet for violence. Still another camp rule challenged by the game is the right of territory. The patrols generally respect each other's territory and belongings in camp, but a central feature of the game is penetrating the other side's territory and carrying off its property.[20] The symbolism of the "flag" in this regard is important, as each patrol campsite is marked by its patrol flag. Seizing a symbolic flag, even when it is a Frisbee, is a violation of the other's symbol of identity.

There are two sources of authority among the boys in the troop, authority through rank and authority through office. Each of these is subject to transformation in the game of Capture the Flag. Authority by rank arises out of the boy's acquiring badges of rank that represent levels of knowledge, skill, and achievement. Authority by rank represents some mixture of intelligence and physical skill, but a good deal more of the former. The boys comment quite frequently on how much the advancement classes are like school, and a boy's attitude toward advancement as well as his actual advancement depend largely upon his attitude toward school. The game of Capture the Flag nicely cuts through matters of strategy and "school smarts." Although the *Handbook* with its adult goals emphasizes the value of exercising stalking skills and strategy, the fact is that the game greatly favors physical ability. The two main activities, running and capturing another boy, are the key to success or failure in the game. Capture the Flag undercuts the ideology of strategy with the game–determining reality of physical skill. Put differently, the athletic boy who does poorly in school and struggles with his Scout advancement through the ranks has the opportunity for unqualified success in this game of physical skill.

The game of Capture the Flag also comments upon the authority of office. Each patrol has its Patrol Leader and Assistant Patrol Leader, and the camp itself has a distribution of offices among the Seniors, such as Senior Patrol Leader, Scribe, Quartermaster, Commissary Director, Campfire Director, Advancement Director, and the like. The game undermines the authority of office in several ways. Choosing sides along lines that erase patrol identifications means that in the game's space and time the normal authority of Patrol Leaders and Assistant Patrol Leaders no longer applies. This makes possible not only verbal aggression through taunts but also physical violence toward a bossy Patrol Leader or Senior. Disputes over rules in this game also tend to make irrelevant the power of the central interpreter of rules, the Senior in charge of the game. But even here a boy must be careful because excessive cheating or arguing will spoil the fun for others and that boy will find himself the target of quite evident peer disapproval.

This view of the ways in which the game of Capture the Flag provides a frame for doubting the normal lines of authority and power in the troop might lead us to conclude that this is only a game of disorder and inversion, but such is not the case. The game simultaneously dramatizes fraternity. It contributes powerfully to the communitas the boys create in the face of the adult agenda for the organization. The game provides two dramatic displays of self-sacrifice for the group, one an explicit feature of the game and the other a peculiar feature that, at first glance, appears not to be part of the game at all.

The first symbolic display of self-sacrifice is provided by the game strategy that involves a forward's drawing defenders away from the flag to give a teammate a better chance of capturing the flag. This is a central strategy even in the official versions of the game, as in the 1915 *Handbook for Boys*. The second dramatic display of self-sacrifice is a good deal more subtle. Every time I have observed the troop play Capture the Flag, I have seen at least one case of moderate injury. Boys trip and fall or hurt one another during a capture. Once a boy suffered a severe insect bite. The response of the players on the occasion of relatively serious injury is to "break frame" and suspend play until the injured boy is cared for or leaves the playing field. Like the boys, I once took these injuries to be outside the normal play frame, events that are natural outcomes of the conditions of play but that follow rules different from the game's.

Now I believe that these "injury events" are most likely "injury displays" that are as much a part of the game as so-called asides are in interpreting a verbal narrative.[21] I call them injury displays not because the boys fake the injuries but because the injured boy becomes for a few minutes the center of a symbolic ritual easily as complex and important as the game itself. Consider what happens when a boy stumbles over a log and goes sprawling across a stretch of granite and brush. Play stops; rules are suspended. Those closest to the boy, including his pursuer (or pursued), stop to see if he is hurt. If he is, the Senior referee and others administer first aid (an important Scout skill), sending for the camp first-aid kit, if necessary, or even sending the boy back to the Staff Area for a more complete patching-up. Others stand nearby, awaiting the outcome of the diagnosis. Boys express concern and encouragement. Sometimes the boy will affirm his tough manhood, "walk it off" and resume playing; at other times, a severe or convenient injury will mean the boy retires from the game to sit with the Senior referee as an observer.[22] What has happened?

Think of the injury and response, the injury display text, as a necessary element of the game of Capture the Flag. Gregory Bateson was fond of thinking about social systems as cybernetic systems, that is, as systems with their own built-in mechanisms for monitoring and correcting error in the system.[23] Bateson's example of this is the now-antique governing mechanism of whirling ball weights on steam engines. The faster the steam engine goes, the faster the centrifugal force of the whirling balls makes the arms horizontal, which in turn reduces the flow of energy to the engine. Thus, the governor for a steam engine is a cybernetic mechanism for keeping the system from running out of control and destroying itself.

This is not a bad analogy for understanding the cybernetic mechanism in the game of Capture the Flag. The game is highly competitive and violent, features that, as we have seen, serve useful functions in the play frame as the occasion for transformed communication about power, rules, and identity in everyday life at camp. But these same qualities that make the game a useful metaphor for dealing with these other issues also threaten to run out of control if not checked by some process intrinsic to the game itself. The injury display is that check. Totally unpremeditated but equally inevitable, the injury event stops the contest and the violence long enough to permit the boys to show the nurturance and caring that the institution values so much. There is, in short, a lesson in androgyny in this cybernetic process, as the boys learn how to mitigate agency (the ability to organize resources to get things done) with communion (the ability to take care of how people feel about the group and their place in it).[24]

The injury display serves one final important function in the game. To be injured in team sports, as in battle, is to have earned the badge of courage and sacrifice. The injured boy most likely feels justified in terms of the game; he was hurt, after all, in service of his fellows. "Walking it off"—that is, enduring the pain and resuming play—is a sure sign of masculine courage.

The game of Capture the Flag had been a brief suspension of their normal patrol affiliations and loyalties, and as they left the game space and time for the walk back to camp, the boys were returning slowly to their patrols, to their "home" loyalty in the troop. Patrol campfires were scheduled for that evening, and the patrols had been instructed to think up "Usonia Commercials" as skits for the next evening's troop campfire.

While the patrols were having their campfires, the Seniors assembled around the advancement table for a meeting with Pete and the Staff. George had made sure a number of Coleman lanterns were on the table and hanging from the fly in order to provide plenty of light. This was probably going to be a long meeting, as the Seniors had to complete the plans for the next day's Treasure Hunt. The Seniors were seated around the table, looking pretty listless, when Pete and the Staff came up from the Staff Area.

Pete sat in his aluminum lawn chair at the head of the table and surveyed the group. He did not look pleased. "You all look pretty tired," he began, "and I wasn't pleased that some of you were late for the color assembly. I told you that if I saw signs that your late hours were interfering with the camp program and the quality of the experience for the Scouts, I was going to confiscate your smut. Well, that's what I've done. Todd, did you get every last piece of smut?"

"Yes," said Todd briskly, though he seemed angry and embarrassed that the Seniors had not been able to keep up their part of the bargain.

Now Pete looked at George. "George," he began, "do you have something to tell me?" Aaron and I knew immediately what was up. Earlier in the day, we had overheard another Senior tell George that they were almost out of peanut butter in the Commissary. Aaron reminded George that it was over just such a thing that Pete had once pounded a hole in the Commissary table, so angry was he that the Commissary Czar that year had deliberately hidden from him the impending shortage, which resulted in no lunch food for "Break Camp" day. The Commissary Czar that year never made Eagle because of that and subsequent fuck-ups. Later we saw Pete, and Aaron alerted him to the problem. Pete decided to wait to see if George would say anything to him voluntarily. Apparently, he had not.

"George?" repeated Pete. "Do you see this?" He pointed to the place on the table where duct tape had been applied to repair the hole Pete had once put there. "Do you know how that got to be that way?

"Because one year a Commissary Director ran out of peanut butter."

"No, not because he ran out of peanut butter, but because he didn't *tell* me about it in time to do anything about it. We had dads in camp yesterday, and someone could have gone out to get us peanut butter. But I didn't know we needed any. Do you get the picture?" Clearly, Pete was disgusted with George.

"Yes," murmured George.

"Do you see the distinction I'm making between running out and failing to tell me?"

"I guess so."

"You'd better know so. I don't care if the kids consume lots of peanut butter—that's fine. I want them to eat if they're hungry. They need the fuel. But failing to tell me about the shortage is like lying to me, and that is one thing I will not tolerate. Not from you and not from any of you. I hate it when a kid lies to me, especially if the lie puts others in jeopardy. So you and I have to talk later about how we're going to solve this peanut butter problem." Pete's performance had made its impact. The tape on the table was an ever-present reminder of a story, and the story was told and retold in the troop as a cautionary tale meant as a warning to Commissary Directors but also to all the Seniors. Pete wanted to make sure that the Seniors understood the moral of the story, namely, that lying to Pete is one of the greatest sins a Senior can commit. Pete will accept fuck-ups much more easily than he will accept lying to conceal a fuck-up.

Pete next raised the matter of advancement and the progress each kid was making. This began a slow and, for the Seniors, tedious round of interviews between Pete and each Senior, during which Pete asked how each Scout was doing in his advancement classes. Pete stated several times that he did not want the Seniors to lighten up on the badge requirements. He wanted the instructors to hold the Scouts to strict standards.

Once Pete was satisfied that the Seniors were paying close attention to the advancement progress of each boy, he turned the discussion to the Treasure Hunt. The Treasure Hunt is a half-day contest in which the patrols follow clues that take them from place to place in search of a "treasure," a six-pack of Coke. Patrols win points as well as the treasure. The Treasure Hunt really has two agendas. One, of course, is for the boys to have fun. The other is for the boys to get the opportunity to practice some of the Scouting skills they learn at camp. As always, the Boy Scout program seeks to make learning fun.

"Last year's Treasure Hunt was great," began Pete, "and I want this year's to be just as great. Who's in charge?"

"Jeff and Les," replied Todd.

"Good. The key to a great Treasure Hunt is having both 'false clues' and 'false false clues' that make the Scouts be alert to something wrong."

"Yeah, we've been working on some," offered Jeff. "Some will be based on breaking a camp rule, like going barefoot or throwing a knife or chewing tobacco."

"Good idea," said Pete. "You also need some clues that have to do with the Scout Law."

"We've got that covered," chimed in Les. "We thought of having a Senior changing a tire on the truck along the route. The Scouts who offer to help him are being 'Helpful,' so they'll get the right clue. Those who don't will get a false clue."

Pete's face brightened. "Good. You'll have to find some way to signal the next clue station as to which patrols offered help and which didn't."

The discussion continued for some time, as Jeff and Les led Pete through the entire Treasure Hunt as they had it plotted out. The Seniors were very tired, but Pete made them go through the hunt, station by station, clue by clue, until he was satisfied that the hunt made sense and that each Senior knew what he was expected to do.

In the middle of this, I excused myself to go to the KYBO, and on my way back I walked by the Eagle Patrol and heard the boys, all in their sleeping bags, talking softly about "rubbers" and "pricks" and "twats." "Didn't you ever hear of a rubber?" an older Scout was asking a younger one. I could see that the sex education part of Scout camp was proceeding quite nicely. When I returned to the meeting, they were almost finished with the clue-by-clue rehearsal of the Treasure Hunt.

"We'll have Roy hide the treasure," said Pete, turning to the alumnus who had come up for the week, "and, Jay, you can accompany Roy to see how it's done." We both nodded assent. Pete finally dismissed the Seniors, who welcomed the chance to go back to the Point and to bed. The Staff (at this point, Pete, Aaron, Tad, Roy, and I) went back to the Staff Area and began gathering things for the Staff campfire. Once we settled down at the campfire, we began discussing some of the problems at camp. Aaron was bothered by the fact that some Seniors were going from Todd to Aaron to Pete, making the same request, until they found someone who would say "yes." Pete agreed that had to stop. Pete then turned to his exchange with George about the peanut butter.

"If there's one thing I won't abide it's deception. I hate it when a kid lies to me, and I want them to know that. George didn't seem to get it. Did you hear him say, 'I guess so'? One of the decodable coverts. I should have pursued that. I'm not sure he really understands that his sin was not running out of peanut butter but neglecting to tell me. I'm really worried he'll do it again. He's a smart enough kid, but he's another one in deep denial."

The conversation broke briefly while Roy fed the fire and we passed around some cheese and crackers.

"How'd the game of Capture the Flag go, Jay?" Pete asked.

I said that I thought the kids enjoyed it and that there was only one minor injury. I didn't offer the group my elaborate folklore- and anthropology-driven interpretations, but I did comment on the cheating.

"I was more interested in the ways the kids broke the rules of the game than in the game itself," I began. That got everyone's attention. "What I mean is that every capture, every event seemed to become a dispute over the rules—like the rule about a defender's standing a Cadillac's length away from the flag." The others laughed.

"Well," said Roy, "that rule used to be a Volkswagen's length, so the distance has gotten bigger." [25]

"But how does a kid know what's a Cadillac's length?" I asked. "This is a game with very permeable rules. Then there's the outright cheating. I saw kids sneaking out of bounds to come around behind the enemy's flag." I waited for a reaction, but there was none. They seemed to be waiting for my academic reaction to this news that sometimes Boy Scouts cheat. So I continued.

"I think cheating is a very important part of the game. The cheater doesn't really threaten the game. The acts of the cheater actually confirm for everybody that there are rules to the game and that there are consequences for breaking the rules. The real threat to the game is the 'spoil sport,' the one who says, 'this is just a game, it's not real,' and maybe picks up in the middle of a game and leaves.[26] The cheater confirms the reality of the game because the cheater works within the rules. But in this case, the cheater also conforms to the rules about breaking the rules. Every game seems to have permissible ways to cheat. You get called on and maybe penalized for breaking the rules, but so long as you've followed the rules for breaking the rules, you're still part of the game and you strengthen the power of the game, even though you're cheating. It's when you break the rules for breaking the rules that you've done real damage to the game. I haven't figured out yet what that would take in the game of Capture the Flag, but I'm sure there are ways a kid could break the rules that would be so outside the rules for breaking the rules that he would have to be expelled from the game. Maybe a guard taking his own flag and giving it to an enemy. Maybe treason of that sort is the cheating I have in mind."

"Yeah, I see that," said Pete. He was thinking about what I had said. "So do you think the Scouts shouldn't cheat?"

"No, on the contrary, I think it's very important that the kids learn how to break the rules, so long as they follow the rules for breaking the rules. It helps them understand all sorts of things, such as the relation between formal and informal rules in an organization, and it teaches them to take punishment when caught. But the disputes teach them verbal and interpersonal skills, too, since part of what's going on when they play the game is practice at 'managing' their relationships. The game would be pretty boring and wouldn't teach them much if everyone played by the rules and if nobody disputed any call. Fortunately, there's enough ambiguity in the rules—like the Cadillac's length rule—that they get practice in negotiating and arguing."

"Yeah, they *do* do that," acknowledged Aaron, laughing.

I was on a roll, thinking through this point about cheating. "And I also think that playing with the rules teaches them some creativity. I think there's a relationship between creativity and 'cutting corners,' so I feel sure that the kids most active in negotiating the rules are also the most creative. At least in one sense."[27]

"That's an interesting point, Jay," added Pete. "I think you're right. Some of the most contentious kids are also the most creative. I worry that with all our rules I'm not giving the kids a chance to be creative. And then sometimes I worry that we don't take things seriously enough, like all our joking and punning—the silly stuff we do."

Pete was referring to several stock jokes traditional in the troop. Someone will ask for duct tape, and someone else will ask, "What kind of tape?" "Duck tape," and everyone present will duck, sometimes shouting "Duck! Tape!" Or Pete will talk of giving a kid an ass-chew, and everyone present will say, "Gesundheit!" Or someone will talk of singing a song "Acapulco" (instead of a capella, without musical accompaniment). Or Pete will talk of doing something "on the sperm [spur] of the moment." Or, as was popular for a while, a Senior or Staff member would ask a certain alum—Richard, nicknamed Dick—quite innocently, "Do you have a pencil, Dick?" ("pencil dick" is a slur at the girth and size of one's penis). And so on. There are dozens of such examples of wordplay in the troop.

"No, Pete," I continued, spinning out this idea of the connection between cheating and creativity, "I think the wordplay is very important for the kids' learning creativity. They hear the adults and older Scouts playing with words and language and meanings. That's important for them to learn. To turn it around, I'd say that a kid who can't play with language or doesn't have a good sense of humor probably has other problems. Certainly, I'd guess that kid isn't very creative, in the sense I mean 'creative.'" We thought about these things for a while.

What I did not add to this discussion, for fear that it would sound too academic and might get me doused in beer, is that Gregory Bateson's double-bind communications model of schizophrenia suggests that some people never become adept at distinguishing between literal and figurative messages. An element of the schizophrenic's dysfunction often is taking figurative language literally. Communications and language are "dangerous" territory for these people. But most of us learn early how to make these distinctions. In fact, one of the ways kids typically get power in a situation is by purposely taking an adult's figurative language literally or by purposely taking an adult's literal language figuratively. All the wordplay at Scout camp was helping make these boys competent players in language games and, ultimately, in all sorts of uses of language. I was also raising a sort of warning flag for Pete and the other adults: watch carefully the kid who can't joke and play with language. He may be headed for severe adjustment problems.

Pete seemed glad to hear my assurances, and we joked among ourselves a little before retiring. Pete has a wonderful, complex sense of humor, but he worries that the seriousness he has to bring to certain aspects of being Scoutmaster threatens to make him seem humorless. I was trying to assure him, indirectly, that I thought there was a proper balance between play and seriousness in the ways he interacted with the boys and alumni.

An artifact of the Treasure Hunt (from author's collection)

Tuesday

★ ★

In the morning we had a regular round of advancement classes. Shortly after lunch, Roy and I went down to the lower Waterfront area on Usonia and took the outboard motorboat to Sandy Pits, a beach that the troop and others often use to launch boats. That was where the Seniors had decided we were to hide the treasure. When we arrived at Sandy Pits, I could see two large canoe trailers chained and locked to trees. These belonged to the troop and were to play an important role in the hunt. We beached the boat and took out the supplies we had brought with us. The first task was to mark a spot on the iron trailer. Roy then began laying out a compass-and-pacing course of the sort required for one of the Scout ranks. The idea is to have a course with compass readings and distances in feet, to test the Scouts' skills at taking compass readings and estimating distances using their own pace. But Roy explained that the task would not be that simple. The Staff usually makes things more difficult by always starting the compass course near some iron that will interfere with the first compass reading. This year the canoe trailer would pose the challenge. In past years, they have used a coil of cable around the rock where the compass course began, or an iron bar in a box of sand on which the compass course was taped. The smart Scouts will realize that the trailer causes magnetic interference and will compensate for it somehow. In any case, even a small mistake in a triangular course can lead to giant errors at the end.

Roy finished making the course and jotting down the compass readings and distances. He had the course end at a stump by the water, and the plan was for a Senior to canoe over to Sandy Pits later with the treasure and use duct tape to tape the six-pack to the underside of the canoe. The canoe would then be beached at the stump where the compass course ended. Our work complete, we got back into the motorboat and returned to camp.

By the time we got back up to the upper assembly area, the troop was assembled, and the Seniors had left camp for their assigned stations. I could see the Scouts were dressed for hiking, wearing hats and good hiking shoes and carrying water bottles. Something was wrong in the Snake Patrol. Sam, a first-year camper, was crying, much to the embarrassment of his patrol. Steve was trying to comfort him about something.

"What's wrong?" Pete asked Todd.

"Steve says that Sam feels sick, like he's going to barf. I doubt it, and so does Steve."

Pete went over to Sam and led him over to the Commissary table, where Pete sat the still weeping boy in front of him. "Sam, you're not sick in your stomach. You're just afraid that you won't make it out there on the hunt, and your mind is making your body sick. So you've got to get over that fear. You're afraid you'll wimp out, aren't you, Sam? Well, the only way you'll be a wimp is if you chicken out. You're not a wimp. You'll make it. There are at least six other guys out there who are feeling the same way you are right now. It happens every year. So, what's it going to be? How do you feel?"

"I guess I feel all right," admitted Sam, wiping his tears away.

"Good," said Pete, and he sent Sam back to join his patrol.

When we rejoined the assembly, Jeff was in the middle of explaining the game boundaries and rules. The rules are relatively simple. Each patrol carries a plastic baggie for collecting the clues, a shovel in case it is necessary to dig for the treasure, and a first-aid kit. Patrol members must travel slowly enough so that they are always in sight of each other. When coming to a station, the patrol must give its "patrol yell," whereupon the Senior at that station reads his rhyming clue twice. He then writes on the back of the clue the order in which the patrol arrived at his station (first through fourth) and the time of its arrival. The patrol puts the clue in its baggie as proof that it visited that station and then moves on to the next station (assuming, of course, that it can solve the clue). A most important rule of the Treasure Hunt is "to obey all rules"—that is, to be alert always to camp rules (such as rules against throwing objects, going shoeless, practicing unsafe use of tools, and such) as well as the more general rules laid out in the Scout Oath and the twelve points of the Scout Law. The Treasure Hunt has a time limit, so patrols who lose the route or have not reached the treasure site by 5:30 are to return to camp.

The Scouts understand that the Seniors must speak in rhyme. Any communication not in rhyme is to be understood as being outside the play frame of the game. This rule, it turns out, is crucial to the "false" and "false false" clues lurking in the game.

I decided that I would follow one patrol through the game, seeing how the Scouts did and how they reasoned out their clues. I chose the Eagles because I was eating with them that day and Eddie seemed to have the most experience as a Patrol Leader. Jeff explained that the first clue was taped to the underside of the patrol tables and that the game would begin when he blew his whistle. He paused dramatically, then blew. It was like an Oklahoma land rush, as the boys scampered back to their patrol sites.[1]

I arrived at the Eagle campsite just as they were retrieving the clue from underneath the camp table. The first clue traditionally is written out in Morse code, knowledge of which once was part of the requirement for First Class rank. Few boys know Morse code these days, so it took the patrol a while to decipher the message using the Morse code key in the *Handbook*. The messages send each patrol to a different first station, but after that the clues direct the patrols to the same stations.

Finally, the Eagles deciphered their message, which sent them to Advancement Rock, where a Senior stood to give them the first rhymed clue:

Don't stand like a bunch of sillies,
Head on down to the place of lilies.

This clue led the patrol to the Lily Pond station, where the next clue read:

Go where some walked like the Lord,
Where they used the water-walking cord.

Alert patrols saw in this clue a reference to the creek swimming site where the troop set up the Rope Swing. But now came the complication.

On the way to the Rope Swing, beside the road, one of the Seniors was washing the troop pickup truck. This seemed rather routine, but it was actually a station, the "false false clue" station. The third point of the Scout Law is "A Scout is Helpful," and the test here was whether or not the patrol would offer to help the Senior wash the truck. If the patrol was alert enough to offer help, then the Senior's spoken rhyme immediately would confirm that this scene was within the play frame:

> Congratulations, by the third point of the Scout Law you did abide,
> Continue to your previous destination side by side.

The Senior would then give the patrol a written copy of this clue. It was the possession of this written clue that would tell the Senior at the Rope Swing that the patrol had passed the test. Patrols that did not offer help were also headed for the Rope Swing, but they would not have this clue in their baggies.

Let me pause here in my description to explain why the troop calls this the "false false clue." The Scouts know that their violation of a camp rule or their failure to note a Senior's violation of a camp rule will result in a penalty, a "false clue" that will send them far out of their way. The "false false clue" poses a game challenge regarding camp or Scout rules, but it is a "*false* false clue" in that failure to meet the challenge results in a brief delay but not a false clue. Furthermore, the "false false clue" station is meant to lull the alert patrol into a false sense of security, leading them to believe that they have come across the "false clue" challenge and have met it successfully. Adding to this construction is the fact that one year's "false clue" challenge might be used the next year as a "false false clue" challenge. The only safe strategy for a patrol is to be constantly suspicious of every event that relates to the large body of camp and Scout rules.

The Rope Swing station was the pivotal station for this Treasure Hunt. The "false clue" station is the most complicated for a Senior to manage, so it demands that one of the brightest Seniors be at that station. I arrived with the Eagle Patrol, they gave their yell, and Eddie presented his baggie of clues to Jason, the Senior manning that station. Jason examined them all, but he was really looking for the "false false clue" slip, which would indicate that the patrol had stopped to help the other Senior wash the truck.

The Eagle Patrol had not figured out the "false false clue," so it had no slip. Without indicating that he hadn't found what he was looking for, Jason presented the Eagles with this rhymed task:

> At this station you sing a song;
> If you're smart it won't take long.

The "smart" patrol sings the troop's short parody version of the longer song "Titanic": "Oh, they built the ship Titanic, and it sunk!"

At this point, the imaginary flowchart of the Treasure Hunt branches. Patrols that met the challenge of the "false false clue" will not be given a second task at this station, but patrols that failed to offer help next hear this rhymed instruction:

> By the third point you were not true,
> Now light that stove until it turns blue.

So the penalty for failing to offer help was that the patrol must spend time setting up and lighting a Coleman camp stove. But both sorts of patrols, those who offered the help and those who didn't, were equally vulnerable to the *true* "false clue" challenge, which came next.

As Jason began writing the time and order on the back of the last clue, he "accidentally" broke his pencil point, muttering "Shit!" to help convince the boys that this was not part of the game. Pulling out a pocket knife, the Senior began sharpening the pencil, breaking at least two camp rules by drawing the blade toward his thumb and by whittling while standing. If a patrol detected this violation, the patrol then would get the true clue:

> Okay, okay,
> I'll put it away.
> Now's the time to take a rest;
> Go where all must wear a vest.

The true clue was referring to the camp Waterfront and life vests.

But the patrol that did not detect the whittling violations would get this "false clue":

> Take this clue all in stride,
> Go on up to Devil's Slide.

This "false clue" sent the unhappy patrols on a hot, hard climb in the direction opposite from the one they should be taking. The Senior at Devil's Slide delivered the bad news to those patrols:

> By the tot'n chip[2] Jason did not abide,
> Now you are here at Devil's Slide.
> The trip you just made didn't mean a thing,
> So head on back to the Rope Swing.

Back at the Rope Swing, the patrol received the true clue sending the members to the Waterfront, but they had paid a forty-five-minute penalty for failing to detect a broken rule.

At the Waterfront, the patrols faced a new task:

Put on this vest the way you were shown,
Or else your chances may be blown.

This task seems like another "false clue" challenge, though it isn't. Just to be sure, the patrol members put the vests on exactly as they had been taught. Then they received the next clue:

While you can still eat, drink, be merry and function,
Head on over to the newly painted junction.

The next stretch was a long hike to a trail junction newly marked with paint in order to avoid lost patrols.
     This station, too, involved a task:

I don't care how much you bitch,
This tent here you still must pitch.

Given the rocky terrain of this site, "pitching" a tent would be worth "bitching" about unless the patrol leader realized that "pitch" can also mean "toss." The patrol alert to wordplay in the game can usually make short work of these tasks. Every year at least one station's clue contains a verbal ambiguity that can be read in a way that shortens the task. One year, for example, a clue was "Make a cup of Kool-Aid for the entire patrol," which could mean making either one cup or an entire pitcher. Through the entire Treasure Hunt, the younger boys learn from the older ones to attend carefully to wordplay and to the metaphorical level of language.
     Upon completing the tent "pitching" task, the next clue advised:

Let's all get down and all get funky,
And head on down to the site that's junky.

Those words referred to a place on the lake known to the troop as "the junky campsite" on account of its popularity with messy campers. Again, the boys faced a hike of more than a mile to that station. As we walked along, some of the Eagle members were beginning to fatigue, straggling and complaining so much that Eddie had to yell at them to keep up.
     At the junky campsite, the Senior offered this clue:

A "hamburger" would be a fancy treat,
So take a bite out of McGeorge's meat.

This clue had an immediate meaning to the campers, since it named a spot where, on the first day of camp, George's dad had met the incoming campers with a large lunch. The troop immediately dubbed the spot McGeorge's in a playful reference to McDonald's. The clue purposely played on the double meaning of "meat," slang for the penis.

At that station, George read the clue that told the boys they were near the end of the hunt:

All is not as you supposed,
McGeorge's is officially closed.
Just too bad about your treat,
You can't have McGeorge's meat.
The trip is getting shorter and shorter,
Beat your feet to Sandy's canoe transporter.

Eddie recognized immediately that this clue referred to Sandy Pits and the troop canoe trailers.

Arriving at the site ten minutes later, the patrol found on the troop's canoe trailer the cardboard sign Roy had made:

Eureka!
From the X this course will lead
To the treasure that you need.
1. 143.8' at 299.7 degrees
2. 146.3' at 70.2 degrees
3. 112.9' at 349.9 degrees

Four compasses sat on the canoe trailer, so upon arrival each patrol was required to lay out the compass course and pace out the distances in order to reach the spot where the treasure was hidden.

By the time we arrived at Sandy Pits, two of the patrols (the Snakes and the Tigers) had already laid out their compass courses and were digging with the shovels they'd brought along. The Tiger Patrol was digging in the mud and water some thirty feet from the treasure, but (amazingly) the Snake Patrol was digging around exactly in the right spot. Ironically, they had moved the canoe over a bit in order to dig in the shallow water. Having not found the treasure after a while, they did their compass course again, then once more. Each time it brought them to the same spot.

Just as they began to lose confidence in their compass work, a first-year Scout suggested looking under the canoe. The older Scouts in the patrol called the idea stupid, worthy of only a first-year camper. Finally, the "stupid" eleven-year-old got a friend to help lift the end of the canoe out of the water, and there, to everyone's amazement, was the treasure. The Snake Patrol posed for its victory pictures, and the cookout began.

The Treasure Hunt had taken over three hours and had led the patrols on a six-mile route around the lake. The boys were all tired and hungry. The Snake Patrol members drank and enjoyed their Cokes rather publicly, a conspicuous consumption of the spoils of the Treasure Hunt. The Cokes were their immediate reward. The other reward was the points they won by finding the treasure. Those points, added to the ones they had accumulated during the week in inspections and at the coming troop campfire that evening, would be useful in the camp's last Nugget Auction on Thursday evening.

Dinner seemed to reanimate the boys. No one could complain about the meal of hot dogs, Kool-Aid, soup, and roasted marshmallows. And, besides, the wire coat hangers they used for roasting the marshmallows doubled as play weapons with which the boys tormented one another as they vied for places near the hottest parts of the fire, playing a game of "dueling hangers," in which the object is to knock the other boy's hot dog or marshmallow into the fire. Inevitably, some camper's marshmallow accidentally caught fire and he had to extinguish it, to the delight of his fellows. Just as inevitably, he insisted that he "likes them that way" and popped the charred sugar into his mouth.

Aaron instructed Todd to hurry the campers as dinner ended. We had to hike a short distance back to camp, and we had a troop campfire ahead of us. As we walked, I reflected a bit on the Treasure Hunt I had just seen and mentally compared it to the few others I had watched this troop engage in. It's clear why the game fits so well into the official agenda of the Boy Scouts. The game requires the boys to exercise some Scout skills, such as the Morse code and compass work. More important, though, the game serves the troop's needs. The boys learn more about the terrain of their camp's region by hiking it and learn the troop's folk names for sites in that region. The game also reinforces specific camp rules, from the complex "true false clue" about whittling to the station where boys had to show they knew how to put on life vests. The game's heightened attention to troop rules makes the boys inspect every event for evidence of rule keeping and rule breaking.

From the anthropologist's viewpoint, the Treasure Hunt is a straightforward game of skill and strategy. If all goes according to plans, the reward of the game will go to the most physically strong, mentally awake, and morally straight.

The paradox is that this game of skill and strategy actually turns a great deal more on other factors. The three great threats to the smooth running of the Treasure Hunt are chance, cheating, and fuck-ups. Luck, both good and bad, persistently undercuts the role of skill and strategy in the game. One year the Eagle Patrol arrived first at the treasure site quite by chance, having misinterpreted a clue. In two other years, all four patrols arrived at the treasure site and began searching before anyone found the treasure. And this year three of the four patrols searched simultaneously. The fourth patrol was a "lost" patrol that had been in second place until it began hiking in circles. One year, when the Staff hid the treasure in a tree, a Scout found it by pure chance. He was climbing the tree in order to get a better view of the area where his patrol was digging for the treasure. Underscoring the role of chance in the game is the fact that getting to "Eureka" first really means nothing, since it is the compass-and-pacing course that ought to determine ultimately who gets closest to the treasure. But, again, elements of skill and chance mix to undo this "ought."

In a remarkable modern parallel with some traditional buried treasure legends, the treasure the boys seek is "guarded" by one last task made all the more difficult by treachery. The final rhymed clue brings the patrol to a site marked "Eureka," but that is not where the treasure is hidden. The "Eureka" sign bears the three sets of compass-and-pace readings, so to get to the treasure they must utilize properly the Scout skills of orienteering by compass and pacing distances. But, as in many folktales, treachery lies behind this seemingly straightforward task. The magnetic vagaries of the earth itself play the first trick to the extent that every spot on earth has a "declination," the difference between true north and magnetic north. The "Eureka" compass readings are given in "true north" degrees, requiring the Scouts to make adjustments for the magnetic declination at their spot on earth.

Humans play the second trick. As we have seen, the Staff hiding the treasure always makes sure that there is a substantial mass of iron at the Eureka site. These obstacles, one natural and one human, help "protect" the treasure by making difficult the final task of taking and measuring the compass course to the treasure. Interestingly, luck plays a part here, too, in that the Scouts' errors on those compass courses sometimes cancel out these obstacles, bringing the boys close to the treasure by the luck of the sum of their errors.

Outright cheating is rare in the game. The only really effective way to cheat would be to get an advance list of the stations and/or advance word of the location of the treasure. Seniors keep strict security on this information, but the security rests upon the solidarity of the Seniors.

The third sort of disruption of the Treasure Hunt is the fuck-up, wherein a Senior fails in his scripted performance. One year the Senior at the "false clue" station misunderstood the signals from the Scoutmaster and gave the false clue to every patrol rather than only to those that put on their life vests incorrectly. A few years later another Senior at the "false clue" station mishandled his role. He failed to respond flexibly to signs that patrols were willing to help him change a tire on the canoe trailer (if Scouts offered to help, they got the real clue), thereby causing all of the patrols to proceed two miles out of the way in pursuit of a false clue.

The element of contingency in the Treasure Hunt lays bare one of American culture's most troubling contradictions.[3] Playing the game draws attention to the true role of luck in a game officially meant to reward skill and strategy. This insight, in turn, necessarily comments upon the supposed role of physical skill and strategy in the pursuit of achievement in the everyday life of the troop at camp. The Treasure Hunt, within the safety of a play frame that can be dismissed as "not real," asserts the falsity of what appears to be real at a Boy Scout camp, namely, that hard work is the means to achievement as measured by ranks and badges. Too often the boys see one another succeed out of luck, deception, or outright "gift." The play frame of the Treasure Hunt game permits the boys to confront this contradiction in a way set aside from everyday life at camp.

The day had been an exhausting one for the boys, and they probably would have preferred to return to their patrol sites for some relaxation and peaceful patrol campfires. But a troop campfire had been scheduled for that evening. I could see the strategy behind that plan. The Treasure Hunt was an intensely competitive event, pitting patrol against patrol, so the troop needed a campfire to bring it together again for a ritual affirming of its shared, collective identity. Besides, one school of thought holds that the best cure for being tired is to engage in something upbeat and energetic, and a troop campfire certainly is that. In any case, we were to have a troop campfire that evening.

Everyone went back to their campsites to change into warmer clothing for the campfire. As I entered the Staff Area, I saw Jeff and Ricky sitting in aluminum camp chairs, facing each other. Ricky had his leg up and his foot in Jeff's lap as Jeff was bending over and rummaging through the Staff first-aid box for something.

I knew it was against camp rules for the Seniors to use the Staff first-aid supplies without permission from someone in a high-level position, so I asked Jeff whether Pete had said it was okay for him to be doing that. "Ricky got some blisters today," explained Jeff as he pulled his head out of the first-aid kit, "so I'm helping him put on some moleskin [a cushioned patch]. Aaron said it was okay."

As I was changing my clothes, I watched this operation. Jeff cleaned Ricky's foot with a wet washcloth, dried the foot, applied some antiseptic, and cut a moleskin patch the size and shape that would protect the area. He then did the same with Ricky's other foot.

In some respects, this event was not so remarkable—boys administered first aid to each other all the time at camp. But this particular vignette impressed upon me how tender and nurturant this care could be. Like the cooking chores, this was another example of how the all-male setting required males to perform tasks often assigned to females in the home world. These role experiments could work out in many ways. The tenderness Jeff was showing Ricky, and Ricky's unselfconscious acceptance of that tender care, struck me as evidence that the relentless construction of the heterosexual adolescent at camp did not preclude some space for androgynous definitions of masculinity.[4]

The campfire began, as always, with "Fireman Bill" and then moved on to a troop favorite, "Chewing Gum." Tommy quickly announced that the next song would be "Comin' Round the Mountain," a well-known American folk song. But, as I had come to expect, the troop has transformed this traditional song into something more appropriate for campfire singing, adding phrases and gestures to each verse and making the song a test of memory, as in "Hasenpfeffer." The song was a great hit with the boys. The three lively songs opening the campfire had rallied them from the fatigue they brought with them as they trudged up to the site, and it was hard to tell that they had already had a long day.

"Let's have a skit now from Bear Patrol," said Tommy. The patrols had prepared parody television commercials, as instructed. The Bear Patrol had made props; they set up a large cardboard box with large lettering: "Usonia Clean Garbage Disposal." Bob, the Patrol Leader, stepped forward to deliver the commercial voice-over. Two boys standing by the box had in front of them what clearly was a white "clean garbage" bucket.

"What to do with awful, clean garbage? Why, use our handy dandy Usonia Clean Garbage Disposal."

At this point, the boys poured the wet, sloppy contents of the white bucket into the box. One of the boys came out from behind the box, eating a piece of hot dog from the garbage. The audience was disgusted, muttering, "Oh, gross!" and similar comments at the thought that a boy would actually eat out of the garbage. The Senior judges gave the patrol suitably low scores, indicating their disgust as well.

"Nexxxxxt," said Tommy, dragging out the suspense, "is . . . 'Commissary Store.'" This caught my attention because I knew that "Commissary Store" is one of the most interesting of the chainlike songs the troop sings and that the improvisations by the boys would tell me something about how they were feeling about the day's events. Pete had brought the song to the troop from his own Scouting days. The song's origin, according to two troop alumni I later interviewed, lies in a University of California, Berkeley, drinking song "The Farm," sung about Stanford University, Berkeley's arch-rival across the Bay. The drinking song's chorus—"My teeth are dull, I cannot chew, it comes from opening cans of brew"—alternates with invented verses, such as "Oh, it's vodka, vodka, vodka, that makes you feel so rodka, on the farm, on the farm." The troop has transformed this song into an appropriate camp song.

Tommy was about to give the troop a downbeat for beginning the song, but Pete interrupted. "I have an announcement about 'Commissary Store,'" he began. "First, I want to remind you that we'll go around once, giving each person one chance to sing a verse. So if you think of something and you've already been passed up, it's too late. The other thing is that both Aaron and I want the verses to be 'M.A.'—'Mom Approved.' That means you can't sing anything here you wouldn't sing in front of your mommy and daddy at the family campfire at the end of camp. Also, I'm making Jeff the 'Senior lawyer,' which means that he can go out of turn in order to say a verse back to a Scout who has made a cutting verse at a Senior." Pete paused, then remembered a few more rules he wanted the boys to follow. "Another rule: every other verse is to be 'traditional'—that is, without reference to people. So if you have a 'put-down' verse, you can sing it after a traditional verse."

The ground rules stated, the song began:

Commissary Store

Chorus
My teeth are dull, they cannot chew.
It comes from opening cans of stew.
It comes from opening cans of stew.

Verses

1. Scout: Oh, it's rats, rats, rats, as big as alley cats.
    All: In the store, in the store.
            Oh, it's rats, rats, rats, as big as alley cats
            In the commissary store.
2. Scout: Oh, it's Stone [George's last name], Stone, Stone, who
            always makes us groan.
    All: In the store, in the store, *(etc.)*
3. Scout: Oh, it's P, B, and J, that spreads like modeling clay. *(etc.)*
4. Scout: Oh, it's Stone's red hair, that stands out like a flare. *(etc.)*
5. Scout: Oh, it's greasy pans and pots, that give us all the
            trots. *(etc.)*
6. Scout: Oh, it's my big brother [George], who's a scum like no
            other. *(etc.)*
7. Jeff: Oh, it's that ugly little Stone [Martin, George's little
            brother], that makes us want to groan. *(etc.)*
8. Scout: Oh, it's P, B, and J that makes my butt decay. *(etc.)*
9. Scout: Oh, it's Terry [Les's last name], Terry, Terry, whose
            teeth are so damn hairy. *(etc.)*
10. Jeff: Oh, it's Carter [the Scout who sang the put-down verse
            about Les], Carter, Carter, who wears his cute pink
            garter. *(etc.)*
11. Scout: Oh, it's tape and twine, enough to blow your
            mind. *(etc.)*
12. Scout: Oh, it's Stone, Stone, Stone, who moans on the
            fence. *(etc.)*
13. Jeff: Oh, it's Scott [the Scout who just sang the put-down
            verse about George], Scott, Scott, whose breath is like
            the pot. *(etc.)*
14. Scout: Oh, it's mice, mice, mice, running through the
            rice. *(etc.)*
15. Scout: Oh, it's Brad and Hare [Jason's last name], that make a
            gay pair. *(etc.)*

[Pete calls for the last verse]

16. All: Oh, that's all there is, there ain't no more.
            In the store, in the store.
            That's all there is, there ain't no more,
            In the commissary store.

As was true in "You Can't Get to Heaven," which the troop had
sung at an earlier campfire, the key to the boy's mastering the formula

for this song is his learning to invent a relatively short couplet. But whereas the rhyme in "You Can't Get to Heaven" depends upon means of transportation (car, boat, etc.), the scheme of "Commissary Store" permits the rhyme to hinge upon the name of a person in the group, opening the way for put-down verses. Name play and wordplay mix here in those verses.[5]

When sexual references enter this song, they are explicitly homosexual—the "hairy teeth," the "cute pink garter," and the "gay pair" lines. This is in contrast with the "Yay! Boo!" version of "Salvation Army," where the sexual references are heterosexual. "Salvation Army" creates a collective fantasy about sex with girls; it is not a cut song, not the occasion for stylized, ritual put-downs. But "Commissary Store" has none of this fantasy sex, turning all of the sexual energy and anxiety of the boys into male insult instead. Perhaps the competition of the day evoked the aggressive and hostile content of "Commissary Store." In any case, the two songs complement one another, each necessary for the other's meaning. Just as it is important to the sexual identity of these adolescent boys for them to engage in collective heterofantasy, so it is important for them to distance themselves from homosexuality through insult. Both publicly construct the heterosexual male.

The boys are thrown together in activities that alternatively require intense cooperation and intense competition with other boys. Loyalty and trust are highly valued in the official Boy Scout literature, but also in the real-life demands of this male group. Homosexual or homoerotic feelings are central to both competition and cooperation within male groups. Homosexuality was the paradoxical key to the Greek contest system, and certainly the homoeroticism present in the male camp activities (including the Insane Day contests) must pose something like the same paradoxical feelings in the boys.[6] The boy distances himself from these homoerotic feelings by means of put-downs and the projection of these feelings onto another. In short, the close comradeship among these boys is possible so long as they share in their expressive culture a scorn for homosexuality. The tension is never resolved, of course, so these themes pervade the lore of the Boy Scout camp.

I noticed three other things about the troop's performance of "Commissary Store" that evening. First, the "Senior lawyer" had quick retorts to the insult verses. Verse 7 responded to 6, 10 to 9, 13 to 12. This immediate put-down is a highly regarded ability in the "cut wars" of adolescent boys. Second, aside from the sexual references are two other themes common at camp—the quality of the food and personal features (red hair, bad breath). Mice and assorted forest critters do get into the food, and the references to mice and rats betray a little bit of nervousness about these pests and their "pollution" of clean food. Finally, verse 12 is an example of teenage humor wherein the joke lies in the Scout's violating the rule that the verse must rhyme. It is also a put-down, linking metaphorically the victim and an alley cat.

The song finished, Tommy asked for the Eagle Patrol to come forward with its television commercial skit. The patrol lined up, with Eddie providing the voice-over. In front of the line of boys is a familiar white bucket. The Eagle Patrol had brought its own clean garbage. "What do you do with clean garbage?" asked Eddie in his commercial voice. Another boy from the patrol, dressed in an orange jumpsuit and wearing a homemade "gas mask," stepped into the campfire circle and addressed the Eagle Patrol: "What have you got there? Don't you know that this clean garbage is *toxic* to our environment?" He picked up the bucket and carried it off into the darkness. "Remember," said the boys in unison, "only you can close down Rancho Usonia and prevent toxic pollution of our soil!" The "Rancho Usonia" reference was to Rancho Seco, the nuclear power plant in the Central Valley. The plant, a twin to the ill-fated facility at Three Mile Island in Pennsylvania, had a troubled history of its own, and there had been throughout the 1980s a concerted social effort to close down the facility.[7]

Two skits in a row about clean garbage struck me as more than mere coincidence, but there was no evidence of collusion between the patrols. The "clean garbage," that lovely oxymoron, had attracted the boys somehow as symbolic material for their dramatizations.

Next Tommy asked the "junior Staff" members to come up and lead "Trail the Eagle." The junior Staff are the Scouts who are almost Seniors and who have special talents qualifying them to help the Seniors teach skills and merit badge classes. The song they led is an official song of the Boy Scouts of America, one of the few official songs the troop sings, and it is meant to inspire the boys to achieve the highest rank.

Tommy changed the pace again with a lively version of "Crawdad Hole," a well-known song among campers and children, and then asked the Snake Patrol to come forward for its commercial skit. This patrol had gone to the most trouble, even writing a script. The central prop was a large Cheerios cereal box that had been transformed with marker and tape into a "Spameos" box, with humorous text added to the back and sides. Steve began with a typical cereal commercial lead-in for "Spameos"; then the boys in the patrol stepped forward one by one to give their "endorsements" of this new cereal. Some posed as athletes, some as doctors "stranded on an island" (as in a real commercial for Bayer aspirin), and some as people on the street. The boys concluded the commercial with a jingle about how great "Spameos" were. The parody was wonderfully funny, showing the boys' mastery of the television commercial and endorsement formula. The commercial again revolved around food, in this case a revolting combination of two familiar food items.

"Saints" was the next song on Tommy's program, and this time the Seniors enjoyed themselves by circulating around the campfire circle screaming the lyrics in the faces of the campers. Energy was high, so Tommy asked everyone to stand for a yell:

Give a Yell
Give a yell!
Give a yell!
Give a good substantial yell!
And when we yell, we yell like ——— *(pause)*
And this is what we yell:
Get a reebo!
Get a rybo!
Get a reebo rybo rum!
Boom! Get a rattrap bigger than a cattrap!
Boom! Get a cattrap bigger than a rattrap!
Boom! Boom! Siss boom bay!
Troop 49, hip-hip-hooray!

This yell is the only tongue-twister among the four traditional yells in the troop, and it's easy for boys to fall behind. As they cut off sharply, the last shouted syllable created the echo the boys had wanted, and everyone sat down, well pleased. Time was running out, so Tommy asked for the last commercial skit, this one from the Tigers.

The Tigers presented a commercial for "portable KYBOs." Tim began with his pitch for the "Troop 49 Portable KYBOs in three convenient sizes." One boy brought forward the large size, consisting of a full-size shovel with a roll of toilet paper on the handle. Another boy presented the medium size, a "cat-hole" shovel with a roll of toilet paper; and a third boy presented the small size, a trowel with toilet paper.

There you have it—two skits on "clean garbage," one on a disgusting cereal made of Spam, and a fourth on portable KYBOs. A good many television commercials are about food, household appliances, and bathroom cleaners, to be sure, so these are reasonable targets for commercial parody. But I could not help noticing that all four skits involved some symbolic treatment of food and filth, of the clean and the dirty. This pattern of skits gave me much to think about.

Tommy led the group in one more song, "Usonia," before we all stood and went into the sequence—"Vesper Song," benediction, "Taps"—that ends all troop campfires. Pete punctuated the end of the campfire with a "Good night, Scouts," and everyone gathered their things for the trek back to camp. Everyone was very tired from the Treasure Hunt, and even the Staff campfire was short and subdued. Like the Seniors, we were falling behind in our sleep, so we welcomed the chance to turn in early.

The Two Bodies at a Boy Scout Camp

Mary Douglas, Victor Turner, and other symbolic anthropologists have created a metaphor that works very nicely as a starting place for thinking about culture. The "two bodies" metaphor, as Douglas dubs it, draws our attention to the relationships between the two bodies in a society—the individual human body and the "body" of people who constitute the small group, the community, and in some cases the nation.[1] The body turns out to be an excellent symbol for society. Like the society, the body is a "bounded system," with an inside and an outside. These boundaries can be crossed at a place we might consider a breach in the boundaries, a danger zone.

In the case of the human body, there are materials that cross through the mouth and nose into the body—air, food, and drink, primarily. And then there are materials that cross the body's boundaries in the other direction, moving from inside to outside: urine, feces, flatus, semen, blood, menstrual blood, milk, tears, saliva, and sweat. Anthropologists note that cultures create taboos to deal with the danger of materials passing in both directions across the boundaries of the body. Not every society has a taboo governing every material ingested or inhaled and excreted, but in the American case, there are certainly food taboos and other ritualized behavior around food, drink, and even air.[2] As for excreta, Americans have their own taboos and other ritual ways of dealing with urine, feces, and menstrual blood (for example). While we do not believe in the extreme power and danger of saliva, we do recognize the health hazards (both real and imagined) of spitting in public. You can learn a lot by looking at the ways a culture treats these materials crossing the body's boundaries.

The brilliance of the "two bodies" metaphor lies in its recognition that talk about one of the bodies really stands for talk about the other sort of body. The two metaphorical bodies "bleed" into one another, we might say. Talk about the human body often is coded talk about the society, and talk about the society often is coded talk about the human body. A culture's "ethnomedicine," its belief systems about health and disease, might provide us with clues to its belief systems about other, social matters. We talk about illness as a disorder, a recognition that order/disorder, clean/dirty, good/evil, and a dozen other such sets of binary oppositions apply to the health of the society as much as to the health of the individual. A society's talk about illness becomes, then, talk about the order of the society itself, and the anthropologist would have us look at our discourse on illness as a symptom of larger anxieties and tensions we might be experiencing as a society. Susan Sontag's masterful essays *Illness as Metaphor* and *AIDS and Its Metaphors* show how the metaphors move from the body to the society and back again, and the considerable body of cultural criticism on our American discourses about HIV/AIDS uses this same insight to show how cultural assumptions about gender, sexuality, and race get coded in presumably "scientific" and "medical" talk about the virus and the disorder it causes.[3]

But enough generalities. Let me ground this theoretical point in the concrete example of Troop 49's summer encampment. The theory leads me to say that there are "two bodies" at the camp. One sort of body is the male body, primarily the adolescent male body. The other sort of body is the social body, and in different contexts this can mean the patrol, the troop, the boy's home world, the community, or the United States. What happens if we think about the metaphorical slippage between these two bodies, about the ways the boy's body sometimes stands for the group and the ways the group's "body" sometimes stands for the boy?

Take the boy's body as a ritual symbol. Begin with the fact that real things happen to the body. The body changes. As hormonal changes begin with the onset of puberty, the boy begins to develop his secondary male sexual characteristics. His genitals enlarge and change, he develops pubic and other body hair, and his voice deepens, sometimes unevenly and with amusing effects. The hormonal changes affect his body shape, giving him growth spurts and changes in the contours and strength of his muscles. His hormones begin urging him toward sexual objects, and his masturbation now can result in orgasms and the ejaculation of semen. He might have "wet dreams," involuntary ejaculation at night. And his hormones might be changing his moods, so that (from a mother's perspective, especially) a sweet young boy becomes a surly teen.

Adults tend to see the adolescent boy's body as something precarious, in that liminal zone on the threshold between childhood and adulthood. Our science tells us about hormones in the adolescent boy, but our everyday experiences also show us the behavioral quirks and mood swings caused by "raging hormones." The adolescent male body threatens to swing out of control. So, in general, the adult society's view is that the adolescent male body is dangerous and in need of control, including self-control.

Our society has a long history of controlling the dangerous adolescent male body. The idea of adolescence and a name for that period in the life cycle were not formulated until the turn of the twentieth century, when they were explicated, most notably, in G. Stanley Hall's massive two-volume work entitled *Adolescence* (1904). But developing male bodies always went through the changes, even without the label.[4] Historian Carroll Smith-Rosenberg, for example, shows how advice manuals for young men in the Jacksonian period of the nineteenth century reveal the society's view of the young male body as a potentially dangerous thing that must come under self-control and regulation. For Smith-Rosenberg the advice about masturbation especially reveals anxieties and strategies about order and disorder, and about the need for self-control for the benefit of the individual boy's body as well as for the society.[5] Smith-Rosenberg shows how the social and political anxieties about the health of American society in the Jacksonian era became coded in this discourse about the male body, the perfect symbol of society.

Similarly, one can read through the successive editions of the *Handbook for Boys* and the *Handbook for Scoutmasters* and find what is to our eyes some rather amusing talk (and silence) about masturbation. At one Staff campfire, Pete talked about the fun he and other young Scouts had had looking at the section on masturbation across several editions of the *Handbook for Boys*. "Everyone knew the page number," laughed Pete, and the nods around the campfire told me that Pete was not the only man who had read with a combination of fascination and humor the ways the adult authors of the *Handbooks* squirmed around this topic.[6]

The very earliest statements in the *Handbook for Boys* come straight out of nineteenth-century notions of male sexuality. The section on "Health and Endurance," written by physician and YMCA officer George Fisher for the first *Handbook,* explains to boys that God has put into their bodies a "special fluid," the "sex fluid," that gives "tone to the muscles, power to the brain, and strength to the nerves." "When this fluid appears in a boy's body," writes Fisher,

> it works a wonderful change in him. His chest deepens, his shoulders broaden, his voice changes, his ideals are changed and enlarged. It gives him the capacity for deep feeling, for rich emotion. Pity the boy, therefore, who has wrong ideas of this important function, because they will lower his ideals of life. These organs actually secrete into the blood material that makes a boy manly, strong, and noble. Any habit which a boy has that causes this fluid to be discharged from the body tends to weaken his strength. . . .[7]

The *Handbooks* preserved these passages until the 1943 edition, when there was a subtle change. Still under the nineteenth-century heading of "Conservation" (i.e., of the body's special fluid), the *Handbook* discusses the changes the sex fluid makes in the boy's physical and moral culture. But this *Handbook* also acknowledges the likelihood of nocturnal emission that may be accompanied by a dream. "It is a perfectly normal experience," explain the authors, but the passage goes on to warn: "Boys need not and should not worry about these experiences. They are natural, but no steps should be taken to excite seminal emissions. That is masturbation. It's a bad habit. It should be fought against. It's something to keep away from. Keep control in sex matters. It's manly to do so. It's important for one's life, happiness, efficiency and the whole human race as well." After recommending cold baths to suppress unnatural urges, the *Handbook* closes with this advice: "Seek advice from wise, clean, strong men. If you feel you need special help you should talk the matter over frankly with your family physician or with your father."[8]

By the 1948 edition, the *Handbook* used by the first wave of baby boomers in the late 1950s, the nineteenth-century fluid conservation approach to adolescent male sexuality was gone, and in its place was the sort of advice a parent might hear from Dr. Benjamin Spock. The *Handbook* urges the boy to have regular medical checkups and to be thoroughly frank with the doctor. "Suppose you are worrying because you have 'wet dreams' or have practiced masturbation once in a while.

If it has happened, don't let it scare you. If it's a habit, break it! Sure, it takes courage and the best way is to keep busy with lots of work and play. But talk it over with your parents, religious leader or doctor; just open up to them and let them set you right." [9] The sixth edition, written by William Hillcourt and published in 1959, continued the reassuring tone, explaining that a "wet dream" is perfectly natural and healthy. "There are some boys who do not let nature have its own way with them," the *Handbook* continues, "but cause emissions themselves. This may do no physical harm, but may cause them to worry. If anything like this worries you, this is not unusual—just about all boys have the same problem." [10] Once again the authors recommend talking to a parent, physician, or spiritual advisor if the worrying continues.

By the eighth handbook, published in 1972, author Frederick L. Hines was acknowledging, "You may have questions about sexual matters such as nocturnal emissions (also called 'wet dreams'), masturbation, and even those strange feelings you may have." [11] Hines does not elaborate on those "strange feelings," but certainly he means heterosexual desire, perhaps even the strong feelings for other males that boys may take for signs of homosexuality. The ninth *Handbook* (1979), one again written by Hillcourt, abandons all mention of masturbation but still acknowledges that the "fluids" created by the "sex glands" may create "strange feelings" ("While all this is going on, you may be wondering what is happening to you.").[12] Boys were told to seek information about their developing bodies from a parent or religious leader or doctor, because "Information about sex you get from your friends may be in error." Later, under the discussion of what it means to be "morally straight," Hillcourt warns the boy that he is capable of becoming a father and that "God has given you this very high trust." Young men can destroy their lives by betraying that trust, writes Hillcourt, but when "you live up to the trust of fatherhood your sex life will fit into God's wonderful plan of creation." [13] Again Hillcourt recommends getting "proper sex education" and seeking advice from "the persons who helped you during your sexual growth," beginning with parents and including religious leaders and physicians.

If possible, the tenth (1990) edition of the *Handbook* has even less to say about the boy's developing body. In the chapter describing what it means to be "Physically Strong," the author merely states, "During the years you are a Scout, you are going through one of the most important growing periods of your life. You are getting taller. Your voice is becoming deeper. You are gaining strength and speed." [14] A later chapter on "Personal Development" devotes two pages to "sexual responsibility," explaining to the boy that "having sex is never a test of maturity," but that "true manliness" consists of acting responsibly toward women, toward children, toward one's beliefs ("For the followers of most religions, sex should take place only between married couples."), and toward oneself (i.e., avoid sexually transmitted diseases).[15] As always, the author recommends that the boy seek information and advice from a parent, religious leader, or sex educator. The eleventh (1998) edition of the *Handbook* drops even the 1990 "physically strong" acknowledgment of the boy's changing body but preserves the discussion of "sexual responsibility."[16] The masturbating Boy Scout looks in vain for any words of comfort or wisdom about this practice.

While the advice to behave responsibly is sound, the euphemisms and eventual silence about masturbation seem to deny what is most obvious to the adolescent boy—namely, that his body is changing and that he is feeling sexual drives wholly new to him and not a little exciting and scary at the same time. The more recent *Handbooks* emphasize keeping the body healthy and "physically strong" (as the Scout Oath has it), talking quite explicitly about the boy's body as something to be shaped and controlled. Training for strength, getting proper nourishment, keeping clean, getting the proper amount of rest and sleep, and avoiding all sorts of drugs require self-control.

As is often the case, when the adults turn silent on a matter of importance to the kids, the group's folklore steps in to provide an avenue for expressing thoughts that might be anxiety-producing or even taboo altogether. I noticed this in the two Senior meetings in the late 1990s, one where the Seniors sang for me their "Choke the Chicken" song and another where the Seniors baited me with the "What did you do last night, Jay?" question, which led immediately to their masturbation song. The great value of folklore is that it is impersonal. As a "traditional" form of cultural expression with no "author," folklore can make matters less personal and less threatening (both psychologically and socially). Humorous songs about masturbation make it a more communal, public, and impersonal event, thereby deflating some of the anxiety surrounding it.

We need to be clear on what masturbation means in this all-male folk group. Recall the fascination with menstruation in the Insane Day wordplay about the watermelon and elsewhere. Women have a clear marker for the transition from girl to woman, and many of the young women in these boys' worlds begin menstruating while the boys are still immature. The boys have no such clear marker of sexual maturity, though the ability to have an orgasm and ejaculate comes close. Immature boys can get some pleasure out of the rubbing involved with masturbation, but the real signal of maturity is ejaculation.

In his book on "rites of passage in male America," Ray Raphael presents a long piece of testimony from one of his informants, "Ralph W.," about the role of masturbation in the male folk group:

One year when I had just turned fourteen I went to summer camp where there were a whole bunch of us sleeping in a dormitory. At that age most of the guys were masturbating pretty regularly, so instead of trying to hide it they made it into a quasi-public event. In each room, posted on the wall, we had a "BTMS" chart—"Beat The Meat Sheet"—with everybody's name on it and the number of times they masturbated. . . . We actually managed to turn our horniness, which was a sort of curse we couldn't escape, into a status symbol. . . . The only problem for me with the "BTMS" was the first half of the summer, whenever I tried to masturbate, nothing happened. I was a little late in maturing and I didn't ejaculate. So there I was with nothing next to my name on the "BTMS"; it didn't count unless you could come. . . . Then finally, somewhere around the middle of the summer, I actually did it. I came. It felt great physically, plus I made it onto the "BTMS." There was a general feeling of satisfaction that I had finally joined the club.[17]

I have never interviewed the Seniors of Troop 49 about their masturbatory habits, but their songs tell me that this is on their minds and that they are going to recognize in a public performance a fact about their bodies and sexuality that the official organization ignores. Of course, the taboo nature of the topic adds to the excitement.[18]

I think there may also be some issue of control in the masturbation humor. The boy's body becomes the site of a contest of control, a contest between the adult leaders and the boys. The adolescent boys' folklore inverts the adult values as expressed in the *Handbook* and elsewhere. That is, whereas the organization stresses controlling the boy's body and working on the boy's acquiring self-control over his body, these songs are about being wildly out of control. Or maybe they assert the boy's right to control his body on his own terms. I heard one father tell a joke at the Staff campfire that I remembered hearing and telling as a Scout forty years earlier. An adult leader finds a boy masturbating in the shower and tells him to "stop that." The boy replies, "Sir, it's my soap and it's part of my body and I'll wash it as fast as I want to." The folklore reasserts the boy's control over his own body, and it is decidedly not the sort of self-control the authors of the *Handbook* had in mind.

As "Ralph W.'s" anecdote about the "BTMS" at camp suggests, other boys are an audience for the changing male body at Scout camp.

The age of the onset of puberty is extremely variable, but in most cases the youngest campers (ages eleven and twelve) still have the immature bodies of children, so the boys' bodies at camp run the whole developmental continuum. Boys are always on the lookout for signs of their own maturation—a pubic hair here, an underarm hair there, a whisker or two maybe—and are always measuring themselves against the boys older and younger than they. When the older boys develop beards, they usually decline to shave in camp, wearing their scraggly beards as visible evidence of mature masculinity.[19]

And it works the other way, unfortunately. The slowly maturing boy outpaced by his age mates can be teased (e.g., about his lame, peachfuzz of a beard), and the teasing juvenilization also tends to be a feminization, as male children and women share the status of not-men. To become a mature male is to become a not-child and a not-female. And this, it turns out, is not such an easy accomplishment.

The boys actually play with being "not female." The transvestitism in the Insane Day themed skits—beginning with the first year's "Gilligan's Island" theme (with its two female characters, Ginger and Mary Ann) through various other themes (e.g., Princess Leia from *Star Wars*) and up to the most recent theme based on *Austin Powers: The Spy Who Shagged Me* (with two female characters)—appears both familiar and strange to the observer: familiar because transvestitism is common in the dramatic skits performed by the members of all-male institutions (boarding schools, the military, fraternities, the Scouts) and strange because one wonders why any fourteen- or fifteen-year-old boy would dress up like a girl for his friends. Gender and sexuality identity seem so precarious for the adolescent male that one wonders why any Senior would upset the performance of heterosexual masculinity by dressing in drag. What saves the meaning of the performance is the play frame— in this case, the dramatic skit frame, in which it is understood that the events within the skit do not represent what they would if the frame were different ("this is play," versus "this is ritual," or "this is everyday life," or "this is how I'd like to dress when we have sex"). The play frame derives its humor from the symbolic inversion—a male becomes a female. And, as anthropologists are fond of pointing out, symbolic inversions actually strengthen accepted meanings. The Senior's dressing in drag is funny precisely because we know he is a male, and in some cases he is a hypermasculine male.[20] The inversion and our taking it as "nonsense" help solidify the "common sense" that these Seniors are heterosexual males. So the risk for the Senior dressing in drag is minimal, so long as everyone concerned maintains the play frame.

The observer cannot help noticing that the boys who dress as females seem to put more into the performance than the mere play frame requires. Most of the Seniors I've seen dress as females work hard on the illusion, carefully selecting the dresses and wigs and speaking in falsetto voices. This is great fun, naturally; the Scouts find the performances extremely funny, as do fellow Seniors and Staff. Still, I am not sure how to explain fully the pleasure some of the Seniors seem to take in performing femininity.

The Seniors' drag performances in the Insane Day skit bring me back to a central theme in this excursus. How does the Boy Scout camp work to create the heterosexual adolescent male? One of the consequences of feminist theory, the intellectual arm of the women's movement begun in the 1960s, has been the widespread recognition that both the masculine and the feminine are largely social constructions. This perspective does not deny that there are (on average) real biological differences between male and female; the perspective simply holds that most of the differences we perceive between "masculine" and "feminine" are our own creations through culture. Even the biology here is very complicated, as there are true hermaphrodites with dual or ambiguous genitals, and the more we know about genetics, the more we realize that our sex (as opposed to our gender) sits on a continuum rather than in a simple binary opposition. Most of the generalizations we want to make about men and women need to be modified by the sort of phrase I used above—"on average"—because we have good reasons to believe that, in many matters of sex and gender, the within-group variation is at least as large as the between-group variation. The average man may be stronger than the average woman in our society, for example, but there are many women stronger than many men.

Feminist and other theories have led us to the realization that male heterosexuality, the sort of masculinity our society idealizes, is not a biological given.[21] The "world-openness" of human biology means that humans are capable of a wide range of sexual behaviors and a wide range of ways to "perform" gender. Until a few decades ago, the heterosexual male was the "unmarked" category in American society, the quintessential human against which the alternatives (child, female, homosexual male) had to be defined. Categories are unmarked because we tend to take them as natural, as not subject to social, cultural construction. All this has changed.

At the turn of the twenty-first century, we now understand male heterosexuality to be a social construction. One of the main "projects," let's say, of the Boy Scout camp is the creation of the heterosexual male. Let me explain each of these statements in turn.

The "fragility of masculinity," as Michael Kaufman calls it,[22] is a social "problem" because the basis of mainstream masculinity in the United States is ideological, not biological. A feminist reading of Freud makes clear just how fragile is this construction. Why begin with Freud? Despite Freud's nineteenth-century bourgeois Viennese and masculine biases, psychoanalytic theory and method remain the most sophisticated tools we have for understanding patriarchy, capitalist society, and the psychologies of both men and women within society; the point is to discover how *both* men and women internalize and consent to patriarchal arrangements. The Oedipus complex and its solution in American society are at the root of patriarchy; put differently, patriarchal culture and the fact that "women mother" (Nancy Chodorow's phrase) work together in a system that creates a certain strength in the Oedipus complex and that favors a "solution" that perpetuates patriarchy.

Crucial to this reading is Freud's understanding of the human infant as essentially bisexual in nature and possibilities. The infant is "polymorphously perverse," as the phrase goes, and both gender and sexuality must be constructed out of this raw material. Thus, all sexualities are constructed through an interaction between developmental constants and culture.[23] For Chodorow and other psychoanalytic feminists, boys and girls face crucially different projects in the developmental drama of separating from the first object of attachment and identification—the mother.[24] In the boy's separation from his mother lies the root separation of intimacy from sexuality. Peter Lyman relies on Chodorow's account, for example, to note that masculine identity arises from the repression of the son's erotic bond to his mother. "With this repression," explains Lyman, "the son's capacity for intimacy and commitment is devalued as feminine behavior."[25] The separated son's sense of powerlessness has a solution not available to the separated daughter—namely, he can identify with the father. "Masculinity," writes Kaufman, "is a reaction against passivity and powerlessness and with it comes a repression of all the desires and traits that a given society defines as negatively passive or as resonant of passive experiences."[26]

Masculine development is a far more "precarious achievement" than is feminine development, for it is based on a negative, on a lack.[27] Both girls and boys must establish independence of identity from the mother, but for the boy this involves a radical separation from the mother. The Oedipal fascination, then identification, with the father seems to be a solution in which the boy turns his back on the feminine source of power and turns toward the father's promise of the phallus as power.[28] But, as Stephen Frosh (following Lacan) says, "[T]he phallus is itself fraudulent; there is no mastery that is complete. . . . Hunting for a centre for his masculinity," continues Frosh, "the boy looks towards the father; but what he discovers is that while masculinity presents an appearance of integration and strength, its inner coordinates will always remain mysterious and unavailable to articulation. Instead, masculinity comes to be defined experientially as a movement *away* from something—from maternal intimacy and dependence—rather than towards something with a clear and vibrant content of its own."[29]

The Oedipal male's repudiation of intimacy and dependence as "feminine," and hence "other," has dire consequences for male sexuality, according to this model. The male sees intimacy and dependence as dangerous, so sexual desire becomes fearful. Sexual desire threatens masculine autonomy, rationality, and control.[30] Men can stabilize their identities only through sexual performances featuring emotional distance, control, and independence. True male sexuality tends to require activity rather than passivity, independence rather than dependence, detachment rather than engagement, and the status of penetrator rather than penetratee; hence, male sexuality is centered on the penis.

Males in groups create customs and patterns of communication meant to bolster this fragile construction. Men's experiences with other men—from the earliest social experiences in play groups—are marked by hierarchy, competition, and aggression. Boys learn to negotiate a place within this competitive hierarchy, and the folklore and other customary behavior of the male group serve to deflect real aggression and violence into the symbolic realm. Elaborate rituals of verbal dueling and other "stylized" forms of verbal and physical aggression take the place of real aggression. Male friendship groups, in a sense, are safe havens in an otherwise dangerous world of male-male interactions. The unstated rules of the stylized interactions become the basis for the safe haven. As Lyman puts it, "[T]he eros detached from sexuality is attached to rules, not to male friends; the male bond consists of an erotic toward rules. . . ."[31]

The hierarchy of the male friendship group requires some performances of passivity in relation to others, and this passivity is both comforting (it provides safety within the group) and anxiety-producing (it requires an unmasculine, hence feminine, performance). The homology between the dependence required of intimacy in sexual relations and the dependence required in close friendships heightens the anxiety. "There is a constant tension between activity and passivity" in the institutions of "male bonding and buddying," explains Kaufman, and it is crucial to the performance of masculinity in the male friendship group that the passivity not be interpreted as feminine.[32] The folklore of the heterosexual male group, therefore, serves the repression of the male's bisexuality, which means the repression of the feminine and homosexual potentials. In practice, the joking and verbal play of the male group make the homosexual and the woman the targets of disapproval; the folklore constructs an active, powerful, heterosexual masculinity at the expense of women (sexism and misogyny) and of gay men (heterosexism and homophobia).

The fragility of the construction, maintenance, and constant repair of masculinity means that the boy and then the man must constantly "prove" his masculinity. Masculinity is never a state comfortably obtained and occupied; each day sees a new onslaught of assaults and tests. Masculinity is a project never complete.

It is the "precarious achievement" of masculinity, as Frosh puts it, that is the central condition of men's lives.[33] Male friendship has a peculiar role in this fragile construction. On the one hand, male friendship can solidify one's heterosexual masculinity, but male friendship also always poses threats to heterosexual masculinity. The management of male friendship becomes, therefore, a major project for men in groups. Men need a "frame" for understanding passivity and intimacy.[34] Put differently, men who are trying to sustain a fragile heterosexual masculinity must understand their passivity and intimacy (such as they are) as not sexual. Typically, men's friendship groups do this in several ways, such as hypermasculine performances, from the verbal (stories, jokes, etc.) to the physical (e.g., playfighting). The men's bodies must be "managed" according to this heterosexual frame, too. Rituals of touching are as "stylized" as the verbal dueling. Playfighting, stylized pats on the butt between athletes, and so on permit the men to touch one another in sometimes intimate ways without permitting a sexual frame for interpreting the touching. Casual nudity in the presence of the other men is another way to establish a frame of heterosexual intimacy; the frame sends the metamessage "I can be naked in front of you because we are both heterosexual and not potential sex partners." The nudity declares that the men are not the object of "the heterosexual male gaze" usually cast upon women; that is, the men will not be feminized by that gaze. "Looking" must be managed carefully. As Deborah Tannen and other ethnographers of nonverbal communication note, even intimate heterosexual men tend to avoid eye contact unless meaning to threaten or intimidate another man.[35] Between males, eye contact signals either a threat or a sexual interest. This is the delicate framing that is threatened by the presence of gay men in the showers, whether in a college dorm, on an athletic team, or in the military. The real problem created by permitting openly gay men in the military is not one of sex; it is one of the fragility of male friendship, a "bonding and buddying" seen as crucial to one's survival in battle.[36]

Given the fragility and difficulty of the project of male friendship, the prospects of a straight man's friendship with a gay man face even greater difficulties. The straight man who bonds easily and intimately with a gay man is practicing "gender treachery." He is, writes Patricia Hopkins, a "genuinely subversive heterosexual man, a kind of gender traitor himself, whose identity is not coextensive with his assignment as a man. Although comfortable with himself, he wouldn't mind being gay, or mind being a woman—those are not the categories by which he defines, or wants to define, his personhood."[37] Beyond his feeling "comfortable" enough to withstand questions about his own masculinity, the straight man wanting to bond with a gay man does not have available to him some of the conversational tools straight men have to bond as heterosexuals. Homophobic humor is out, though misogynist humor might be used by both parties to signal similarity (they are not women). The stylized rituals of touching and looking need even more delicate management. The crossover codes of camp can be a conversational resource for the friendship to the degree that they can share the code and use it in creating their intimate, dyadic traditions.[38]

Think now about the Boy Scout camp's "project" of turning boys into heterosexual males. The misogyny and homophobia of the boys' (and sometimes the men's) folk cultures now make sense as strategic moves to define boys as not female and not feminine males (i.e., homosexuals). The daily misogyny of the folk humor and the large-scale, ritualized misogyny of the Poison Pit serve to distance the developing boys from their mothers and from the dependence those mothers represent. The homophobic humor, likewise, distances the boys from the feminine. At every turn, the folk culture of the boys and men at camp works to repress the feminine.

There are potential social costs arising from this misogyny and homophobia. The boys and men may carry home from camp attitudes that denigrate women, and they may mistreat the women in their public and private lives. The homophobia reinforced by camp culture may have unhappy consequences in the home world. The boys might act on these beliefs by being verbally or even physically abusive toward gay men. Moreover, the psychoanalytic perspective sees additional psychological "costs" of this repression of the feminine elements in the boys' naturally bisexual selves.

One of the troop fathers said at the end of a brief joking event about farts, "You know, the only things we seem to talk about up here are sex and farts." The group laughed in acknowledgment of the truth of his observation, but let me take this observation seriously: why is there so much folk speech at the camp about farts and feces?[39]

First, we must admit that there is an extraordinary amount of talk about farts and feces in Troop 49's camp. The central icon of the folk speech is the KYBO. The Senior held responsible for keeping the KYBO working (making sure there is toilet paper there, making sure there are cans of campfire ashes for spreading on the feces to suppress the smell and discourage flies) is called the "KYBO King," and he might have an assistant called the "Prince of Poop." Over the years, there have been various sorts of humorous signs up at the KYBO. One was a pilfered (maybe found) Pacific Gas and Electric sign, "Warning: Gas Leak," and written on the cardboard that covers the two seats have been such mottoes as "Usonia Food Fund—Please Donate Generously" and "No deposit, no return." One KYBO King took a Kellogg's Raisin Bran box and marked it up to indicate "two scoops" of ashes— "Only you can prevent forest flies." The broken ax handle used a few years for distributing the feces as they pile up was labeled "high KYBO floater," and a broken canoe paddle used for the same purposes a few years later had a face with a large tongue drawn on it.

The KYBO signs confirm that a good deal of the folk speech at camp connects food and feces. In the 1970s, when the troop relied heavily on U.S. Department of Agriculture surplus canned food, a particularly nasty beef with gravy was served over instant mashed potatoes or rice. Some Seniors nicknamed the meal "SOS" ("shit on snow"). For one Insane Day, a dad wanted to use Baby Ruth candy bars as "turds" for the Poison Pit. Recall, too, the series of patrol commercial skits, each featuring garbage or feces. The Scouts are not the first group to link food and feces; there are many examples in children's folklore and worries about the contamination of food by feces extend well into adult male folklore.[40]

Other elements of the troop's folk speech contain this same fixation on the anal. The upper assembly area is called Upper Ass, and the troop regularly hikes to Big Bare Ass Slide and Little Bare Ass Slide. A stern lecture is called an ass-chew.

How can we account for this anal fixation in the Scout camp's folklore?

As a beginning, we might observe an affinity between what psychoanalytic theory calls "anal-erotic character" and the nature of the Boy Scouts as an organization. In this regard, the Boy Scouts typify a larger cultural pattern. Compared cross-culturally, American parents tend to socialize the child's anal system earlier than most other societies; that is, we toilet train our children earlier and more forcefully. This pattern varies across class and ethnicity, and toilet training has become a great deal more relaxed in the past three decades. In general, though, psychologists and anthropologists see the average, middle-class American parents as rather anxious about toilet matters. Look at our bathrooms and at the advertisements for bathroom cleaners, and you will see evidence of our cultural fixation on cleanliness, a key element of which is flushing human feces out of sight.

Even within this general culture of concern about maintaining cleanliness and about socializing the anal system, an organization like the Boy Scouts displays many of the character traits we consider anal-erotic. Freud wrote a brief essay entitled "Character and Anal Eroticism" in 1908, in which he identified three character traits—orderliness, parsimony, and obstinacy—that may be the result of a fixation on the erotogenic nature of the anal canal.[41] Ernest Jones later expanded Freud's catalog of traits, arguing that sometimes it can be a *process* (such as a "moral" or tedious task) that symbolizes defecation. At other times, certain *objects* (most notably dirt, dung, bodily excretions, money, and children) become the "unconscious copro-symbols" onto which the individual transfers his or her feelings about the act of defecation.[42] William Menninger continued the description of the anal-erotic character with his 1943 essay correlating six infantile events in the anal phase with both positive and negative expressions in adult character.[43]

The Boy Scouts of America is an organization that values highly those traits that Menninger and others would call anal-erotic. Several of the twelve points of the Scout Law—"A Scout is Thrifty," "A Scout is Trustworthy," "A Scout is Clean"—are exactly those that Menninger considers socially acceptable anal-erotic traits. Moreover, the institution heavily emphasizes duty ("On my honor, I will do my best to do my duty . . ."), which Menninger links with the anal phase of infant megalomania. The Boy Scout *Handbook* is a document rich in anal-erotic values, devoting many pages to orderliness and cleanliness. The collecting behavior that pervades the institution is also an anal-erotic trait. "All collectors are anal-erotics," insists Jones, "and the objects collected are nearly always topical copro-symbols."[44] The system of advancement in the Boy Scouts depends upon the boy's collecting badges, and many of the badges require that the boy collect something—such as birds, rocks, stamps, coins, or leaves.[45]

The adult men at camp reinforce the anal-erotic traits with their constant attention to cleanliness, orderliness, and duty, but the boys' own folklore and customs confirm that everything at camp works toward the anal-erotic. The six-pack of cans of Coke that is the treasure in the Treasure Hunt can be read as a copro-symbol of feces; usually, the Cokes are buried in the sand, like the boys' own feces on a hike, but one year the Cokes were hidden among the rocks in one of the dams. Indeed, the Treasure Hunt itself is a complex ritual full of anal-erotic symbolism. Jones and Menninger both see "interest in the discovery of treasure-trove" as a trait that combines several anal-erotic impulses.[46] The size and shape of the cans of Coke could be seen as similar to animal droppings, completing the feces = treasure equation.[47] Note, as well, that the treasure is always Coca-Cola ("Coke: It's the Real Thing!"), never Fresca or 7-Up or root beer or even Pepsi. This is not an insignificant detail, given the phonetic pattern common in words associated with feces—for example, cloaca, colon, caca (or kaka), KYBO. In fact, the two favorite beverages of this group—Coke and cocoa—fit this pattern.[48] The Nugget Auction continues the anal-erotic symbolism of the Treasure Hunt.[49]

The male folk culture's fixation on farts (or *flatus,* in the polite nomenclature of the psychoanalytic profession) is an important part of this anal-erotic complex of traits. Menninger argues that attitudes toward flatulence are correlated with both expulsive pleasure (with occasional soiling) and aggressive defiance.[50] The fartlore of this troop displays the pleasurable and defiant nature of flatulence.[51] The folklore includes the wordplay ("Q: Who cut the cheese? A: Why, do you want to lick the knife?"), pranks (e.g., lighting farts with a match, or at least telling stories about such events), and assorted insults. Farting in the group can be aggressive and hostile, as in those cases I have recounted where the Seniors used farting to undermine the serious agenda of a Senior/Staff meeting. Even so, the troop also has a customary aesthetic about farting in Senior meetings. Recently, one Senior raised his leg dramatically to fart while another Senior was speaking, and one of the Staff members had to tell him not to make such a disruptive show of it; "Just do it," he advised, "that's the Troop 49 way." So emitting a "classy fart" (i.e., without drawing attention to it) can be read as an act of bonding.

And then there were the nine classifications of a fart Pete recited for me at one of the Staff campfires:

> There's the pip, the poop, and the anti-poop,
> The fizz, the fuzz, and the fizzy-fuzz,
> The ring-tail, tear-ass, and the rattler.

Menninger cites a version of this same item in his discussion of "direct carryovers primitively expressed" from the infantile phase of curiosity.[52]

What are we to make of all this folk speech pointing to the anal-erotic character of the Boy Scout camp culture? Those who object to the psychoanalytic approach might make the case that in long-term camping the disposal of waste is a real problem, one that creates a certain amount of anxiety that the folk speech and humor play with in order to reduce the anxiety. There's some truth to that view, but most of this speech play around food, feces, and flatus can be found in the male friendship groups far away from the woods. And if this were merely a matter of living in the woods, then we would expect to find the same amount of food/feces and fart play at an all-girls camp. There is very little ethnographic study of girls' camps, but the work some of my students have done over the years about Girl Scout camp confirms my suspicion that the elements of the anal-erotic complex simply do not appear in the girls' folklore. It's a "male thing," say the women I've talked with about this, to be so obsessed with feces and farting.

I puzzled over this for a long time before my reading of Freud's "History of an Infantile Neurosis" (1918) helped me see the meanings of this anal-erotic complex in the context of feminist psychoanalytic theory about the construction and defense of fragile masculinity. This long case study—a compelling piece of writing, I might add—is more commonly know as "The Wolf Man," owing to the striking dream reported by Freud's patient. Key to Freud's analysis was the patient's report of his dream of seeing white wolves sitting in a tree outside his bedroom window and Freud's slow, methodical unraveling of the connections among the wolves, their whiteness, the open bedroom windows, the bare tree, the patient's early seduction by his sister, his mother's intestinal disturbances, his poor relations with his father, his report of witnessing the primal scene between his parents, and his fear of castration.

Freud discovered in this dream the transformation of the male bi-sexual self (a notion that Freud long held but developed only in 1905 in *Three Essays on the Theory of Sexuality*) into a self that settles upon the masculine at the expense of the feminine. Two of the patient's symptoms—his dealings with money and his intestinal troubles at the time he came to Freud—confirmed Freud's ideas about the anal-erotic character.[53] The patient was excessively fond of "anal jokes and exhibitions." Freud deftly saw that the anus was the organ by which his patient identified with the "feminine impulses of tenderness."[54] The patient's repressed feminine attitude toward men surfaced as intestinal symptoms. Under these conditions, the patient's feces acquired increasing symbolic importance. Feces, money, and baby are all equivalent expressions of *gift*, a feature also common with castration. The triumph of the patient's masculinity is illusory: "We are not confronted by a triumphant masculine sexual trend, but only by a passive one and a struggle against it."[55] The patient's obsessional neurosis, his problems with money, his extreme intestinal distress, and his unhappy relationship with his father are all the prices he paid for the repression of his feminine side.

Returning to the Boy Scout camp, we see that these boys are "normals" in a way Freud's patient was not. But there are too many suggestive analogies between the Wolf Man symptoms and the Boy Scout expressive behavior to dismiss the possibility that we are witnessing in the Boy Scout rituals and speech a slightly healthier version of the transformed symbols rooted in the repression of the feminine qualities of the self in service of the creation of a heterosexual male identity. The symptoms are sometimes verbal, as in the speech play; sometimes nonverbal, as in the Treasure Hunt; and sometimes somatic, as in the occasional intestinal problems (gastritis, diarrhea, colitis, constipation) the boys talk about.

This anal–erotic complex is a "cost" the boys pay for the repression of the feminine element in the naturally bisexual self. The Scout camp's project of creating the heterosexual male, therefore, has costs for women (in the misogyny), costs for gay men (in the homophobia), and costs for the boys themselves. These three costs are connected in important ways. It is unlikely, for example, that heterosexual men will abandon their misogyny and homophobia until they reclaim for themselves some androgynous balance of the masculine and feminine in their own identities and performances of gender.

An interesting possibility for growth of this sort exists in the Boy Scout camp, where the boys must assume both the traditionally male tasks and the traditionally female tasks of everyday living. Boys cook food for and serve other boys, for example, but I also have in mind the emotional and other work boys do for one another in the absence of women, who usually do that emotional work. A boy injured in a game may be told to "walk it off" like a man, of course, but in some cases he is ministered to and comforted. Seniors and older Scouts (like a Patrol Leader) might be more likely to comfort a homesick boy than to ridicule him. Even certain sorts of caring touching—usually in the form of first aid—break the usual pattern of stylized, aggressive male touching at camp. One Senior's careful attention to the feet of another could be framed safely as an act of medical care, but the touching is still remarkable in its contrast to the usual playfighting frame for the boys' touching one another.

Thinking about the various meanings of the boy's body at the Scout camp and the ways the boy's body comes to be seen as a symbol of American society leads inevitably to the other two "G's" that have plagued the Boy Scouts in the form of lawsuits. The "two bodies" perspective also reminds us that the boy's body is a "contested" zone, the site of a struggle (between adults and between adults and the teens themselves) over the meanings of a teenage boy's body. I hope it will not break too much the rhythm of the daily camp narrative to offer one more excursus on the heels of this one before returning to the story of the encampment. The debates over whether the Boy Scouts should admit openly gay boys and men and whether the organization should admit girls and women can benefit greatly, I think, from these ruminations on the two bodies at the Scout camp.

The "Problem" of Gays and Girls in the Boy Scouts

In the spring of 1980 in Oakland, California, Skyline High School senior Timothy Curran made brief headlines by insisting upon his right, as a gay man, to take a male date to the senior prom. The story briefly got good press, but the generally liberal and tolerant San Francisco Bay area had larger and more dramatic stories to tell about the emergence of gay rights activism in Northern California in the early 1980s. The media's disclosure of Curran's homosexuality, however, drew the attention of the leaders of the East Bay's Mount Diablo Council of the Boy Scouts of America, who were not pleased that an Eagle Scout and registered Scout leader in the Council was declaring openly his homosexuality. Curran received notice that his membership in the organization was being terminated due to his homosexuality, a condition the organization (he was told) considered immoral and inappropriate as a role model for young men. With the assistance of the American Civil Liberties Union (ACLU) and the National Gay Task Force, Curran filed suit against the Boy Scouts of America, asking for his reinstatement as a Scout leader and for $520,000 in damages.[1]

The case dragged on for a decade, during which time the national leadership of the Boy Scouts of America, headquartered in Irving,

Texas, held fast to its position that there was no place for homosexual boys or men in the organization. In November of 1990, Los Angeles Superior Court Judge Sally G. Disco, who was hearing the Curran case, handed down a ruling that "the Boy Scouts were a business and thus subject to state civil rights law, which bars discrimination on the basis of sexual orientation, race or religion."[2] That ruling appeared to be a blow to the Boy Scouts' assertion that it is a private organization constitutionally protected in its rights of association and membership. But in her May 1991 decision, Judge Disco held that the constitutional right to engage in association with others and to exclude unwanted members from such association took precedence over California state law barring discrimination.[3] Curran and the ACLU appealed Disco's decision.

An article in the *San Francisco Chronicle* captured the Boy Scouts' position:

> The official position of the Boy Scouts is that homosexuality is inconsistent with scout oaths and laws to be "morally straight" and "clean in word and deed," said Marty Cutrone, director of field service for the Boy Scouts in the San Francisco Bay Area Council.
>
> "We just don't feel homosexuals present the right kind of role model," Cutrone said. "We are a private organization aimed at traditional families."[4]

The Boy Scouts' claim to being a private organization faces some reasonable skepticism. While the organization receives no federal assistance (beyond its charter from Congress in 1916, not a small gesture), it relies upon public benefits in several forms. First, the organization receives support from the United Way, which itself has a nondiscrimination policy. Indeed, the United Fund of the San Francisco Bay Area decided in 1991 that the Boy Scouts' policy violated the United Way ban on discrimination, and the charitable organization withdrew subsidies to local councils.[5] The matter of funding became even more complicated in the Bay area when the San Francisco Board of Supervisors used the city's considerable financial dealings with the Bank of America to put pressure on the bank to withhold corporate funding from the Boy Scouts.[6]

The Boy Scouts also benefits from certain state and local governments and governmental agencies. In the fall of 1991, the school boards in Oakland and in San Francisco banned Scouting programs that operated on school property during school hours.[7] In 1992, the California Highway Patrol (CHP) had to reconsider its sponsorship of the Explorer Scout program that permitted 217 boys to learn about law enforcement by "working alongside CHP employees," and similar Explorer programs in the El Cajon and Laguna Beach police departments had to face the same issue.[8] In 1998, the Berkeley Waterfront Commission voted to withdraw the free docking an Explorer Sea Scouts post had enjoyed at the Berkeley Marina for sixty years, citing the city's clear ban on discrimination on the basis of sexual orientation.[9]

All these cases are a subset of a larger set of legal cases that were argued in the courts as part of the culture wars of the 1990s, wars largely between an "orthodox" side fighting in defense of traditional values and a "progressive" side arguing for greater tolerance for the diversity of American customs and values.[10] The case law being made in the Boy Scout cases addresses the right of private individuals and organizations to discriminate on the basis of values. Thus, the courts have had to address the rights of student religious organizations and prayer groups to use public school meeting facilities, the rights of churches to require their employees to belong to the religion or to subscribe to a particular moral code, the rights of landlords to refuse to rent to unmarried adults living together, and so on. Is the Boy Scouts of America a private organization, the courts asked themselves, and if so, does it have a right to limit its membership to those who subscribe to its announced values?

Through the 1990s, different courts came to different conclusions on this question. In early March of 1998, a New Jersey appeals court ruled in the case of James Dale, an Eagle Scout and Assistant Scoutmaster who had been barred from the Scouts in 1990 when his Rutgers University newspaper mentioned that Dale is gay.[11] The New Jersey court held that the Boy Scouts "are essentially a public accommodation like a hotel or restaurant" and that they must adhere to the state's antidiscrimination law. But the judge went even further in his opinion:

> "There is absolutely no evidence before us, empirical or otherwise, supporting a conclusion that a gay Scoutmaster, solely because he is a homosexual, does not possess the strength of character necessary to properly care for or to impart B.S.A. humanitarian ideals to the young boys in his charge," Judge James M. Harbey wrote. . . . "Plaintiff's exemplary journey through the Boy Scouts of America ranks is testament that these stereotypical notions about homosexuals must be rejected," the judge wrote.[12]

Meanwhile, things were not going as well for Tim Curran's case in California. Later in March of 1998, the California Supreme Court, considering together the Curran case and the case of the Randall twins (the atheists discussed in the excursus on God), held unanimously that "under California's 1959 civil rights law, the Scouts are not a business establishment and so are free, as is any private club, to set membership policies as they see fit."[13] Hence, reasoned the California court, the Boy Scouts can bar homosexuals and atheists from membership. The court declared that "it was not making a moral or ethical judgment on the Scouts' policies,"[14] but the attorney for the organization took the decision as such an endorsement. "'I think it's still true that a majority of Americans describe themselves as members of religious groups which hold that homosexuality is immoral,' [Boy Scout attorney George] Davidson said. 'The Boy Scouts is committed to bringing the values of the oath of law [*sic*] to youth the best way they know how.'"[15]

With conflicting opinions offered by the California and New Jersey Supreme Courts on what sort of organization the Boy Scouts of America is, observers in 1998 waited for a case to get to the U.S. Supreme Court. That Court declined in December of 1998 to consider the case of the gay police officer from El Cajon, California, who sued the Boy Scouts for banning him from a leadership position in an Explorer post emphasizing law enforcement.[16] But in 1999, the Court agreed to hear the New Jersey case.

Meanwhile, the national office of the Boy Scouts of America, buoyed by the general drift of the court decisions throughout the 1990s, had stepped up its purge of not only homosexual boys and leaders, but also their sympathizers. In February of 1992, a troop in San Jose, California, defied the national office by adopting a resolution renouncing the policy of discrimination against gay members.[17] The national office moved immediately against the troop, threatening to revoke its charter. "Our organization charters units that adhere to our rules," explained a spokesman for the Boy Scouts, "and if a group doesn't agree with them, then we have no choice but to revoke their charter. . . . We can't let some little troop go off on its own and make its own rules."[18] The "little troop," in turn, invoked Scouting principles to defend its stand:

> In San Jose, the scoutmaster, Michael Cahn, said the 26-member troop would not back down. "We feel that if you see something that's wrong and you ignore it, then you're part of the problem," Mr. Cahn said. "We feel the national scouting organization is wrong for their anti-gay stand." . . .
>
> Mr. Cahn said that there were no homosexuals in his troop, and that no parents had complained about the resolution. David Williams, a 17-year-old seeking the top rank, Eagle Scout, said: "The

Constitution says all men are created equal. So I don't see any reason why we should discriminate against homosexuals."[19]

The Boy Scout purge included Dave Rice, a sixty-nine-year-old veteran Scout leader from Petaluma, California. Rice, a heterosexual who has been in Scouting for fifty-nine years and was a Redwood District Scout executive for sixteen of those years, was booted from the organization for being "a visible part of the campaign to get the Boy Scouts to end their exclusion of gay youngsters and adults."[20] Rice had not given much thought to the question until 1980, when the Curran case hit the papers. A Scoutmaster himself then, Rice "wondered what he'd do if a gay boy came to him." Working with gay and lesbian fellow workers for the National Park Service at Fort Mason and Fort Point led Rice to the realization that "they were just like everyone else," and by 1991 he concluded that he had to do something about the policy. "While making clear his deep love for Scouting," explains the newspaper account of the press conference he finally called after exhausting the Boy Scout appeal process, "he expressed concern that the movement's administration has fallen under the spell of the 'religious right.' And he singled out what he considers to be a dangerous new BSA tactic. Last spring, its leaders told Unitarian Universalist churches, which sponsor Scout troops, that they may not verse the boys in the denomination's belief that there's nothing wrong with homosexuality."[21] Indeed, the Boy Scouts eventually punished the Unitarian Universalist Church and its Scout members by revoking the religious medal boys can earn.

Rice and the "little troop" in San Jose were not the only ones to resist the Boy Scout policy in the 1990s. In October of 1992, three San Francisco Bay area men—Ken MacPherson, William Boyce Mueller (grandson of William D. Boyce, the Chicago publisher credited with organizing the group that founded the Boy Scouts of America), and Allan Shore—formed an organization called Forgotten Scouts, "a group for gay former Scouts and those who support their cause." It joined the resisting landscape that already included a more radical group called Queer Scouts, which staged a "kiss-in" on July 3, 1991, in front of the San Francisco regional headquarters of the BSA.[22]

By the end of the 1990s, then, the legal situation was this. While the Supreme Court of the United States had not spoken definitively on the matter, the supreme court of the most populous state had agreed with the Boy Scouts that it was a private organization that could discriminate against homosexuals and atheists. Outside of a few communities where gay and lesbian activists have economic and political clout, most local governments and private corporations have been able to support the Boy Scouts without getting into legal trouble for violating anti-discrimination policies. Meanwhile, the Boy Scouts continued to banish from the organization any individuals or groups (including a whole religious denomination) that make a public attempt to criticize or undermine the official policy banning gay men and boys from membership.

While the case law on attempts by girls to break the gender barrier in the Boy Scouts is much thinner than the case law on religion and homosexuality, adult claimants seem to have made some inroads. Actually, women have had a toe in the Boy Scout tent for several years. The Explorer program was created in the 1930s in response to the need to create a program still attractive to boys after they reached high school (ages fourteen to eighteen). While some Explorer posts operated like troops, many were specialized around an activity (Sea Scouts, Air Scouts) or around a vocation (e.g., law enforcement). In 1969, the Explorer program became a coeducational program. Its successor, the Venturing program, accepts young men and women ages fourteen through twenty.[23] (The 1999 Annual Report Membership Summary on the BSA website records 202,486 Venturers, but without a gender breakdown.) So for many years now, there have been young women in the Boy Scouts, in a way. Older women have also been involved in Scouting as the den mothers of Cub Scout dens, the small groups that combine into a pack, usually led by a male Scout volunteer. Despite the presence of women in the organization, the Boy Scouts always stood strong on three points: girls cannot enter the Boy Scouts before age fourteen (really, the completion of eighth grade), girls cannot earn Eagle Scout, and a woman cannot be a Scoutmaster. Again, the presence of a heterosexual male role model seems to be the key quality the organization wants in a Scoutmaster and in its other adult leaders.

Lawsuits in the 1990s challenged all three of these principles. Ken Nelson, a Scoutmaster in Quincy, California, organized a troop in early 1991 and included (with the eager consent of the boys) seven girls, ages nine to fourteen, two of whom are his own daughters.[24] The Reno-based Nevada Area Council discovered this and rescinded the girls' memberships. The ACLU consulted with Nelson about suing the BSA. The girls did not want to join the Girl Scouts. "'I got bored in the Girl Scouts,' say [sic] Andrea Nelson, 14. 'All we did was sew buttons and sell cookies.'"[25] Her father added: "'I got my first job because I was an Eagle Scout . . . and this is an opportunity I want my daughters to have.

I think their [the BSA's] attitude stinks.'"[26] Meanwhile, an eight-year-old girl, Margo Mankes, of Miami, Florida, sued to attend the five-day summer camp for Cub Scouts her brothers were attending.[27] A Cub pack had admitted her, but the Boy Scouts canceled her membership, saying "no girls allowed." A U.S. district court denied her petition to force the Scouts to let her attend camp.

If the younger girls are having a tough time breaking the gender barrier of the Boy Scouts, their mothers and other adult women are having better luck. In response to several lawsuits, the Boy Scouts decided in February of 1988 to begin permitting women to be adult volunteer leaders in the Boy Scouts. As Michael Kimmel argues in *Psychology Today,* it is unlikely that the Boy Scouts has given in on this point because the leadership has had a conversion experience so that they now believe that women can be just as effective and appropriate leaders of boys as can men.[28] Rather, the national office cited the "costs" of litigation in time and money and must have concluded that this was an issue on which they could lose in court. Thus, the national office decided it would be better to make the change than to have one (possibly even broader) forced on it by the courts. Then, too, there is the fact that there is a shortage of adult male volunteers; perhaps the change of heart has more to do with the need for volunteer leaders than with issues of gender equality.[29] The BSA's action suggests that the organization prefers even a female leader as a role model for boys to a homosexual male one.

Still, girls eight to fourteen cannot be Cub Scouts or Boy Scouts, and Venture crews cannot be attached to a Boy Scout troop (hence, female members of these Venture crews cannot earn Eagle). So, by 1999, the Boy Scouts had been victorious on barring girls, gays, and atheists from membership, losing only on the matter of female volunteer leadership. In all of these cases, the ACLU and others have chosen to challenge the BSA on the basis of nondiscrimination passages in the civil rights laws concerning public accommodations, and in almost every case the Boy Scouts of America has been upheld as a private organization that may discriminate on the basis of gender, sexual orientation, and religion.

On June 28, 2000, the Supreme Court of the United States, in a 5–4 decision, ruled that the Boy Scouts of America is a private organization, which, through its constitutional guarantees of freedom of speech and freedom of association, cannot be forced to accept as members people whose "'acceptance would derogate from the organization's expressive message.'"[30] In a jubilant news release issued by the Boy Scouts that same day, the organization said succinctly what had been its claim in the Dale case and in the Curran case before that:

> The Boy Scouts of America, as a private organization, must have the right to establish its own standards of membership if it is to continue to instill the values of the Scout Oath and Law in boys. . . . We believe an avowed homosexual is not a role model for the values espoused in the Scout Oath and Law. Boy Scouting makes no effort to discover the sexual orientation of any person. Scouting's message is compromised when prospective leaders present themselves as role models inconsistent with Boy Scouting's understanding of the Scout Oath and Law.[31]

This battle seems over; but is it?

I have been arguing in this book that the Boy Scouts of America—that is, the legal corporation and the bureaucrats working in the office buildings of the national office and the council offices—is not the "real" Boy Scouts in the sense that a boy experiences Scouting through a concrete folk group of men and boys. Troops have a great deal of autonomy, so that Scouting resembles a more decentralized religious denomination (e.g., Congregationalism or Baptists) than a centralized one (e.g., the Roman Catholic Church or the Church of Jesus Christ of Latter-Day Saints). Troops are not under constant surveillance by the Scout officials, and aside from the routine scrutiny of a troop's performance, a troop is unlikely to be examined closely unless it does something very public—for good or for ill. And many troops—not simply Troop 49—define themselves proudly as different from (and superior to) the national or council office, especially when they think the national office has strayed from the basic message of the Boy Scouts.

So one possible outcome of this court decision is that little will change. The press release from the BSA actually seems to suggest a U.S. militarylike "don't ask, don't tell" policy ("Boy Scouting makes no effort to discover the sexual orientation of any person"), though this seems to put the organization in the strange position of welcoming totally closeted gay males while excluding "avowed" gay males, which I don't think it really wants, either. In any case, "don't ask, don't tell" has been the de facto policy of the Boy Scouts since its founding; after all, the offense committed by Eagle Scouts Curran and Dale is that they made their homosexuality public.

An official "don't ask, don't tell" policy, combined with the actual practices of many troops—mostly under the radar of the national and council offices—probably means that little will change. Some gay men and boys in troops will remain closeted. Some troops will have cultures accepting of "avowed" gay men and boys, though the troops will treat this as "no big thing."

Still, some pressures will continue on the Boy Scouts of America. As I write these words, several government agencies are taking the Boy Scouts at its word and moving against special privileges it has enjoyed from public agencies.[32] The ACLU is challenging a dollar-a-year rental arrangement the Boy Scouts has with the City of San Diego for a large portion of Balboa Park. We can expect to hear more of these in the months and years to come.

The other fallout from this decision is that some men and boys within the organization will have to decide whether they want to remain in Scouting. If you believe your organization is wrongheaded in some way, do you stay in the organization and try to reform its policies from within? Or do you resign from the organization and form or join an alternative organization, maybe trying to reform the original organization from outside? This is the classic social movement dilemma.

Leading the campaign to get the BSA to change its policy voluntarily is a newly emergent social movement organization, Scouting for All. An organization cofounded in 1999 by teen Eagle Scout Steven Cozza of Petaluma, Scouting for All is an alliance of straight and gay men and women. It has created an elaborate website (www.scoutingforall.org) for organizing volunteers to protest the BSA's policies through letters and marches, to help troops write their own nondiscrimination policies, to pressure governments and sponsoring organizations to withdraw subsidies, and to support gay boys and men who are either inside the BSA or trying to obtain membership. Scouting for All also has asked Eagle Scouts to turn in their Eagle badges in protest, not to the BSA national office but to Scouting for All: "We will hold it in trust for you, pending the day when you can retrieve it from us because Scouting has ceased to discriminate."[33] Here and elsewhere in their materials, as is often true in the rhetoric of social movement organizations, Scouting for All appeals to the basic values of Scouting itself—tolerance, justice, and so on—as the basis for a critique of the organization.[34]

The *Los Angeles Times* devoted a large story in its August 31, 2000, edition to those who are facing this dilemma on a personal level. Pictured is Eagle Scout Howard Menzer, a fifty-four-year member of Scouting, from his Bronx boyhood to an adult volunteer, who says he is "ashamed of the policies, not the organization." The story reports that "some former Eagle Scouts, including gays and straights, have turned in their badges, renouncing the Scouts completely. Others, like Menzer, are deeply conflicted, torn between their conscience and their loyalty to a group that helped shape who they are."[35] Menzer led an "eight person demonstration" in San Diego, the local version of the larger National Day of Protest rallies that Scouting for All organized in forty cities.[36] In largely symbolic gestures, eleven members of Congress urged President Clinton to resign as honorary president of the BSA, and Representative Lynn C. Woolsey (D–Petaluma) "has introduced legislation to revoke the Boy Scouts' federal charter."[37]

Aside from the two dozen Eagle Scouts who turned in their Eagle medals in protest at the Irving, Texas, national headquarters, another "22 Eagle Scouts nationwide have posted their names on a Web site list of those who have turned in their medals to Scouting for All." One of those who turned in his Eagle Scout medals—"one of the treasures of my life," he said—was the Reverend Gene Huff, a seventy-two-year-old Presbyterian minister in San Francisco. Huff urged men and boys to stay in Scouting but to work against "this abominable policy."[38] Parents already are having to talk with their Boy Scout sons about the policy and its conflicts with the family's values.

The U.S. Supreme Court decision of June 28, 2000, then, marks a beginning as much as an end. The narrow decision settled the contradictory rulings from New Jersey and California, but now begins the interesting period in which forces internal and external to the Boy Scouts will try to change the organization's policy.

Even if one grants the Boy Scouts its claim to being a private organization with the legal right to discriminate, we still might ask whether it is good policy for the organization to exclude women and homosexual men and adolescents. The previous excursus on the "two bodies" at a Boy Scout camp might actually have some bearing on this question. Given the way a Scout troop and camp experience undertake the cultural project of creating heterosexual masculinity, is it a good idea or a bad one for the organization to accept openly homosexual men and women of any sexual orientation? Let me address the homosexuality question first and then the gender question.

In a newspaper interview in November of 1991, national spokesperson Blake Lewis elaborated the organization's moral argument in

favor of excluding gay men and boys. "Our position" on barring homosexuals from the organization, he explained,

> "comes from the Scout Oath and Law. They specifically state that
> scouts must be morally straight. . . . Anyone who can follow our
> rules can join scouting."
>
> According to Lewis, "moral straightness" is so strongly empha-
> sized because role modeling and the influence of troop leaders and
> volunteers are essential parts of scouting.
>
> "Gays are a negative role model. . . . Scouting stands for a very set
> group of traditional values, and the gay lifestyle is incompatible with
> these values," Lewis said. . . .
>
> Scout leaders have an incredible impact on young people, he
> said. Leaders, therefore, are responsible for setting consistent, stable
> examples. This responsibility also extends to matters of sexual ori-
> entation.
>
> "Young people are building their value sets. . . . They're still col-
> lecting information on their sexual orientation and that's another
> reason we don't want gays in the program," Lewis said.
>
> Still, Lewis said that the Boy Scouts is an organization that does
> not address issues of sexuality, preferring to leave that to the parents
> of individual scouts.
>
> "We're not going to teach sexual education, and at the same
> time we don't want to expose people at a young age to these issues,"
> he said.
>
> Despite the recent surge of publicity surrounding the Boy Scouts'
> anti-gay policy, Lewis said he believes the issue is almost irrelevant
> to scouting.
>
> "This issue is being raised by special interest groups trying to force
> their cause," he said.[39]

The BSA argues that homosexuality is immoral and that homosexuals make improper role models for (presumably heterosexual) young
men. These could be separate claims, since one could hold that homosexuality is morally acceptable but that it is inappropriate to "con-
fuse" adolescents on their path toward conventional sexual orientation.
Perhaps there is a role somewhere for organizations that provide adult
gay role models for gay adolescents, suggested one spokesperson for the
BSA, but that organization should not be the Boy Scouts of America.
This position harkens a bit to the racial segregationist era of the Boy
Scouts, but that era ended, and many Scout troops are racially inte-
grated. As on college campuses and elsewhere, there is some voluntary

segregation as some adult leaders create racially homogeneous troops out of the notion that, say, an exclusively African-American or Latino troop will provide a better setting for building the self-esteem, leadership qualities, and general competence those boys will need in society. The Boy Scouts of America is unlikely to tolerate an exclusively homosexual troop, however, so clearly the matter of sexual orientation has a power more salient than race for this organization. This seems obvious, but the details of the Boy Scouts' evolving attitudes toward male sexuality over the past ninety years are actually more complex than the official statements imply.

The Boy Scouts, both in England and in the United States, was born in a period of extreme anxiety and confusion over the meaning of masculinity.[40] Biographies of Lord Baden-Powell and histories of the English movement make clear the crisis of masculinity for a certain social class there.[41] There was a similar "crisis" of masculinity for that generation of middle- and upper-class Americans, and in response to that crisis some figures collaborated to create organizations that would counter the "feminizing" and other weakening forces connected with the modernization of the society. The Boy Scouts of America, founded in 1910, arose out of that milieu. If we look at three key founders—Ernest Thompson Seton, Daniel Carter Beard, and James E. West—we see in their individual biographies the tensions and paradoxes of masculinity in late Victorian America. Seton had created his Woodcraft Indians in the early years of the twentieth century as a revitalizing youth movement based on the developmental psychology of G. Stanley Hall. Similarly, Beard's Sons of Daniel Boone, founded in 1905, adopted the rhetoric of "muscular Christianity," which dominated late-nineteenth-century discourse about adolescents, sports, outdoor activities, and morality. West's case was exemplary; like Teddy Roosevelt, West was a sickly child who, through sheer physical determination, made himself a vital recreationist. Seton's Indians were coeducational, but the rhetoric of all three men echoed familiar views on the need to revitalize American manhood in the face of the modern transformation of American life. When these men and others came together to found the Boy Scouts of America in 1910, it seemed clear that they were dedicated to making boys into model men, using a model drawn from the late nineteenth century.

Yet a closer look at Seton reveals a far more androgynous figure than one might imagine. In fact, all the sexual ambiguities Dorothy Ross finds in her excellent biography of G. Stanley Hall could be applied to Seton.[42] And, although Beard cultivated a far more masculine image, there is plenty of evidence that he, like Seton and Hall, combined in his own personality traits that would have been called both masculine and feminine in late Victorian America. In my view, we don't need to probe the sexual orientations of these individuals in order to see the central point—namely, that in their own personalities the founders of the BSA were "role models" for an androgynous masculinity not dissimilar from the new masculinities that emerged in response to parallel social and economic pressures on masculinity in the 1990s.

This historical perspective also leads us to examine the motivation that led so many men to join the organization as leaders after 1910. Jeffrey Hantover has argued that the occupations and other markers of the social location of these men suggest that they were suffering a status revolution, in terms of both the precariousness of their social class standing and the precariousness of their masculinity. Stuck in occupations previously deemed "feminine," or at least passive and sedentary, these men saw the Boy Scouts as an organization for shoring up their masculinity.[43] Shifting our gaze to the 1980s and 1990s, the emergence of the gay rights movement and of alternative masculinities (e.g., the mythopoetic men's movement of Robert Bly and others) creates circumstances that assault traditional notions of masculinity.[44] The reaction of Scout leaders to the gay challenge seems a predictable response; if many adult leaders of the Boy Scouts rely upon the organization to shore up a conventional masculine identity under assault elsewhere in society, then it is understandable that these men would resist muddying the masculinity of the Boy Scouts.

Add to this 1990s crisis in traditional masculinity the increasing influence of the religious right in the national offices of the Boy Scouts. As I indicated in my excursus on God, the men who created the Boy Scouts were not particularly religious, at least not in the sense purported by the leaders of the Boy Scouts at the end of the twentieth century. But these roots do not mean that the organization is as religiously neutral as the founders would have wanted. Dave Rice's claim that the "religious right" has taken over the Boy Scouts' national office may have some truth. Certainly, the influence of the Mormon Church (the Church of Jesus Christ of Latter-Day Saints) and the Roman Catholic Church in the organization was substantial at century's end, and it would be surprising to see Mormons and Catholics take a position on homosexuality and atheism different from the one enunciated by the Boy Scouts.[45]

The official literature of the Boy Scouts makes clear that the goal of the organization is to create a heterosexual male who meets the culture's definition of mature masculinity. At the same time, the literature clearly makes the homosexual male "the other," a figure whose feminine qualities and immoral qualities (an interesting conflation of the feminine and the immoral here) help define the masculine by showing what it is not.

In the excursus on the "two bodies," I reviewed what the *Handbooks* have to say, or mainly not say, about male sexuality. After many decades of silence on the subject of homosexuality, though, the 1968 edition of the pamphlet for the Personal Fitness merit badge, written by Dr. J. Roswell Gallagher, chief of the Adolescent's Unit at Boston's Children's Medical Center, finally explicitly addresses homosexuality. After assuring the reader that masturbation is a natural but "temporary part of the process of sexual maturation," Gallagher goes on to say:

> Another subject about which there is much misinformation is homosexuality. This term is generally used to describe a fixed adult pattern of behavior in which an individual is sexually attracted only to members of his own sex. Many boys before they become interested in girls develop strong friendships with other boys. This is perfectly normal and will lead to many strong friendships for the rest of their lives. It does not mean that they are homosexuals or are not manly or will not develop an interest in girls. As they grow up and widen their circle of friends and activities, they will become attracted to the opposite sex.[46]

There is here, of course, the assumption that the "normal" boy will emerge into full heterosexuality.

Despite Dr. Gallagher's brief foray into the developmental issue of sexual confusion, all other Boy Scout talk about homosexuality makes the moral argument, foreshadowing the position taken in the 1990s. Hillcourt's 1959 *Handbook* takes a page to explain what it means to be "morally straight," the last phrase of the Scout Oath. This is a crucial discussion on account of the reliance upon the phrase in the Boy Scouts' rejection of homosexual members. Previous *Handbooks* had little to say about "morally straight." The 1948 edition relates morality to keeping God's commandments,[47] and the earlier *Handbooks* do not even seek to interpret the phrase. Elsewhere in the 1959 edition, when explaining the meaning of the Scout Oath, Hillcourt writes vaguely and generally about "strong character" and about duty to God, country, others, and self.[48] His discussion of what it means to be "morally straight" comes late in the *Handbook,* after the discussions of sex and having "a healthy attitude." Key to the discussion is what Hillcourt calls "a precious thing"—the conscience. The conscience is an inner voice that helps boys know right from wrong. Moreover, "[y]our conscience speaks to you about your relationship to other people—respecting their rights, treating them justly, giving them a fair chance."[49] This seems to lay the groundwork for tolerance toward homosexuality and respect for the rights of homosexuals.

Hillcourt's 1979 discussion repeats the injunction regarding others: "Respect their rights. Treat them justly. Give them a fair chance."[50] But Hillcourt then goes on to make clear that the morally straight boy will become a heterosexual man. "As a young man you are capable of becoming a father. God has given you this very high trust. . . . When you live up to the trust of fatherhood your sex life will fit into God's wonderful plan of creation."[51] Hillcourt is making a plea here for boys to act sexually responsibly and to avoid unwed teenage fatherhood, but notable is the heterosexual assumption built into the discussion.

So by the 1980s, when Curran began his lawsuit, publications by the Boy Scouts were delivering two potentially conflicting messages. On the one hand, being "morally straight" included respecting others' rights, treating them justly, and avoiding prejudice. On the other hand, the literature assumed that heterosexuality is the normal, appropriate sexual orientation for boys and men. The literature never claimed that homosexuality is immoral, only that the sexual orientation of a mature man is heterosexual. It was only in their public oral arguments and eventually in their legal arguments that the BSA claimed that homosexual adult leaders could not be "appropriate" role models for young men.

Before evaluating this claim in light of the "two bodies" perspective, there is one more important matter to consider—sexual molestation. This has been a fear of the Boy Scouts since its founding in 1910. When I was doing archival research in the Philadelphia Council for a graduate seminar paper in 1968–69, an older Scout executive confided in me that they used to worry that some of the men volunteering to work with the boys did so from the wrong motives. Some men just wanted to be around the boys, this man explained, letting his facial expression convey his meaning. The period he was remembering would have been the 1920s. Over the years, there have been numerous sexual scandals, from an elaborate one where a New Orleans Scoutmaster was accused of running his troop as a boy prostitute ring, to cases of individual leaders accused of molesting boys in their charge.[52] According to documents obtained from the Boy Scouts of America by Michael Rothschild, a Sacramento attorney handling one of the molestation lawsuits, about "1,800 Scoutmasters suspected of molesting boys were removed" by the organization in the twenty years between 1971 and 1991, "but some simply went elsewhere and continued to abuse Scouts."[53] The Boy Scouts, with some good reasons, claims both that the percentage of child molesters among the volunteer adults is relatively small (1 in 13,000) and that, as one spokesman for the organization said in response to these numbers, molestation " 'is a phenomenon that happens to every organization committed to youth development and that the Scouts are leaders in fighting such abuse.' "[54] The lawsuits generally have charged, though, that the Boy Scouts prefers to keep these matters quiet and too often permits the molester to move on and continue his predatory habits.

These continuing scandals are enormously embarrassing to the organization, leading in the mid-1980s to a new set of rules governing the interaction of boys and men. For example, I arrived at camp one summer (the summer of 1989) to learn that there was a new "rule of three." Two adults could be alone with one boy or two boys alone with one adult, but an adult could no longer be alone with a boy. The Boy Scouts created training materials—including a film, *A Time to Tell* (1989)—and new materials for the *Handbook,* but recall, too, that Pete thought these efforts were window dressing meant to minimize the legal and financial responsibility of the national organization.[55] He now thinks the materials have become more thoughtful in their advice to boys and parents about the prevention of and proper responses to the sexual abuse of children, but (again) he thinks the organization was slow to come around to thinking of the boy first.

Scouting for All and other critics of the BSA's position and rhetoric agree that pedophiles should be kept out of the Boy Scouts. The public's general conflation of homosexuality and pedophilia is what causes the mischief in the view of these critics. Screening volunteer youth workers for pedophiles is no easy matter. The solution reached by the Boy Scouts has been to bar all homosexuals from leadership, assuming that it will exclude most of the pedophiles that way. But there are several problems with this solution. The first is that the policy contributes to the public confusion in equating homosexuality with pedophilia. Pedophilia is as repugnant to most homosexuals as it is to most heterosexuals. But even granting that there are homosexuals among the pedophiles in society, it seems to me that an openly gay Scout leader would be the least likely person to engage in pedophilia. Because of the special scrutiny, his behavior would need to be the least problematic. Some of the case studies presented by Patrick Boyle, for example, confirm what even the national office warns of in its educational materials for the boys—namely, that the pedophilic Scout leader appears not as the proverbial "dirty old man in a trench coat" but as a highly skilled, friendly, and persuasive adult who gains the boy's trust by doing precisely what we would want a Scout leader to do, things such as listening to the boy's reports of personal troubles and comforting the boy when he is homesick, upset, or injured. One of the Scoutmasters Boyle interviewed for his book nicely summarizes this dilemma. After describing the elaborate protections he had to take in helping a boy remove a tick in his groin (having another adult present, using a towel for privacy), a Maryland Assistant Scoutmaster explains the problem:

> "The toughest thing is when a kid wants to talk to you," Cheesman says. "I had this kid, his parents were getting a divorce. He comes up to me, he couldn't sleep. A couple of us were sitting around, shooting the breeze. He says, 'I gotta talk to ya.'
>
> "All of a sudden he puts his arms around me and starts crying. And you're trying not to embarrass the kid in front of the other kids. You don't want kids making fun of him because he's crying. What are you gonna do? The kid put his arms around you. You just have to pat him on the back and say things are gonna be okay."[56]

The *Handbook* urges the boy to talk with his parents, his Scout leader, or his religious leader when things are bothering him or worrying him. What sort of nurturance and modeling of mature masculinity, one wonders, can male Scout leaders and religious leaders display when they are worried that their nurturing behavior is precisely the sort of confidence-gaining behavior pedophiles might use?

Moreover, although there are no figures on this and the evidence is merely anecdotal, pedophilia may be the least common sort of sexual exploitation that goes on at a Boy Scout camp. Far more common is the molestation of boys by other boys. This is not the mutual, exploratory play of consenting boys; I am referring to the genuinely coercive molestation of some boys by others, though (just as in date rape) the line between consensual and nonconsensual sex play might be confusing and the person with the greater power might use persuasion rather than physical force as the means of obtaining consent. Boys molesting boys, like men molesting boys, might be a small problem when counted against the millions of boys who camp together and the millions of nights boys share tents and cabins out of the surveillance of adults, but it is a problem that the Boy Scouts does not acknowledge. Nor can it do anything about this sort of molestation; there is no way of screening for the boy who will coerce a younger or smaller boy into sexual touching and maybe more.

The fear of molestation, it seems, is a weak reason for wanting to exclude openly homosexual teens and men from the Boy Scouts. To exclude all avowed homosexuals because some might molest a boy is to approach the problem from the wrong direction and to punish thousands of gay teens and men, while at the same time making it highly unlikely that there will be fewer sexual predators among the members.

Almost as feared as molestation is the male gaze. The presence of young men who understand their sexual orientation as homosexual (or possibly as bisexual—a possibility only increasing teen confusion in sexual orientation) *would* be disturbing to other boys, given the present social construction of the masculine culture of a Boy Scout troop, just as the presence of openly homosexual men in the military will be threatening to men who consider themselves exclusively heterosexual. The presence of a known homosexual or bisexual male in these settings threatens to *feminize* the heterosexual males. The male gaze, traditionally leveled at women, now finds a new target and feminizes the target.

But is a gaze an assault? This question poses a dilemma for heterosexual men, for if the male gaze at other men is an assault, an aggressive and threatening gesture against which heterosexual men are seen to have rights of protection (i.e., the right to privacy), then the heterosexual male gaze at women is equally assaulting. The problem for heterosexual men is that the homosexual is in some contexts assumed to be *hypermasculine,* is taken as an extreme case of the typical male inability to control his sexual urges. And this hypermasculinity makes the heterosexual male uncomfortable, as he assumes the gay male will "hit on" him.

Does the heterosexual boy have a right to privacy from the gaze of gay boys and men? This gets complicated because casual nudity between presumed heterosexual boys is an important part of the performance of their heterosexuality. So privacy becomes an issue only in the case of the gay gaze. Do the heterosexual boys have a right not to be made uncomfortable? Changing the category, would we be prepared to say that a boy in the Scouts or a young man in the military has a "right" not to be in the presence of an African American where that makes him uncomfortable? If we would not say this, as a matter of public policy—if, indeed, we would say that the public good is served by requiring citizens to learn to live with the diversity of human beings—then it is difficult to defend the notion that heterosexual men have a right of privacy to be defended against the gaze of homosexual and bisexual men.

So we return to the most likely reasons why the Boy Scouts must dig in its heels over permitting homosexuals into the organization—namely, that homosexual behavior is immoral and that homosexuals make bad role models because (1) immoral behavior makes a poor role model for anyone and (2) homosexual behavior makes a poor role model for heterosexual men.

The morality or immorality of homosexuality is one of those topics in the culture wars that seems incommensurable, incapable of compromise or even civil debate. Rhetoric runs hot on both sides. An organization like the Boy Scouts, one that stands for traditional morality, currently faces a dilemma. On the one hand, the organization recognizes and endorses the existence of cultural differences; Scouts are to be more than tolerant of differences; they are to celebrate differences when it comes to race, ethnicity, religion, and nationality. But when sexual orientation became a kind of cultural difference after the Stonewall Riot of 1969 and the emergence of a gay rights movement, the threat of homosexuality to the fragile construction of heterosexuality meant that the Boy Scouts could not be tolerant of this difference; too much was at stake. So the claim is made that homosexuality is immoral, not "morally straight" (the pun is too apt).

But morality, one assumes, comes primarily from religious teachings, and the Boy Scouts traditionally has been nonsectarian and ecumenical in its stance toward religious diversity. To maintain the position that homosexuality is immoral amounts to preferring some religions over others on this matter. The Boy Scouts has already punished the Unitarian Universalist Church for its stand on homosexuality, and one wonders what will happen if and when the Episcopal, Evangelical Lutheran, Methodist, and Presbyterian churches come to ordain openly gay clergy and endorse gay marriages (as they are considering doing as of this writing).[57] Will those be the next churches to find their religious medals being eliminated from the Boy Scout list?

Of course, the Boy Scouts can say that homosexuality is "immoral" as agreed to by most Americans and by most of the religions Americans belong to—that was precisely the claim made by the Scouts' attorney, above. In this case, the "immorality" view stems not from a particular religion's dogma but from a view that there is some sort of moral consensus in the culture that homosexuality is immoral. But what is the scope and nature of that consensus?

The role of religion as a source of morality in American democracy is a topic fraught with complications. The courts usually are reluctant to use their decisions to create and defend a common morality, not least because most Americans do not want their government to create one official morality for all citizens.[58] Law and morality are distinct systems of thought in our political system, though the law depends upon there being a strong "civil sphere" or "public sphere" to balance the power of the state and the market.[59] Part of that healthy public sphere is organized religion; the courts count on institutions other than the law for the maintenance of morality in the society. The law therefore represents a very minimalist definition of what people in the society can agree is moral.

Sociologists who have examined public opinion polls and interviewed samples of middle-class Americans in the last twenty years have found pretty much the same thing—Americans value the principle of individual choice in morality as much as they value their own moral systems.[60] So, while most middle-class Americans (70 percent in the survey examined by Alan Wolfe) think homosexuality is wrong, most also favor tolerance toward homosexuals.

If it is a private organization, the Boy Scouts of America has every right to demand a particular code of morality in its members. But it should realize that, in this case, it is acting like a church and is departing from the founders' principles. If, indeed, as seems likely, religious conservatives have "taken over" the national offices of the Boy Scouts, we do have an incommensurable debate. Ask the Unitarian Universalist Church.

If, on the other hand, the Boy Scouts of America is an organization that has modeled and should model democratic processes in a diverse, multicultural society and if the Boy Scouts amounts to more than the people in the national office in Irving, Texas, then perhaps we can set aside the "morality/immorality" question as inappropriate for an institution the likes of the Boy Scouts. What the debate really comes down to, in my mind, is the following fascinating question: Can a homosexual adult male be an appropriate role model for a heterosexual teen?

As an initial attempt at answering this question, let me first reverse the terms and ask this: can a heterosexual male adult be an appropriate role model for a gay teen? Many closeted gay teens have gone through the Boy Scouts, earning Eagle and any number of honors within the organization. I assume that most of the adult Scout leaders—their adult male mentors—were heterosexual men. What were these men modeling for the boys? Officially, they were modeling the Scout virtues and skills, which (apparently) the gay boys learned. Unofficially, but high on the agenda of what the Boy Scouts is about, they were modeling adult heterosexuality. As we have seen, masculinity is defined and constructed by means of hundreds of small verbal and physical interactions throughout everyday life at camp. Every time an adult or boy urges a boy not to chicken out in an activity, every time a boy calls another boy a "fag," every time a boy tells his friends a dirty joke, every time a boy brags about a real or imagined sexual encounter with a girl, every time a boy is asked to continue playing a game despite a twisted ankle, every time a boy is called a "crybaby" when he is homesick or loses a contest, every time a boy experiments with how many ways he can get the word "fucking" into a sentence, the group is socializing the boy into what it means to be a man.

Most times, the sort of masculinity implied by these events and gestures is heterosexual, but that is not necessarily so. It is more accurate to say that these are performances of a certain sort of masculinity—a tough, aggressive masculinity—which ironically can be found as readily among homosexual men as among heterosexual men.[61] But in the camp I studied, there are also performances of different sorts of masculinity; sometimes it is the tough, aggressive, physical masculinity, but at other times I found examples of cooperative, gentle, compassionate, nurturing masculinity.

In short, I would have to say that heterosexual men can be appropriate role models for gay teens if by "appropriate role model" we mean that the adults perform a more complex, broader spectrum of masculinity than the cultural stereotype allows. A Scout leader does not model actual sexual behavior, one assumes; as of yet, the Boy Scouts does not inquire into the sexual practices and fidelity of the heterosexual male volunteers. Rather, under the best circumstances, the male leader models what it means to be a "good man." A heterosexual adult who is a good man can model this for every adolescent boy in his charge, regardless of the boy's state of fixed or puzzled sexual orientation.

At the same time, we should recognize the pain to the closeted gay teen as he endures the homophobic performances of masculinity at camp. One of the ways a heterosexual adult leader can model being a "good man" for the boys is to refuse to engage in the homophobic performances and to ask the boys to refrain from the misogyny and homophobia in the boys' everyday folklore. Pete models this sort of mature masculinity for the boys and men of Troop 49; he won't tolerate homophobic or misogynist utterances at troop campfires, assemblies, or dining tables. This stance may have little chance of stamping out the misogyny and homophobia in the more private folklore performances, out of earshot of the adults, but at least it makes the statement that "the public culture of this troop does not tolerate antifemale and antigay expressions." (I shall take up shortly the question of whether the creation of heterosexual masculinity *requires* expressions of misogyny and homophobia.)

Having answered the question, Can a heterosexual male leader be an appropriate role model for a gay teen? in the affirmative, I can return to the initial question and ask whether an openly homosexual male leader can be an appropriate role model for the boys, regardless of their sexual orientation. Again, my answer would be "yes," if we are talking about modeling for the boys what it means to be a "good man." Homosexual men are capable of performing masculinity in the same broad range as heterosexual men, just as homosexual men are as capable of expressing misogyny as are heterosexual men. I would expect that the openly gay man will not model heterosexism and homophobia for the boys.

These are my best guesses, based on my experience with the Boy Scouts and my familiarity with the interdisciplinary research on masculinity. We have no systematic study of the impact of the adult Scout leader's sexual orientation on his performance as a leader. A study comparing homosexual and heterosexual volunteers in the Big Brothers and Big Sisters programs in San Francisco, however, found that sexual orientation had no significant influence on such performance factors as empathy and nurturance. Sexual orientation, concluded the authors, "cannot be used to predict a successful volunteer. One wonders why it continues to be used as an exclusionary criterion for adults interested in working with children."[62] More research is needed to confirm the results of this study, but these results suggest that it is the personality and integrity of the volunteer that make for a successful role model.

I have argued here for the inclusion of openly homosexual men and teens in the Boy Scouts. For the sake of both the heterosexuals and the homosexuals in the organization, learning that the performance of a range of masculine behaviors is separate from the sexual orientation of the performer is an important lesson. This is why the poorly conceived and mismanaged "don't ask, don't tell" policy created for the military by President Clinton would not be a satisfactory solution for the Boy Scouts. Aside from the personal costs to the boy or man who must pretend to go along with and be amused by the homophobic humor that is part of the folklore of camp, keeping the gay men and teens closeted in the organization misses an opportunity to teach everyone involved that there are many ways to perform masculinity, that these styles are not necessarily connected to sexual orientation, and that our criteria for judging "good men" from "bad men" should be their wisdom, generosity, compassion, nurturance, and ethics, not their sexuality.[63]

The Boy Scouts might object to my list of the qualities of an appropriate role model for boys; not that it would exclude any of these criteria, but it probably would accuse me of loading the list in favor of the more feminine qualities we associate with a certain sort of performance of masculinity, a more androgynous sort of masculinity than the popular culture usually provides as the "script" for being a man. What about strict-but-fair discipline, religious reverence, courage, decisiveness, and so on? There is nothing in this additional list to exclude the leader on the basis of his sexual orientation.

Perhaps we should reword my "good man" and "bad man" distinction and talk, instead, about good fathers and bad fathers or, better, fathers who are good role models for adolescent boys and fathers who are not such good role models. If the Scoutmaster is a surrogate father in American culture, then what sort of father is he, and what sort of "family" is modeled by the troop he leads? This plunges us once again into the culture wars, as the nature of fathers and fatherhood in American culture is the topic of much public debate.[64] George Lakoff's 1996 book, *Moral Politics,* offers what I find a useful way to talk about good fathers and bad. Lakoff shows how the metaphors for the nation and the metaphors for the family move back and forth, so that the culture wars between the traditionalists and the progressives really come down to different models of the family and different models of the father as "head" of the family in a patriarchal society like ours. "At the center of the conservative worldview," writes Lakoff, "is a Strict Father model."[65] The Strict Father heads "a traditional nuclear family" and has the primary responsibility and authority to set and enforce rules. The Strict Father loves his children, of course, but it sometimes takes "tough love" to ensure that children respect and obey authority. "Strict father morality," continues Lakoff, "assigns highest priorities to such things as moral strength (the self-control and self-discipline to stand up to external and internal evils), respect for and obedience to authority, the setting and following of strict guidelines and behavioral norms, and so on."[66]

In contrast, the "liberal worldview centers on a very different ideal of family life, the Nurturant Parent model."[67] In this model, parents stress love, empathy, and nurturance. Parents still expect children to acquire responsibility, self-discipline, and self-reliance, but in this case those qualities are the result of the loving respect and care in the family. Children obey their parents not out of fear of punishment but out of love and respect. The Nurturant Parent model of the family emphasizes communication skills. "Nurturant parent morality," explains Lakoff, "has a different set of priorities. Moral nurturance requires empathy for others and the helping of those who need help. To help others, one must take care of oneself and nurture social ties. And one must be happy and fulfilled in oneself, or one will have little empathy for others."[68]

Lakoff musters many persuasive examples to show how the political differences between liberals and conservatives in the 1990s can be understood as coming out of two very different models of the family. What makes Lakoff's book so distinctive, however, is that he bothers to ask a further set of questions: "Who's Right? And How Can You Tell?" A linguist and cognitive scientist, Lakoff finds in the scientific and social scientific literature three good reasons for choosing the Nurturant Parent model of the family and morality:

> Reason 1. The Nurturant Parent model is superior as a method of childrearing.
>
> Reason 2. Strict Father morality requires a view of human thought that is at odds with what we know about the way the mind works.
>
> Reason 3. Strict Father morality often finds morality in harm; Nurturant Parent morality does not.[69]

Lakoff draws upon social scientific research on child-rearing practices and outcomes to support his first reason, and he draws upon cognitive science research to support his second reason.[70] His third reason is, purely and unapologetically, a moral argument, but one that also points out a logical flaw in the Strict Father morality. "Strict father morality," concludes Lakoff,

> is not just unhealthy for children. It is unhealthy for any society. It sets up good vs. evil, us vs. them dichotomies and recommends aggressive punitive action against "them." It divides society into groups that "deserve" reward and punishment, where the grounds on which "they" "deserve" to have pain inflicted on them are essentially subjective and ultimately untenable. . . . Strict Father morality thereby breeds a divisive culture of exclusion and blame. It appeals to the worst of human instincts, leading people to stereotype, demonize, and punish the Other—just for being the Other.[71]

The official culture of the Boy Scouts presents an interesting combination of these two models. The Boy Scouts began with what seemed a very nineteenth-century model of masculinity, a model emphasizing duty, self-reliance, obedience, and courage. At the same time, the models of masculinity offered by Seton and Beard were more androgynous, an interesting mix of the Strict Father and the Nurturant Parent.

Careful readings of successive editions of the *Handbook for Boys* and the *Handbook for Scoutmasters* tell the same story. The official culture of the Boy Scouts sometimes describes the Scoutmaster as a Strict Father, but more often (and increasingly in the last half of the century) the ideal Scoutmaster combines the Strict Father with the Nurturant Parent.

My ethnographic evidence, along with anecdotal testimony from former Scouts, supports Lakoff's argument that the Nurturant Parent model produces the best results. On the ground, day to day, the most effective Scout leader judiciously combines the two models of parenting, with the Nurturant Parent as the dominant mode. There is the occasional purely Strict Father Scoutmaster, but most adolescent boys do not respond very favorably to that model of Scouting. Far more effective, in my experience, is the Scoutmaster who carves out a way to be a Nurturant Parent with occasional performances of the Strict Father. The most effective Scout leaders perform what we might call an androgynous masculinity, and gender role research tells us that such men (and presumably the boys for whom they model this performance of masculinity) are much happier and mentally healthier than men and boys who stick more closely to the stereotypical masculine role, which resembles Lakoff's Strict Father.[72] Adolescent boys have very keen "crap detectors" (Ernest Hemingway's phrase), and they are more likely to respect a male leader who respects them, who sets clear standards for their behavior, who is willing to talk with them about the standards and perhaps even negotiate some of those standards, who provides nurturance when it is needed, and who has the boy's happiness and self-fulfillment in mind.

I would say, then, that there are very good reasons for the Boy Scouts to seek Scoutmasters and other volunteer male leaders who demonstrate an androgynous masculinity much broader in its range than stereotypical male performances. The more models of masculinity available to the boys, the better, I would say, and this principle argues in favor of the inclusion of both homosexual and heterosexual men and boys.

I come, finally, to a question I have put off until now. Does a pluralistic, flexible masculinity appropriate to twenty-first-century American culture *require* misogyny and homophobia in its creation and maintenance? This question forces us to speculate on the implications of feminist psychoanalytic theory and the "two bodies" perspective for the debates over girls and gays in the Boy Scouts.

Theory explains why the social construction of masculinity incorporates strategies for separating the masculine self from the feminine, and theory explains the social and psychological consequences of those strategies. But the theory also suggests a possible alternative pattern. Nancy Chodorow, for example, argues that our patriarchal arrangement, in which "women mother," helps create the circumstances in which it is so vital for the male child to separate himself from the mother. Chodorow proposes that a change in child-rearing arrangements, in which fathers participate equally in the earliest care for and socialization of the child, would largely obviate the necessity for the male child to separate so dramatically from the mother and everything feminine.[73] More androgyny in both parents and children presumably would end the need for misogyny and homophobia in the construction and maintenance of masculinity. This is not an androgyny that erases all differences between men and women; biology still makes some differences, on average. This is an androgyny that, not so incidentally, actually meets the avowed goals of both the Boy Scouts and the Girls Scouts, which is to say that the desired androgyny expands the culturally expected performance of "male" to include qualities and behavior usually reserved for women, just as it expands the culturally expected performance of "female" to include qualities and behavior usually reserved for men. Misogyny and homophobia would wither away in this utopian rearrangement of child-rearing practices.

I call this rearrangement "utopian" not because I think it is an impossible goal imaginable only in science fiction; the change will be very slow, though. In the meantime, and in the absence of such a change in fundamental child-rearing arrangements, we must not conclude that misogyny and homophobia are an inevitable part of the social construction of masculinity in organizations like the Boy Scouts. Presenting a larger, broader range of types of performances of "masculinity" in the adult male leadership, accompanied by a broadening of the range of acceptable performances of masculinity by the boys themselves, can reinforce a public culture in the Boy Scouts where expressions of misogyny and homophobia are unwelcome. The strategies that take the place of the misogyny and homophobia, which (after all) are strategies necessitated by the fact that masculinity is defined as a negative, stem from defining masculinity as a positive. That means filling the concept of masculinity with content describing the qualities we would want in any human being with whom we shared friendship and a sense of belonging to the same community. With proper attention to defining masculinity positively, misogyny and homophobia would wither away eventually, first in the public culture of the Boy Scout troop and then in the private folk culture of the adolescent boys themselves.

Nonetheless, as may be inferred from the last sentence, I think adolescent boys probably need a same-sex organization.[74] If girls were allowed to join the Boy Scouts in the eight- to fourteen-year-old age group, there would be some natural segregation of the sexes anyway.[75] Girls and boys both would create smaller friendship groups—folk groups—and there would be peer socialization in those settings, communicating to the children a clear separation between a mixed-gender public culture and the single-gender folk group. Single-sex groups would make easier the connection between the private and public cultures of these organizations for kids, and in the case of the Boy Scouts the public culture of the troop would help put pressure on the private culture of the male friendship/folk group to change its performances of masculinity.[76]

Actually, the governing truth in this whole discussion is (as I have argued above) that the individual Boy Scout troop is the real site of the social construction and maintenance of what it means to be a Scout. The men who run the national office of the Boy Scouts, the "professional Scouters," think that they are the Boy Scouts; but they are not. The boy does not experience the Boy Scouts through the national office, though he does read the *Handbook* and other materials created by that office. The boy experiences the Boy Scouts through the concrete group of men and boys who constitute his troop; all of the official Boy Scout culture gets filtered through the individual troop experience. It was individual troops, for example, that admitted gay members and girls because the members thought that this was the right thing for them to do for their group. Other troops make other decisions. One of the Assistant Scoutmasters in Troop 49, an Eagle Scout, said to me: "You know, I'm really angry that these guys in the national office are trying to turn the organization into something different from what I know it should be." The pride in a troop's rebellion against the national office is a constant theme I have found in talking with Scouts and former Scouts in and beyond Troop 49; an important source of the identity of a troop can be its rejection of the "Mickey Mouse" regulations of the national office.

In the absence of a national policy on gays and girls, troops would continue to make up their own minds on these matters, and it would be relatively easy to create a new troop if the existing troop in a neighborhood or community was not especially welcoming of gay members or girls. Nothing is to be gained by forcing a homosexual or female member onto a troop hostile to the new member, just as nothing is to be gained by forbidding a troop to accept homosexual or female members. Troops should be empowered to model the diverse society for which (presumably) they are socializing their members.

Fewer women and girls would want into the Boy Scouts if the Girl

Scouts provided a more interesting and more financially secure organizational setting in which girls could learn a full range of human behavior beyond the traditionally female. Boy Scout troops are sponsored
by adult organizations (religious organizations, men's clubs, etc.) and in
most cases are financially sound enough to provide an assortment of
activities. Girl Scout troops typically do not have organizational sponsors in the community, and the girls must peddle their cookies up and
down the streets in order to earn money for their activities. Title IX of
the Education Amendments of 1972 has shown us what social goods
can come of funding girls' athletics at the same level as we fund boys'
athletics. We should learn a lesson from the history of Title IX and
reinvent the ways we support Girl Scouts and other organizations that
help girls tackle their own developmental projects, such as the difficult
matter of female friendship in groups larger than dyads.

In conclusion, the trajectory of the Boy Scouts' own literature,
added to the fact that the real culture of the Boy Scouts is the group
folk culture created by a face-to-face gathering of boys and men, suggests to me that the Boy Scouts could and should change its stance on
the matter of admitting openly homosexual or bisexual men and boys
into the organization. The claim that homosexuality is immoral and,
therefore, violates the oath that the boy will be "morally straight" does
not stand up to the scrutiny of the organization's history. The *Handbooks'* explanation that the "morally straight" boy respects the rights of
others and does not prejudge them seems to me compatible with a
tolerant view of different sexual orientations. The matter of appropriate role models speaks only to a narrow definition of masculinity, one
that is rapidly being rejected in the society. A boy who emerges from
the Boy Scouts with a rigid, traditional view of masculinity, in short,
will not have had role models appropriate for the twenty-first century.

Some observers of the Boy Scouts consider it a nineteenth-century
institution that is so misogynist and homophobic in its organizational
ideology and culture that it damages young men and should be abolished. The same abolitionist argument has been made about college
fraternities, on the same grounds. I am not an abolitionist when it
comes to the Boy Scouts. I believe the organization can be redeemed.
I know from my fieldwork that the culture of the national organization
lags considerably behind the cultures of individual troops.

Even though I recommend the redemption rather than the abolition
of the Boy Scouts, I am not overly optimistic. There are men in the
organization who have great stakes in fostering a narrow, inflexible,
exclusively heterosexual definition of masculinity. These men are suffering powerful anxiety about masculinity, and a Boy Scouts of Amer-

ica that admits homosexuals and bisexuals will have lost its usefulness in their social and psychological defenses against alternative definitions of masculinity. These men are on the losing side, at least for this generation, and I wish they would compromise. But they are not the real Boy Scouts of America, after all, and I pin my hopes on those troops—like the one in San Jose—that are interested in fostering new definitions and practices of what it means to be a man.

1940s/50s Boy Scout Troop
(photographer unknown; photo from author's collection)

Wednesday

★ ★ ★ ★ ★ ★ ★ ★ ★ ★ ★ ★ ★ ★ ★ ★ ★ ★ ★

I awoke with the realization that camp was winding down. In two days, we would break camp and begin our slow transition back to the real world, to the normal, routine, everyday life. I had begun to take for granted the exquisite scenery and special smells of the wilderness, and I vowed to savor them a bit more in the remaining few days of camp. I breakfasted with the Snake Patrol, where the cook served up scrambled eggs and fried Spam. The boys were still on a "high" from their victory in the Treasure Hunt, and around the table they told and retold the story of their discovery.

I decided to visit Les's campcraft class in the morning. "Campcraft" is the name Seton and the other authors of the first *Handbook for Boys* used to describe the skills useful in camping outdoors, skills ranging from hiking and building shelters to canoeing, rowing, and sailing. That morning Les was teaching a small class how to lash poles together with rope. This is an old skill and its use is evident all around camp. From the Rope Slide to the smallest constructions in patrol campsites, rope lashings were the fundamental method for joining poles. Each boy in the class had two small (no longer than about eighteen inches) segments of tree branches. They were crowded around Les, who was hunched over two poles on the ground, each about two feet long; the poles crossed at a right angle. I peeked over his shoulder to watch the lesson. He carefully created a clove hitch on the vertical stick, above the crosspiece, and began weaving the rope around and behind each branch of the cross, keeping the rope taut; he did this three times for his three "wraps." He then began his "fraps," another two turns around just the rope between the two poles. He pulled the frapping tight, which tightened even more the lashing around the poles, and he tied it off with another clove hitch. "There," he said with great pride, holding up the cross of poles for all the boys to see and giving two arms of the cross a hard scissorslike squeeze to show how his tight lashing kept them at a right angle. "You see that?" The boys nodded. "Now make one yourself." Each boy laid his sticks at a right angle on the ground and began reproducing Les's construction methods. Things went better for some than for others, and when a boy was finished, Les would test the lashing by working the sticks to and fro. If the lashing slipped or the sticks moved too much, Les would tell the boy, "That's too loose. Take it apart and do it again." Finally, each boy had produced a lashing meeting Les's test, and none too soon, as we heard the whistle announcing free swim.

People sometimes joke about Boy Scouts and their knots, but as I was walking toward the Waterfront to sun myself and provide another set of watchful eyes for the swimmers, I recalled how much pride I had as a Scout when I learned how to tie a range of knots. That seems like such a simple thing, yet it felt very powerful each time I mastered a knot. And, still, each time I tie a half-hitch or a square knot for some project around the house, that sense of power returns to me briefly. I imagine, without having asked them, that these boys walked away from that class with some of the same feelings. They now knew how to do something concrete, how to build something out of tree branches. They might never do another lashing outside of Scout camp, but I knew they would never forget that skill.

On that walk to the Waterfront, I also reflected on all that was happening in that brief moment of instruction. I knew already that the part the boys hate most about any of these advancement classes is the part that seems most like school and schoolwork, such as reading an assigned section of the *Handbook* or a merit badge pamphlet and answering orally questions about the materials. "How many different sorts of —— are there?" "Name the steps in CPR." And so on. The boys love classes when they learn by doing. Psychologists and educators now appreciate that there are different sorts of intelligence, and surely one of the most important things going on at the Scout camp is the experience of learning something manually, through vision and touch.[1] Boys who might not be doing so well in school, who don't read the Scout *Handbook* and merit badge books any better than they read their textbooks in school, still have a successful experience learning something like lashing. Nobody fails. Everyone gets an "A" because he does it over and over again until he gets it right. The skill seems real, tactile, and the pleasure repeats itself every time they tie a knot or sharpen a kitchen knife on a whetstone at home or perform any number of the everyday skills they learned at Scout camp.

The fact that everyone gets an "A" in these learning situations reflects one of the lasting impacts Seton had on the Boy Scouts, even though he left the organization in 1915. This is Seton's principle of "Honors by Standards," and it is worth quoting Seton in full:

> The competitive principle is responsible for much of what is evil. We see it rampant in our colleges to-day, where every effort is made to discover and develop a champion, while the great body of students is neglected. . . . A great deal of this would be avoided if we strove to bring all individuals up to a certain standard. In our non-competitive tests the enemies are not *"the other fellows,"* but time and space, the forces of Nature. We try *not to down the others, but to raise ourselves.*[2]

Unlike in the Greek contest system, in Seton's program a person's "winning" does not depend upon another person's "losing"; the contest is not a zero sum game.[3]

An early *Handbook for Scoutmasters* (1924) makes clear to the adult leaders the difference between this principle and the usual understanding of competition. The opening paragraphs of the chapter on Scout contests, for example, emphasize this distinction in bold type, a sign that the authors assume most adults coming into the organization to expect contests to be zero sum games:

> Scout contests and competition differ from ordinary physical contests in that emphasis is placed not only on group competition, but an opportunity is provided whereby the boy can compete against his own record or against a record which is set up. As well as this form of competition, each patrol or group is concerned in bringing up its weaker members and indeed does so.

Scout contests do not represent the development of one champion in each event—but rather that every Scout develops his "best" in every event, thus giving each Scout breadth of experience.[4]

The honors-by-standards principle values learning a large repertoire of skills ("breadth," as the *Handbook for Scoutmasters* calls it), rather than specializing in a single skill and trying to excel in that skill alone. The contests come only after each boy has learned the skills required for the contests, and the contests are almost always between small groups, usually patrol against patrol. The goal is to learn the skills, a mastery that cannot be taken from the boy. The contests are for fun and are meant to build speed and proficiency in the skills.

The other remarkable thing that happened in that brief campcraft class, I reflected, was Les's own experience of teaching the boys something. Boys teaching boys. What a simple notion that is, with such important consequences. Boys are giving the gift of knowledge to one another. They're doing that all the time, of course, and sometimes the knowledge is a dirty joke or how to spit. But at the other end of the scale are these lessons, where one boy passes on to another a skill he learned earlier from still another boy, continuing the chain of knowledge across the generations of boys in the troop. The skill itself and the skill of teaching it are gifts one keeps by passing them on.[5]

Les's class also reminded me of the ways learning these skills empowers the boys. In the troop, as in any organization, there is some power to an office, an authority granted. But the real authority, the real power in the organization falls to a man or a boy because he "has the right stuff." He knows his stuff. He knows how to paddle a canoe or build a fire or butterfly a wound. In the mastery of these skills lies power, and it is a power the boys both recognize and crave.

The rest of that day was pretty ordinary, but I knew that an important event was coming up—the Investiture of the new boys into full membership in the troop. As the boys cleaned up after dinner, the Staff and Seniors began setting up the Investiture site and attending to other arrangements for the ceremony. The Investiture is one of the troop's most serious ritual occasions. It resembles the initiation ritual of Greek letter societies and other fraternal and sororal organizations in American culture. There is magic and mystery in these sorts of ceremonies, meant to evoke awe in the initiates.

Although formal women's organizations and even some informal women's friendship groups have initiation rituals, they are far more common in men's groups. Masculinity is a fragile construction, it seems, so it needs more elaborate rituals for its maintenance. For young women, the transition from girlhood to womanhood is clear enough with the onset of menstruation. For young men, the transition is always more elusive. The boy never really fully achieves a mature masculinity that need not be tested and proved again; the tests and proofs (and failures) are ongoing. In Troop 49, the transition from "investite" (the troop's joking wordplay on "transvestite") to Tenderfoot marks one of those moments where a test has been accepted and passed.

Most initiations, certainly male initiations, typically have three stages, as first outlined by Arnold van Gennep.[6] The first stage is one of separation, in which the initiates are set aside from daily space and time. Then follows a second stage of transition, a ritual time when the initiates are, as Victor Turner so aptly puts it, "betwixt and between" categories.[7] They are neither the boys they were before the initiation began nor the men they will be once the initiation is complete. The third stage sees the incorporation of the initiates into the company of men, or perhaps we should say into the "body" of men, a meaning that the word "incorporation" so nicely captures. The boy's body and the "corporate" body of men become interchangeable, symbolically.

Van Gennep noted that this tripartite structure of the male initiation ritual establishes a sort of death-rebirth metaphor for what is happening to the boy, and there are some anthropological examples that show how traumatic this metaphorical death (and mortification, to use Kenneth Burke's term)[8] can be. In modern American organizations like college fraternities or traditionally male occupational groups (especially military, police, firefighters, loggers, and so on), hazing comes close to the most dramatic anthropological examples in showing how the initiate's male body can be "mortified" so that he can rise again, being reborn into the new social status as a member of the group.

The Order of the Arrow (OA), the group within Scouting most like a college fraternity, does not, strictly speaking, haze an initiate. But the "Ordeal" Member, as one at the first level of membership is called, does go through the separation and some of the mortification of the body meant to strip away his preordeal status and "purify" him for the "redemption" that comes with his incorporation into the organization. In my own case, for example, I joined other initiates at an Everglades camp in a physically grueling service project—hauling, sawing, and placing by hand old telephone poles as part of constructing the seating and staging area for the campfire circle at the camp. We had to accomplish the project in complete silence, putting a notch in the arrows we had carved and hung around our necks every time we broke our silence. Three notches and you were out.[9] We each slept alone that night out in the tall grass surrounding camp, wondering what poisonous snake would find our sleeping bags and warm bodies just the thing on a cold night in the swamp. The OA's ritual of initiation is a full Indian pageant, as one might expect, replete with solemn drama, oaths, and symbols of brotherhood.

The initiation drama staged by Troop 49 is not quite as dramatic as the OA's, but it has its own powers. The troop's initiation customs enact the classic formula. For the weeks at camp and even the weeks before camp, the new boys are in many ways separate from the group. The new boys do not have troop neckerchiefs. More dramatically, the new boys must stand inside the circle when the troop creates its ring of touching bodies at the end of each campfire. Those campfires enact for all those present the physical separation of the new boys' bodies from the individual and collective bodies of the troop. The Investiture ritual brings the initiates into the "body" of the troop, metaphorically and also quite literally.

The new boys' bodies serve the symbolism of the event in a second way. The root of the word "investiture"—vestment or garment— refers to the ritual practice of adorning the body of the initiate with clothing or other symbols of belonging or of power. And so it is with Troop 49 and its distinctive neckerchief. The Investiture ceremony is the ritual occasion on which the new boys receive their new neckerchiefs, the indisputable sign of belonging to the troop.

I joined Pete, Jeff, and George as they worked at a table in the Staff Area. Pete was lettering the Tenderfoot badge cards for the ten investites, while Jeff and George were busy making troop neckerchiefs. This involved taking two triangular neckerchiefs, one gold and one maroon; laying them out with the long sides together; and taping them together with masking tape. These taped neckerchiefs would be temporary, strong enough to get the boys through the next few days until the end of camp, but once home the mothers (usually) would sew the neckerchiefs together to make a permanent troop neckerchief.

These unique neckerchiefs are not the only way that the troop has taken the official Boy Scout uniform and altered it to signal better to each other some of the insider knowledge shared only by members.[10] These alterations undermine the authority of the national office and its rules about the "proper" Scout uniform. The point of a uniform for a youth organization, after all, is that it is "uniform." To some extent, youth organizations like Scout troops, private schools, and even some public schools require young people to wear uniforms because it adds to the sense of order and discipline the adults think the youths need. Uniforms also help erase social-class differences. All kids wear the same clothes, regardless of family income. The Scouts are quite explicit about this. No boy is denied membership because his family cannot afford the uniform. A uniform will be found for every boy.

Young people usually dislike the uniforms for exactly the reasons adults like them. Adolescents especially like to use their bodies as the canvas on which they paint their identities. Clothing, hairstyles and hair color, makeup, body hair, piercing, tattooing—all of these can be manipulated to help the adolescent fashion his or her statement, even if the collective result is that the adolescents resemble each other.[11] So it is not surprising to find that adolescents subvert the adult intentions of uniforms in any way possible.

The difference in the Boy Scouts is that in Troop 49 and in some other troops the adult leaders collaborate with the boys to create C&Ts that undermine the "uniformity" of the Boy Scout uniform and turn the troop uniform into a "folk costume" unique to the group. Start with the neckerchief. Insider, esoteric knowledge recognizes the unique neckerchief, but, as I've mentioned, there is further symbolism in how the troop wears the neckerchief. Troop custom dictates that the yellow portion comes over the right shoulder and the maroon portion comes over the left. If through haste or other accident someone puts on the neckerchief backward, members will point to the offender and ask, "What color is blood?"—a reminder that the maroon goes over the heart.

Not all of the troop's neckerchiefs look alike. Older alumni have faded neckerchiefs, usually with thin white cording sewn along the edges. Older neckerchiefs were made of cotton, and constant washing made the colors fade. Thus, the more faded the neckerchief, the longer the alum's association with the troop. One Senior was the butt of much humor one year, when the neckerchiefs were still cotton, because he tried bleaching his neckerchief to give it the old look. But the bleaching created an obvious, washed-out color nothing like the naturally faded neckerchiefs. Now the neckerchiefs are made of polyester—more durable but, alas, nonfading. Paradoxically, then, the most prestigious neckerchiefs in the troop are very old, naturally faded, corded, and probably falling apart. Their fragility makes them the owners' "dress neckerchiefs," worn only for the most solemn troop ceremonies.

The two rolled ends of the neckerchief are threaded through a "slide," and the slide is tightened to come up to about the point where the uniform shirt opens. There are official Boy Scout slides sold by the national office, but the organization lets the slide be one of the items with which a boy or troop can customize the uniform. The national office for many years has sold craft kits for making slides (carving a neckerchief slide, for example, can be a project for the Wood-working merit badge) and has sold slides commemorating national jamborees, summer camps, and the like. Order of the Arrow lodges often have their own neckerchief slides. Troop 49 tends to shy away from the commercial slides. Traditionally, investites at Usonia receive an ULMUD slide—a piece of black plastic pipe about an inch long. They then receive the traditional slide—a ring of yellow polyethylene rope fashioned into a "never-ending band symbolizing the everlasting fellowship that all Troop 49 members enjoy"—at the Court of Honor a few days later.

If the national office allows diversity in the choice of neckerchief and slide, it does not approve of deviance when it comes to the uniform shirt. The uniform shirt is the background for the patches that mark the boy's official Boy Scout identity, from troop number and commu-nity patch to patches of office (e.g., Patrol Leader) and rank (e.g., First Class). The national headquarters is so serious about the uniform shirt that the *Handbook* prints templates to guide the boy (he, not his mother, is supposed to do the sewing) in placing and spacing the patches. The left breast pocket, for example, is for the badge of rank, while the right breast pocket can bear "temporary" badges commemorating camp-outs, fifty-mile hikes, and such. Troop 49 C&Ts, however, elaborate on these official patches and places. One much-coveted patch is hand-drawn, featuring a pulsating big toe and text identifying a particular hike and its year. Also much coveted is the red "Usonia" community strip. For many years, the Boy Scout uniforms bore on the left shoul-der curved red strips with the community's name in black; below this strip was the troop number (also black on red). At some point (the late 1960s, I think), the national headquarters eliminated the community strips and substituted larger council patches. A red community strip with the troop's hometown name on it is a high-prestige item.

To the trained eye, then, the boy or man wearing his Troop 49 Scout uniform both literally and figuratively wears his identity "on his sleeve." He may have individualized his uniform, but he does so mainly with symbols shared with others in the troop.

After a while, Pete looked up from his cards and asked me to go over to the Investiture site to check on arrangements there. I knew vaguely where the site was and headed in that direction, listening for the sound of voices. The site is secret; you won't find it on any map, and although it is close to camp, boys would not normally go there, as it is not on the way to any other troop site. The Investiture site is in a small, sandy depression surrounded by high boulders. It is an ideal ritual site, set off from the everyday world by a box of granite walls, most easily accessible from only one end, with a few small pine trees at the other end. If the site of Church Rock was chosen for its expansive view, leading the boys to look outward and upward from their finite group to the infinity of Nature and of God, then the Investiture site was chosen for its intensive focus, turning attention away from the outside world and onto this very small, focused event that has so much meaning for the group.

I found the site without much trouble. Todd was directing the setting of the stage, so to speak, for the ritual drama of the Investiture. The boys had brought a Commissary table that they put near the pine trees at the far end of the rectangle formed by the high boulders. Behind the table they had strung a rope and had hung the American flag and the troop flag, as a background for Pete and the ceremony. On the table was a candelabra made of four pieces of wood, forming a triangle with three candles in the top level and six candles on each side. There was also a single candle in a small wooden base.

Pete came to the site shortly after I arrived and brought with him the neckerchiefs and Tenderfoot cards and pins. He laid them out neatly on the table. "The troop is assembling now," said Pete, "so let's get ready." He went over the ceremony quickly with the Seniors present. I left the site to join the troop; I wanted to see the site from their viewpoint as they entered. As I came up to the Parade Ground, Todd was giving the troop last-minute instructions. Once dismissed, the troop walked single-file toward the Investiture site. At the edge of camp, the line stopped, and the investites were blindfolded for the remainder of the walk. Each investite had another boy as his escort, who would help him walk to the site and would stand behind him during the ceremony; each escort blindfolded his investite with his own neckerchief.

Todd was leading the troop, and when he got to the entrance to the Investiture site, he banged two rocks together three times.

Pete answered, in a solemn tone: "Who is it that knocks?"

"Ten wandering boys," responded Todd, equally solemnly, "who seek the fellowship of Scouting and Troop 49."

Then Pete: "Let them enter."

Todd led the troop in, and two patrols lined up on each side of the rectangle, perpendicular to the ceremonial head table. The escorts brought the investites in last, lining them up across the rectangle from the head table.

"Remove their blindfolds," ordered Pete. "You see before you the altar of Scouting. On the altar are fifteen candles, these six [pointing to the sides] and these six for the twelve points of the Scout Law, and these three [pointing to the top] for the three points of the Scout Oath. Before them is a single lit candle, representing the Spirit of Scouting. The troop will help you approach the altar as they light the candles."

The Scout closest to Pete stepped up to the table, used the single candle to light the first candle on his left, turned, raised his right arm to make the Scout Sign, and said: "A Scout is Trustworthy." At that point, a disembodied voice from behind the rocks read from the *Handbook* the printed text for that point of the Scout Law. Two Seniors were behind the rocks, off to Pete's right, and they took turns reading the text. At the conclusion of the reading, the first Scout returned to his place, and the escorts moved their charges one step toward the table.

The ceremony went through each of the twelve points of the Scout Law. By the twelfth point, "A Scout is Reverent," the investites had moved right up to the table. Pete asked the investites to come around the table, put their left hands on the troop flag, raise their right hands in the Scout sign, and say together the Scout Oath. As they recited the oath, Pete lit each of the three top candles at the appropriate times. Pete then asked the investites to return to their places in front of the table and asked the escorts to lay the neckerchiefs across the investites' shoulders and back.

Pete explained, for the first time for these investites, the meaning of the neckerchief. "The gold goes over the right shoulder and stands for sunshine and happiness that we enjoy, especially here at Usonia. The maroon goes over the heart and stands for the two stars on the Scout badge, for truth and knowledge." Pete then explained that "the two colors are joined together by a never-ending slide which symbolizes the everlasting fellowship you will enjoy as a Troop 49 member. And remember this: the troop slogan is 'Once a member, always a member!' Because it is very special to be invested at Usonia, you get an ULMUD slide. At the Court of Honor on Saturday, you'll receive your regular troop slide."

Pete asked the escorts to pin the Tenderfoot badges to the shirts of the investites, and while the escorts did that, Pete explained that the boys would get to pin Tenderfoot badge pins on their mothers at the

Court of Honor. Pete came around to the front of the table and gave each boy his Tenderfoot card and a Scout handshake. Pete then returned to his place behind the table.

"Now, at this point," said Pete, "I always tell a story. Sometimes they are true and sometimes not, but they always have a point about a special point of the Scout Law—'A Scout is Brave.' This story concerns three members of the troop, one of whom became an Eagle and has been on staff at Usonia. These three boys were bored, milling around at the church before an outing, so they went over to a fast-food place; got some packages of ketchup, mustard, and relish; and played at stomping on them in the church courtyard. They knew it was wrong, yet no one said anything, so for these Scouts the flame for 'Brave' was snuffed out." Pete extinguished the candle that represented "A Scout is Brave." "And they certainly weren't 'Thrifty,' so that flame was snuffed out [Pete snuffed that candle]. And it made a terrible mess, so the flame for 'Clean' was snuffed out." Pete snuffed out the candle representing that point of the Scout Law.

"The next week, at the troop's regular meeting, by fortunate coincidence, there was to be an Investiture. Before the meeting, the church custodian told me about the mess he had found and how he had spent a good deal of time hosing down the courtyard and walls to prevent stains. I told him I would find out who did it and asked him what sorts of chores the guilty Scouts could do around the church to help out. He told me that wasn't necessary, but I told him that it *was* necessary for the boys to make restitution. So he told me that the boys could come to the church on Saturday to help do some other chores to make up for the mess they made.

"So the troop had its meeting and Investiture. At the point of the ceremony where I tell a story, I related these events as if they were made up. But at the end of the story I announced that this was a true story about members of the troop and that it had actually happened on the previous Saturday. I said that I hoped those Scouts would come forward later to tell me they did it and make restitution. Well, they actually did, and I was proud of them then and I'm still proud of them. Because they relit the flames of Brave, Thrifty, and Clean." As he said this, Pete relit each of the extinguished candles. "Why? Because the flame of the Spirit of Scouting was strong enough in those three Scouts that they were able to reestablish the Scout Law in their hearts."

Pete came around the table to stand with the troop and had the investites turn to face the whole troop. "Some of you were at the last Eagle Court of Honor and heard me say that there are two times in your life in Troop 49 that the troop will salute you. Once is when you're invested and the other is when you earn Eagle. Maybe all of you won't make Eagle, but it would be great for an investiture class of ten to all make Eagle. Anyway, we're going to salute you; then you should return our salute. Scouts, salute! New members, return the salute!" Todd immediately stepped forward to lead three "hip-hip-hoorays," and the Scouts mobbed the investites to congratulate them. Todd announced, "Scout Circle!" and the troop held the C&T closing ceremony, this time with no one inside the circle. The new members clearly were very proud that they could now join the circle.

Some Seniors stayed behind to take down the ritual trappings of the ceremony, while the rest of us returned to camp. The boys, especially the new members, were ebullient. The patrols held sedate campfires, while Pete assembled the Seniors for a meeting. Before the meeting could even begin, Pete realized that he had not brought up his clipboard and notes, so he left to fetch them from the Staff Area. While the Seniors sat huddled in a circle waiting for Pete to return, a few of them broke out in a song that apparently they had learned or invented recently. With something like a rap song beat, the song had this chorus:

> *Chorus*
> Choke, choke,
> Choke, choke my chicken.
> Choke, choke,
> Choke, choke my chicken, baby.
>
> *Sample verse*
> Choke it at the KYBO,
> Choke it every hour,
> On the hour
> For an hour.

The boys tossed the verses back and forth like the usual chain song, inventing verses connecting the song to the troop and camp. They found the song enormously funny. "Choke the chicken" is slang for male masturbation, so this song had joined the more traditional "Last Night I Stayed at Home and Masturbated." The singing stopped as Pete approached the group.

Pete called the meeting to order. "First, I want to have us go over advancement. Tomorrow is the last full, regular day of camp, and I want to be sure every boy has his advancement done by Saturday's Scoutmaster conferences." Jeff went down the list of boys, and each

Senior reported how that boy was doing in his advancement classes. Pete made suggestions here and there, trying to maximize the advancement of each boy without relaxing at all the troop's strict standards. When Pete was satisfied with the advancement reports, he asked the Seniors if they needed to discuss the Treasure Hunt. Everyone thought things had gone pretty well, so this item did not take much time. Finally, Pete outlined plans for breaking camp on Friday. This took some time, as Pete consulted the Camp Bible (a loose-leaf three-ring binder with the accumulated wisdom of many years of running camp) and made sure that every Senior had an assignment and understood it.

"This has been one of the best camps yet," said Pete, "thanks largely to the work of you Seniors. I want you to work at making tomorrow, the last regular day, a perfect one." He then went around the table, asking each Senior what he was going to do the next day to make things go "perfectly." After a few slow responses, each Senior had a ready answer. Morale and spirit were high as Pete dismissed them and wished them a good night.

As we settled down for a the Staff campfire, Aaron announced that there was a problem. Todd had come to him with a complaint that one of the Seniors, Les, apparently had told the Eagle Patrol, his old patrol, where the treasure was going to be hidden the morning of the Treasure Hunt. One of the Seniors had overheard a conversation between members of the Eagles, quizzed the nervous boys on this, and reported the information to Todd. The Seniors were quite angry at Les and were shunning him. "The Seniors want to handle this themselves," said Aaron. "It was their trust he violated, so they want to be the ones to punish him. But Todd thought we should know what is happening."

"Well," said Tad, "it really doesn't matter that he told the Eagles. They still have to have all the clues in their baggies, and it didn't seem to make much difference who got to the treasure site first. All the patrols seemed equally incompetent in finding the actual burial spot of the treasure. It's the violation of the Senior trust that's most serious."

Pete was making an unhappy face, one alternating between anger and disgust. "That kid really gets to me," said Pete, his eyes flaring. "He lies to me, and that's something I won't abide. What's worse, his family makes a show at being very religious, and Les always has this morally superior, disdainful attitude toward things we do in the troop. I've had more than one run-in with his dad about things Les reports we do. Les is the perfect hypocrite. I'll have a talk with him, but I know

now that the conversation will just infuriate me. He'll have that same sanctimonious look on his face, while all the time lying to me. I guess his shunning by the Seniors is about the best thing to do, but he doesn't much belong in that group, anyway. That's why he hangs out so much with the younger Scouts. I really don't know why he stays in the troop. He's very disruptive and basically an outlaw as a Senior. Maybe he'll wise up as to how unwelcome he is and drop out."

We all stared at the fire, taking in what Pete had said. We had all witnessed some version of Les's marginality in the Senior Patrol and the unusual amount of time he spent with the Eagle Patrol and other boys. It was sad that he ingratiated himself with the younger boys by betraying the Seniors. Worse, Les's act had undermined the structure of mentorship at camp.

Our mood changed when Pete suggested a Staff canoe ride. There was a full moon that night, and it is a troop C&T for the Staff to take a late night canoe ride under the full moon. Roy volunteered to stay in camp while the rest of us went down to the Waterfront, put on life vests, grabbed paddles, paired up, and chose our canoes.

The night was still and the water like a mirror reflecting the bright moonlight, mountains, and trees at the edge of the lake. You have to be in the mountains on this sort of cloudless, full moon night to understand how bright it can be—almost like daylight. We did not speak as we paddled our canoes away from the shore and across the glassy water toward T.I. Once beached on the sandy shore of T.I., we finally stood around and talked in soft whispers for a while, taking in the beauty of the night and remarking how light it was. Soon the chill caught up with us, and we returned to the canoes for the warmth the paddling gave us. As we were coming back to the Waterfront, I pointed out to Tad (my canoe mate) how the rock ledge was reflected perfectly in the water. "Wow," breathed Tad, as taken by the beauty of the sight as I was. We glided for a while, not letting our paddling disturb the surface of the water. Finally, we all paddled to the Waterfront, put away the canoes and equipment, and silently filed back to camp, where we turned in.

That moonlight canoe ride seemed to me like another ritual at the end of a day featuring a more elaborate troop ritual. In this case, the canoe ride reaffirmed our Staff bond after the disturbing story about Les and his betrayal. The necessary cooperation between two people paddling the same canoe, a cooperation that had to be felt and negotiated with the whole body without verbal communication, enacted this bond. The beauty and whispered silence of the canoe ride provided a spiritual experience, perfectly punctuating the evening. Some would say that the canoe ride was restorative, though none of us talked about it. None broke the silence as we each climbed into our sleeping bags, as if chatter of any sort would break the ritual spell.

Scout and flag, Guam Float
(photographer unknown; photo from author's collection)

Thursday

★ ★ ★ ★ ★ ★ ★ ★ ★ ★ ★ ★ ★ ★ ★ ★ ★ ★ ★ ★

This was to be the last regular day at camp, and the boys seemed to have mixed feelings. They felt some sadness that camp was drawing to a close, but a part of them also missed home and would be glad to return to a comfortable routine. Everyone, Scouts and Seniors alike, focused their energies on the advancement classes. This was the last chance to complete requirements for the badges that would be awarded Saturday evening at the Court of Honor. Advancement was the individual boy's measure that he had had a "productive" camp as well as a fun time.

Seniors spent their spare time beginning the process of breaking down camp, disassembling elements that would not be needed over the next twenty-four hours. This was the beginning of the transition from one frame to another. Camp would slowly disappear; the next day the boys would depart from camp and enter a transitional zone, rejoining their families who would have driven up from the valley to settle into a public campground along the highway. The boys would camp Friday night and Saturday night with their families, and Sunday morning the boys would return fully into the home world.

The day went pretty well. I helped with the breaking down of camp as much as I could. At lunch with the Tiger Patrol, the talk was about the upcoming Nugget Auction that evening, the last fun event in camp. The Tiger Patrol was doing pretty well on points, and its members were eager for this last chance to buy some treats. Over their lunchmeat sandwiches, the boys traded advice about the bidding, while Tim assured them he knew what he was doing. They seemed especially keen to win some Cokes.

Finally, the evening campfire began. The Seniors were as creative for this auction as they had been for the last. Among the new "zonks" was a small rock taped to a footlong string. Taped to the rock was a piece of paper reading

> SENIOR FORECASTING ROCK
> If dry, clear.
> If wet, rainy.
> If horizontal to the ground, wind.
> If spinning, tornado.
> If bouncing, earthquake.

A fabrication of cardboard, stick, and string became a "Senior Mouse Trap," a reference to the continuing problem of mice in the tents holding the stored food. An "open" can of cocoa turned out to be a zonk. The Seniors had used all the cocoa, refilled the can with sand, and replaced a thin layer of cocoa on top to provide the illusion that the prize was authentic.

Watching the Seniors' animated performances and the boys' exuberant bidding, shouting, and taunting, I began to see clearly how the Nugget Auction, the Treasure Hunt of two days earlier, and Insane Day of the previous week formed a sort of sacred triangle of play events for dealing with some of the most troubling contradictions facing these boys. Pete told me once that the "three best traditions" the troop borrowed from his old troop in Berkeley were these three games. Each of the three creates a different metamessage about the relationship between hard work, luck, and reward. What's more, each comments differently upon a fourth frame, everyday life at camp, and all four comment upon a fifth, the boys' everyday life back at home and at school.

The games of Insane Day are ritual contests of physical skill and strategy, involving little or no luck; as such, they confirm for the boys the causal connection among physical skill, strategy, and success. Insane Day fits a larger pattern of culture, in this regard, as scholars have found a strong cross-cultural correlation between high-achievement training and involvement in games of physical skill or of physical skill and strategy.[1] The rituals of Insane Day override the contradiction of the Boy Scout camp and help make the overt, official messages of the institution seem true, even if that requires hiding temporarily the fact that Boy Scouts often achieve their badges and ranks and other rewards through means other than hard work.

If Insane Day ritual contests confirm the connection among physical skill, strategy, and success, then the third game, the Nugget Auction, is a pure gambling event that puts the lie to the lessons of Insane Day by linking chance and success. The Treasure Hunt and the Nugget Auction share the same theme. The Treasure Hunt is the labor, the combination of pluck and luck that produces the consumable commodity—food. Just as the treasure, the Cokes, was food, so the items for which the patrols bid at the Nugget Auction are food. The metamessage that links the Treasure Hunt and the Nugget Auction concerns work, value, commodity, and money.

But the Nugget Auction shifts suddenly the relationship among work, rewards, and value. In the Nugget Auction, chance—not hard work or skill, but chance—is the means to successful acquisition of the desired commodities. The patrol that has worked hardest at keeping its patrol site clean, done its camp chores most diligently, paid the fewest fines, and prevailed in troop contests brings to the Nugget Auction the most points, the most wealth. But this patrol may not be able to acquire the most commodities. A patrol that bids on an item and gets zonked has lost all the work and maybe the virtue that went into earning the points. It is significant that the boys do not appear to blame themselves for their losses, nor does the injustice wrought by the Nugget Auction dampen their enthusiasm for earning the currency with which they gamble for food.

The camp system keeps food a valued commodity and points a scarce currency. We see this most clearly when the system breaks down temporarily. The troop allows "care packages" from home, boxes of cookies, candy, gum, and the occasional birthday cake, all of which have to be shared with the patrol. At one point in the early 1980s, though, the care packages got seriously out of hand.[2] Packages arrived almost daily, sometimes two or three to a patrol. The Staff began to perceive that they were losing a considerable source of leverage over the behavior of the campers. With food treats plentiful, the patrols lost interest in earning points through work and virtue or losing them through transgression. The system worked again once the Staff imposed limits on the receipt of care packages. Once more the Staff and Seniors had control over the food treats, and the Nugget Auction assumed again its power to engage the campers.

It would appear, then, that conflicts induced by the American middle-class achievement training, conflicts heightened by the hypermasculine, achievement-oriented atmosphere of a Boy Scout camp, can be assuaged in two quite different ways, each reflecting an aspect of the cultural contradictions of modern American institutional life. Insane Day's games of physical skill and strategy are good models of mastery over the environment and the social system. But the boys' experience in the Boy Scout institution, an experience not far removed from experiences in the large bureaucratic work settings that lie in their futures, creates considerable uncertainty that physical skill and strategy actually will enable them to master the physical, social, and cultural environments of that world. Facing increased uncertainty and feelings of impotence in modern institutional settings, represented by the bureaucratic troop, the boys are drawn to games of chance wherein they can experiment with mastery of models of uncertainty and gain, as some have put it, "strength to endure bad times in the hope of brighter futures." [3] The Nugget Auction provides this experiment with mastery over uncertainty.

So the game of the Treasure Hunt is about American capitalism, but not in the way I originally supposed. The games of Insane Day do model the Protestant ethic, the entrepreneurial spirit of production, the aggressive male certainty that skill and strategy are the means to success and achievement—but they model an America that no longer exists in our most common institutional experiences. The Nugget Auction lies closer to home, a model of passive strategies of uncertainty appropriate to bureaucratic settings and oriented toward consumption rather than production. The avowed values of the Boy Scout institution stand on the nineteenth-century side of the great transformation in America's political economy and in the social psychology of American institutional experience. Insane Day asserts a faith, perhaps an insane faith at the beginning of the twenty-first century, in the efficacy of skill, strategy, and plain hard work. The boys' actual experience in the institution stands on the twenty-first-century side, where the sense of powerlessness and passivity replaces faith and where consumption delivered more often by contingency (luck or "the fix") than by work seems a truer model of everyday life.

We can see now why the boys prefer both Insane Day and the Nugget Auction to the Treasure Hunt, so much so that several boys get "cold feet" each year just before the hunt. In 1980, all the campers save one signed a petition asking that the Treasure Hunt not be played that year. Most boys turned out to have fun, after all, but they approached the game with great ambivalence. The boys' uneasiness about the Treasure Hunt stems from its crucial difference from the two "safe" games. Insane Day and the Nugget Auction are "fun" precisely because they pose no tough questions. The Treasure Hunt unnerves the boys to the degree that, as play, it stresses the falsity of the supposed simple, direct causal relationship between hard work and reward. It confronts the boys with the terrible secret that underlying an activity that seems to be governed by physical skill and strategy is a *casual* contingency that undermines it all.

This insight into the Treasure Hunt game helps sort out a minor debate among folklorists about the meaning of American buried treasure tales.[4] The ambivalence folklorists find in the tales is not ambivalence toward sudden wealth but ambivalence toward work. Americans' ambivalence toward the tales is akin to the campers' ambivalence toward the Treasure Hunt. Both genres raise disquieting questions about the cultural contradiction involving work, chance, and achievement. Both the tales and the game remind the players that skill and strategy are uncertain paths to reward, that underlying the American mythology of achievement, progress, and virtue is the subversive element of chance that pumps certain irony into American experience. John Huston's 1948 film, *The Treasure of the Sierra Madre,* like the 1935 B. Traven novel on which Huston based the screenplay, ends in ironic failure as the winds blow the gold dust back into the mountains.[5]

Perhaps the ultimate lesson of this pattern in tales, games, and even mass-mediated cultural mythologies is that the self should seek identification through consumption rather than through production, for it is in the former process that luck turns from being subversive to enhancing the excitement of the activity. Disneyland's popular Pirates of the Caribbean ride, according to one interpretation, ironically equates death with hoarding treasure and makes the capitalist argument for the aliveness of consumption.[6] The Boy Scout Treasure Hunt somehow bears the same message. Eating the goods at the end of the Treasure Hunt and at the end of the Nugget Auction confirms that meaning lies in the public, ritual process of consumption, *not* in production. Never mind that there are formal ceremonies elsewhere in camp for reaffirming the virtue of achievement, of production. During the play space and play time of the Treasure Hunt, the boys learn how contingency and consumption are linked inextricably in American experience.[7]

Of course, none of this is on the minds of the boys as they bid for the items displayed by the Seniors. This triangle—Insane Day, Treasure Hunt, and Nugget Auction—does its ideological work precisely because it has encoded American themes in barely recognizable forms. The deep anxieties about the real relationships among hard work, reward, and virtue have been displaced in the coded language of the play frame. At the same time, the play frame is precisely the place where people can invert the usual order of things, entering a subjunctive, "what if?" mode of communication. The triangle does not solve the problem for the boys. But it might assuage their fears enough that they learn to live with the tension that they will feel throughout their entire lives in American society.

The ritual closing of the campfire program was more solemn than ever, tinged with the sadness that camp was ending. The sharing of wins at the final campfire helps "soften the sadness," as Pete says, and this last round of wins takes the longest time, as each boy has at least one win to share. Speaking to the circle of boys and men standing around the campfire, Pete thanked everyone for a "great camp."

"This has been one of the best camps ever," said Pete, really meaning it, I think. "I am so proud of you all. Sometimes I get discouraged about the troop when we have some troubles or things are not going so well. But then we have a camp like this and it makes me proud to know you. We still have to finish breaking camp tomorrow, and I'll have the Scoutmaster conferences with each of you throughout Saturday. And then, of course, we'll have the Court of Honor and a Swingin' Campfire. Get a good night's sleep."

Pete began singing the traditional Boy Scout closing song, and we all joined in:

> Softly falls the light of day
> As our campfire fades away.
> Silently each Scout should ask,
> "Have I done my daily task?
> Have I kept my honor bright?
> Can I guiltless sleep tonight?
> Have I done and have I dared
> Everything to be prepared?"

We spoke together the Scoutmaster's Prayer and sang "Taps" one last time. "Good night, Scouts," said Pete. The last troop campfire of the summer was over.

The mood at the Staff campfire that evening was contemplative. We were all pretty tired and knew we had a long day of labor ahead of us. We were sad that camp was ending. Maybe it was the mood, but my thoughts turned to the words of the song we had sung at the end of each troop campfire. "Have I kept my honor bright?" the song asks. "Can I guiltless sleep tonight?" Honor and guilt—twin concepts that seem to belong to the nineteenth-century world of the Boy Scout founders, from Lord Baden-Powell to Seton and Beard and West. "On my honor," swears each Scout as he recites the Scout Oath. "On my honor, I will do my best to do my duty. . . ." These are concepts easily politicized in today's culture wars. One side in the culture wars decries the absence of honor and duty in secular society; the other side finds these concepts old-fashioned, putting group rules ahead of individual rights and freedom. The boys probably recite the oath and sing this song without much thought to the words they have memorized. Or maybe not. What are we to make of the centrality of the concept of "honor" to the Boy Scouts of America, and if we take the boys' point of view, what happens to the meanings of the term?

There is plenty of evidence that the men who founded the Boy Scouts made "honor" the supreme virtue in the movement. One of these men was John L. Alexander, a YMCA activist and a convert to William Forbush's Knights of King Arthur, a youth organization that predated the Boy Scouts and took as its theme the English feudal Christian code of honor. Alexander brought to his Boy Scout work his and others' preoccupation with honor. When Alexander and the rest of the Committee on Standardization undertook to "Americanize" the British Scout Oath and Law, they decided to begin the American Scout Oath with "On my honor. . . ." The paragraph in the first *Handbook for Boys* explaining the first point of the Scout law—"A Scout is Trustworthy"—links trust to honor. "A scout's honor is to be trusted," explain the authors. "If he were to violate his honor by telling a lie, or by cheating, or by not doing exactly a given task, when trusted on his honor, he may be directed to hand over his scout badge."[8]

In writing of the "Scout virtues" in the introductory chapter of that first *Handbook,* Alexander makes it clear that

[t]he most important scout virtue is that of honor. Indeed, it is the basis of all scout virtues and is closely allied to that of self-respect. When a scout promises to do a thing on his honor, he is bound to do it. The honor of a scout will not permit of anything but the highest and the best and the manliest. The honor of a scout is a sacred thing, and cannot be lightly set aside or trampled on.[9]

Alexander also contributed a later chapter devoted to "Chivalry," where he calls for "modern knighthood," a modern chivalry appropriate to the reform ethos of the Progressive Era. "Might still tries to make right," warns Alexander, "and while there are now no robber barons or outlaws with swords and spears, their spirit is not unknown in business and commercial life." Warming to this jeremiad against capitalist greed, Alexander continues: "Vice and dishonesty lift their heads just as strongly to-day as in the past and there is just as much need of respect for women and girls as there ever was."[10]

Alexander's rhetoric here seems to leave little doubt that the founders of the Boy Scouts fixed on honor as the most important Scout virtue because its status had become so shaky by 1910. These men perceived a crisis in the status of honor as a piece of the masculine character, and they saw the Boy Scouts as a means to revitalize this concept in American boys.

The founders included little analysis of the causes of the decline in honor in modern American society, though they seemed to be reacting to several developments at the turn of the twentieth century. As many historians have noted, in the 1890s these men were reacting to what they saw as the "feminization" of the American boy, by female schoolteachers, by overprotective mothers, and by a society that was going "soft" without the masculinizing effects of war.[11] These men were also witnessing gargantuan changes in the nature of the American economy and the ways people arranged their institutional lives. Business and science, each in its own way, assaulted religion, replacing spirituality with a purportedly "new materialism." The United States had matured as a producing economy and was shifting into a consumption-oriented economy, with all of the institutions (department stores, catalog sales, the invention of consumer credit, and so on) that commodity capitalism requires. Not that the economy was making this transition so smoothly; the 1880s and 1890s saw several jolting downturns in the economy and a great deal of labor unrest.[12]

These changes in the structure and nature of the American economy affected people's experiences of institutional order and disorder. "The middle and upper class generations born after 1910," writes historian Thomas C. Cochran of what he calls the "inner revolution" in the American worldview, "found themselves surrounded by the rubble of once imposing structures of truth."[13] The "entrepreneurial" personality died in that rubble, to be replaced by the "organization man" of the twentieth century, as the work experience of Americans came to be played out increasingly in bureaucratic organizations. Nineteenth-century concern with "character," explains another historian, was replaced with twentieth-century concern with "personality."[14] Whereas the term "character" suggests the sort of "moral gyroscope" David Riesman thought was typical of the "inner-directed" personality and is compatible with religious understandings of the world, the term "personality" seems more related to the sort of moral "radar" Riesman associated with the conformist, "other-directed" personality and relies on ideas from psychology rather than from religion.[15] The recent slogan, "Character Counts," that the Boy Scouts use on their materials, signals the values of the 1890s far more than those of the 1990s.

In a provocative essay entitled "On the Obsolescence of the Concept of Honor," sociologist Peter L. Berger contrasts two terms, "honor" and "dignity," in order to understand the cognitive change the modernization of consciousness brings.[16] Berger's thesis is quite simple. Modernity brings with it the demise of the concept of honor and the rise of the concept of dignity. The two concepts describe very different links between the self and society. Whereas the concept of honor "implies that identity is essentially, or at least importantly, linked to institutional roles," the modern concept of dignity "by contrast implies that identity is essentially independent of institutional roles." The shift to a world of dignity, where "the individual can only discover his true identity by emancipating himself from his socially imposed roles," is a product of the forces of modernization, epitomized primarily by technology and bureaucracy.

This shift also lies behind the founders' intense interest in displays of "everyday heroism."[17] This topic stood at the intersection of several lines of thought, including social Darwinism and the puzzle of altruistic behavior. If the individual understood his identity as grounded in the group and in institutional roles, then altruism was comprehensible; if, however, the individual discovered his true identity only by emancipating himself from those roles, then altruism was impossible. To one person, altruism and doing one's duty were a high human virtue; to the other, altruism and doing one's duty were no more than foolish betrayals of the true self.[18]

The founders of the Boy Scouts, men of the 1890s, became obsessed with the concept of honor and with related concepts like heroism, altruism, and duty precisely because they were living through this great transformation and were entering a new world where the concept of honor was becoming, in Berger's term, "obsolete"—which is a way of saying that in 1910 these founders were facing a world in which their own lives and values—their own characters—were obsolete. They were trying to create a revitalization movement that would bring boys back to nineteenth-century values and save them from the twentieth century.[19]

The founders were trying to revitalize the concept of honor through two strategies. One was purely rhetorical; the *Handbooks* and other publications and public pronouncements put the "Scout's honor" at the center of the movement. The second strategy aimed to revitalize honor by putting the boy as much as possible into situations where he and his behavior were governed by the group, namely, by the Boy Scout patrol and troop. The patrol system at the heart of the Scout program is meant to create everyday behavior, "practices" and "experiences," we might say, in which the boy resists the modern pressures for him to value his individualized "personality" above his group-based "character."

The cultural crises of the 1890s and the 1990s bear a remarkable resemblance. By invoking the slogan "Character Counts" and by talking about traditional values in response to the legal challenges to exclusion of atheists, homosexuals, and girls, the national leadership of the Boy Scouts continues the founders' efforts to revitalize the concept of honor and fight back the forces of modernization.

Looking at the rhetoric of the national organization, however, might not be the best way to judge what honor means to the boys and men in the movement. I have to remind myself to return to the field, to see how Troop 49 defines honor every day through its collective practices. Pete's lectures on "truthfulness," "duty," and "trust" do some of this work, but far more important are the practices that connect the boys to their folk groups, to the patrol and to the troop. The boys acquire a sense of honor through their experience of belonging to the group and maturing with and within the group. This is why Pete substitutes "classy" for "cool." "Cool" represents a radical, isolated individualism, while the meanings of "classy" exist only in relation to the individual boy's connection to the troop. Even if they sing their final campfire song without thinking much about the words, the Scouts are learning to judge their performances against the group's standards and to see their behavior in terms of how it reflects on the group.

The lake (photograph by author)

Friday, Saturday, & Sunday

★ ★ ★ ★ ★ ★ ★ ★ ★ ★ ★ ★ ★ ★ ★ ★ ★ ★ ★

Friday morning was devoted to finishing advancement, but the Staff and the dads and alumni who began arriving Friday morning were busy breaking down camp. Pete asked me to move among the patrol sites after breakfast, making sure they had packed their personal belongings and had broken down the patrol boxes to be loaded later on the large flatbed truck that would carry the camp equipment back home. The boys, I sensed, were feeling the same mixed emotions as I was. I was anticipating home, and especially such luxuries as hot showers, but I was also saddened by the thought that the weeks in the mountains were almost at an end. The familiar constructions of camp were disappearing before our eyes, as the troop proudly practiced the backpacker's credo that you should leave a wilderness site with little evidence that you had trod upon that space.

We had a Commissary lunch, standing around and eating sandwiches amid the hubbub of breaking camp. After lunch, Todd assembled the patrols. Each boy had all his personal belongings in his backpack, and Todd led the troop off toward LBAS, where they would take a final, cooling swim before they hiked out to "the green gate" on the highway, the appointed rendezvous site where parents picked up the boys in the late afternoon. Some families would camp out at the public campground where the rest of Troop 49's activities would take place that weekend. Others had rented rooms or cabins at the nearby lodge. Hot showers and real mattresses beckoned.

The Seniors and adults remained in camp to finish breaking down the equipment and loading it onto the flatbed truck. All the camp tables had to be disassembled, ULMUD disassembled, the KYBO taken down, and so on. The troop has done this enough times that everyone seemed to know what they were doing, and we finished by 4:00 Friday afternoon, almost a troop record for breaking camp. I hiked back to my car and drove out the way I had come, arriving at the public campground around 5:00. After chatting briefly with some of the alumni and parents at the campground, I found Tad, and we drove over to the lodge where Pete and his wife, Helen, had rented a room. Pete, Helen, Tad, Aaron, and I had a glass of wine together, and then Tad, Aaron, and I went off to have dinner at a restaurant. At the bar, one of the troop fathers came over to buy us a beer and to thank us for "taking care of" his son at camp. The conversation was rather awkward, even a bit sad. I was reminded of my earlier thoughts about the anthropological "mother's brother" phenomenon, wherein the father turns over the socialization of a son to the boy's maternal uncle. We were those uncles for this man's son, and he was thanking us for doing what he could not do. We thanked him for the beer and watched him return to the family across the room. We waved to the family, watching the boy that we had known in one setting for three weeks settle back into being a son and a brother. After dinner, we returned to the campground and talked around an impromptu campfire. Tired, I excused myself and set up my sleeping area beside my car, just my air mattress and sleeping bag on a tarp. This was my next-to-last night to sleep under the stars that summer.

★ ★ ★

Saturday's activities began at 9:00 in the morning. Jeff's father, Clark, was chairman of the troop Advancement Committee, and he had organized the fathers for Boards of Review. The Boards "examine" Scouts on the badges they have earned, not so much to test them on material as to inquire what sorts of things the boys learned in working on the badge or rank. The Boards are friendly, really as much for the benefit of the troop fathers as for the boys. The Board of Review sessions give the fathers a glimpse into the official agenda of the organization and into what goes on for the three-week summer encampment.

Meanwhile, I could see Pete sitting in his aluminum lawn chair under a tree, talking with a boy seated in a chair facing him. Pete has a twenty- to thirty-minute conference with each Scout. The goal of the Scoutmaster's conference is for Pete and the boy to have a private conversation about how camp went for the boy, what his patrol thinks of him, what he likes best and worst about camp, what the boy's future goals are, and the like. Pete asks if anything is bothering the boy. He also asks the boy what point of the Scout Law means the most to him. Pete's next-to-last question is always "Are there any deep, dark secrets, and bad stuff going on that I should know about?" And, finally, he asks, "What do you like the most about the troop and Scouting? What are your biggest wins?"

Normally these conferences are private, but Pete permitted me to sit in on one of them, Stan's, with Stan's permission. Pete had to deal with Stan's complaints about Eddie, his Patrol Leader. Pete offered advice about dealing with fights within the patrol, dealing with a bossy Patrol Leader, and so on. Pete gave this conversation the form of a Socratic dialogue. Stan thus discovered for himself some of the solutions and strategies he would have to adopt in order to be happier and more successful in his patrol and in the troop.

Listening to this Socratic dialogue, I began reflecting on the reservoir of understanding Scoutmasters like Pete have to draw upon when dealing with adolescent boys. There are plenty of scientific psychological theories of adolescence, and these have always informed the program of the Boy Scouts of America, from G. Stanley Hall's recapitulation theory of the late nineteenth century to the present. These theories usually show up in successive editions of the *Handbook for Scoutmasters*. Pete, though, has little use for academic theories about male adolescents. "People who have theories about boys," he proclaimed in one Staff campfire conversation, "usually have never actually worked with boys."

Anthropologists have a name for theories of the sort that we, in our ethnocentric way, call science: psychology, sociology, botany, entomology, and so on. All cultures have "ethnosciences," say the anthropologists, where the prefix "ethno" announces that this is a belief system held by a specific people. For example, every culture has an "ethnopsychology," a theory of the mind, of emotions, of motives, of individual behavior—in short, of all the phenomena we associate with the "science" of psychology.

Pete holds a very workable ethnopsychology of the white, middle-class, male adolescent. Like sports team coaches and other people who work closely with young men, successful Scoutmasters come to understand the boy's psychology from the boy's point of view. Pete's decodables are a perfect example of this ethnopsychology. His is an inductive understanding, gleaned from years of teaching high school and spending summers in the mountains with hundreds of boys aged eleven through seventeen. He intuits very effectively the boundaries and structures these boys need; he finds a productive balance between freedom and control; he helps them develop a working understanding of the necessary balance between individual rights and the individual's responsibilities to the group; he lets boys try and fail, if necessary, within a safe environment. As Pete says, the troop is the only place where you can fuck up in most ways and still redeem yourself.

No adolescent psychology textbook or any version of adolescent psychology as translated by the authors of the *Handbook for Scoutmasters* can arm the Scoutmaster with these understandings and practices. Some men take to this work, and others don't. Pete has learned his teaching skills well; maybe he learned to teach in the Boy Scouts and became a high school teacher with those skills already in hand. Pete likes the Socratic dialogue as a teaching tool. He likes to see the boys arrive at the right answer themselves, if they can. He expects their obedience to camp rules, for example, not because the Boy Scout owes blind obedience to authority (as some would have it). Rather, Pete wants the boy to arrive himself at the rationale for the rule. He wants the boy to develop a duty to the group not out of some abstract notion declared in the Scout Oath (which the boys come to speak automatically and mindlessly anyway, without much thought to the words) but out of the boy's own mixed drives to be autonomous and, at the same time, to belong to a male friendship group, to have the close bonding and sense of loyalty those friendships entail. In a sense, Pete's ethnopsychology of the adolescent male actually resembles G. Stanley Hall's and Ernest Thompson Seton's. Pete follows Seton's program, I would say, even when it leads him away from the "official" Boy Scout ways of doing things (as a Setonian approach almost certainly must lead one). Pete has Seton's genuine love for boys and a faith that even the kid who looks like a mess, who seems to be a perennial fuck-up, can be redeemed by participation in the troop. As I observed in the excursus on gays and girls in the Boy Scouts, the genius of Pete's skill as a Scoutmaster lies somewhere in his ability to bring the structure of the Strict

Father model of the family to what is more fully a Nurturant Parent model.

Walking around after my visit with Pete and Stan, I noticed that the boys were reacting in predictable ways to the presence of women. Some boys were noticing friends' sisters, and some girlfriends had come up with the boys' families. Boys were now sons and brothers. The transition from an all-male world was well under way, but I knew that some of the boys were probably suffering transition shock, much like the boy in Pete's story who asked his sister to "pass the fucking butter."

Later in the afternoon, Aaron, Tad, and I went shopping for some steaks and accompaniments for dinner; no Spam. We had a large meal, and the alumni enjoyed standing around, sharing memories and stories. One of the troop alumni had set up a small tent with a slide projector automatically showing tray after tray of the slides Pete had accumulated over the years, and every once in a while I would go over to that tent to watch the slides and listen to the alumni and Seniors talk about what they were seeing. Some of the slides were of an Insane Day from years earlier, and the Seniors were stunned at how much those slides looked like the present. They were getting a visual lesson in the continuity of the troop's traditions. After dinner, everyone changed into their dress uniforms for the upcoming Court of Honor, which began at 7:00.

The Court of Honor rivals the Investiture as a sacred ritual for the troop. The Court of Honor is the public occasion for conferring badges and ranks upon the Scouts. The American and troop flags hung vertically from a rope as background for this ceremony, and Pete sat behind a table on which were arrayed the various pieces of paper and badges that the boys had earned. The Scouts sat on the ground to Pete's right, at a right angle to the table, and the audience of parents, families, alumni, and friends sat in lawn chairs and on blankets opposite Pete.

Todd asked everyone to stand for the Pledge of Allegiance, and then he led the troop in a recitation of the Scout Oath. Everyone sat down and the Court of Honor began. Clark and Jeff went through the advancement lists, announcing each badge or rank and calling forward the boys who had earned that badge. The boys came to the table, saluted Pete (who returned the salute), and turned to face the crowd. A father from the appropriate Board of Review came forward for each badge and spoke briefly to the audience about the badge, its requirements, and what sorts of things the boys learned. The audience applauded after each badge. When boys came forward to get their badges of rank (Tenderfoot, Second Class, First Class, Star, and Life), each mother (or father) came forward to pin the badge on the son's uniform. The boy then turned to put a pin of that rank on the mother or, in a few cases, the father. Pinning the badge on his mother nicely reconnects the boy with the world of women. So much of what was happening at Scout camp worked to create the heterosexual male by separating him from his mother and by disregarding or even disrespecting the feminine. While camp radically separates the developing boy from the feminine, the boy's pinning the badge on his mother serves to reconnect the boy to the feminine.

The Court of Honor lasted a good amount of time, as camp is a productive advancement time, and near the end we needed the lanterns that had been strung over the audience for light. The Court of Honor finally ended, and Pete invited everyone to attend the "Swingin' Campfire" at the large campfire site nearby.

The Swingin' Campfire is a public event, and it is here that the boys need to remember to keep things "MA"—Mother Approved. Put differently, don't sing or say anything you wouldn't sing or say in front of your mother because your mother *is* there. Tommy led the campfire, which had a good sample of the troop's traditional songs and yells. The campfire ended in the usual way, and Pete wished the boys his last "Good night, Scouts" of the camp season. The boys all went with their families to their campsites or lodge rooms, as the troop alumni and Staff milled around, waiting to have the campfire site to themselves. They were waiting to begin another troop tradition, the "After-Campfire Campfire."

The After-Campfire Campfire is a troop reunion, pure and simple. Pete's two sons, Dick and Bill, were there, Bill with his wife. About a dozen troop alumni had come up, men ranging in age from nineteen to early thirties, and many brought their wives and girlfriends to the campfire. Some of the Seniors tried to hang around for this campfire, but they seemed to know that it was not quite "cool" that they were there, and Tad asked them to leave.

One of the alumni threw more wood on the fire, and we created a circle of aluminum lawn chairs around the campfire. People brought out the beers and snacks that had been hidden away during the official portions of the evening. It was strange to see women in the circle, and I knew what was coming. Finally, Pete strummed a chord on his ukulele as a signal that the After-Campfire Campfire was beginning. Like the regular troop campfires, the After-Campfire Campfire begins traditionally with the same song ("One Ball Alley," with the Camp Director for that year as the butt of the song's humor), but in this case the ribald song sets the tone and lets the audience know that this is going to be an obscenely male event.

The campfire is a songfest and jokefest, interspersed with small-group conversations around the circle, and there is a flavor of college fraternity humor in everything, which is to say that most of the songs and jokes would be classified as sexist, racist, homophobic, or a combination of the three. Pete early launched us into a song traditional for this campfire. It is a traditional chain song, with the chorus

> Ay, ay, ay, ay,
> In China they never eat chili,
> So sing me another verse
> Worse than the other verse,
> And waltz me around again, Willie.[1]

The verses to this song, volunteered by those around the campfire, took the form of familiar obscene limericks, each followed by the chorus. I was surprised when Roy's woman friend, Stacey, jumped in for a turn; Stacey's obscene limerick gave courage to a few other women to offer a verse, but mainly the song bounced back and forth between the men.

The song led to a joke-telling session, filled with jokes about penises and other subjects of male humor. Finally, Robert's wife had the courage to tell a joke, and she asked for the floor.

"Here's one for the women," she said. "How do you say 'small' in 3 two-letter words?" She paused for dramatic effect. "'Is it in?'" Everyone laughed.

Some of the women, though, seemed unsure about how to respond to the whole evening. As I gazed around the campfire at the women, some seemed alternatively stunned and appalled at the crude songs and jokes coming out of the mouths of their husbands and boyfriends, while others joined in the fun. The misogyny of most of the songs and jokes must have been shocking to the newcomers. After one joke, I heard Bill's wife say, almost unheard, "That's the kind of joke I punch my husband for telling."

The After-Campfire Campfire is a complex folk event, and it sits right at the border between the all-male world of camp and the everyday world of men and women living, working, loving, and fighting together. The campfire is a play event, and it enacts the true paradox of play. It's not surprising to me that a group of men (almost all of them Eagle Scouts) would sit around a campfire drinking beer, singing the most obscene songs a college rugby team or fraternity could dream up, and telling jokes just as obscene. This is an old and familiar folk phenomenon, the bonding of men over drink and dirty talk. But this is a very unusual campfire for the men of Troop 49; even the evening Staff campfires, without Scouts present, show the men to be thoughtful, respectful, and even somewhat androgynous in their talk. Paradoxically, the men of Troop 49 become the most masculine—hypermasculine, one might say—when the women, the women these men love and respect, are present.

My first thought was that these women were getting an unwelcome glimpse into the otherwise secret world of the male friendship group and that they did not like what they were seeing. This was a side of their husbands and boyfriends better left unseen, ignored, for in other contexts these were loving, affectionate men who were respectful toward women. Here, in full view, was an ugly misogyny that (I imagined) might make the women wonder which was the real husband or boyfriend—the considerate and sensitive man they knew and loved on an everyday basis or the man who joked and sang obscenely with his male friends?

After lengthy conversations with Pete and Tad about the After-Campfire Campfire, I see now that the event is more fully paradoxical than I initially realized. It's true that for some newcomers, some women, the event is shocking and disturbing. At least I thought I could see that in their faces, and I even witnessed a spat between a twenty-something alumnus and his girlfriend, sparked (I thought) by the tension of the event.

But, as Pete and Tad rightly point out, lots of the wives and girlfriends come back to this After-Campfire Campfire year after year, and some even contribute to the singing and joking. So the women are getting something out of it. Let me try to sort this out.

From the men's point of view, the After-Campfire Campfire is a parody of male culture. The play frame of the event makes it possible to make this campfire an inversion of the troop's other campfires. In a sense, the other troop campfires (and maybe especially the Swingin' Campfire, with families and even young children present) seem more like rituals and less like play compared with the vibrant, inversive, transgressive play frame of the After-Campfire Campfire. The play event is fun precisely because it isn't "classy" (though I'm certain that the participants believe that there is such a thing as a "classy" way to perform even this campfire).

But the After-Campfire Campfire is more than mere transgressive fun. It is doing some ideological, psychological, and social work, too.

For example, for the men who have spent the past three weeks in camp, the stylized performance of hypermasculine talk in the presence of women is a way of punctuating the three weeks' worth of all-male culture and preparing the participants for the feelings of dependence and interdependence they are already experiencing and anticipating in the presence of their wives and girlfriends. Even these men, who seem to me to be fashioning some fairly androgynous meanings of masculinity, feel enough fragility in their performances of masculinity that this stylized hypermasculinity feels like a necessary last gesture in the transition from an all-male world to a world with women.

The men of Troop 49 are also "testing" their women with this event. The question is whether the women can enter the troop's traditional play frame and play with the men. "We think the women should feel privileged to be there," explained Tad when he, Pete, and I later talked about the event. "We are saying to them, in effect, 'We regard you women so highly that we are sharing this event with you.'"

Pete added to Tad's observation: "You know, the men are gambling when they take their women to the After-Campfire Campfire. They are gambling that their women will understand how important this group of friends is to the troop alumnus. They are gambling that the woman will come away from the campfire with the right feelings. Usually, the gamble pays off, and the woman passes the test. Sometimes the guy loses—the woman flunks the test. But not too often."

Hearing this testimony, I thought of Gregory Bateson's point that simply sharing a play frame voluntarily signals to the participants something about their relationship. Just as ritual insults require a play frame that confirms the closeness and trust of the participants, so voluntary play in the frame of the After-Campfire Campfire might signal a closeness and trust between the men and women.[2]

What are the women getting out of this? The presence of Helen, Pete's wife, at the After-Campfire Campfire makes it legitimate for other women to be there, too. Helen works tirelessly for and with the troop, but she also knows what to leave alone. Her presence at the campfire doubtless makes the other women more comfortable and might even (says Pete) make the men exhibit more courtesy toward the women (especially during "backstage" moments that occur between the "onstage," over-the-edge displays of hypermasculinity).

Women might get some pleasure from seeing their men behave in ways that confirm for them the superiority of women. Many women have the sense that men carry a thin veneer (if any at all) of being civilized, and it is the source of much folk and popular humor that women work hard at civilizing men. Seeing their loved ones lapse into the crudeness of the After-Campfire Campfire paradoxically might confirm for the women the importance of their role as the civilizers of men.

And then there's the pleasure the women might take in the obscenity itself. The play frame of the After-Campfire Campfire frees the women to act in ways they would not normally act in front of their male partners (or at least not in public). Women can be as obscene as men, we know, but we expect public displays of crudeness and obscenity from men, just as we expect women to avoid them. Women more often rely on carefully framed places and times to share their obscenities with other women and with some men.[3] So there was a lot of bending of the norms of both male and female behavior in this play frame.

The campfire wound down slowly, as people near one another broke into smaller, quieter conversations and some, tired, said their goodbyes and went off into the dark, cold night. Most of the women had left by 2:30. By that time, only a few alumni, Tad, Aaron, and I were left. We doused the fire with buckets of water.[4] The campfire circle finally was totally dark, and we turned on our flashlights as we gathered our things and trudged back to the camping area. I laid out my tarp and sleeping bag and slept soundly until Tad shook me awake only a few hours later, with dawn barely breaking. "Come on, Jay. I want to introduce you to one last Troop 49 C&T. It's traditional for us to go skinny-dipping in the lodge lake before breakfast."

I shook the sleep from my eyes. The night had been cold, and I didn't really want to climb out of my down sleeping bag with only two hours' sleep, but I knew I could not turn down an invitation to a troop C&T. I dressed quickly and Tad, Aaron, and I drove over to the lodge, parked, and walked the short distance to the lakeshore. The sun had not yet appeared over the mountain tops, but the sky was getting lighter, and I could see the beautiful, still lake and forest. Skinny-dipping was the traditional way to end the camp season, but a couple was sitting nearby, enjoying the sunrise, and the group quickly determined that skinny-dipping in front of the woman was not "cool." So we all stripped down to our underwear and plunged into the water. I expected it to be colder. It was cold, to be sure, but the air was so cold that the water actually seemed warm in comparison. We swam and splashed around for a while. I insisted on taking a final picture, to document the tradition. Finally, we all got out of the water, toweled ourselves dry, and went into the lodge for breakfast. The food was good and the coffee strong (how I had missed my morning coffee), and we engaged in animated chat about the campfire and camp.

After breakfast, we said our goodbyes. I got into my car and began the long drive home, descending from the mountains to the foothills, to the flat valley, and finally to my home and family.

Real Boy Scouts

The lingering memory of a clear Sunday morning with a mist rising from the warm lake and young men posing for a picture makes a poetic ending to this story about Troop 49, but there is more to say. Pete retired from his high school teaching job in the mid-1990s, and by 1998 he was ready to hand over the leadership of Troop 49 to the next generation. One troop father acted as Scoutmaster for a year, while Pete enjoyed the invented office of "Scoutmaster emeritus," from which he exercised his privilege of giving advice and wisdom when asked. In 1999, Tad took over as Scoutmaster, and throughout most of the summer encampment, Pete kept away from camp, joining the group only for the Court of Honor, the Swingin' Campfire, and the After-Campfire Campfire. The transition of leadership was complete, and Pete was eager to have everyone understand that, despite Tad's closeness to Pete, it was Tad who was Scoutmaster. As in any organization with a charismatic leader, especially a Boy Scout troop that had a single Scoutmaster for nearly thirty-two years, the question remains how much the distinctive culture of the troop is the projection of a single person's personality and how much the culture has a strength and resilience beyond any one leader. Tad seems to be doing well in his new role, and he is working hard to rebuild the troop's membership, which saw a decline near the end of the decade.

As I reflect on the lessons to be learned from Troop 49's example and from Pete's leadership, I want to return to some of the issues I raised in the introduction. I claimed there that the close, ethnographic examination of the ways boys create their everyday lives might help cut through the overheated rhetoric about boys, offer some insight into the present public discourse about the "boy problem," and point to some ways parents and other adults who work with male teens can do those young men some good.

One way to approach this task is to look briefly at what the therapists who are writing the books on boys say about them and then compare this map of boys' psychology and social lives with the culture Troop 49, under Pete's philosophical guidance, has created. In the language of anthropologists, I am comparing Pete's "folk psychology of male adolescence" with what the practitioners of the scientific psychology of male adolescence say.

William Pollack's 1998 book, *Real Boys,* is a good place to begin.[1] Actually, from the ethnographer's point of view, Pollack has a pretty good grasp of the cultures of boys. After amassing the examples and statistics showing how much boys are at risk in our society in the late 1990s, Pollack points to two ever-present elements of boys' lives— separation and shame—as the conditions that lead finally to the "Boy Code," Pollack's umbrella term for the defense mechanisms boys adopt to compensate for the traumas of separation and shame.

By separation, Pollack means that developmental process I noted earlier in my discussion of Nancy Chodorow's work. Because the boy needs to separate from the mother in order to establish his own identity, masculinity is almost always defined as a negative, that is, as "not feminine." In Pollack's view, we (society) force boys to separate from their mothers a bit too early and a bit too much. So anxiety about this separation gnaws at boys, even as they "know" that they are supposed to be independent. One author even labels this "post-traumatic stress."[2]

At the same time that boys are suffering the anxiety of separation, they are also socialized to avoid expressing emotions, a trait our society tends to consider feminine. Most of the writers about the "boy problem" agree on this point—namely, that our society trains boys to suppress and deny their emotions, including sadness, fear, and jealousy, while permitting girls a broader expression of emotions as appropriately "feminine." This "emotional mis-education of boys," as a pair of writers calls it, adds to the stress of separating from the feminine.[3] Boys are permitted to express one emotion—anger—and in the absence of other outlets, that anger sometimes becomes rage.[4]

Making things worse, boy peer culture tends to use shame as a socializing device. Boys tend to create larger friendship groups than do girls, and those friendship groups tend to be hierarchical. As Deborah Tannen notes, boys see talking in the friendship group as a performance in front of an audience, and often at stake in those performances is the place of the boy in the group's hierarchy.[5] Boys develop an elaborate expressive culture in their friendship folk group, a culture that includes boasting, teasing, taunting, insulting, and even physical playfighting. As I argued earlier, boys develop this aggressive, combative peer culture in part as a substitute for the real violence boys and men are capable of visiting on one another. The play frame of the oral, aggressive culture creates a safe zone that helps bond the friendships.

Shame enters this expressive culture, as boys might tease each other about not being quite masculine enough. The play frame gets tested in these episodes where the boys shame a member of the group. What is even more significant for Pollack and the other therapists writing about boys' lives is that parents, coaches, teachers, and other adults also employ shame as a device to steer the boy away from dependence, emotionality, weakness, and other signs that might be read as "feminine." Boys learn from both peers and adults that they are to be independent, strong, stoic, aggressive, fearless, dominant, and powerful. And anything but feminine. These qualities, says Pollack, describe the Boy Code.[6] This code might include the masculine "cool pose," a style of masculinity scholars have noted in many men of color as a defense mechanism against the feminizing stereotypes used against them by white men.[7] But if Pollack and other writers are right, most boys of every ethnic background learn to perform some version of the "cool pose" as a defense against dependence, weakness, emotionality, and other things feminine. Boys constantly have to prove their masculinity; it is always a process, never an achieved goal. What others see as arrogance in boys covers the fragility of the masculinity they are attempting to construct and repair daily.

Pollack and his fellow therapists see the Boy Code as a pathology that hurts boys and everyone around them. As therapists, Pollack and the others aim to help their individual patients understand their anger and depression, help them see that they need to free themselves from the Boy Code and learn (for example) individuation without separation.[8] But these books are also filled with concrete advice to parents, teachers, and others (coaches, Scoutmasters, and so on, one assumes) about how to help boys create in their everyday lives the circumstances and resources that help them resist the Boy Code.

As I read these books, I am struck by how much they resemble the thinking of G. Stanley Hall, the "inventor" of "adolescence," at the end of the nineteenth century. As I read Michael Gurian's list of the basic principles of "boy culture"—including competitive performance, skill-building, preference for large groups, search for independence, love of adventure, personal sacrifice for the group, and structuring life as if it were a sport—I could as easily be reading Hall or Ernest Thompson Seton.[9] The strong resemblance between Seton's boy psychology in the 1890s and that of these therapists in the 1990s (including, I should add, a firm belief in the power of the boy's biology and of human evolution) reinforces our notion that the two decades responded in similar ways to a perceived crisis in masculinity.

The way the men and boys of Troop 49 construct the Boy Scout experience speaks to ongoing public debate about boys and what (if anything) we should do to "save them." Pete's philosophy as Scoutmaster and his theory of male adolescence compare quite favorably with the experts' theories and advice. For example, Pete recognizes the damaging role of shame in boys' cultures and works to eliminate that peer control mechanism; he forbids anything approaching hazing, and he mitigates embarrassment. Pete recognizes the "cool pose" for what it is, so he consciously substitutes the notion of "classy," which expresses pride rather than a false front. Pete is not afraid to model emotions beyond anger (though he does model that one, too), as when he cried with Todd in their talk about Todd's increasing distance from the troop. And, as I discussed earlier, Pete manages to combine elements of the Strict Father and the Nurturant Parent.

The culture of Troop 49 is so much a projection of Pete's personality and ideas about male adolescence that it is hard to separate discussions of the two, but it is worth noting that the culture of the troop embodies many of the qualities and strategies the experts on boy culture recommend. Some of these qualities and strategies, frankly, come from the Boy Scout program itself (and can be traced, as I said, to the ideas and practices introduced by Seton). I am thinking here of Seton's honors by standards—a notion of competition quite different from the common one dividing winners from losers—and the fundamental strategy of having boys construct and maintain their friendships through, as Pollack calls it, "doing together." Whereas girls tend to rely on talk to sustain and repair their friendships, boys tend to talk less and let shared activity—"doing together" or doing "side by side"—be the way they communicate about their friendship.[10] There is also some truth to the BSA's claim that the patrol and troop are the functional equivalent of the boy's "gang," giving him a natural-sized friendship group, an identity that is both individual and collective, highly visual markers of those identities, and opportunities to perform duties and provide leadership in the service of others. The culture of Troop 49 features all of these practices.

It is important to note, though, that it takes a troop of living men and boys to create what we might consider a "healthy" group culture for the still-maturing adolescent male and that many troops (Troop 49 is a good example) forge a group culture that is to some extent in opposition to the official Boy Scout institution. Morality, for example, cannot be legislated. For some time now, moral philosophers and social scientists who study the social construction of everyday morality have known that a set of rules is no guide to how people actually deal with ethical and moral dilemmas. You cannot live unambiguously by the Scout Oath and Law, for everyday life presents the boy and man with situations needing an interpretive reading of the law, preferably a reading done in conversation with others. In some situations, for example, a boy might have to choose between being "Loyal" and being "Obedient."[11] The quality of moral instruction in the Boy Scouts, then, depends less on the printed texts and more on the personal qualities of the men and older adolescents who provide moral instruction to the boys. As in education, where some professionals try to create a "teacher-proof curriculum," it is foolish to think that the institution can make up for the broad diversity of adults training the children by standardizing the printed texts. The increasing moral rigidity of the BSA national office deflects our attention from the simple fact that the BSA has little control over the quality of the men "delivering" its program.

I imagine, for example, that Scout executives will cringe when reading in these pages about Pete's fuck-up principle. They won't like the obscene phrase, but even more they will not want to acknowledge that even the best Boy Scouts fuck up. That principle, recall, sees the troop as a "safe" place for a boy to fail and still redeem himself. Pete has some unforgivable fuck-ups on his list, but in most cases he will give a kid the chance to prove himself again and again. When Pete teaches the Tenderfoot class to the first-year campers and they get to a discussion of the Scout Oath, Pete draws the boys' attention to the wording of the first line: "On my honor, I will do my best to do my duty. . . ." "Do my best," explains Pete, acknowledges that you will sometimes fuck up but that you will try to do the right thing. Pete won't abide lying, but he also detests sanctimonious behavior and hypocrisy, which he finds in great quantities among professional Scouters and among some volunteers.

Pete and the other adult leaders of Troop 49 also show respect for the folk cultures of male adolescents. Respecting the privacy of Senior Point is one element of this respect, but I have in mind a broader willingness to tolerate a certain range of adolescent behavior and to permit the peer group some latitude in how it socializes its members, resolves

internal disputes, and inserts its own creativity into the traditional practices it inherits from previous generations of adolescents in the troop.

Finally, I think it is promising that Troop 49 operates according to a
social and political philosophy that has come to be called "communitarian" by social critics. Since the 1980s, sociologist Amitai Etzioni has
taken considerable intellectual leadership in explaining and promoting
this "third way" in American public philosophy, attempting to chart a
course between the "individualists," who place autonomy above all social values, and the "social conservatives," who value order most.[12] The
communitarian position criticizes individualist thinking as imagining
the freestanding individual, whereas we have every reason to believe
that individuals and autonomy exist only in terms of attachments to a
democratic group. The communitarian position criticizes social conservative thinking as too willing to impose a single moral order on all
people. For the communitarian trying to balance the good in both autonomy and order, the "new golden rule" reads, "Respect and uphold
society's moral order as you would have society respect and uphold
your autonomy."[13] As Etzioni explains, the new golden rule "requires
that the tension between one's preferences and one's social commit-
ments be reduced by increasing the realm of duties one affirms as moral
responsibilities—not the realm of duties that are forcibly imposed but
the realm of responsibilities one believes one should discharge and
that one believes one is fairly called upon to assume."[14] A prominent
site for citizens' learning how to manage the tensions between individual preferences and social duties (moral responsibilities) is what the
nineteenth-century French social critic and commentator on American culture, Alexis de Tocqueville, called "intermediary bodies," what
some later critics have called "mediating structures."[15]

At its best, a Boy Scout troop can operate as a mediating structure
in which the boys and men together experience and work through all
of the tensions, dilemmas, and contradictions between autonomy and
social order. The tension of this setting is exacerbated by the fact that
the boys are struggling simultaneously with the social and the psychological pushes toward autonomy. Troop 49's culture, at its best, provides a safe community in which the boy can discover through conversation and action how to expand the voluntarily agreed-upon range of
duties and moral responsibilities, while also learning how to construct
an "autonomy" that, as Etzioni puts it, "encompasses both what is typically considered as individual freedom and needs for self-expression,
innovation, creativity, and self-government as well as legitimation of
the expression of subgroup differences."[16]

This view of a Boy Scout troop, as a messy work-in-progress grappling with some of the most important tensions in our culture, departs considerably from the BSA's view of Scouting. The social conservatism of the official organization would make a Boy Scout troop unworkable as a mediating structure if the troop took seriously the national organization's pronouncements and dictates. Fortunately, a great many troops do not.

So back to one of my original questions. Is Scouting a viable "solution" to the "boy problem" at the beginning of the twenty-first century, or will it make things worse? If by "Scouting" one means the national office and council offices and their bureaucrats, then I see little chance that Scouting will improve the quality of public life and civic responsibility. But if by "Scouting" one means, as I do, the actual experience created by the men and boys of a particular troop, then I think there is potential for a troop to operate as a healthy mediating structure. A troop does not receive such a culture with its official charter. Rather, the culture of a mediating structure has to be constantly constructed, tested, and repaired. The public good that comes out of such a troop has to be earned, and the process that creates that good is easily destroyed. That is the lesson of this ethnography of Troop 49. There are hundreds of troops like it, and there is no troop like it. Some days the program works, and some days it fails, but in either case we can learn from Troop 49 and from other troops like it what we adults might do for our adolescent boys, and what we might leave alone.

Based on my experience, then, I would say that the Boy Scouts is neither the Hitler Youth of its worst detractors nor the virtuous community of its stalwart defenders. The Boy Scout experience is plural. It creates many different kinds of men capable of performing a broad range of masculinity. Whether recent developments will narrow that range remains to be seen. I remain optimistic because I know that the messiness of culture, the disorderliness of play, and the always fresh creativity of adolescents are almost certain to carry the day against the forces of orderly sameness.

Studying Boy Scouts in a Natural Setting

I described briefly in the introduction how I came to work with Troop 49 and how I have written this book as if it recounted a single summer's two-week encampment. I hoped that the brief account in the introduction would orient and satisfy the general reader, but I offer in this appendix a somewhat more extended account of my work and of why I approached the fieldwork and writing tasks as I did. Other scholars certainly will want to know more about my methods, but so might some general readers.

My Relationship with the Troop

From the beginning, I was completely candid with Pete, with the other adults (fathers and troop alumni), and with the boys that I was writing about the troop. The boys understood my presence in the early years as Tad's university teacher. By the 1980s, I was officially on the troop records as one of twenty or more Assistant Scoutmasters (mainly alumni) in Troop 49. For most of the fieldwork, I wore my old khaki Scout uniform shirt with the Troop 49 neckerchief for the dress occasions; the uniform (especially my Eagle badge) legitimated my Scouting experience. My old Florida troop number and badges (including the Order of the Arrow Lodge patch) puzzled the boys some, but the neckerchief seemed to override the other signals. Later I transferred my badges to a new tan Scout shirt and began wearing the Troop 49 number and the appropriate council patch. The uniform marked me as a member of the troop.

Most of the time in camp I had no official role or authority, other than the natural authority of an adult, so the boys were usually relatively relaxed in my presence. I must say "relatively" because I could not pass as an adolescent boy, so it is likely the boys censored themselves somewhat in my presence. Still, they said and did so many things in my presence that I must have seemed invisible to them at least part of the time. They never tested me by breaking any of the more serious rules in my presence (as Gary Alan Fine's informants did him in his fieldwork with a Little League baseball team), though they did break some of the smaller rules, such as pranking on the edge of hazing.[1] In some cases, I did not know they had broken a rule until Pete or someone later told me that what I had seen was against the rules.

Occasionally, Pete would be shorthanded in terms of Staff and would need me to provide an adult presence at an activity, such as free swim or a game of Capture the Flag, but even then I was able to sit on the sidelines most of the time and not make a fuss about my presence and authority. All told, I believe I had as good a glimpse as any adult could have had of the camp and troop from the boys' point of view.

My Fieldwork Methods

My fieldwork methods were rather conventional. I kept a field journal, writing in it as many times during the day as possible. I never wrote in front of the boys; that would have altered their behavior, certainly. But I often sneaked away at the end of an event to write down as quickly and as thoroughly as possible a narrative account of the event, some stream-of-consciousness notes, snippets of conversation, and so on. At times, I could go off alone to my bunk or sometimes to a remote rock with a beautiful Sierra Nevada vista to write long entries in my journal.

I took hundreds of color slides and black-and-white photos, which is not very intrusive in that scene, since the Scoutmaster and Staff often take pictures at camp. Often I would place these slides in a slide viewer, looking at them as I was writing and finding them a useful memory aid; the slides helped take me back to certain events and moments, helped me recover the "feel" of a moment.

I openly tape-recorded a few events, usually campfire programs. Once, back home and with the cooperation of the Scoutmaster, I gathered together a number of the troop alumni, I put a tape recorder out in front of them, and we had a remarkable three-hour conversation about the strengths and weaknesses of the troop and its encampment. Otherwise, I did not tape-record interviews or other conversations. Sometimes I was able to jot down some exact phrasing immediately after a conversation.

I was fortunate that Pete, Tad, Aaron, and many of the other alumni are very self-conscious and thoughtful about the distinctiveness of the troop's culture. Thus, I was able to talk with them about some of the things I observed, and I even tried out in these conversations some of the interpretations I was building. These conversations were always profitable, and I have tried to indicate where and when my interpretations of an event were sparked by or elaborated by something Pete or another troop member said. Sometimes my interpretations matched their implicit understandings of a custom or event. Sometimes my interpretations came from so far outside the "natural" language of their understandings of the troop (notably the psychoanalytic interpretations) that they simply laughed at my "academic" penchant for "reading too much" into an event. At times, I was able to teach Pete and the others something about their troop culture. At other times, they taught me. My first try at understanding the After-Campfire Campfire, for example, didn't work me very far out of the puzzlement I felt, but a conversation with Pete and Tad about the event helped me appreciate what I should have seen all along—namely, that the unexpected content and tone of that campfire are a perfect example of the paradox of messages in the play frame.

Many ethnographers have turned away from the prevailing genre of realist ethnography, which draws its narrative authority from the authority of positivistic science, and have come to live comfortably with the notion that we really are more collaborators with our subjects than we are independent and objective observers.[2] This has been the case for me, as many of my understandings of the meanings of what I saw those summers in camp arose very much in the give-and-take of conversations. Moreover, my aim was not merely to take but also to give, so I have endeavored as much as possible to offer my own interpretations as a sort of gift back to the troop, as when I sought to reassure Pete that all the punning and other wordplay in the troop were a healthy and necessary part of what the boys were learning, not a silly distraction from the business at hand.

Narrative Strategies

More unusual and possibly controversial are my decisions to create composite characters and to collapse over twenty years' worth of fieldwork observations into a narrative account of a single two-week encampment. As I explained in the introduction, after writing for so long about the Boy Scouts for academic audiences, I wanted to write this book for a general audience. I see culture criticism as a sort of political and social practice, and I wanted my writing about the Boy Scouts to enter the public conversation about the lives of adolescent boys and about the Boy Scouts as a cultural institution. I feel strongly that adults talk to each other about the "problems" of children without paying much attention to real children. The only antidote I see to this tendency for adults to worry and debate about the "children" they "invent" as projections of their own experiences and anxieties is for the scholar to try to insert into the public conversation some accounts of the lives of children as seen through children's eyes. This is a quality I value in child psychiatrist Robert Coles's work—that he sits on the floor to color or paint with kids and actually listens to what they tell him.[3] This book is my gesture in that direction

I judged that a coherent, sequential narrative of Troop 49's encampment as a two-week event would make the troop's culture most accessible to the general reader. I felt confident that I could write such an account and make it all "true" in the sense that everything I report actually happened, but not necessarily in the sequence presented here. Some characters in this story of Troop 49 I could take as they are; some worked better as composite characters.

In reading and teaching anthropologist Barbara Myerhoff's *Number Our Days,* her alternately funny and sad ethnography of a Jewish community center in Venice Beach, California, I was impressed by the way that she managed to "smuggle" some anthropological theory talk almost seamlessly into a very readable account of that community, including herself as an actor.[4] My use of certain narrative strategies here—such as the Staff campfire, my asides, and the excurses—had the same aim of bringing useful ideas to bear upon a day's events. Every conversation that I have reported as part of a Staff campfire did actually occur, though not always at a Staff campfire and not necessarily in the same sequence.

A Boy Scout troop, of course, is different from the individual child patient of a Robert Coles or the autonomous adult organization that Myerhoff studied. But my goal has been the same as theirs—namely, to tell a story about some people's lives in order to alter how we might think about those people and possibly to make those people's lives better. Every person has a story to tell, and every group has a story. But in the necessary triage of stories, I would argue that the story of Troop 49 needs to be told, read, and discussed because it touches so many cultural issues that, in turn, affect other lives.

NOTES

Introduction

1. The book referred to in the second paragraph is William B. Forbush's *The Boy Problem,* with a foreword by G. Stanley Hall (Boston: Pilgrim Press, 1902).

2. See the BSA website, http://www.scouting.org.

3. James Davison Hunter, *Culture Wars: The Struggle to Define America* (New York: Basic Books, 1991), and James Davison Hunter, *Before the Shooting Begins: Searching for Democracy in America's Culture Wars* (New York: Free Press, 1994).

4. Rick DelVecchio, "Scouts May Lose Sponsors' Support," *San Francisco Chronicle,* 4 July 2000, pp. A13–A14.

5. Gregory K. Lehne, "Homophobia among Men: Supporting and Defining the Male Role," in *Men's Lives,* 2nd ed. rev., ed. Michael S. Kimmel and Michael A. Messner (New York: Macmillan, 1992), 381.

6. On the Cold War and the crisis of masculinity, see Tom Engelhardt, *The End of Victory Culture: Cold War America and the Disillusioning of a Generation* (New York: Basic Books, 1995); Robert J. Corder, *Homosexuality in Cold War America: Resistance and the Crisis of Masculinity* (Durham, N.C.: Duke University Press, 1997); and (indirectly) Garry Wills, *John Wayne's America* (New York: Touchstone, 1997).

Day 1

1. Elna S. Bakker, *An Island Called California* (Berkeley: University of California Press, 1972).

2. "Care package" seems to be a generic name used by counselors, campers, and parents since World War II. CARE, the international relief organization created to meet the needs of war victims and refugees, became well known in the 1950s, and middle-class children growing up in that era often participated in class and school projects gathering materials and raising money for CARE packages to be sent overseas. Campers in the 1950s began using the term "care packages" for the parcels of treats parents sent from home, the word "care" nicely marking the loving connection between home and camp. College freshmen still get what they call "care packages" from home.

3. Anthropologist Gregory Bateson invented the idea of "frames" in order to understand a broad range of communicative interactions. See his classic essay, "A Theory of Play and Fantasy," in his *Steps to an Ecology of Mind* (1952; reprint, New York: Bal-

lantine, 1972), 177–93. Erving Goffman, one of the great theorists and practitioners of symbolic interactionism, the dramaturgical approach to social reality, was so taken with the idea of frames that he borrowed Bateson's idea and elaborated it into a book, *Frame Analysis: An Essay on the Organization of Experience* (New York: Harper & Row, 1974). Goffman was especially interested in the ways con artists create their confidence games. In Goffman's view, all socially constructed frames are created, sustained, and repaired (if necessary) in ways similar to the confidence game.

4. Peter L. Berger and Thomas Luckmann, *The Social Construction of Reality: A Treatise in the Sociology of Knowledge* (Garden City, N.Y.: Anchor/Doubleday, 1966).

5. Just as I am disguising the number of this troop and providing pseudonyms for the men and boys, so I am using "Usonia" as the name of the reservoir beside which they camp. Architect Frank Lloyd Wright coined the word to describe average, middle-class citizens of the United States and the "Usonian" houses he designed for them, and I borrow it here.

6. Just as Troop 49's number is fictitious, so is Troop 8's.

7. Pete also sadly notes that the other troops, who received the direct orders from the ranger and did not have the resources to challenge his arbitrary ruling in court, began moving their camps every week for three or four weeks, which meant that they had to drastically reduce their camp setups and lost several days of their Scouting program to these logistics.

8. This changed in the late 1990s. Now many of the Assistant Scoutmasters and fathers bring small tents.

9. I like Elliott Oring's approach to defining the term "folklore." After reviewing a history of attempts at defining the terms "folk" and "folklore," Oring argues that it makes more sense to talk about the orientation that folklorists take when studying cultures. As he puts it in his essay "On the Concepts of Folklore" (in *Folk Groups and Folklore Genres,* ed. Elliott Oring [Logan: Utah State University Press, 1986], pp. 17–18): "folklorists seem to pursue reflections of the *communal* (a group or collective), the *common* (the everyday rather than the extraordinary), the *informal* (in relation to the formal and institutional), the *marginal* (in relation to the centers of power and privilege), the *personal* (communication face-to-face), the *traditional* (stable over time), the *aesthetic* (artistic expressions), and the *ideological* (expressions of belief and systems of knowledge)." The folklorist invokes not all of these orientations for every group or event, but this makes a helpful checklist for understanding how the folklorist's interests would include a Boy Scout troop in the late twentieth century.

10. These qualities mark what Erving Goffman calls a "total institution . . . a place of residence and work where a large number of like-situated individuals, cut off from the wider society for an appreciable period of time, together lead an enclosed, formally administered round of life." See his *Asylums: Essays on the Social Situation of Mental Patients and Other Inmates* (Garden City, N.Y.: Anchor/Doubleday, 1961), 3. I have found Goffman's term useful for describing summer camps and some other settings where we find children's folk groups and folklore. See Jay Mechling, "Children's Folklore in Residential Institutions: Summer Camps, Boarding Schools, Hospitals, and Custodial Facilities," in *Children's Folklore: A Source Book,* ed. Brian Sutton-Smith, Jay Mechling, Thomas W. Johnson, and Felicia R. McMahon (New York: Garland, 1995; reprint, Logan: Utah State University Press, 1999), 273–91.

11. In the summer of 1996, I encountered for the first time the second generation

of the Scouts I was studying, as there were in camp two boys who were the sons of a Scout I came to know in the 1970s.

12. I could hear a few of the Seniors beside me substitute "turds" for "birds" in the wilderness, but they were not singing loudly enough for Pete to hear, as he would have disapproved of their doing that in front of the Scouts.

13. There is a considerable scholarly literature in humanistic cultural geography on the meanings of place, but a defining work is Yi Fu Tuan's *Space and Place: The Perspective of Experience* (Minneapolis: University of Minnesota Press, 1977).

14. Although Troop 49 does not use this term, many summer campers beyond the Boy Scouts know Kool-Aid by the folk term "bug juice," an instance of the folk speech having to do with food contamination. For more on contamination lore, see George W. Rich and David F. Jacobs, "Saltpeter: A Folkloric Adjustment to Acculturation Stress," *Western Folklore* 32 (1973): 164–79, and Gary Alan Fine, "The Kentucky Fried Rat: Legends and Modern Society," *Journal of the Folklore Institute* 17 (1980): 222–43.

15. The Boy Scouts of America quite explicitly talks about the patrol as the positive equivalent of the boys' "gang." The Boy Scouts early settled on eight boys as the usual size of the patrol because the social scientists studying juvenile delinquency had determined that eight was the "natural" size of the boys' gang. The patrol system at the heart of the Boy Scout program counts on the patrol as the functional equivalent of the gang. For some of this history, see David I. Macleod, *Building Character in the American Boy: The Boy Scouts, YMCA, and Their Forerunners, 1870–1920* (Madison: University of Wisconsin Press, 1983).

16. For some of the history of the uniform, see Jay Mechling, "Dress Right, Dress: The Boy Scout Uniform as a Folk Costume," *Semiotica* 64, no. 3/4 (1987): 319–33, and Jay Mechling, "The Collecting Self and American Youth Movements," in *Consuming Visions: Accumulation and Display of Goods in America, 1880–1920,* ed. Simon J. Bronner (New York: Norton, 1989), 255–85. One of the BSA's founders, Ernest Thompson Seton, disliked the military style of the proposed uniform, preferring some version of a handmade costume (such as his Woodcraft Indians wore).

17. William Hillcourt, *Boy Scout Handbook,* 9th ed. (Irving, Tex.: Boy Scouts of America, 1979).

18. Pete disapproves of such behavior and talk, so this goes on outside his presence. Pete wants the boys to learn behavior appropriate to audience and place, and he wants the Seniors to enforce this rule. Les has doubly violated Pete's rules here—in his language and in his failure to instruct the boys to watch their language and behavior at the table.

19. See Gregory K. Lehne's definition of "homophobia" in his essay "Homophobia among Men: Supporting and Defining the Male Role," in *Men's Lives,* 2nd ed. rev., ed. Michael S. Kimmel and Michael A. Messner (New York: Macmillan, 1992), 381.

20. Barrie Thorne, *Gender Play: Girls and Boys in School* (New Brunswick, N.J.: Rutgers University Press, 1993).

21. Alan Dundes, "Into the Endzone for a Touchdown: A Psychoanalytic Consideration of American Football," in his *Interpreting Folklore* (Bloomington: Indiana University Press, 1980), 203. Also see Alan Dundes, "The Strategy of Turkish Boys' Verbal Dueling Rhymes," *Journal of American Folklore* 83 (1970): 325–49.

22. Gregory Bateson calls the communication establishing the frame "metacom-

munication," a level at which people communicate something about their communication. The participants somehow agree to a "metamessage," a message about messages, according to which they will interpret the messages as not meaning what they would mean in everyday conversation. See "A Theory of Play and Fantasy."

23. There is a large literature on games of ritual insults—playing the dozens, sounding—in male African-American folk groups. See, for example, several essays on the subject in Alan Dundes, ed., *Mother Wit from the Laughing Barrel: Readings in the Interpretation of Afro-American Folklore* (1973; reprint, Jackson: University Press of Mississippi, 1994). For an excellent statement on the ways ritualized aggression works to avoid real violence between men, see Michael Kaufman, "The Construction of Masculinity and the Triad of Men's Violence," in *Men's Lives,* 2nd ed. rev., ed. Michael S. Kimmel and Michael A. Messner (New York: Macmillan, 1992), 28–50. This was reprinted from *Beyond Patriarchy: Essays on Pleasure, Power, and Change,* ed. Michael Kaufman (Toronto: Oxford University Press, 1987).

24. Bateson makes the important point that one of the things communicated through the metacommunicated message "This is play" is the relationship between those who agree to the frame.

25. Erving Goffman, *Asylums;* Jay Mechling, "Children's Folklore in Residential Institutions."

26. Nude swimming has pretty much disappeared from the troop, as improved roads into the lakes have increased the foot traffic of women hikers and campers. Also, the recently adopted official BSA "Youth Protection" policy, nicknamed the "rule of three," has outlawed any form of skinny-dipping. See the discussion of this rule on Day 2.

27. The famed "circle jerk" is another play frame in which adolescent males can engage in behavior that might suggest homosexuality but, in fact, confirms the heterosexual orientation of the participants. The circle jerk consists of a group of males who form a circle and masturbate ("jerk off") themselves simultaneously. Usually, the male who ejaculates first "wins" the circle jerk. Pete has heard a version of this story in which the boys ejaculate on a cookie in the middle of the circle and the last guy done has to eat the cookie. In other versions, the circle jerk becomes the premise of a practical joke, in which the boys in on the joke explain to the "dupe" that they are going to do the circle jerk with the lights off. The boys make appropriate sounds and then turn on the light when the dupe ejaculates—he is the only one masturbating. As homoerotic as this play is (not to mention the narrative recounting of the play, even if only as a contemporary legend), it also bears the same metamessage as other nude play. "We can play this way because we do not see each other as sexual objects." An important element of the circle jerk is that each male is masturbating himself. Touching the genitals of another male would break the heterosexual play frame. I did not observe this game in the troop, and I don't know whether any of the boys participated in such behavior.

28. This is a variant of the song "Last Night I Stayed Up Late to Masturbate," reported by Ed Cray, *The Erotic Muse: American Bawdy Songs* (Urbana: University of Illinois Press, 1992), 339–41.

29. See the essay "The Mother's Brother in South Africa" in A. R. Radcliffe-Brown, *Structure and Function in Primitive Society* (Glencoe, Ill.: Free Press, 1952).

Excursus on God

1. Leah Garchik, "Personals," *San Francisco Chronicle,* 5 August 1985, p. 10.

2. Ibid.

3. "Boy Scout Ousted over God Is Reinstated," *San Francisco Chronicle*, 14 October 1985, p. 8.

4. Michael deCourcy Hinds, "In Tests of Who Can Join, Scouts Confront Identity," *New York Times*, 23 June 1991, National edition, pp. 1, 12. The Church of Jesus Christ of Latter-Day Saints (LDS, or the Mormons) has had a special relationship with the Boy Scouts since 1913, and the church considers Scouting a very important organization for the training of young LDS men. The church is the second largest sponsor of Scout troops, after public schools. The church's website has a link to a site called "LDS Scouting Resources" (http://gemstate.net/scouter/), telling a good deal of the history of the relationship between the BSA and the LDS Church.

5. Hinds, "In Tests of Who Can Join," 12.

6. Matt Lait, "Lawyer for Atheist Twins Rests Case against Scouts," *Los Angeles Times*, 7 December 1991, Orange County edition, p. B1.

7. Matt Lait, "Boy Scouts Lose Bid to Keep Twins Out of Group," *Los Angeles Times*, 31 July 1992, Orange County edition, pp. B1, B8.

8. Thom Mrozek, "Girl Scout Promise to 'Serve God' Challenged," *Los Angeles Times*, 19 November 1991, Orange County edition, p. B6.

9. "Girl Scouts Revising Pledge to Accept Religious Diversity," *New York Times*, 25 October 1991, National edition, p. A12.

10. The fact that Girl Scout troops do not have sponsoring organizations that include such powerful institutions as the LDS and Roman Catholic churches makes it easier for the organization to compromise on the language.

11. Hinds, "In Tests of Who Can Join," 12.

12. The two basic biographies of Seton are John H. Wadland's *Ernest Thompson Seton: Man in Nature and the Progressive Era, 1880–1915* (New York: Arno Press, 1978), and Betty Keller's *Black Wolf: The Life of Ernest Thompson Seton* (Vancouver: Douglas and McIntyre, 1984). Seton's own autobiography is *Trail of an Artist Naturalist* (New York: Scribner's, 1940).

13. For the basic history of the founding of the Boy Scouts, see W. D. Murray, *The History of the Boy Scouts of America* (New York: Boy Scouts of America, 1937), and David I. Macleod, *Building Character in the American Boy: The Boy Scouts, YMCA, and Their Forerunners, 1870–1920* (Madison: University of Wisconsin Press, 1983). Seton wrote his own history of the Boy Scouts, no doubt in self-defense against the official historians of the organization he argued with and left in 1915, but he never published the manuscript. See "A History of the Boy Scouts by: Ernest M. T. Seton, Chief Scout—1910–1915," c. 1927, Seton Papers, Seton Village, Santa Fe, N.M.

14. Ernest Thompson Seton, *The Book of Woodcraft and Indian Lore* (Garden City, N.Y.: Doubleday, Page, 1921), 11–12, 19–59; Ernest Thompson Seton, "The Message of the Redman; or, The Gospel of Manhood," *Totem Board* 11 (1932): 3–36; Ernest Thompson Seton, *The Gospel of the Redman* (New York: Doubleday, 1937).

15. There is no published biography of Beard, but see Allan Richard Whitmore's "Beard, Boys, and Buckskins: Daniel Carter Beard and the Preservation of the American Pioneer Tradition" (Ph.D. diss., Northwestern University, 1970). For Beard's autobiography, see *Hardly a Man Is Now Alive* (New York: Doubleday, Doran, 1939). For more details from those sources, see Jay Mechling, "The Collecting Self and American Youth Movements," in *Consuming Visions: Accumulation and Display of Goods in America, 1880–1920*, ed. Simon J. Bronner (New York: Norton, 1989), 258–60.

16. Daniel Carter Beard, *American Boys' Handy Book: What to Do and How to Do It* (New York: Charles Scribner's Sons, 1882).

17. Whitmore, "Beard, Boys, and Buckskins," 146–64, contains a discussion of the single-tax novel, *Moonblight; and Six Feet of Romance* (New York: Charles L. Webster, 1892).

18. Daniel Carter Beard, *The Boy Pioneers: Sons of Daniel Boone* (New York: Charles Scribner's Sons, 1909).

19. Macleod, *Building Character,* 146–48.

20. Boy Scouts of America, *Handbook for Boys* (Garden City, N.Y.: Doubleday, Page, 1911), 250.

21. Ibid., 16.

22. Boy Scouts of America, *Handbook for Boys,* 5th ed. (New Brunswick, N.J.: Boy Scouts of America, 1948), 20–21.

23. Ibid., 39.

24. Ibid., 441–44.

25. For more on the ways that symbolic demography overdetermines the ways the baby boomers look at children and adolescents, see Gary Alan Fine and Jay Mechling, "Minor Difficulties: Changing Children in the Late Twentieth Century," in *America at Century's End,* ed. Alan Wolfe (Berkeley: University of California Press, 1991), 58–78.

26. Stephanie Coontz, *The Way We Never Were: American Families and the Nostalgia Trap* (New York: Basic Books, 1992).

27. William L. O'Neill, *American High: The Years of Confidence, 1945–1960* (New York: Free Press, 1986), 212.

28. Ibid. For other discussions of religion and religiosity in the 1950s, see Paul A. Carter, *Another Part of the Fifties* (New York: Columbia University Press, 1983), and John Patrick Diggins, *The Proud Decades: America in War and Peace, 1941–1960* (New York: Norton, 1988).

29. Carter, *Another Part of the Fifties,* 135–37.

30. Ibid., 138–39.

31. Robert Bellah, "Civil Religion in America," *Daedalus* 96 (1967): 1–21. For further thoughts on this concept, see Robert N. Bellah, *The Broken Covenant: American Civil Religion in Time of Trial* (New York: Seabury, 1975); John F. Wilson, *Public Religion in American Culture* (Philadelphia: Temple University Press, 1979); Harold Bloom, *The American Religion: The Emergence of the Post-Christian Nation* (New York: Simon and Schuster, 1987); and Robert Wuthnow, *Producing the Sacred: An Essay on Public Religion* (Urbana: University of Illinois Press, 1994).

32. John Murray Cuddihy, *No Offense: Civil Religion and Protestant Taste* (New York: Seabury, 1978).

33. William Hillcourt, *Boy Scout Handbook,* 6th ed. (New Brunswick, N.J.: Boy Scouts of America, 1959), 82.

34. Ibid., 95.

35. William Hillcourt, *Norman Rockwell's World of Scouting* (New York: Abrams, 1977). Hillcourt provides a brief sketch of the founding of the organization and of three of the men—Seton, Beard, and West—who were its founders. But the bulk of this heavily illustrated book is about Rockwell's paintings.

36. Ibid., 144.

37. The first National Jamboree was held in 1937 in Washington, D.C., and the third in 1953 in Irvine, California. The Golden Anniversary National Jamboree was held in 1960 in Colorado Springs. See R. D. Bezucha, *The Golden Anniversary Book of Scouting* (New York: Golden Press, 1959), 154–55.

38. The best book on the religious reverence we hold for George Washington is Garry Wills's *Cincinnatus: George Washington and the Enlightenment* (Garden City, N.Y.: Doubleday, 1984).

39. Stephen Braun, "Boy Scouts in a Knot of Controversy," *Los Angeles Times,* 14 July 1991, p. A1.

40. In the 1970s, a membership drive and program, called Boy Power, was plagued by scandal, as some districts and councils inflated their membership figures in order to get more dollars. See "Scandals Drive Many Kids Out of the Scouts," *San Francisco Sunday Examiner & Chronicle,* 17 July 1977, p. A18.

41. James Davison Hunter, *Culture Wars: The Struggle to Define America* (New York: Basic Books, 1991), 43–44.

42. Ibid., 44–46.

43. Michael Rosenthal, author of *The Character Factory: Baden-Powell and the Origins of the Boy Scout Movement* (New York: Pantheon Books, 1986), wrote a letter to the editor of the *New York Times* (8 July 1991, p. A10) contesting the Boy Scouts' claim that Baden-Powell intended the movement only "for boys who believe in God."

44. On the "crisis in white masculinity" reflected in American mass-mediated culture, see, e.g., Fred Pfeil, *White Guys: Studies in Postmodern Domination and Difference* (London: Verso, 1995). This crisis is reflected in such 1990s films as Joel Schumacher's *Falling Down* (1993); in fact, the films starring Michael Douglas make a major subgenre of this phenomenon.

Day 2

1. Instructions for making twist on a stick appear in 1943 revised edition of the *Handbook for Boys* (New York: Boy Scouts of America, 1943), 236.

2. Victor Turner, *Dramas, Fields, and Metaphors: Symbolic Action in Human Society* (Ithaca, N.Y.: Cornell University Press, 1974).

3. Don Handelman, "Play and Ritual: Complementary Frames of Meta-Communication," in *It's a Funny Thing, Humour,* ed. Anthony J. Chapman and High C. Foot (Oxford: Pergamon Press, 1977), 186–91. See also Don Handelman, "Reflexivity in Festival and Other Cultural Events," in *Essays in the Sociology of Perception,* ed. Mary Douglas (London: Routledge & Kegan Paul, 1982), 162–90, and Don Handelman, *Models and Mirrors: Toward an Anthropology of Public Events* (Cambridge: Cambridge University Press, 1990).

4. Brian Sutton-Smith shows how "it" games, like tag, can provide an impersonal role and game script for children who do not normally have much power to experiment with the power a role like "it" gives. For example, see P. V. Gump and Brian Sutton-Smith, "The 'It' Role in Children's Games," *The Group* 17 (1955): 3–8.

5. Folklorists warn against overextending the use of "folk drama." Only skits at the campfire should be called folk drama, though certain other events at the campfire ap-

proach the definition. See Thomas A. Green, "Toward a Definition of Folk Drama," *Journal of American Folklore* 91 (1978): 843–50.

6. Seton insisted upon lighting every campfire by friction with a bow and drill, one of the many Indian ways Seton used to invest the campfire with romantic meaning.

7. This sort of beginning helps make Barre Toelken's point that it is sometimes difficult for the outsider, the folklorist, to say when a folk event actually has "begun." See Barre Toelken, *The Dynamics of Folklore*, rev. and exp. ed. (Logan: Utah State University Press, 1996).

8. A troop alumnus in his twenties compiled and printed a songbook for the troop in the late 1970s. The first edition of *The BEST Songs of Troop 49* lists sixty-six songs, and the fifth edition (1997) lists ninety-one songs.

9. These categories and the scoring system clearly come from television's *The Gong Show*, a popular half-hour "bad amateur talent show" from the 1970s that was well known to the boys when this custom began, but is obscure to the current generation. This is a good example of the process by which children's folklore appropriates familiar material from the popular media and puts the material into service for the folk group.

10. "Raw oysters" is slang for thick globs of phlegm, which they resemble.

11. Mary Knapp and Herbert Knapp, *One Potato, Two Potato: The Secret Education of American Children* (New York: Norton, 1976), 161–90.

12. Simon Bronner describes and analyzes children's "sick" jokes and "grosser than gross" jokes in his *American Children's Folklore* (Little Rock, Ark.: August House, 1988), 113–42. Most of the analysis occurs in the footnotes to the annotated edition of this book.

13. Bronner presents three variants of this well-known "gross rhyme," though he does not say it was a song for his sources. See ibid., 82.

14. Brunvand refers to tales of this type as "cumulative tales" or "chains" (Types 2000 to 2199), noting that some interesting versions—like the "Yay! Boo!" chains—remain largely uncatalogued. See Jan Harold Brunvand, *The Study of American Folklore: An Introduction*, 2nd ed. (New York: Norton, 1978), 138; see also Brunvand's citation (p. 174) of collections of camp songs.

15. On ritual insults among white boys, see Bronner's review of the scholarship, *American Children's Folklore*, 239.

16. In 1998 the Seniors made an error that threw off every patrol and spoiled the fun of the hunt. Because of that, the Staff reluctantly decided to omit the Treasure Hunt in 1999.

17. Even on the nights of patrol campfires, there is a group sport—usually Whiffleball or Capture the Flag—that fortifies the larger troop identity before the boys go off to their individual patrol sites.

18. In one of my first essays on Troop 49, I offered an extended psychoanalytic interpretation of the meanings of fire—and especially urinating on fire—in male initiation rites. See Jay Mechling, "The Magic of the Boy Scout Campfire," *Journal of American Folklore* 93 (1980): 35–56.

19. This was one of the seventy instincts he listed in "A History of the Boy Scouts by: Ernest M. T. Seton, Chief Scout—1910–1915," c. 1927, Seton Papers, Seton Village, Santa Fe, N.M.

20. Ernest Thompson Seton, *The Book of Woodcraft and Indian Lore* (Garden City, N.Y.: Doubleday, Page, 1921), xxii.

Day 3

1. See Jay Mechling, "Heroism and the Problem of Impulsiveness for Early Twentieth-Century American Youth," in *Generations of Youth: Youth Cultures and History in Twentieth-Century America,* ed. Joe Austin and Michael Nevin Willard (New York: New York University Press, 1998), 36–49.

2. William Hillcourt, *Boy Scout Handbook,* 9th ed. (Irving, Tex.: Boy Scouts of America, 1979), 40.

3. David Riesman, with Nathan Glazer and Ruell Denney, *The Lonely Crowd: A Study of the Changing American Character* (New Haven, Conn.: Yale University Press, 1950).

4. On the chance that there might be some readers unfamiliar with *Gilligan's Island,* here is a brief synopsis. The situation comedy television series ran from 1964 to 1967 (three seasons, with ninety-eight episodes) on CBS and then had significant audiences in syndicated reruns in the 1970s and 1980s. The storyline is simple. A group of people take a cabin cruiser out for what is meant to be a "three-hour tour." A storm comes up and wrecks the boat on a deserted island, so the group has to create a little society there on the island. The characters include the Skipper; his crew member Gilligan (played by Bob Denver); a millionaire older couple, Mr. and Mrs. Howell; Ginger, the glamorous movie star; the Professor; and Mary Ann, a cute and basically sensible young woman. The series has acquired "campy cult" status (see, for example, the website, http://www.gilligansisle.com).

In subsequent years, the Seniors have "themed" Insane Day (now more usually called "T.I.") around other popular culture texts, such as the *Star Wars* films, *The Simpsons* television show, and in 1999 the film that was so popular that summer, *Austin Powers: The Spy Who Shagged Me,* a comic spoof on the James Bond films. A running joke through all these subsequent years, however, has been that Gilligan always appears as a cameo character in the themed drama.

5. Boys have made some version of these comments at every Insane Day I have witnessed. In the summer of 1999, the Senior playing Austin Powers made many clever ad-libs, including comments about abortion and "that reminds me of my last date," all in the English accent actor Mike Myers used in playing Austin Powers in the film. None of the adults asked him to stop the comments. (After all, most of the Scouts had seen the movie that summer, and the movie was much racier than any of the comments the Seniors were making.)

6. Folklorists have documented a traditional vocabulary of folk speech used in the place of words not permitted in swearing. Thus, "heck" traditionally replaces "hell," just as "Jiminy Cricket" replaces "Jesus Christ."

7. In recent years, Insane Day has been scheduled for a weekend day, and the dads have brought barbecue kettles and food to the island and prepared dinner for the tired boys. This makes good sense after a tiring day, but as one of the fathers said to me, "You know, we do more and more cooking for these kids on the weekends, and they are coming to expect it. In the old days, we kids did all the cooking. We're spoiling these kids."

8. Venture Scouting has replaced exploring. See the description of the program in the eleventh edition (1998) of the *Handbook* and on the BSA website (http://www.scouting.org/factsheets).

9. Douglas E. Foley uses his ethnographic work in a small Texas town's high school to develop a performance model for understanding how adolescents reproduce class

culture. In part, Foley is trying to take the suggestive research of Paul Willis and others, who have studied the ways working-class kids in England condemn themselves to a continual working-class existence, and modify the model to make better sense of the ways social class operates as a force in the United States. See Foley's *Learning Capitalist Culture: Deep in the Heart of Tejas* (Philadelphia: University of Pennsylvania Press, 1990).

10. There is a considerable literature on gender and sports. Two early works providing a useful context for this scholarship are Janet Lever's "Sex Differences in the Complexity of Children's Play and Games," *American Sociological Review* 43 (1978): 471–83, and Brian Sutton-Smith, "The Play of Girls," in *Becoming Female: Perspectives on Development,* ed. Claire B. Kopp (New York: Plenum Press, 1979), 229–57. Barrie Thorne's *Gender Play: Girls and Boys in School* (New Brunswick, N.J.: Rutgers University Press, 1993) brings this scholarship up to date.

11. See Michael A. Messner, *Power at Play: Sports and the Problem of Masculinity* (Boston: Beacon Press, 1992), and Michael A. Messner and Donald F. Sabo, *Sex, Violence and Power in Sports: Rethinking Masculinity* (Freedom, Calif.: Crossing Press, 1994). For an exploration of the relations between men's sports and men's sexualities, see Brian Pronger, *The Arena of Masculinity: Sports, Homosexuality, and the Meaning of Sex* (New York: St. Martin's Press, 1990).

12. Carol Gilligan, *In a Different Voice: Psychological Theory and Women's Development* (Cambridge, Mass.: Harvard University Press, 1982).

13. Robert Horan, "The Semiotics of Play Fighting at a Residential Treatment Center," in *Adolescent Psychiatry,* vol. 15, ed. Sherman C. Feinstein (Chicago: University of Chicago Press, 1988), 367–84.

14. Alan Dundes, "Into the Endzone for a Touchdown: A Psychoanalytic Consideration of American Football," *Western Folklore* 37 (1978): 75–88. Dundes appeared on Phil Donohue's television show and participated in numerous television and radio interviews, explaining his views. Not surprisingly, his interpretation met with considerable hostility from some men.

15. Alan Dundes, "The American Game of 'Smear the Queer' and the Homosexual Component of Male Competitive Sport and Warfare," *Journal of Psychoanalytic Anthropology* 8 (1985): 115–29.

16. Alan Dundes, "The Strategy of Turkish Boys' Verbal Dueling Rhymes," *Journal of American Folklore* 83 (1970): 325–49.

17. Poison Pit is a traditional folk game, appearing in some collections of children's folklore as Adder's Nest, Poison Pot, and This Drain Is Dangerous. See Iona Opie and Peter Opie, *Children's Games in Street and Playground* (Oxford: Clarendon Press, 1969), 236–37. Seton included the game in his 1906 edition of *The Birch Bark Roll of Woodcraft* and in the first edition (1911) of the *Handbook for Boys,* calling the game "Stung, or Step on the Rattler—Sometimes Called Poison."

18. I had one of those "aha" experiences one winter evening, sitting in front of a fire while reading Alan Dundes's essay "Projection in Folklore: A Plea for Psychoanalytic Semiotics," *Modern Language Notes* 91 (1976): 1500–33.

19. Bruno Bettelheim makes this point in *The Uses of Enchantment: The Meaning and Importance of Fairy Tales* (New York: Knopf, 1976).

20. I mean "campy" here in Susan Sontag's sense, not summer campy, though it is both. See Susan Sontag, "Notes on Camp," *Partisan Review* 31 (1964): 515–30.

21. Barbara Babcock-Abrahams, "Why Frogs Are Good to Think and Dirt Is Good to Reflect On," *Soundings* 58 (1975): 167–81.

22. Anthropologists and others have been interested in symbolic inversion for quite some time, but Barbara Babcock's introduction to her edited collection, *The Reversible World: Symbolic Inversion in Art and Society* (Ithaca, N.Y.: Cornell University Press, 1978), nicely traces the intellectual history of this idea, including the rhetorical theories of Kenneth Burke (especially his notion of "the aesthetic negative") and the all-important symbolic anthropology formulated by Victor Turner. See also "Introduction: Secular Ritual: Forms and Meanings," the introductory chapter by editors Sally F. Moore and Barbara G. Myerhoff to the collection *Secular Ritual* (Amsterdam: Van Gorcum, 1977), 3–24.

23. For a more complete discussion of the cultural meanings of male cross-dressing, see Marjorie Garber, *Vested Interests: Cross-Dressing and Cultural Anxiety* (New York: Harper Perennial, 1993). When Susan Faludi visited the Citadel, the famously all-male military school that was forced (as a publicly supported college in South Carolina) to accept women, she discovered that the young male cadets valued the military school frame that permitted their performances of femininity to be shielded from outside view. A great deal of the play and ritual at the Citadel has the homoerotic flavor of other all-male total institutions (including ritual nudity). Faludi also found that some of the cadets liked to hang out at the Treehouse, a "mixed" bar with both straight and gay patrons, and with a drag show on weekends. "The cadets go for the drag queens," one performer explained to Faludi, and most of the drag queens she interviewed had dated cadets. The cadets are not necessarily gay, she notes, but both the Citadel and the Treehouse were safe, framed places "where the rules of gender could be bent or escaped, if only in part and for a time and under the most laborious of conditions." See Susan Faludi, *Stiffed: The Betrayal of the American Male* (New York: Morrow, 1999), 150.

24. The book that seemed to launch the interdisciplinary study of the invention of tradition is Eric Hobsbawm and Terence Ranger, eds., *The Invention of Tradition* (Cambridge: Cambridge University Press, 1983). For the folklorists' take on this, see Tad Tuleja, ed., *Usable Pasts: Traditions and Group Expressions in North America* (Logan: Utah State University Press, 1997).

25. I think *The Brady Bunch* has the same status for this age group and for the cohort called generation X, born roughly between 1962 and 1982. Witness the parodic theater play and film versions of *The Brady Bunch* in the 1990s.

26. Neil Postman, *The Disappearance of Childhood* (New York: Dell, 1982).

27. See, for example, Marcia Kinder, *Playing with Power in Movies, Television, and Video Games* (Berkeley: University of California Press, 1991).

28. I elaborate this argument, with detailed examples, in Jay Mechling, "Children and Colors: Children's Folk Cultures and Popular Cultures in the 1990s and Beyond," in *Eye on the Future: Popular Culture Scholarship into the Twenty-First Century,* ed. Marilyn F. Motz, John G. Nachbar, Michael T. Marsden, and Ronald J. Ambrosetti (Bowling Green, Ohio: Bowling Green State University Press, 1994), 73–89.

Day 4

1. Pete invented the term "flavor nuggets" (also found in instant pudding and in poorly stirred hot cereal) years ago "in an attempt to convert a liability into an asset."

More recently, the boys have invented the term "nature nuggets" to refer to the stray pine needles, dirt, and other unplanned additions from nature.

2. These requirements have changed over the years, and I am describing here the requirements in the eleventh edition of the *Boy Scout Handbook* (Irving, Tex.: Boy Scouts of America, 1998).

3. John Henry Wadland, in his *Ernest Thompson Seton: Man in Nature and the Progressive Era, 1880–1915* (New York: Arno Press, 1978), argues convincingly his thesis that Seton possessed an ecological consciousness.

4. *Boy Scout Handbook*, 11th ed., 544.

5. This is a widely known camp song, originally sung by soldiers and sailors in World War II. See Simon Bronner, *American Children's Folklore* (Little Rock, Ark.: August House, 1988), 110–11, 285–86 n. The military origins of the song echo the regimented feel of a summer camp to some children. The new verses reported here were collected in July of 1989.

6. "Rad" is slang for radical, an adjective meaning good.

7. The spreading of campfire ashes to cover the feces and reduce the smell and number of flies tends to leave a fine layer of dust on everything at the KYBO.

8. "The trots" is slang for diarrhea.

9. The troop's traditional substitution of the word "revolution" for the gospel song's word, "revelation," began in the 1970s, when the older Scouts and leaders shared leftist politics. Today's Scouts probably don't even notice the substitution, or understand it if they do notice.

10. "Community of memory" is a phrase from Robert N. Bellah, Richard Madsen, William M. Sullivan, Ann Swidler, and Steven M. Tipton, *Habits of the Heart* (Berkeley: University of California Press, 1985).

11. On traditional campfire stories and legends and their functions at camp, see Bill Ellis, " 'Ralph and Rudy': The Audience's Role in Re-creating a Camp Legend," *Western Folklore* 41 (1982): 169–91; also see Bronner, *American Children's Folklore,* 153–54.

12. In 1991, Rhino Records issued a two-CD set (R2 70743) to commemorate the twentieth anniversary of Dr. Demento (Barry Hensen). This compilation of novelty songs includes "Dead Puppies," by Ogden Edsl. As the liner notes say of this song (one of the two most-requested songs in the history of Dr. Demento): " 'Dead Puppies' was born in 1977, child of the OGDEN EDSL WAHALIA BLUES ENSEMBLE MONDO BIZARRIO BAND, which used to perform in every Midwestern city where its name would fit on the marquee. Lead singer Bill Frenzer wrote the song with bandmate Richie Thieman, with pipe organ by fellow Edslite William Carey."

13. This is the Troop 49 version and differs slightly from the version on the recording. I was amazed to find, while reading a long *Washington Post Magazine* article on the reporter's visit to a Virginia Boy Scout summer camp, that the boys there enjoyed singing "Dead Puppies." See Peter Carlson, "The Call of the Wild," *Washington Post Magazine,* 5 August 1990, pp. 11–17, 29–30.

Day 5

1. For a review of the folklore and other scholarship on children's pranks, see Marilyn Jorgensen, "Teases and Pranks," in *Children's Folklore: A Source Book,* ed. Brian Sutton-Smith, Jay Mechling, Thomas W. Johnson, and Felicia R. McMahon (New York: Garland, 1995; reprint, Logan: Utah State University Press, 1999), 213–24.

Simon J. Bronner discusses college pranks (an extension of adolescent pranks) in *Piled Higher and Deeper: The Folklore of Student Life* (Little Rock, Ark.: August House, 1995), 114–37.

2. The slang phrase "brown-nosing," meaning to heap insincere compliments on a superior, refers to the notion that to "kiss ass" gets one's nose brown from the superior's anus. The boys know this phrase, as in "brown-nosing" a teacher.

Day 6

1. The present requirements for Eagle still insist upon the First Aid merit badge but let the boy choose between Lifesaving and Emergency Preparedness.

2. For the biography of Baden-Powell, see Michael Rosenthal, *The Character Factory: Baden-Powell and the Origins of the Boy Scout Movement* (New York: Pantheon Books, 1986), and Tim Jeal, *The Boy-Man: The Life of Lord Baden-Powell* (New York: Morrow, 1990).

3. Fitzhugh's novels bore the imprimatur of the Boy Scouts of America, unlike most of the series novels that, beginning in 1910, put Boy Scout characters in the middle of traditional adventures.

4. On Wilson's "liberal democratic internationalism," see Tony Smith, *America's Mission: The United States and the Worldwide Struggle for Democracy in the Twentieth Century* (Princeton, N.J.: Princeton University Press, 1994).

5. In June of 1996, the Supreme Court of the United States ruled that VMI could not remain a male-only, state-supported college.

6. I elaborate this point in my essay "Dress Right, Dress: The Boy Scout Uniform as a Folk Costume," *Semiotica* 64, no. 3/4 (1987): 319–33.

7. Birkby, Robert C., *Boy Scout Handbook,* 10th ed. (Irving, Tex.: Boy Scouts of America, 1990), 567.

8. The Boy Scouts of America struggled with these questions from the beginning. Macleod recounts the struggles the first Chief Scout Executive, James E. West (1876–1948), had with the National Council over exemptions from some requirements for handicapped boys. West had some sympathy for handicapped boys as he himself endured childhood with a crippling condition. See David I. Macleod, *Building Character in the American Boy* (Madison: University of Wisconsin Press, 1983), 157–58. For later history of the BSA's struggle with this issue, see "Age Limits Dropped for Handicapped Scouts," *San Francisco Chronicle,* 6 May 1978, p. A2, and "A Victory for Disabled Scouts," *San Francisco Chronicle,* 25 May 1979, p. A6.

9. In the 1950s, when historians and social scientists worked collaboratively on the study of national character, "achievement orientation" was a key concept. See David C. McClelland, *The Achieving Society* (New York: Free Press, 1961).

Days 7 & 8

1. On the sociobiology of alcohol consumption, see Pertti Alasuutari, *Desire and Craving: A Cultural Theory of Alcoholism* (Albany: State University of New York Press, 1992), and Richard Rudgley, *Essential Substances: A Cultural History of Intoxicants in Society* (New York: Kodawha International, 1993). For recent data on teen drinking, see Michael T. Windle, *Alcohol Use among Adolescents* (Thousand Oaks, Calif.: Sage, 1999).

2. Caillois calls this category *ilinx.* The other categories are *agon* (competition), *alea*

(chance), and *mimicry* (simulation). See Roger Caillois, *Man, Play, and Games,* trans. Meyer Barash (New York: Free Press, 1961).

3. For examinations of alcohol use in American history, see John C. Burnham, *Bad Habits: Drinking, Smoking, Taking Drugs, Gambling, Sexual Misbehavior, and Swearing in American History* (New York: New York University Press, 1993); Mark E. Lender, *Drinking in America: A History* (New York: Free Press, 1982); and William J. Rorabaugh, *The Alcoholic Republic, an American Tradition* (New York: Oxford University Press, 1979).

4. Boy Scouts of America, *Handbook for Boys* (Garden City, N.Y.: Doubleday, Page, 1911), 226.

5. If the *Handbook* for these years was low key, the juvenile fiction offered more colorful portraits of boys who smoked and drank.

6. William Hillcourt, *Boy Scout Handbook,* 6th ed. (New Brunswick, N.J.: Boy Scouts of America, 1959), 424.

7. Frederick L. Hines, *Scout Handbook,* 8th ed. (New Brunswick, N.J.: Boy Scouts of America, 1972), 336–40.

8. Ibid., 336.

9. William Hillcourt, *Boy Scout Handbook,* 9th ed. (Irving, Tex.: Boy Scouts of America, 1979), 514.

10. Robert C. Birkby, *Boy Scout Handbook,* 10th ed. (Irving, Tex.: Boy Scouts of America, 1990), 389–90.

11. Actually, since I began studying Troop 49, there has arisen quite an extensive literature on leadership because colleges have made leadership the topic of academic study and teaching. There are leadership courses for Scouts and Scouters, just as there are leadership courses for college students, business people, and so on.

12. Boy Scouts of America, *Handbook for Boys* (Garden City, N.Y.: Doubleday, Page, 1911), 153.

13. Boy Scouts of America, *Handbook for Boys,* 4th (rev.) ed. (New York: Boy Scouts of America, 1927), 444.

14. Boy Scouts of America, *Handbook for Boys,* rev. ed. (New York: Boy Scouts of America, 1943), 378.

15. Boy Scouts of America, *Handbook for Boys,* 5th ed. (New Brunswick, N.J.: Boy Scouts of America, 1948), 434.

16. William Hillcourt, *Boy Scout Handbook,* 6th ed. (New Brunswick, N.J.: Boy Scouts of America, 1959), 434; Boy Scouts of America, *Boy Scout Handbook,* 7th ed. (New Brunswick, N.J.: Boy Scouts of America, 1965), 434; Frederick L. Hines, *Scout Handbook,* 8th ed. (New Brunswick, N.J.: Boy Scouts of America, 1972), 27.

17. Robert C. Birkby, *Boy Scout Handbook,* 10th ed. (Irving, Tex.: Boy Scouts of America, 1990), 593. This passage is almost identical to the one William "Green Bar Bill" Hillcourt wrote for the *Boy Scout Handbook,* 9th ed. (Irving, Tex.: Boy Scouts of America, 1979), 463. As a university professor, I would turn over to the Campus Judicial Board a student who committed an act of plagiarism such as Birkby's, but truthfully the texts move across editions and across "authors" and "editorial committees" such that it is hard to keep track of who wrote what and when. The passage on Eagle Service project leadership in the 1998 *Handbook* (eleventh edition) is an abbreviated version of the 1990 passage.

18. William Hillcourt, *Handbook for Patrol Leaders* (New York: Boy Scouts of America, 1929), 6.

19. Ibid., 18.

20. William Hillcourt, *Handbook for Patrol Leaders,* rev. 2nd ed. (New Brunswick, N.J.: Boy Scouts of America, 1950), 7.

Day 9

1. A. B. Gomme, *The Traditional Games of England, Scotland, and Ireland* (New York: Dover Publications, 1964), 183.

2. Iona Opie and Peter Opie, *Children's Games in Street and Playground* (Oxford: Clarendon Press, 1969), 147.

3. William Welles Newell, *Games and Songs of American Children* (1883; reprint, New York: Dover Publications, 1963).

4. Gomme, *Traditional Games,* 183–84, and Opie and Opie, *Children's Games,* 147, offer examples of traditional taunts.

5. Boy Scouts of America, *Handbook for Boys* (Garden City, N.Y.: Doubleday, Page, 1911), 306.

6. Boy Scouts of America, *Handbook for Boys,* 3rd ed. (New York: Boy Scouts of America, 1915).

7. Don Handelman, "Play and Ritual: Complementary Frames of Meta-Communication," in *It's a Funny Thing, Humour,* ed. Anthony J. Chapman and High C. Foote (Oxford: Pergamon Press, 1977), 185–92.

8. This is Handelman's point.

9. Mary Douglas, "Jokes," in her, *Implicit Meanings: Essays in Anthropology* (London: Routledge & Kegan Paul, 1975), 90–114.

10. Dramas, play, jokes, and dreams are all connected in this way. Gregory Bateson makes this point in his "A Theory of Play and Fantasy," in *Steps to an Ecology of Mind* (1952; reprint, New York: Ballantine, 1972), 177–93, but so does Sigmund Freud, *Jokes and Their Relation to the Unconscious* (1905; reprint, New York: Norton, 1960).

11. Roger D. Abrahams, "Personal Power and Social Restraint in the Definition of Folklore," in *Toward New Perspectives in Folklore,* ed. Américo Paredes and Richard Bauman (Austin: University of Texas Press, 1972), 18.

12. Don Handelman observes in the natural-setting games he studies the creation of stylized opposition within a broader frame of solidarity. The "exhibition of conflict," he argues, actually proves the strength of the group's cohesion. See Don Handelman, "Rethinking 'Banana Time': Symbolic Integration in a Work Setting," *Urban Life* 4 (1976): 439.

13. Roger D. Abrahams, "Introductory Remarks to a Rhetorical Theory of Folklore," *Journal of American Folklore* 81 (1968): 147–48.

14. Victor Turner, *The Ritual Process: Structure and Anti-structure* (Ithaca, N.Y.: Cornell University Press, 1969). Douglas ("Jokes") makes the same claim for jokes.

15. James Fernandez, "The Mission of Metaphor in Expressive Culture," *Current Anthropology* 15 (1974): 119–45.

16. This is an important point that Gregory Bateson ("A Theory of Play and Fantasy") makes about frames.

17. Abrahams, "Personal Power," 18.

18. See Richard Sennett, *Authority* (New York: Vintage Books, 1980), on fraternity and authority as emotional bonds in modern society.

19. See Brian Sutton-Smith, "Play, Games, and Controls," in *Social Control and Social Change,* ed. J. P. Scott and S. B. Scott (Chicago: University of Chicago Press, 1971), 73–102, on games as models of power.

20. Dundes, no doubt, would see this "penetration" into enemy territory as structurally and metaphorically similar to the "penetration of the endzone" in football, which suggests that Capture the Flag is also about feminizing the other team.

21. Robert A. Georges, "Do Narrators Really Digress? A Reconsideration of 'Audience Asides' in Narrating," *Western Folklore* 40 (1981): 245–52.

22. I say "convenient" injury because an injury might provide an acceptable excuse for the boy who wants to leave the game.

23. See, for example, Gregory Bateson, "The Cybernetics of 'Self': A Theory of Alcoholism," in *Steps to an Ecology of Mind* (1952; reprint, New York: Ballantine, 1972), 309–37.

24. Janet T. Spence and R. L. Helmreich, *Masculinity and Femininity: Their Psychological Dimensions, Correlates, and Antecedents* (Austin: University of Texas Press, 1978), 18.

25. By 1999, it had grown to "a stretch limo's length."

26. This point is historian Johann Huizinga's. See his influential book *Homo Ludens: A Study of the Play Element in Culture* (Boston: Beacon Press, 1955).

27. For more on the relationship between creativity and cheating, see Jay Mechling, "On the Relation between Creativity and Cutting Corners," in *Adolescent Psychology,* vol. 15, ed. Sherman C. Feinstein (Chicago: University of Chicago Press, 1988), 346–66.

Day 10

1. From the outset, the Boy Scouts of America saw value in the Treasure Hunt as a game that combined fun and physical exercise with the potential for getting boys to practice their Scout skills. Seton's chapter on "Games and Athletic Standards" in the first *Handbook for Boys* (1911) offered a lengthy description of "The Treasure Hunt." The game slowly disappeared from subsequent editions of the *Handbook for Boys,* but it continued in two leaders' manuals. The second *Handbook for Scoutmasters* (New York: Boy Scouts of America, 1924), for instance, groups kinds of hikes according to how they serve the three points of the Scout Oath: "physically strong, mentally awake, and morally straight." The *Handbook* briefly describes the Treasure Hunt as a hike serving several "mentally awake" goals (p. 56). The third *Handbook for Scoutmasters* (New York: Boy Scouts of America, 1937), most elaborately describes the Treasure Hunt, including such crucial elements as written clues, compass readings, pacing, Scout trail marks, and an edible treat as the treasure (pp. 656–58). Similarly, the various editions of the *Handbook for Patrol Leaders* recommend the Treasure Hunt, as does *The Rally Book,* which describes all sorts of "contests, camp-o-rals, rallies, and demonstrations" for Scout gatherings. See William Hillcourt, *Handbook for Patrol Leaders* (New York: Boy Scouts of America, 1929), 223; William Hillcourt, *Handbook for Patrol Leaders* (New Brunswick, N.J.: Boy Scouts of America, 1950), 135–36; and Boy Scouts of America, *The Rally Book* (New York: Boy Scouts of America, 1929), 239.

2. The "Tot'n Chip" (Toting Chip) is a card certifying that the boy has passed a test on how to use knives and axes safely.

3. See, for example, Michael Zuckerman, "The Nursery Tales of Horatio Alger," *American Quarterly* 24 (1972): 191–209.

4. I cannot resist adding some recognition of the erotic nature of attending to someone's feet. Quentin Tarantino's film *Pulp Fiction* (1994) features a hilarious argument between the two hit men (played by Samuel L. Jackson and John Travolta) about whether a man's massaging a woman's feet is sexual; Travolta's character insists it is, while Jackson's insists it is not. Travolta's character ends the discussion by posing this question: would you ever massage a man's feet? I make this point not to suggest that the scene between Jeff and Ricky was homosexual or even homoerotic, though maybe it was the latter for them. I do not know. My point simply is that this is the sort of male-to-male contact that is so highly charged with possible homoerotic feelings that it is precisely the sort of contact you would expect these adolescent boys to avoid in their construction of heterosexual selves. Yet both Jeff and Ricky seemed comfortable with this framed version of this sort of touching (i.e., "this is a first-aid event, so the touching in this frame does not mean what it would mean if I were bathing and massaging his feet back at our campsite").

5. See Martha Wolfenstein, *Children's Humor: A Psychological Analysis* (1954; reprint, Bloomington: Indiana University Press, 1978), 66–77, on work play and name play.

6. Compare Alvin W. Gouldner, *Enter Plato: Classical Greece and the Origins of Social Theory* (New York: Basic Books, 1965), 45–54, and Lionel Tiger, *Men in Groups* (New York: Vintage, 1969).

7. Voters actually did close down Rancho Seco in the late 1980s.

Excursus on the Two Bodies

1. Note how our language recognizes this metaphor. We talk about "the corporation" as a legal entity enjoying the rights and responsibilities of individuals. We talk about "incorporating" individuals into our group. And so on.

2. Americans' late-twentieth-century concern over the purity of air and water, including the antismoking campaign, reflects the danger we see in the air.

3. Susan Sontag, *Illness as Metaphor* (New York: Vintage, 1978), and Susan Sontag, *AIDS and Its Metaphors* (New York: Farrar, Straus and Giroux, 1989). Most HIV/AIDS "culture criticism" uses the body/society metaphor. For a good example, see Paula A. Treichler, "AIDS, Homophobia, and Biomedical Discourse: An Epidemic of Signification" in *AIDS: Cultural Analysis, Cultural Criticism,* ed. Douglas Crimp (Cambridge, Mass.: MIT Press, 1987), 31–70.

4. For the history of the idea of adolescence, see Joseph F. Kett, *Rites of Passage: Adolescence in America, 1790 to the Present* (New York: Basic Books, 1977), and Grace Palladino, *Teenagers: An American History* (New York: Basic Books, 1996).

5. Carroll Smith-Rosenberg, *Disorderly Conduct: Visions of Gender in Victorian America* (New York: Knopf, 1985).

6. Dr. Joceyln Elders, a Surgeon General under President Clinton, was forced to resign her post in the wake of an uproar over her suggestion in a forum on sex education that perhaps children could abstain from sexual intercourse better if they were taught how to masturbate and not feel guilty about it.

7. Boy Scouts of America, *Handbook for Boys* (Garden City, N.Y.: Doubleday, Page, 1911), 232–33.

8. Boy Scouts of America, *Handbook for Boys,* rev. ed. (New York: Boy Scouts of America, 1943), 448–49.

9. Boy Scouts of America, *Handbook for Boys,* 5th ed. (New Brunswick, N.J.: Boy Scouts of America, 1948), 412.

10. William Hillcourt, *Boy Scout Handbook,* 6th ed. (New Brunswick, N.J.: Boy Scouts of America, 1959), 425.

11. Frederick L. Hines, *Scout Handbook,* 8th ed. (New Brunswick, N.J.: Boy Scouts of America, 1972), 334.

12. William Hillcourt, *Boy Scout Handbook,* 9th ed. (Irving, Tex.: Boy Scouts of America, 1979), 516.

13. Ibid., 526.

14. Robert C. Birkby, *Boy Scout Handbook,* 10th ed. (Irving, Tex.: Boy Scouts of America, 1990), 375.

15. Ibid., 527–28.

16. Boy Scouts of America, *Boy Scout Handbook,* 11th ed. (Irving, Tex.: Boy Scouts of America, 1998), 376–77. For this edition, Robert Birkby's authorship credit has disappeared from the front matter, but his name appears as "author" under the long list of credits, 450–51.

17. Ray Raphael, *The Men from the Boys: Rites of Passage in Male America* (Lincoln: University of Nebraska Press, 1988), 76–77.

18. Pete tells me that, as a way of letting the Seniors know how normal he thinks masturbation is, he will sometimes tell them the story about the cookie contest, the circle jerk around the cookie where the last boy to ejaculate has to eat the cookie. Pete thinks that both the cookie contest and the circle jerk are apocryphal events, but he sees the value in making a point indirectly with folklore.

19. There is plenty of evidence for the folk symbolic equating of male hair and strength.

20. We see this in powder puff football, a high school custom in which the female cheerleaders dress in the football players' uniforms for a game of touch football, while the male football players dress as female cheerleaders and perform femininity. And in the 1999 Insane Day based on Austin Powers, the Senior who played "Lotta Fagina," the femme fatale, was a muscular teen who played football at the high school.

21. See, for example, Jonathan Ned Katz, *The Invention of Heterosexuality* (New York: Penguin/Plume, 1995).

22. Michael Kaufman, "The Construction of Masculinity and the Triad of Men's Violence," in *Men's Lives,* 2nd ed. rev., ed. Michael S. Kimmel and Michael A. Messner (New York: Macmillan, 1992), 28–50.

23. See Katz, *The Invention of Heterosexuality.*

24. Nancy Chodorow, *The Reproduction of Mothering: Psychoanalysis and the Sociology of Gender* (Berkeley: University of California Press, 1978).

25. Peter Lyman, "The Fraternal Bond as a Joking Relationship," in *Men's Lives,* 2nd ed. rev., ed. Michael S. Kimmel and Michael A. Messner (New York: Macmillan, 1992), 143–54.

26. Kaufman, "The Construction of Masculinity," 34–35.

27. I follow here the account by Stephen Frosh, *Sexual Difference: Masculinity and Psychoanalysis* (London: Routledge, 1994), 109–13, but this argument is common in the feminist psychoanalytic literature, as in Nancy J. Chodorow, *Femininities, Masculinities, Sexualities: Freud and Beyond* (Lexington: University Press of Kentucky, 1994).

28. While the phallus as a masculine cultural symbol is strong, a real penis—a sure sign of being a male—is merely flesh; as Susan Bordo puts it, "[T]he penis haunts the phallus." See Susan Bordo, "Reading the Male Body," in *Building Bodies*, ed. Pamela L. Moore (New Brunswick, N.J.: Rutgers University Press, 1997), 31–73, and her more extended treatment in her book *The Male Body: A New Look at Men in Public and Private* (New York: Farrar, Straus and Giroux, 1999).

29. Frosh, *Sexual Difference*, 111–12.

30. Ibid., 102–3.

31. Lyman, "The Fraternal Bond," 151. This "erotic toward rules" begins very early. When Gilligan returned to and radically reinterpreted the Kohlberg data on moral reasoning in children, she noticed that boys usually invoked legalistic and procedural understandings of justice (for example), whereas girls usually invoked a morality emphasizing connectedness. See Carol Gilligan, *In a Different Voice: Psychological Theory and Women's Development* (Cambridge, Mass.: Harvard University Press, 1982).

32. Kaufman, "The Construction of Masculinity," 41.

33. Frosh, *Sexual Difference*, 109.

34. Gregory Bateson, "A Theory of Play and Fantasy," in *Steps to an Ecology of Mind* (1952; reprint, New York: Ballantine, 1972).

35. Deborah Tannen, *You Just Don't Understand: Women and Men in Conversation* (New York: Morrow, 1990), 269.

36. What complicates this even more, of course, is the role homoeroticism plays in the "bonding and buddying," even in the military.

37. Patricia Hopkins, "Gender Treachery: Homophobia, Masculinity, and Threatened Identities," in *Rethinking Masculinity: Philosophical Explorations in Light of Feminism*, ed. R. A. Strikwerda and L. May (Lanham, Md.: Rowmen & Littlefield, 1992), 126. Hopkins takes the term "gender treachery" from Margaret Atwood's novel *The Handmaid's Tale* (1986).

38. Elliott Oring, "Dyadic Traditions," *Journal of Folklore Research* 21 (1984): 19–28.

39. The following analysis is an abbreviated form of that found in my essay "High KYBO Floater: Food and Feces in the Speech Play at a Boy Scout Camp," *Journal of Psychoanalytic Anthropology* 7, no. 3 (Summer 1984): 256–68.

40. Iona Opie and Peter Opie, *The Lore and Language of Schoolchildren* (Oxford: Clarendon Press, 1959), 162–67; Leonard R. N. Ashley, "Scoff Lore: An Introduction to British Words for Food and Drink," *Names* 16 (1968): 238–72.

41. Sigmund Freud, "Character and Anal Eroticism," in *The Standard Edition of the Complete Psychological Works of Sigmund Freud*, vol. 9, trans. James Strachey (1908; reprint, New York: Norton, 1959), 168–75. For a more recent consideration of the issue of bisexuality, see Marjorie Garber, *Vice Versa: Bisexuality and the Eroticism of Everyday Life* (New York: Simon and Schuster, 1995).

42. Ernest Jones, "Anal Erotic Traits," in *Papers on Psycho-Analysis* (1918; reprint, Boston: Beacon Press, 1948), 425.

43. William C. Menninger, "Characterologic and Symptomatic Expressions Re-

lated to the Anal Phase of Psychosexual Development," *Psychoanalytic Quarterly* 12 (1943): 161–93.

44. Jones, "Anal Erotic Traits," 430.

45. I elaborate this point in Jay Mechling, "The Collecting Self and American Youth Movements," in *Consuming Visions: Accumulation and Display of Goods in America, 1880–1920,* ed. Simon J. Bronner (New York: Norton, 1989), 255–85.

46. Jones, "Anal Erotic Traits," 430; Menninger, "Characterologic and Symptomatic Expressions," 181.

47. On the transformation connecting dirt, mud, stones, money, coins, and feces, see Jones, "Anal Erotic Traits," 426–27; Menninger, "Characterologic and Symptomatic Expressions," 181; Paulo de Carvalho-Neto, *Folklore and Psychoanalysis,* trans. Joseph M. P. Wilson (Coral Gables, Fla.: University of Miami Press, 1968); and Sandor Ferenczi, "The Ontogenesis of the Interest in Money," in his *Sex and Psychoanalysis,* trans. Ernest Jones (1914; reprint, New York: Dover, 1956).

48. Freud, "Character and Anal Eroticism," 171–72.

49. See the long footnote 3 in Jay Mechling, "Patois and Paradox in a Boy Scout Treasure Hunt," *Journal of American Folklore* 97 (1984): 38.

50. Menninger, "Characterologic and Symptomatic Expressions," 174.

51. Mary Knapp and Herbert Knapp, *One Potato, Two Potato: The Secret Education of American Children* (New York: Norton, 1976), 211–16; Weston LaBarre, "The Psychopathology of Drinking Songs: A Study of the Content of the 'Normal' Unconscious," *Psychiatry* 2 (1939): 209; Bruce R. Merrill, "Childhood Attitudes toward Flatulence and Their Possible Relation to Adult Character," *Psychoanalytic Quarterly* 20 (1959): 550–64.

52. Menninger, "Characterologic and Symptomatic Expressions," 180.

53. Sigmund Freud, "From the History of an Infantile Neurosis," in *The Standard Edition of the Complete Psychological Works of Sigmund Freud,* vol. 17, trans. James Strachey (1918; reprint, London: Hogarth Press, 1955), 72–75.

54. Ibid., 111.

55. Ibid.

Excursus on Gays and Girls

1. "Oakland Gay Sues Scouts," *San Francisco Chronicle,* 1 May 1981, p. A2.

2. "Judge Rules Scouts Can Block Gay Man as a Troop Leader," *New York Times,* 23 May 1991, National edition, p. A9.

3. Ibid.

4. Michael McCabe, "Boy Scouts under Attack in Court," *San Francisco Chronicle,* 1 July 1991, p. A8.

5. Margaret Perkins, "United Way Shuts Off Scout Funding," *Alameda Journal,* 21–23 April 1992, p. 1; Clarence Johnson, "Boy Scouts Stand Firm on Anti-gay Rule," *San Francisco Chronicle,* 25 July 1991, p. A17.

6. Theresa Moore, "Gay Groups Announce Bank of America Boycott," *San Francisco Chronicle,* 25 August 1992, p. A12.

7. Nanette Asimov, "Scouts Hold Fast to Homosexual Ban," *San Francisco Chronicle,* 18 September 1991, p. A15.

8. David Tuller, "CHP Won't Sever Ties with Scouting over Gay Ban," *San Francisco Chronicle,* 10 December 1992, p. A27; Leslie Earnest, "Laguna Might End Scout Pact Because of Gay Ban," *Los Angeles Times,* 17 March 1994, Orange County edition, p. B5.

9. Elaine Herscher, "Berkeley May Sink Boy Scouts' Free Berths at Marina," *San Francisco Chronicle,* 8 April 1998, p. A17.

10. The terms "orthodox" and "progressive" are James Davison Hunter's. See his two books, *Culture Wars: The Struggle to Define America* (New York: Basic Books, 1991), and *Before the Shooting Begins: Searching for Democracy in America's Culture Wars* (New York: Free Press, 1994).

11. "Appeals Court Says Boy Scouts Can't Ban Gays," *San Francisco Chronicle,* 3 March 1998, p. A3; Robert Hanley, "Jersey Court Rules against Scouts' Ouster of Gay Man," *New York Times,* 3 March 1998, p. A18.

12. Joyce Wadler, "A Matter of Scout's Honor, Says Gay Courtroom Victor," *New York Times,* 11 March 1998, National edition, p. A19.

13. Todd S. Purdum, "California Supreme Court Allows Boy Scouts to Bar Gay Members," *New York Times,* 24 March 1998, National edition, p. A1. The decision was something of a surprise, as the court had decided in earlier cases that the Boys Club in Santa Cruz was a business establishment that could not discriminate against girls.

14. Harriet Chiang, "State Top Court Says Boy Scouts Can Ban Gays," *San Francisco Chronicle,* 24 March 1998, p. A6.

15. Ibid., A1.

16. "Justices Refuse to Hear Appeal against Scouts," *San Francisco Chronicle,* 1 December 1998, p. A2.

17. Dan Turner, "Boy Scout Troop Defies National Policy on Gays," *San Francisco Chronicle,* 5 February 1992, p. A15.

18. "Troop's Gay Policy Conflicts with Boy Scout's," *New York Times,* 6 February 1992, National edition, p. A11.

19. Ibid.

20. Carol Ness, "Scouts Expel Longtime Leader," *San Francisco Examiner,* 13 September 1998, p. B1.

21. Ibid., B21.

22. Perry Lang, "New Group to Lobby Scouts on Gays," *San Francisco Chronicle,* 4 October 1991, p. A24; David Tuller, "Group Challenges Scout's Gay Barrier," *San Francisco Chronicle,* 18 July 1992, p. A13.

23. The Venturing program is described in the tenth (1990) and eleventh (1998) editions of the *Boy Scout Handbook* and on the BSA's website at http://www.scouting.org.

24. Jane Braxton Little, "Girls Press Fight to Be Eagle Scouts," *Contra Costa Times,* 23 March 1991, p. 10A.

25. John Flinn, "Boy Scouts Prepared for the '90s," *San Francisco Sunday Examiner & Chronicle,* 7 April 1991, p. A15.

26. Ibid.

27. "Aspiring Cub Gets Her Day in Court," *Alameda Times-Star,* 23 June 1991, p. A4.

28. Michael S. Kimmel, "Ms. Scoutmaster," *Psychology Today,* May 1988, 64–65.

29. Allen Salzman, "The Boy Scouts under Siege," *American Scholar* 61 (1992): 596.

30. Linda Greenhouse, "Supreme Court Backs Boy Scouts in Ban of Gays from Membership," *New York Times,* 29 June 2000, p. A1.

31. Boy Scouts of America, "Boy Scouts of America Sustained by United States Supreme Court," news release, 28 June 2000, on the BSA website (http://www.scouting.org/press/000628/index.html).

32. Rick DelVecchio, "Scouts May Lose Sponsors' Support," *San Francisco Chronicle,* 4 July 2000, pp. A13–A14.

33. http://www.scoutingforall.org/callforaction.shtml, p. 3.

34. For example, Scouting for All quotes the *Handbook*'s gloss on the seventh point of the Scout Law, "A Scout is Obedient," and the advice that if the Scout thinks that rules and laws are unfair, then he should work "to have them changed in an orderly manner" (*Handbook,* 11th ed., 1998, 50). Scouting for All works, it says, for an orderly change of the BSA's unfair rules (though Scouting for All also points out that the exclusion of homosexual boys and men appears nowhere as a rule in the official documents of the BSA).

35. Renee Tawa, "On Their Honor, They Will Try to Bend the Scout Law," *Los Angeles Times,* 31 August 2000, Orange County edition, p. E1.

36. Ibid., E3.

37. Ibid.

38. Ibid.

39. Shannon K. Hensley, "Boy Scouts of America under Attack: Scouts Defend 'Morally Straight' Organization," *University of California, Davis, Aggie,* 12 November 1991, p. 4.

40. See, for example, Gail Bederman, *Manliness and Civilization: A Cultural History of Gender and Race in the United States, 1880–1917* (Chicago: University of Chicago Press, 1995). For more broad outlines of the history of masculinity, but also of the specific crisis of masculinity at the end of the nineteenth century, see Peter N. Stearns, *Be a Man! Males in Modern Society,* 2nd ed. (New York: Holmes & Neier, 1990); E. Anthony Rotundo, *American Manhood: Transformations in Masculinity from the Revolution to the Modern Era* (New York: Basic Books, 1993); and Michael Kimmel, *Manhood in America: A Cultural History* (New York: Free Press, 1996).

41. Michael Rosenthal, *The Character Factory: Baden-Powell and the Origins of the Boy Scout Movement* (New York: Pantheon, 1986); Tim Jeal, *The Boy-Man: The Life of Lord Baden-Powell* (New York: Morrow, 1990).

42. Dorothy Ross, *G. Stanley Hall: The Psychologist as Prophet* (Chicago: University of Chicago Press, 1972).

43. Jeffrey P. Hantover, "The Boy Scouts and the Validation of Masculinity," *Journal of Social Issues* 34 (1978): 184–95.

44. See Elizabeth Walker Mechling and Jay Mechling, "The Jung and the Restless: The Mythopoetic Men's Movement," *Southern Communication Journal* 59 (1994): 97–111, and Elizabeth Walker Mechling and Jay Mechling, "American Cultural Criticism in the Pragmatic Attitude," in *At the Intersection: Cultural Studies and Rhetorical Studies,* ed. Thomas Rosteck (New York: Guilford Press, 1998), 137–67. The second essay offers a long analysis of the 1995 film *Braveheart* as a "symptom" of the crisis in white heterosexual masculinity in the 1990s.

45. Allen Salzman pointed in 1992 to a fact still true—that the "Mormon Church is the biggest single Scout sponsor. . . . Together, Mormons and Catholics support more than one-fourth of all Boy Scout activities in America." Allen Salzman, "The Boy Scouts under Siege," 591.

46. J. Roswell Gallagher, *Personal Fitness* (New Brunswick, N.J.: Boy Scouts of America, 1968), 13–14.

47. Boy Scouts of America, *Handbook for Boys,* 5th ed. (New Brunswick, N.J.: Boy Scouts of America, 1948), 25.

48. William Hillcourt, *Boy Scout Handbook,* 6th ed. (New Brunswick, N.J.: Boy Scouts of America, 1959), 82–83.

49. Ibid., 436.

50. William Hillcourt, *Boy Scout Handbook,* 9th ed. (Irving, Tex.: Boy Scouts of America, 1979), 525.

51. Ibid., 526.

52. For a detailed history of lawsuits, court cases, and responses by the Boy Scouts, see Patrick Boyle, *Scout's Honor: Sexual Abuse in America's Most Trusted Institution* (Rocklin, Calif.: Prima Publishing, 1994). And the cases continue. For a few examples since Boyle's research, see Kate Taylor, "Scout Leader Pleads Guilty to Felony Sex Charges," *San Francisco Chronicle,* 4 May 1993, p. A14; Susan Woodward, "O.C. Scout Camp Chaplain Admits Abusing 50 Boys," *Los Angeles Times,* 9 June 1994, Orange County edition, p. A1; and Erin McCormick, "Boy Scouts Sued Over Not Halting Sex Abuse," *San Francisco Examiner,* 23 July 2000, pp. B1, B6.

53. "Boy Scouts' Files Detail Sex-Abuse," *New York Times,* 15 October 1993, National edition, p. A9.

54. Ibid. The article quotes Richard Walker, a spokesman for the BSA national office in Irving, Texas.

55. Katherine Seligman, "Scout Films Warn Kids, Adults of Molest Dangers," *San Francisco Examiner,* 17 October 1993, p. B5.

56. Boyle, *Scout's Honor,* 313.

57. On the clash between the BSA and the Unitarian Universalist Association, including the issue of homosexuality, see Gustav Niebuhr, "Unitarians Are Disputing Boy Scouts on Emblems," *New York Times,* 1 August 1998, p. A11. The 1999 Annual Convention of the Episcopal Diocese of California adopted a resolution encouraging "the BSA to open its organization to youth and leaders irrespective of their sexual orientation" and to "encourage individual churches who charter scout units to open a dialogue with these units, their leaders and their parents, and obtain from them a pledge not to discriminate against youth and leaders on the basis of sexual orientation." The resolution also pledged to support Scouting for All's efforts to change the BSA's policies. See *Pacific Church News,* December 1999/January 2000, p. 13.

58. Mary Ann Glendon's *Rights Talk: The Impoverishment of Political Discourse* (New York: Free Press, 1991) is very good on this, but there are several excellent books on the matters of common morality, the public sphere, and democracy. See, e.g., Michael J. Sandel, *Democracy's Discontent: America in Search of a Public Philosophy* (Cambridge, Mass.: Belknap/Harvard University Press, 1996).

59. See, for example, Michael Novak, *The Spirit of Democratic Capitalism* (New York: Simon and Schuster, 1982).

60. Alan Wolfe, *One Nation, After All* (New York: Viking, 1998).

61. I say "ironically" because the performance of stereotypical masculinity and hypermasculinity by gay men has been criticized from within the gay community as contributing to precisely the oppressive stereotype that progressive men are trying to demolish.

62. Minnie M. Whitehead and Kathleen M. Nokes, "An Examination of Demographic Variables, Nurturance, and Empathy among Homosexual and Heterosexual Big Brother/Big Sister Volunteers," *Journal of Homosexuality* 19 (1990): 100.

63. Pete does not agree with me that the Scoutmaster should bear the obligation to teach *all* human values. He has personal reservations about the BSA's antigay policy and, if asked about it, would (he says) confine his "official" comment to citing the blurb in the *Handbook* describing the meaning of the fourth point of the Scout Law: "A Scout is Friendly. A Scout is a friend to all. He is a brother to all Scouts. He seeks to understand others. He respects those with ideas and customs that are different from his own." (Pete quotes here from the tenth [1990] edition of the *Handbook,* page 7; the changed text in the 11th (1998) edition does not change the message.)

64. For a solid historical background, see Robert L. Griswold's *Fatherhood in America* (New York: Basic Books, 1993). An example of a book calling for a return to traditional fatherhood is David Blankenhorn's *Fatherless America: Confronting Our Most Urgent Social Problem* (New York: Basic Books, 1995).

65. George Lakoff, *Moral Politics: What Conservatives Know That Liberals Don't* (Chicago: University of Chicago Press, 1996), 33.

66. Ibid., 35. When I explored these ideas with Pete, his description of the Strict Father model was "putting the 'rule of law' before the 'rule of heart.'"

67. Ibid., 33–34.

68. Ibid., 35.

69. Ibid., 337.

70. See his chapter 21, "Raising Real Children," 339–65, and his chapter 22, "The Human Mind," pp. 366–78.

71. Ibid., 383.

72. Sandra L. Bem, "The Measurement of Psychological Androgyny," *Journal of Consulting and Clinical Psychology* 42 (1974): 155–62; for Bem's more recent thinking about gender, see her book *The Lenses of Gender: Transforming the Debate on Sexual Inequality* (New Haven, Conn.: Yale University Press, 1993).

73. See Nancy Chodorow's "Afterword: Women's Mothering and Women's Liberation," in *The Reproduction of Mothering: Psychoanalysis and the Sociology of Gender* (Berkeley: University of California Press, 1978).

74. See Michael Ruhlman, *Boys Themselves: A Return to Single-Sex Education* (New York: Holt, 1996).

75. Barrie Thorne, *Gender Play: Girls and Boys in School* (New Brunswick, N.J.: Rutgers University Press, 1993).

76. There is no published ethnographic account of a Girl Scout camp to parallel the one I offer here, though there are some essays in print and some work by folklore graduate students. Thick accounts of the culture of a Girl Scout camp would help put my descriptions and interpretations in a useful comparative dimension. What I have read, especially in research papers written by my undergraduate students writing about

their Girl Scout and Campfire Girl camp experiences, fits what we might expect from Chodorow's and other gender theories—namely, that adolescent girls have a set of developmental challenges different from those faced by boys and that the expressive culture and rituals created by and for these girls—such as campfire songs—address those particular challenges, such as the nature of female friendship, ways for girls to be "competitive" without damaging group cohesion, and so on. For some of the few hints at these matters, see Patricia Atkinson Wells, "The Paradox of Functional Dysfunction in a Girl Scout Camp," in *Inside Organization: Understanding the Human Dimension,* ed. Michael Owen Jones, Michael Dane Moore, and Richard Christopher Snyder (Newbury Park, Calif.: Sage, 1988), 110–17. Simon Bronner has some Girl Scout texts in his *American Children's Folklore* (Little Rock, Ark.: August House, 1988).

Day 11

1. These notions in scientific educational psychology are as old as the ideas of John Dewey, but sometimes this wisdom from the past needs to be rediscovered and grounded in current practices and thinking. What we can add now to Dewey's original insights, for example, are the findings in brain and cognitive sciences, such as those used by Frank R. Wilson, *The Hand: How Its Use Shapes the Brain, Language, and Human Culture* (New York: Vintage/Random House, 1998). Psychologists now are very interested in "situated learning" and the role of apprenticeship in teaching and learning. See, e.g., Barbara Rogoff, *Apprenticeship in Thinking: Cognitive Development in Social Context* (New York: Oxford University Press, 1990); Jean Lave and Etienne Wenger, *Situated Learning: Legitimate Peripheral Participation* (New York: Cambridge University Press, 1991); and Michael Cole, Yrjo Engstrom, and Olga Vasquez, eds., *Mind, Culture, and Activity: Seminal Papers from the Laboratory of Comparative Human Cognition* (New York: Cambridge University Press, 1997).

2. Ernest Thompson Seton, *The Book of Woodcraft and Indian Lore* (Garden City, N.Y.: Doubleday, Page, 1921), 7. For Seton, the principle of "Honors by Standards" was a part of his Populist politics—he was a friend of Hamlin Garland—and he believed that the American Indians, in whom he saw this principle of "Honors by Standards," were the world's "successful socialists" (p. 55). Seton understood all too well the connection between the Greek contest system and world capitalism, and one of the reasons why he left the Boy Scouts was that he saw the pernicious influence of capitalism and militarism in the organization's leadership. By the mid-1920s, Seton was complaining to friends that the "philistines" were in command of the Boy Scouts and that people like Chief Executive James E. West were "totally lacking any knowledge of things spiritual." See Julia M. Seton, *By a Thousand Fires* (New York: Doubleday, 1967).

3. On the Greek contest system and its relationship to our culture, see Alvin W. Gouldner, *Enter Plato: Classical Greece and the Origins of Social Theory* (New York: Basic Books, 1965). Gouldner argues that the Greek contest system undermines the social order. Walter J. Ong speculates on the consequences of our adopting the Greek contest system for the social construction of sexuality. See his *Fighting for Life: Contest, Sexuality, and Consciousness* (Amherst: University of Massachusetts Press, 1981).

4. Boy Scouts of America, *Handbook for Scoutmasters,* 2nd ed. (New York: Boy Scouts of America, 1924), 319.

5. I don't want to overromanticize this "gifting" with my language, but I recognize in my own life that it was my Scouting experience that made me want to be a teacher. I recall distinctly the almost magical feeling of learning a skill and then teaching it to

another boy. I had received a gift and passed it on, and I took great vicarious pleasure in the student's pleasure in learning a skill.

6. Arnold van Gennep, *The Rites of Passage,* trans. Monika B. Vizedom and Gabrielle L. Caffee (Chicago: University of Chicago Press, 1960).

7. Victor Turner, "Betwixt and Between: The Liminal Period in Rites de Passage," in *Symposium on New Approaches to the Study of Religion,* ed. June Helm (Seattle: American Ethnological Society & University of Washington Press, 1964), 4–20.

8. Kenneth Burke, *The Rhetoric of Religion: Studies in Logology* (Boston: Beacon Press, 1961).

9. But nobody was "out" my year (I did manage to get two notches!), and in retrospect I wonder if any boy ever failed that OA ordeal. Ray Raphael points out that in "the extensive ethnographic literature produced within the last century there are virtually no first-hand reports of individuals who have actually failed the initiation ritual required by their society." Ray Raphael, *The Men from the Boys: Rites of Passage in Male America* (Lincoln: University of Nebraska Press, 1988), 13. Amazing—the male initiation "ordeal" that everyone fears and nobody fails.

10. I discuss this matter more completely in my essay "Dress Right, Dress: The Boy Scout Uniform as a Folk Costume," *Semiotica* 64, no. 3/4 (1987): 319–33.

11. Dick Hebdige, *Subculture: The Meaning of Style* (London: Methuen, 1979).

Day 12

1. John Roberts and Brian Sutton-Smith, "Child Training and Game Involvement," *Ethnology* 1 (1962): 174.

2. Pete points out that the care packages got out of control largely because the parents cheated. "At one point," he explains, "we restricted the size of the package to 'a shoe box,' but one parent sent up a boot box, over twice the size of a normal shoe box, so the other parents followed suit. Another rule was 'one package per Scout, per week,' but parents soon circumvented this by having grandparents and other relatives send up goodies." In 1998, the Staff instituted a ban on care packages. The only exception is birthday cakes for kids having birthdays during camp, and even then the cake gets shared by the entire troop.

3. John Roberts and Brian Sutton-Smith, "Cross-Cultural Correlates of Games of Chance," *Behavior Science Notes* 1 (1966): 131, 143.

4. Alan Dundes, "Folk Ideas as Units of Worldview," in *Toward New Perspectives in Folklore,* ed. Américo Paredes and Richard Bauman (Austin: University of Texas Press, 1972); Richard Dorson, "American Folklore vs. Folklore in America," *Journal of the Folklore Institute* 15 (1978): 97–111; Stephen Stern and Simon J. Bronner, "American Folklore vs. Folklore in America: A Fixed Fight?" *Journal of the Folklore Institute* 17 (1980): 76–84; Richard M. Dorson, "Rejoinder to 'American Folklore vs. Folklore in America: A Fixed Fight?'" *Journal of the Folklore Institute* 17 (1980): 85–89; Patrick B. Mullen, "The Folk Idea of Unlimited Good in American Buried Treasure Legends," *Journal of the Folklore Institute* 15 (1978): 209–20; John Lindow, "Swedish Legends of Buried Treasure," *Journal of American Folklore* 95 (1982): 257–79.

5. B. Traven, *The Treasure of the Sierra Madre* (Cleveland, Ohio: World Publishing, 1935); James Naremore, ed., *The Treasure of the Sierra Madre* (Madison: University of Wisconsin Press, 1979).

6. Louis Marin, "Disneyland: A Degenerate Utopia," in *Glyph: Johns Hopkins*

Textual Studies No. 1 (Baltimore, Md.: Johns Hopkins University Press, 1977), 50–66.

7. Mary Douglas and Baron Isherwood, *The World of Goods: Toward an Anthropology of Consumption* (New York: Norton, 1979).

8. Boy Scouts of America, *Handbook for Boys* (Garden City, N.Y.: Doubleday, Page, 1911), 15.

9. Ibid., 9.

10. Ibid., 240. One wonders if the current national leadership of the Boy Scouts knows of, or what they might think of, the deep socialist convictions shared by Seton, Beard, Alexander, and a few other founders. None of this is acknowledged in the "official" BSA versions of the biographies of these men and the history of the founding.

11. See Ann Douglas, *The Feminization of American Culture* (New York: Knopf, 1977). The question of what William James called "the moral equivalent of war" fascinated this generation of men, whose fathers had tales of the Civil War and its tests of manhood but who had no war of their own until the sinking of the *Maine* in Havana harbor in 1898. See William James, "The Moral Equivalent of War [1910]," in William James, *The Essential Writings,* ed. Bruce W. Wilshire (Albany: State University of New York Press, 1984), 349–61.

12. These trends are fleshed out by many historians of the period. See, for example, John Higham's classic essay, "The Reorientation of American Culture in the 1890s," in *The Origins of Modern Consciousness,* ed. John Weiss (Detroit, Mich.: Wayne State University Press, 1965), 25–48; Robert Wiebe, *The Search for Order, 1877–1920* (New York: Hill & Wang, 1967); Alan Trachtenberg, *The Incorporation of America: Culture and Society in the Gilded Age* (New York: Hill and Wang, 1982); Thomas J. Schlereth, *Victorian America: Transformations in Everyday Life* (New York: HarperPerennial, 1991); Simon J. Bronner, ed., *Consuming Visions: Accumulation and Display of Goods in America, 1880–1920* (New York: Norton, 1989); and Charles W. Calhoun, ed., *The Gilded Age: Essays on the Origins of Modern America* (Wilmington, Del.: Scholarly Resources, 1996).

13. Thomas C. Cochran, *The Inner Revolution: Essays on the Social Sciences in History* (New York: Harper and Row, 1964), 16.

14. Warren I. Sussman, *Culture as History: The Transformation of American Society in the Twentieth Century* (New York: Pantheon, 1984).

15. David Riesman, with Nathan Glazer and Ruell Denney, *The Lonely Crowd: A Study of the Changing American Character* (New Haven, Conn.: Yale University Press, 1950).

16. This essay appeared first in the *European Journal of Sociology* 11 (1970): 339–47, and then as an excursus in the book Berger wrote with Brigitte Berger and Hansfried Kellner, *The Homeless Mind: Modernization and Consciousness* (New York: Vintage/Random House, 1973), 83–96.

17. For an expanded discussion of this issue, see Jay Mechling, "Heroism and the Problem of Impulsiveness for Early Twentieth-Century Youth," in *Generations of Youth: Youth Cultures and History in Twentieth-Century America,* ed. Joe Austin and Michael Nevin Willard (New York: New York University Press, 1998), 36–49.

18. Sociologist Ralph H. Turner has used different terms—"institutionals" versus "impulsives"—to try to capture the same transformation Berger is writing about. See Ralph H. Turner, "The Real Self: From Institution to Impulse," *American Journal of Sociology* 81 (1976): 989–1016.

19. The concept of the "revitalization movement" comes from anthropologist Anthony F. C. Wallace, "Revitalization Movements," *American Anthropologist* 58 (1956): 264–81.

The Final Weekend

1. Ed Cray presents this song under the title "I-Yi-Yi-Yi" and says that "for sheer length, this is the champion song of all time," mainly because the participants can sing any number of the hundreds of known limericks. See Ed Cray, *The Erotic Muse: American Bawdy Songs* (Urbana: University of Illinois Press, 1992), 216–22.

2. I say "voluntary" because this metacommunication about relationship can signal different sorts of relationships. Participants of equal power will feel one sort of relationship. Those dragged unwillingly into a play frame by more powerful people certainly can understand how the frame signifies their relationship, but the message is not about equality and respect. I don't know if any of the women at this campfire felt unwillingly trapped there; I am assuming most were there voluntarily and at any time could excuse themselves to go to bed (as some did).

3. Some of my women students have written ethnographies of their sports teams and sororities, and these accounts make it clear that women can be every bit as obscene as men, only usually more privately.

4. One year I witnessed a "pissing" out of the fire—pissing on the embers, really. This seemed to me then and now to be an example of a last male gesture before returning to the world of interdependence between men and women. My folklore student Rurik "Rik" Goyton describes and analyzes the custom of "pissing out the fire" he witnessed (and participated in) as a camp counselor at a coeducational camp. The male members of a leadership program called Campers in Leadership Training (CILT), for counselors-in-training ages fifteen through seventeen, traditionally stay to "piss out the fire" of the last campfire of the two-week training session. Goyton's crucial point is that the boys seem to use this exclusively male ritual of "sword fighting" with streams of urine as a last gesture punctuating two weeks' worth of "political correctness" training about gender and sexuality. It is as if the boys need to repair their masculinity before making the transition between camp training and everyday life. See Rurik Goyton, "Pissing Out the Fire: Reasserting Masculine Identity in a Closure Ritual," in *Prized Writing: The Essay 1997–1998* (Davis: University of California Campus Writing Center, 1998), 56–60.

Epilogue

1. William Pollack, *Real Boys: Rescuing Our Sons from the Myths of Boyhood* (New York: Holt, 1998). Also in this genre are three best-selling books by Michael Gurian—*The Wonder of Boys* (New York: Putnam, 1996), *A Fine Young Man* (New York: Putnam, 1998), and *The Good Son* (New York: Tarcher/Putnam, 1999); Dan Kindlon and Michael Thompson, *Raising Cain* (New York: Ballantine, 1999); and Eric H. Newberger, *The Men They Will Become: The Nature and Nurture of Male Character* (Reading, Mass.: Perseus Books, 1999). Decidedly antifeminist on these matters is Christina Hoff Sommers's *The War against Boys: How Misguided Feminism Is Harming Our Young Men* (New York: Simon and Schuster, 2000). For thoughtful reviews of Sommers's book, see Nicholas Lemann's "The Battle over Boys," *New Yorker,* 10 July 2000, pp. 79–83, and Richard Bernstein, "Boys, Not Girls, as Society's Victims," *New York Times,* 31 July 2000, p. B6.

2. Gurian, *A Fine Young Man,* 24.

3. Kindlon and Thompson, *Raising Cain,* 4.

4. Pollack, *Real Boys,* 44; Gurian, *The Wonder of Boys,* xviii; and Kindlon and Thompson, *Raising Cain,* 219, et passim. On the history of the socialization of anger in children, see Carol Ziswitz Stearns and Peter N. Stearns, *Anger: The Struggle for Emotional Control in America's History* (Chicago: University of Chicago Press, 1986).

5. Deborah Tannen, *You Just Don't Understand: Women and Men in Conversation* (New York: Morrow, 1990), 24–25.

6. Pollack, *Real Boys,* 23–24, cites the work of Deborah David and Robert Brannon, who name four "injunctions" at the heart of this code: "The 'sturdy oak'; 'Give 'em hell'; 'The big wheel'; and 'No sissy stuff.'" See Deborah David and Robert Brannon, eds., *The Forty-Nine Percent Majority: The Sex Male Role* (Reading, Mass.: Addison-Wesley, 1976).

7. Richard Majors, *Cool Pose: The Dilemmas of Black Manhood in America* (New York: Lexington Books, 1992). The paradox for African-American men is that the stereotypes sometimes feminize the black man, and at other times they do as much damage by hypermasculinizing him.

8. Pollack, *Real Boys,* 173.

9. Gurian, *The Wonder of Boys,* 28–49.

10. On this phenomenon of "doing together," see Pollack, *Real Boys,* 195–96, 245–47, and Gurian, *The Wonder of Boys,* 34–37.

11. One of the interesting features of the Percy Keese Fitzhugh Boy Scout novels is that they put boys in situations where they face such dilemmas and the novels show the boys how they might work through such dilemmas.

12. Etzioni has written over a dozen books explaining and elaborating the communitarian paradigm but for a good introduction see his *The New Golden Rule: Community and Morality in a Democratic Society* (New York: Basic Books, 1996). It is also worth noting that when Robert Bellah and his colleagues wrote a new "Introduction to the Updated Edition: The House Divided" (1996) for *Habits of the Heart: Individualism and Commitment in Everyday Life* (Berkeley: University of California Press, 1985), they embraced a "democratic communitarianism" (p. xxix).

13. Etzioni, *The New Golden Rule,* xviii.

14. Ibid., 12.

15. Tocqueville's continuing influence on American social thought about civic culture shows up everywhere. Bellah and his colleagues borrowed Tocqueville's felicitous phrase "habits of the heart" for their title. Among the many editions of Tocqueville is *Democracy in America,* trans. George Lawrence, ed. J. P. Mayer (New York: Doubleday, Anchor Books, 1969). On "mediating structures," see Peter L. Berger and Richard John Neuhaus, *To Empower People: Mediating Structures and Social Policy* (Washington, D.C.: American Enterprise Institute, 1977). See also Jay Mechling, "Folklore and the Public Sphere," *Western Folklore* 56 (Spring 1997): 113–37.

16. Etzioni, *The New Golden Rule,* 24.

Methodology Appendix

1. See Gary Alan Fine, "Appendix 2: Participant Observation with Children, " in *With the Boys: Little League Baseball and Preadolescent Culture* (Chicago: University of

Chicago Press, 1987), 222–44, and Gary Alan Fine, "Methodological Problems of Collecting Folklore from Children," in *Children's Folklore: A Source Book,* ed. Brian Sutton-Smith, Jay Mechling, Thomas W. Johnson, and Felicia R. McMahon (New York: Garland, 1995; reprint, Logan: Utah State University Press, 1999), 121–39.

2. See James Clifford and George E. Marcus, eds., *Writing Culture: The Poetics and Politics of Ethnography* (Berkeley: University of California Press, 1986), and for a feminist perspective on these issues, see Ruth Behar and Deborah A. Gordon, eds., *Women Writing Culture* (Berkeley: University of California Press, 1995).

3. Coles is an enormously prolific writer, but a good place to enter his writing about children is *The Moral Life of Children* (Boston: Atlantic Monthly Press, 1986). Also see his *The Call of Stories* (Boston: Houghton Mifflin, 1989) for some thoughts on the relationship between writing ethnographic accounts and writing fiction.

4. Barbara Myerhoff, *Number Our Days* (New York: Simon and Schuster, 1978).

INDEX